First World War
and Army of Occupation
War Diary
France, Belgium and Germany

52 DIVISION
157 Infantry Brigade
Highland Light Infantry
6th (City of Glasgow) Battn. (Territorial)
28 September 1917 - 31 March 1919

WO95/2898/3

The Naval & Military Press Ltd
www.nmarchive.com
Published in association with The National Archives

Published by

The Naval & Military Press Ltd

Unit 10 Ridgewood Industrial Park,

Uckfield, East Sussex,

TN22 5QE England

Tel: +44 (0) 1825 749494

www.naval-military-press.com

www.nmarchive.com

This diary has been reprinted in facsimile from the original. Any imperfections are inevitably reproduced and the quality may fall short of modern type and cartographic standards.

© Crown Copyright
Images reproduced by permission of The National Archives, London, England, 2015.

Contents

Document type	Place/Title	Date From	Date To
Heading	WO95/2898-3		
Heading	52nd Division 157th Infy Bde 1-6th Bn Highland Lt Infy Apr 1918-Mar 1919		
Heading	157th Brigade. 52nd Division Disembarked Marseilles From Egypt 17.4.18 1/6th Battalion Highland Light Infantry April 1918		
War Diary	Balutah Firing Line Ref. Map Arsuf K.6.	01/04/1918	02/04/1918
War Diary	Sarona	03/04/1918	03/04/1918
War Diary	Surafend Camp Ludd	04/04/1918	06/04/1918
War Diary	Kantarah	07/04/1918	07/04/1918
War Diary	Sidi Bishr Alexandria	08/04/1918	11/04/1918
War Diary	HMT Caledonia	11/04/1918	17/04/1918
War Diary	Marseilles	18/04/1918	18/04/1918
War Diary	In Train	19/04/1918	22/04/1918
War Diary	St. Valery	23/04/1918	29/04/1918
War Diary	La Lacque Ref Map France 1/10000 36 (a)	30/04/1918	30/04/1918
Miscellaneous	1/6th Bn. Highland Light Infantry Administrative Instructions	30/03/1918	30/03/1918
Operation(al) Order(s)	Battalion Order No. 48	31/03/1918	31/03/1918
Miscellaneous	1/6th Highland Light Infantry Preliminary Instruction Re Move	01/04/1918	01/04/1918
Miscellaneous	Battalion Administrative Instructions	03/04/1918	03/04/1918
Heading	War Diary 1/6th H.L.I. 1st-31st May 1918 Volume III		
War Diary	La Lacque	01/05/1918	06/05/1918
War Diary	Neuville St Vaast	07/05/1918	07/05/1918
War Diary	Vimy 2nd Line Trenches	08/05/1918	11/05/1918
War Diary	Chaudiere Defences	12/05/1918	16/05/1918
War Diary	Chaudiere Defences (front Line)	17/05/1918	19/05/1918
War Diary	La Chaudiere Line (Bde Reserve)	20/05/1918	24/05/1918
War Diary	St Eloy	25/05/1918	31/05/1918
Miscellaneous	1/6th Bn. H. L. I.	30/04/1918	30/04/1918
Miscellaneous	Sketch Of 6th Bn. H. L. I. Trenches		
Operation(al) Order(s)	Battalion Order No. 2	02/05/1918	02/05/1918
Operation(al) Order(s)	Battalion Order No. 3	05/05/1918	05/05/1918
Operation(al) Order(s)	Battalion Order No. 4	07/05/1918	07/05/1918
Operation(al) Order(s)	Battalion Order No. 5	10/05/1918	10/05/1918
Operation(al) Order(s)	Battalion Order No. 6	12/05/1918	12/05/1918
Miscellaneous	Defence Scheme Of "Betty" Area		
Miscellaneous	Operation Order For Raid On Enemy Trench Meril by Lieut. Col. J. Anderson, C.M.G. D.S.O.	18/05/1918	18/05/1918
Operation(al) Order(s)	Battalion Order No. 8	18/05/1918	18/05/1918
Miscellaneous	Addendum No. 2 To 157th Brigade No. 2	19/05/1918	19/05/1918
Operation(al) Order(s)	Battalion Order No. 9	23/05/1918	23/05/1918
Miscellaneous	Reference 2/696	25/05/1918	25/05/1918
Miscellaneous	Addendum No. 1 To 157th Bde. No. Z/696	16/05/1918	16/05/1918
Miscellaneous	Reference Z/696	23/05/1916	23/05/1916
Miscellaneous	O.C. 6th H.L.I. Z/696	16/05/1918	16/05/1918
Miscellaneous	Addendum No. 1 To 157th Bde. No. Z/696	16/05/1918	16/05/1918
Miscellaneous	O.C. H.Q. C.O. R.S.M & File	11/05/1918	11/05/1918
Heading	1/6 HLI Vol 3		

Heading	D.A.G. 3rd Echelon War Diary June 1918		
War Diary	St Eloy	01/06/1918	01/06/1918
War Diary	Firing Line Hudson Trenches	02/06/1918	09/06/1918
War Diary	Thelus Post	10/06/1918	14/06/1918
War Diary	Firing Line Hudson And Ottawa Tr, Etc	14/06/1918	16/06/1918
War Diary	Firing Line Hudson Tr Etc	17/06/1918	20/06/1918
War Diary	Mont St. Eloi	21/06/1918	29/06/1918
War Diary	La Chaudiere Sector (Front Line)	30/06/1918	30/06/1918
War Diary	La Chaudiere Sector	30/06/1918	30/06/1918
Miscellaneous	Strength as at.	31/05/1918	31/05/1918
Operation(al) Order(s)	Battalion Order No. 9	01/06/1918	01/06/1918
Miscellaneous	O.C. 6th H.L.I.	31/05/1918	31/05/1918
Operation(al) Order(s)	157th Infantry Brigade Order No. 102	31/05/1918	31/05/1918
Miscellaneous	Administrative Order No. 11 Issued With Reference To Brigade Order No. 102	01/06/1918	01/06/1918
Miscellaneous	Proposed Raid Scheme	05/06/1918	05/06/1918
Miscellaneous	Alternative Raid Scheme	05/06/1918	05/06/1918
Operation(al) Order(s)	157th Infantry Brigade Order No. 103	06/06/1918	06/06/1918
Miscellaneous	Reference Battn Order No. 10 Para II	07/06/1918	07/06/1918
Operation(al) Order(s)	Battalion Order No. 11	13/06/1918	13/06/1918
Operation(al) Order(s)	157th Infantry Brigade Order No. 105	12/06/1918	12/06/1918
Operation(al) Order(s)	Battalion Order No. 12	19/06/1918	19/06/1918
Miscellaneous	Amendment To Brigade Administrative Instructions No. 103	18/06/1918	18/06/1918
Miscellaneous	Handing Over Of Communication Issued With Bde Order No. 107	17/06/1918	17/06/1918
Miscellaneous	C Form Messages And Signals		
Operation(al) Order(s)	157th Infantry Brigade Order No. 107	20/06/1918	20/06/1918
Miscellaneous	157th Infantry Brigade Administrative Instructions No. 103		
Operation(al) Order(s)	Battalion Order No. 13	28/06/1918	28/06/1918
Operation(al) Order(s)	157th Infantry Brigade Order No. 108	27/06/1918	27/06/1918
Miscellaneous	157th Infantry Brigade Administrative Instructions No. 105	27/06/1918	27/06/1918
Miscellaneous	Communications Issued With Bde Order No. 108	27/06/1918	27/06/1918
Heading	1/6th Bn. H. L. I. War Diary Volume III July 1918		
War Diary	La Chaudiere Sector (Front Line)	01/07/1918	05/07/1918
War Diary	Vimy Sector (Reserve Line)	06/07/1918	10/07/1918
War Diary	Toast Sector (Front Line)	11/07/1918	16/07/1918
War Diary	Neuville St Vaast	16/07/1918	17/07/1918
War Diary	Mont St Eloi	18/07/1918	20/07/1918
War Diary	Raimbert	21/07/1918	30/07/1918
War Diary	Barlin	31/07/1918	31/07/1918
Miscellaneous	Table Shewing Increases & Decreases In Battn. Camp Strength		
Operation(al) Order(s)	157th Infantry Brigade Order No. 106	02/07/1918	02/07/1918
Operation(al) Order(s)	Battalion Order No. 17	10/07/1918	10/07/1918
Miscellaneous	Reference B.D. No. 17 Para 8	10/07/1918	10/07/1918
Miscellaneous	O.C. 6th H.L.I.	03/07/1918	03/07/1918
Miscellaneous	G.O.C. Left Section	06/07/1918	06/07/1918
Operation(al) Order(s)	157th Infantry Brigade Order No. 110	03/07/1918	03/07/1918
Miscellaneous	157th Infantry Brigade Administrative Instructions No. 106	03/07/1918	03/07/1918
Map	Map Issued With 52nd Div Order No. 3		
Miscellaneous			
Operation(al) Order(s)	Battalion Order No. 14	03/07/1918	03/07/1918

Miscellaneous	O.C. 5th H. L. I.	03/07/1918	03/07/1918
Operation(al) Order(s)	Battalion Order No. 16	10/07/1918	10/07/1918
Miscellaneous	Orders For Scouts		
Miscellaneous	O.C. 6th Bn. H. L. I.	09/07/1918	09/07/1918
Operation(al) Order(s)	Brigade Order No. 111	10/07/1918	10/07/1918
Miscellaneous	1/6th Bn. H. L. I. Defence Scheme		
Miscellaneous	Appendix I List Of Co Ordinates		
Miscellaneous	Appendix II Company Boundaries		
Miscellaneous	Appendix III Communications		
Map	Map "A"		
Map	Map "B"		
Map	Map "C"		
Operation(al) Order(s)	Battalion Order No. 18	14/07/1918	14/07/1918
Miscellaneous	Alarm Orders	18/07/1918	18/07/1918
Operation(al) Order(s)	Battalion Order No. 19	19/07/1918	19/07/1918
Miscellaneous	Billet Standing Orders	20/07/1918	20/07/1918
Map	Map		
Miscellaneous	Battalion Preliminary Move Orders by Lieut-Col. J. Anderson. C.M.C.D.S.O. Commdg 1/6 Bn H.L.I.	25/07/1918	25/07/1918
Miscellaneous	157th Brigade Proposed Raid Scheme	01/07/1918	01/07/1918
Operation(al) Order(s)	Battalion Order No. 20	29/07/1918	29/07/1918
Operation(al) Order(s)	Battalion Order No. 21	31/07/1918	31/07/1918
War Diary	Roclincourt	01/08/1918	01/08/1918
War Diary	Front Line Oppy Sector	02/08/1918	07/08/1918
War Diary	Support Line Oppy Sector	08/08/1918	14/08/1918
War Diary	Oppy Sector (Front Line)	14/08/1918	16/08/1918
War Diary	Mont St Eloi	17/08/1918	17/08/1918
War Diary	Chateau-De-La Haie	18/08/1918	20/08/1918
War Diary	Agnes-Les-Duisans	21/08/1918	23/08/1918
War Diary	Brickworks S2d53c	24/08/1918	24/08/1918
War Diary	Attack On Hindenburg Line	25/08/1918	27/08/1918
War Diary	Attack On Fontaine Croisilles	27/08/1918	28/08/1918
War Diary	Mercatel	29/08/1918	31/08/1918
Miscellaneous	Table Shewing Increases & Decreases In Battn Camp Strength		
Miscellaneous	Amendment To Battalion Order No. 22	01/08/1918	01/08/1918
Operation(al) Order(s)	Battalion Order No. 24	05/08/1918	05/08/1918
Operation(al) Order(s)	Battalion Order No. 25	06/08/1918	06/08/1918
Operation(al) Order(s)	Battalion Order No. 26	12/08/1918	12/08/1918
Operation(al) Order(s)	Battalion Order No. 29	16/08/1918	16/08/1918
Operation(al) Order(s)	157th Infantry Brigade Order No. 122	15/08/1918	15/08/1918
Miscellaneous	Table "A"		
Miscellaneous	157th Infantry Brigade Administrative Instructions No. 113	15/08/1918	15/08/1918
Miscellaneous	A Form Messages And Signals		
Operation(al) Order(s)	Battalion Order No. 30	17/08/1918	17/08/1918
Miscellaneous	A Form Messages And Signals		
Operation(al) Order(s)	157th Infantry Brigade Order No. 130	24/08/1918	24/08/1918
Miscellaneous	A Form Messages And Signals		
Operation(al) Order(s)	157th Infantry Brigade Order No. 132	25/08/1918	25/08/1918
Operation(al) Order(s)	157th Infantry Brigade Order No. 131	24/08/1918	24/08/1918
Miscellaneous	B.M.X 1304	26/08/1918	26/08/1918
Operation(al) Order(s)	157. Bde Order No. 134	26/08/1918	26/08/1918
Miscellaneous	Addendum 157. Bde Order No. 134	26/08/1918	26/08/1918
Operation(al) Order(s)	157th Inf. Bde. Order No. 135	27/08/1918	27/08/1918
Diagram etc	Diagram		

Heading	6th H.L.I. Inf Sep 18		
War Diary	Mercatel	01/09/1918	01/09/1918
War Diary	Fat Switch	02/09/1918	02/09/1918
War Diary	Croisilles	03/09/1918	03/09/1918
War Diary	Pronville	03/09/1918	07/09/1918
War Diary	Croisilles	08/09/1918	16/09/1918
War Diary	Inchy-En-Artois	17/09/1918	20/09/1918
War Diary	Moreuil	21/09/1918	22/09/1918
War Diary	Inchy-En-Artois	17/09/1918	19/09/1918
War Diary	Moeuvres	23/09/1918	24/09/1918
War Diary	Moreuil (In Reserve)	25/09/1918	26/09/1918
War Diary	Sand Lane (Hindenburg/Front Line)	27/09/1918	27/09/1918
War Diary	Ref Map 57c NE 1/20,000	27/09/1918	27/09/1918
War Diary	Cambrai Rd Canal Du Nord	28/09/1917	28/09/1917
War Diary	(Ref Sheet 57c Ne)	28/09/1917	30/09/1917
Miscellaneous	Table Showing Increases & Decreases In Battn. Camp Strength During Month Of September 1918		
Miscellaneous	Appendix	01/09/1918	01/09/1918
Operation(al) Order(s)	157th Infantry Brigade Order No. 136	31/08/1918	31/08/1918
Miscellaneous	157th Infantry Brigade Administrative Instructions Issued With Brigade Order No. 136	31/08/1918	31/08/1918
Miscellaneous	C Form Messages And Signals		
Miscellaneous	SE La O.C 6 HLI		
Miscellaneous	Appendix	02/09/1918	02/09/1918
Operation(al) Order(s)	157th Infantry Brigade Order No. 137	01/09/1918	01/09/1918
Miscellaneous	Ref 157th Inf Bde Order No 137 Para 4 A	02/09/1918	02/09/1918
Miscellaneous	Appendix	03/09/1918	03/09/1918
Miscellaneous	BM 15/24	02/08/1918	02/08/1918
Miscellaneous	BM 15/26	02/09/1918	02/09/1918
Operation(al) Order(s)	157. Inf Bde. Operation Order No. 138	02/09/1918	02/09/1918
Miscellaneous	C Form Messages And Signals		
Miscellaneous	A Form Messages And Signals		
Miscellaneous	Appendix	16/09/1918	16/09/1918
Miscellaneous	Battalion Order By Major W. Menzies Anderson, M.C. Commdg, 1/6th Bn. High. L.i.	16/09/1918	16/09/1918
Miscellaneous	Location List		
Miscellaneous	Appendix	19/09/1918	19/09/1918
Miscellaneous	Warning Order	18/09/1918	18/09/1918
Operation(al) Order(s)	157th Infantry Brigade Order No. 142	18/09/1918	18/09/1918
Miscellaneous	A Form Messages And Signals		
Miscellaneous	Appendix	21/09/1918	21/09/1918
Miscellaneous	C Form Messages And Signals		
Miscellaneous	A Form Messages And Signals		
Operation(al) Order(s)	157th Infantry Brigade Order No. 143 1/2	21/09/1918	21/09/1918
Operation(al) Order(s)	Battalion Order No. 50	24/09/1918	24/09/1918
Operation(al) Order(s)	155th. Inf. Brigade Order No. 119	24/09/1918	24/09/1918
Miscellaneous	Appendices 1 & 2	25/09/1918	25/09/1918
Miscellaneous	O.C. 6th H.L.I.	25/09/1918	25/09/1918
Operation(al) Order(s)	157th Infantry Brigade Order No. 145	25/09/1918	25/09/1918
Miscellaneous	157th Infantry Brigade Administrative Instructions Issued With Reference To 157th Infantry Brigade Order No. 145	25/09/1918	25/09/1918
Operation(al) Order(s)	Operation Order No. by Lt Col W. Menzies Anderson M.C. Commdg H.I.J.O.	26/09/1918	26/09/1918
Miscellaneous	157th Infantry Brigade Instructions No.1		
Miscellaneous	157th Infantry Brigade Instructions No.2	26/07/1918	26/07/1918

Type	Description	Date From	Date To
Miscellaneous	Appendix I&II	27/09/1918	27/09/1918
Miscellaneous	Enemy Material Captured	27/09/1918	27/09/1918
Miscellaneous	Casualty Report	27/09/1918	27/09/1918
Miscellaneous	O.C. 6th H.L.I.	29/09/1918	29/09/1918
Miscellaneous	Appendix	29/09/1918	29/09/1918
Heading	1/6th H.L.I Oct 1918		
Heading	1/6th Battalion Highland Light Infantry War Diary For Month Of October 1918		
War Diary	From K2b Canal Du Nord Ref: Sheet 57c 1/40000	01/10/1918	01/10/1918
War Diary	Cantigneul Mill (F 30a)	01/10/1918	02/10/1918
War Diary	Pillbox Nr Cantigneul Mill (F30a)	03/10/1918	04/10/1918
War Diary	Copse	04/10/1918	04/10/1918
War Diary	Copse A 26 d.3.0.	05/10/1918	05/10/1918
War Diary	Canal Du Nord (K2b)	06/10/1918	06/10/1918
War Diary	Canal Du Nord (K3b)	07/10/1918	07/10/1918
War Diary	In Train Petit Houvin Grand Rullecourt	08/10/1918	09/10/1918
War Diary	Grand Rullecourt	10/10/1918	18/10/1918
War Diary	Grand Rullecourt to St Eloi	19/10/1918	19/10/1918
War Diary	St Eloi	19/10/1918	20/10/1918
War Diary	Henin Lietard	20/10/1918	21/10/1918
War Diary	Flers	22/10/1918	23/10/1918
War Diary	Flers to Montreuil	24/10/1918	24/10/1918
War Diary	Montreuil (Flimes Area)	25/10/1918	26/10/1918
War Diary	Montreuil to Landas	27/10/1918	27/10/1918
War Diary	Ref Map Sheet 44 1/40,000 Landas	28/10/1918	29/10/1918
War Diary	Rumegies	30/10/1918	31/10/1918
Miscellaneous	Table Shewing Increases & Decreases In Battn. Camp Strength		
Miscellaneous	Warning Order	30/03/1918	30/03/1918
Miscellaneous	157th Infantry Brigade Administrative Instructions No.3	30/09/1918	30/09/1918
Miscellaneous	O.C. 5th H.L.I.	01/10/1918	01/10/1918
Miscellaneous	Addendum To Warning Order		
Miscellaneous	Battalion Orders By Lt Col W. Menzies Anderson M.C. Commdg. 1/6 H.L.I.	01/10/1918	01/10/1918
Operation(al) Order(s)	Battalion Order No. 56	07/10/1918	07/10/1918
Operation(al) Order(s)	157th Infantry Brigade Order No. 151	18/10/1918	18/10/1918
Miscellaneous	A Form Messages And Signals		
Operation(al) Order(s)	157th Infantry Brigade Order No 152	19/10/1918	19/10/1918
Miscellaneous	Appendix	19/10/1918	19/10/1918
Miscellaneous	B.M. 4/43	20/10/1918	20/10/1918
Operation(al) Order(s)	Battn. Order No. 60 By Lieut-Col W. Menzies Anderson D.S.O. M.C. Commdg 1/6th Bn H.L.I.	20/10/1918	20/10/1918
Miscellaneous	After Order	20/10/1918	20/10/1918
Operation(al) Order(s)	157th Infantry Brigade Order No. 153.	20/10/1918	20/10/1918
Miscellaneous	Appendix	20/10/1918	20/10/1918
Operation(al) Order(s)	Battn Order No. 61 By Lieut-Col W. Menzies Anderson D.S.O. M.C. Commdg 1/6th Bn H.L.I.	23/10/1918	23/10/1918
Operation(al) Order(s)	157th Infantry Brigade Order No 154	23/10/1918	23/10/1918
Miscellaneous	157th Infantry Brigade Administrative Instruction	23/10/1918	23/10/1918
Miscellaneous	Messages And Signals		
Miscellaneous	C Form Messages And Signals		
Miscellaneous	Road Work	23/10/1918	23/10/1918
Miscellaneous	Road Work	24/10/1918	24/10/1918
Miscellaneous	A Form Messages And Signals		
Miscellaneous	C Form Messages And Signals		
Miscellaneous	A Form Messages And Signals		

Type	Title	From	To
Miscellaneous	Reconnaissance Of Forward Areas	25/10/1918	25/10/1918
Miscellaneous		27/10/1918	27/10/1918
Operation(al) Order(s)	157th Infantry Brigade Order No. 156	27/10/1918	27/10/1918
Miscellaneous	Appendix 2	04/10/1918	04/10/1918
Miscellaneous	A Form Messages And Signals		
Operation(al) Order(s)	157th Infantry Brigade Order No. 157	27/10/1918	27/10/1918
Miscellaneous	Appendix	27/10/1918	27/10/1918
War Diary	Rumegies	01/11/1918	04/11/1918
War Diary	Rumegies to P 17 b 88 Hydropathic	04/11/1918	07/11/1918
War Diary	Croisette (Hydropathic Near St Amand)	08/11/1918	08/11/1918
War Diary	Lorette (Out Post Line)	09/11/1918	09/11/1918
War Diary	Lorette to Ville Pommeroeul	09/11/1918	10/11/1918
War Diary	Ville Pommeroeul to Vacresse	10/11/1918	11/11/1918
War Diary	Erbisoeul	11/11/1918	13/11/1918
War Diary	Mons Jurbise Rd Nr Jurbise	14/11/1918	15/11/1918
War Diary	Pave N Of Mons	16/11/1918	30/11/1918
Miscellaneous	Table Shewing Increases & Decreases In Battalion Camp Strength		
Miscellaneous	C Form Messages And Signals		
Miscellaneous	A Form Messages And Signals		
Miscellaneous	Warning Order	03/11/1918	03/11/1918
Miscellaneous	C Form Messages And Signals		
Operation(al) Order(s)	157th Infantry Brigade Order No. 158	03/11/1918	03/11/1918
Miscellaneous	Table "A"		
Miscellaneous	C Form Messages And Signals		
Miscellaneous	To All Recipients Of 157th Infantry Brigade Order No. 160		
Operation(al) Order(s)	157th Infantry Brigade Order No. 160	07/11/1918	07/11/1918
Miscellaneous	BM.2/62	07/11/1918	07/11/1918
Miscellaneous	Addendum No.1 To 157th Infantry Brigade Order No. 159	07/11/1918	07/11/1918
Miscellaneous	Warning Order	02/11/1918	02/11/1918
Operation(al) Order(s)	157th Infantry Brigade Order No. 159	06/11/1918	06/11/1918
Operation(al) Order(s)	157th Infantry Brigade Order No. 161	18/11/1918	18/11/1918
Miscellaneous	Appendix IV O.V. 5th H.L.I.	12/11/1918	12/11/1918
Miscellaneous	Outposts During The Armistice	12/11/1918	12/11/1918
Miscellaneous			
Miscellaneous	Appendix V O.V. 5th H.L.I.	14/11/1918	14/11/1918
Miscellaneous	C Form Messages And Signals		
Miscellaneous	1/6th Bn Highland Light Infantry Training Programme	30/11/1918	30/11/1918
Miscellaneous	1/6th Bn Highland Light Infantry Training Programme	07/12/1918	07/12/1918
War Diary	Pava Mons-Jurbise Road	01/12/1918	31/12/1918
Miscellaneous	Table Shewing Increases And Decreases In Battalion Camp Strength		
War Diary	Pave Mons Jurbise Road	01/01/1919	31/01/1919
Miscellaneous	Table Shewing Increases And Decreases In Battalion Camp Strength		
War Diary	Pave Near Mons	01/02/1919	28/02/1919
Miscellaneous	Table Shewing Increases And Decreases In Battalion Camp Strength		
War Diary	Jurbise	01/03/1919	11/03/1919
War Diary	Jurbise to Maizieres	12/03/1919	20/03/1919
War Diary	Soignies	21/03/1919	27/03/1919
War Diary	Soignies Belgium	28/03/1919	31/03/1919
Miscellaneous	Table Shewing Increases And Decreases In Battalion Camp Strength		

wool, 2858 (10)

wool, 2858 (3)

52ND DIVISION
157TH INFY BDE

1-6TH BN HIGHLAND LT INFY
APR 1918-MAR 1919

157th Brigade.
52nd Division.

Disembarked MARSEILLES from EGYPT   17.4.18.

1/6th BATTALION

HIGHLAND LIGHT INFANTRY

APRIL 1918.

WAR DIARY or INTELLIGENCE SUMMARY

Army Form C. 2118.

VOLUME No. III. APRIL 1918

1/6 H.L.I.

Place	Date	Hour	Summary of Events and Information	Remarks and references to Appendices
BALUTAH Firing Line Ro/Maj ARSUF K.G.	1/4/18	0715 0300 1000–1200 1000	C.O. + 3 Griffith Officers visited firing line. Artillery shelled vicinity of PIMPLE HILL followed by rifle M.G. + Trench mortars fire about 0700. Lewis Gunners + Sniper Scouts practised firing at targets in no mans land. Our Snipers on SNIPERS HILL claim to have wounded two of the enemy - range 300. Advanced Party (Capt Tull + 200 OR) proceeded to SARONA.	S
	2/4/18	1415 0930	Adjutant visited firing line. Guide Officers reconnoitred + cleaning patrols. Enemy shelled heavy battery in vicinity of both sectors with S.9. Batt^n were relieved into the firing line by "GUIDE'S" Batt^n + moved to SARONA into bivouac arriving there at 0530 on 3/4/18 (See Appendix 2/4/18)	S S Appendix 2/4/18
SARONA	3/4/18	0730 1830	Advance cecl. party under Capt. B.G. Tipp left for LUDD SURAFEND CAMP. Brigade left for LUDD SURAFEND CAMP	S
SURAFEND CAMP LUDD	4/4/18		All stores as detailed, bivouac sheets + blanket per man about 2230 + moved into tents at SURAFEND CAMP (See appendix 3/4/18) remainder returned to A.O.D. LUDD. Advanced baggage was also taken to station dump.	Appendix 3/4/18 S
	6/4/18		All vehicles returned to Railway Depot + Animals landed in to Remount. All Rank went through Gas Test whole Divisional Gas officers - a bell tent was used for the purpose, water proof sheet + Gas helmet down.	S

7.H.
Salute

Army Form C. 2118.

WAR DIARY
or
INTELLIGENCE SUMMARY.
(Erase heading not required.)

Instructions regarding War Diaries and Intelligence Summaries are contained in F. S. Regs., Part II. and the Staff Manual respectively. Title pages will be prepared in manuscript.

Place	Date	Hour	Summary of Events and Information	Remarks and references to Appendices
SURAFEND CAMP LUDD	6/4/18	0900	All remaining both baggage sent to Station with loading party	
		1130	Batth paraded & proceeded to Station — Entrained 1351 for Base	
KANTARAH	7/4/18	0730	Arrived KANTARAH & moved into bell Tents for the day	
			Batty was made up to 37 Officers & 864 Other ranks. — Advanced baggage party under Capt Hon. T BOYCE rejoined	
		1530	All both baggage taken to Station by loading Party	
		2245	Batth paraded & proceeded to Station entraining at 2245 for ALEXANDRIA.	
SIDI BISHR ALEXANDRIA	8/4/18	0830	Train arrived SIDI BISHR & Battalion moved into tents already erected	
			10% men allowed leave to Town. 1 Officer 5 OR. supplied as Town piquet	
			Bathing Parade — Lieut Col Anderson C in C. OSO rejoined from NZ R Mgd/Bde.	
	9/4/18	0900	Bathing Parade	
			20% Bn. allowed in town leave — Batth on duty, supplied Town & piquets & guards.	
	10/4/18	0930	Batth paraded marched to SIDI BISHR Station & entrained for Docks arriving at Docks about 11.30 both embarked on board HMT CALEDONIA	
			all Coy on board at 1345.	
			Lt Col ANDERSON appointed O.C. Troops.	
		1530	Conference of O.S.C. Troops & Adjutants at E.S. O's Office & orders for voyage.	
	11/4/18	0830	H.M.T. CALEDONIA pulled out to outer harbour has been	
		1430	sailed & joined a convoy containing the whole 52 Regt. a DO	
		1630	Strong escort was furnished T.B. D's lived & attacked presumably a submarine	

Army Form C. 2118.

WAR DIARY
or
INTELLIGENCE SUMMARY.
(Erase heading not required.)

REF. MAP: ABBEVILLE Sheet XIV

Place	Date	Hour	Summary of Events and Information	Remarks and references to Appendices
HMT CALEDONIA	11/4/18 (Contd)	1130 1250	Practice alarm for boat station	
	12/4/18	1030	Daily inspection by O.C. Troops	
Do	13/4/18	1030	Daily Inspection. Rifles put into armoury	
Do	14/4/18	1030	Practice Alarm — All ranks inspected at their boat stations	
Do		1000	Church parade	
			Escort of six Japanese T.B.Ds. were received by 3 JapM. + 3 British T.B.Ds. as many men as possible slept on deck as extra precaution whilst Cape Bon crew reached	
Do	15/4/18	1030	Practice/no alarm daily inspection	
Do	16/4/18	1030	Daily inspection — Rifles withdrawn from armoury	
Do	17/4/18	1030	Arrived at MARSEILLES and disembarked about 1400 & proceeded to No. 8 Camp MONT FURON. Leave was given to Officers & 10% men to visit the town	
MARSEILLES	18/4/18			
IN TRAIN	19/4/18	1230	Batln. left Camp & proceeded to station where Trg. Entrained with 410th F.C. by R.S.O	
	22/4/18		The train journey lasted till 22/4/18 with two halts of 1½ hours when hot tea was served. NOYELLES sur Mer.	
	22/4/18	1100	Batln. arrived at ABBEVILLE + detrained. B/ln. + hot meal B/ln. marched to ST VALERY & went into billets	
ST VALERY	23/4/18		Physical Training, Specialist Training, Route marching, Gas Training	

Army Form C. 2118.

WAR DIARY
or
INTELLIGENCE SUMMARY.
(Erase heading not required.)

Place	Date	Hour	Summary of Events and Information	Remarks and references to Appendices
ST. VALERY	24/4/18		Ref map ABBEVILLE Sheet 14. Physical, Specialist, & Gas Training. Route marching by Coys. C.O. visited all Companies. Lt Col Anderson resumed temporarily command of 157th Batt on 22/4/18. Major Wardean taking over command of the Batt. Transport & bycles were drawn.	Q
	25/4/18		Physical, Specialist & Gas Training. Bn sept to Shorn with gasmasks on. Route marching in Battledress. Brass drums received for use of Bn touts.	Q
	26/4/18		G.O.C. 52nd Div visited battn. Specialists, Gas Physical Training. Route marching with Steel helmets. Lecture on Gas Shells to by an Officer detailed by F.H.Q. attended by 95 all ranks. Block containers of Gas helmets exchanged for Brown ones.	Q
	27/4/18		Physical Gas & Specialist Training - Orders to move received.	Q
	28/4/18	1300	Btn left In NOYELLES STATION & travelled to BERGUETTE along with 157th Bde H.Q. 1 Coy 157 M.I - 1 Coy 157 M.I.	Q
		1800	Remainder of Batt left ST VALERY In NOYELLES entraining In BERGUETTE at 134.	
	29/4/18	0830	Arrived BERGUETTE and proceeded La LACQUE Camp. where baths occupied huts. Col Anderson took over command of Batt on return of Brig Gen from leave.	
LA LACQUE REF MAP FRANCE 36(a).	30/4/18		Physical, Specialist & Gas Training - all details now Gas helmets - 350 OR ranks paraded for hot baths. Route marching - Bayonet fighting throw petty. Recon of area of C.O. under Brig Gen.	Heavy rain during day

Appendix I   1/6TH BN. HIGHLAND LIGHT INFANTRY.   Copy No. 8

ADMINISTRATIVE INSTRUCTIONS.
Issued Preliminary to Battalion Order No 48

Reference Map. ARSUF.(K 6) 1/20,000.   30/3/18.

---

1 TRENCH & AREA STORES.
(a) All trench and area stores will be handed over as per lists issued (any alterations required to be made will be notified to Orderly Room at once). The Quartermaster will arrange for handing over of all Headquarters Stores. Receipts will be obtained and rendered to Orderly Room, by 1000 on morning after relief.

(b) The R.S.M. will arrange to leave here the following Regtl. Stores taking over a similar quantity at SURAFEND Camp on Arrival,
         80 boxes S.A.A.
    144   50 " Grenades.

~~a proportion~~ of rods and cartridges for rifle grenades. 120 White, 50 Red and 50 Green Very Lights will be taken by R.S.M. - all others will be handed over as area stores.

2. TRANSPORT.
(a) Advanced Stores of Battalion (Details later) will be sent to SARONA on 31st inst and 1st prox., but under no circumstances will more than 4 limbers be sent together. The Transport Officer will ensure that this order is made known to all Transport personnel. All Field Kitchens, water carts, and stores of the Battalion Transport Section will be moved to SARONA on the 31st inst.

(b) Transport will be Brigaded in the same site as previously i.e. on the Sand Dunes S.W. of SARONA.

(c) 50 Camels will be allotted to Battalion for move.

3. ADVANCED PARTIES.
An advanced Party as under will parade (with all kit) at Battalion Hdqrs. at 0830 on 1/4/18 and will proceed to New Bivouac Area at SARONA, take over any stores etc, to be handed over (also all advanced baggage) and await arrival of Battalion, on night of 2nd/3rd prox.

     Capt. K.G. TIDD.
     Capt. & Q.M. T. BOYCE.
     1 N.C.O. & 3 men per Coy.
     Headquarters X 2 Other Ranks (To be detailed by Q.M and 2 servants of above Officers.

The Transport Officer will arrange for 2 limbers to be at Battalion Headquarters at 0830 on 1/4/18.

4. SUPPLIES, & WATER.
(a) The Divisional Train will **not** deliver supplies to unit on day of relief, for consumption following day.
Supplies for consumption on day after relief will therefore be drawn on that day from SARONA DUMP, at 0830.

(b) Water. Drinking water will be drawn daily from the source behind Billet No 25, at 1640.
Horses will be watered at the troughs S.W. end of SARONA.

5. MEDICAL
Dressing Station will be situated as previously in 21 ARGYLL Street.

6. POSTAL
The Field Post Office will move from HADRAH to SARONA on 1/4/18.

7. SANITATION
All surplus boxes and waste material will be burned to-morrow and on 1/4/18. This should not be left over till the last day.

8. ACKNOWLEDGE.

Issued at 2750. 31/3/18.

     Capt.
     Adjutant 1/6th H.L.I.

Copy No 1 To O.C. A. Coy.   Copy No 5. To T.O.
" " 2 " " B "   " " 6 " Q.M.
" " 3 " " C "   " " 7 C.O. Hdqrs & W.D.
" " 4 " " D. "   " " 8 War Diary.

SECRET. Appendix 2.

Copy No 8

BATTALION ORDER NO 48.
BY
MAJOR W.M.ANDERSON, COMMDG 1/6TH.BN.H.L.I.

Ref.Maps – PALESTINE Sheets 10 & 13, and ARSUF (K 6)   31st March 18

1. INFORMATION.
  (a) The 157th Infantry Brigade will be relieved in the RIGHT Section by the 21st Infantry Brigade, on the night of 2nd/3rd ~~March~~ April 1918, and on relief will move to Bivouac Area near SARONA.
  (b) 1/6th Bn.H.L.I will be relieved by Guides Battalion.

2. MOVE.
  When relieved Companies will move independently to SARONA via MUANNIS BRIDGE.
  Coys will arrange for an Officer to reconnoitre route in daylight, prior to relief. Each Coy will detail an Officer to superintend the crossing of the river by Coy and to ensure that Orders regarding Transport crossing bridges is strictly enforced.
  Headquarters when relieved will move to new Bivouac Area under Lieut. J.P.Wilson.

3 ADVANCE PARTIES.
  (a). Advance Party from this Battalion will proceed to SARONA as ordered in Administrative Instructions.
  Cooks will proceed to SARONA with Dixies, immediately after Dinner on 2/4/18.
  (b) 2 Officers, 2 N.C.Os, and 4 men from the relieving unit will be attached to this battalion as an Advanced Party from 31st March, inclusive.

4 GUIDES.
  (a) Each Coy will detail 1 N.C.O. to report to Orderly Room at hour to be notified later, to act as guide for the relieving Coy.
  (b) Capt. K.G.TIDD O.i/c Advance Party will arrange for 5 guides, (i,e, 1 per Coy and 1 for Hdqrs.) to be at MUANNIS BRIDGE on night 2nd /3rd prox., to guide Coys and Hdqrs., to bivouac areas.

5 AREA & TRENCH STORES.
  All trench and area Stores as per lists issued, existing communications, Defence Schemes, Defence Maps, Maps of No Man's Land, Aeroplane photographs, and Log Books, also all maps other than 1" and 1/250,000 will be handed over and receipts obtained.
  Receipts for all articles handed over will be rendered to Orderly Room by 1000 on 3/4/18.

6. SANITATION
  All trench and bivouac areas will be thoroughly cleaned ready for Inspection by Commanding Officer, at 1600 on 2/4/18. All Soakage pits, and Dumps must be filled in by this hour.

7. ALARM.
  In the event of an Alarm during the relief, units on the move will halt and send an Officer to the nearest Brigade Hdqrs., to report position and to receive Orders.

8. TRANSPORT.
  (a) All blankets surplus to 1 per Other Rank, rolled in bundles of 20, securely tied and labelled, surplus Officers Baggage, and surplus Coy Stores, stacked in Coy areas, will be ready for loading on limbers at 1000 on 1/4/18.
  Headquarters surplus blankets, surplus Officers Baggage, and stores will also be ready at same hour.
  (b) Remaining blankets, rolled as before, with greatcoats and bivouac sheets rolled in bundles of 10 and 20 respectively, securely tied and labelled, Officers kits, and all remaining baggage will be stacked ready for loading in Coy areas at 1000 on 2/4/18.
  Headquarters baggage will also be ready at this hour.
  (c) Transport Officer will arrange for all available ~~G.S.~~ G.S. limbered wagons to report at Battalion Hdqrs on 1st and 2nd April.

9. REPORTS.
  Completion of relief will be wired "PRIORITY" to Battalion Headquarters.
  Completion of move into bivouac area at SARONA will be reported verbally to Capt. K.G.TIDD.

10. ACKNOWLEDGE.

SECRET. Appendix 2.

Patrick [Ykus] Capt.
Adjutant 1/6th H.L.I.

Issued at..0730...31/3/18.

```
Copy No 1 To O. C. A. Coy.
 "   "  2 "  "   "  B.  "
 "   "  3 "  "   "  C   "
 "   "  4 "  "   "  D   "
 "   "  5 "  T.O.
 "   "  6 "  Q.M.
 "   "  7 "  C.O. Hdqrs. & War Diary.
 "   "  8 "  War Diary.
```

Appendix 3

1/6th Highland Light Infantry.

To Transport Officer.   Preliminary Instructions Re. Move.

On arrival at SAKONA you will accompany units during move. On arrival at SAKONA you will return the following articles to the Quartermaster :-
Fringes, brow band.
Clippers, horse.

The Battalion will be encamped at LUDD for 2 days prior to entrainment. On the first day Transport will be required to return all bivouac sheets etc., to Ordnance. On the 2nd day all, harness and saddlery, vehicles and muzzles, horse, ropes, baggage -20 pairs, will be returned to 52nd Divisional Dump, LUDD, through the Quartermaster.
Equipment carried on vehicles according to G. 1098 will be retained and will accompany unit during the move. After vehicles have been returned, animals will be returned to Remounts with the following equipment. Nose bag, head collar, head rope.
Note. All harness will be placed in sacks before being returned. Sacks will be drawn from the Quartermaster.
Receipts must be obtained for every animal and article returned.

GS

1st April.1918.

Adjutant 1/6th H.L.I. Capt.

SECRET. Appendix 4   Copy No. 8

BATTALION ADMINISTRATIVE INSTRUCTIONS.
BY
MAJOR W.M.ANDERSON, COMMDG., 1/6TH BN.H.L.I.
3rd April 1918.

1. The 157th Infantry Brigade Group will be prepared to commence entrainment by 0700 on April 8th.
   Train Timings will be communicated to Coys. immediately they are received.

2. 48 hours rations will be drawn on April 5th for consumption on April 6th and 7th.

3. On April 4th the Battalion Transport Section will be required to transport all baggage, equipment, and stores (which cannot be carried on the person when vehicles have been withdrawn) to LUDD Railway Station.
   Capt.R.C.Tidd will superintend the removal of above stores and a Guard of 1 N.C.O. and 3 men will be detailed by the R.S.M.
   A site for stacking the above stores will be pointed out previously by the Staff Captain.

4. Subsequent to removing baggage etc., the Quartermaster Sgt. will arrange for all equipment special to the E.E.F. as detailed in list issued to him, also all tents in use at SURAFEND Camp to be returned to A.O.D. Depot. This will include 1 blanket per man and portable latrine equipment.
   All bivouac sheets will be returned to A.O.D. Receiving Depot. Subsequent to returning these articles and on the same day the Quartermaster Sgt. will draw 1 waterproof sheet and 1 Box Respirator per man from A.O.D. Depot LUDD.
   Q.M.S. will report compliance to Adjutant.

5. On April 5th the Transport Officer will arrange for all vehicles to be returned to a temporary A.O.D. Receiving Depot established near SURAFEND Camp.
   Subsequent to the return of vehicles harness will be handed in to the same Depot. (Saddles in sacks as already detailed). Animals will finally be led with head rope, head collar and nose bag to Field Remount Section, LUDD and there handed over.

6. It should be clearly understood that the A.O.D. Receiving Depot at LUDD can only accept vehicles, harness and bivouac sheets-all other stores will be returned to A.O.D. Depot LUDD.
   Receipts must be obtained for all animals and articles returned.

7. Lieut. J.P.Wilson, through the R.S.M. will arrange for return of D.A.A. of surplus Lewis Gun magazines (+35 per gun to be returned) to Ammunition Depot LUDD.

8. The Quartermaster Sgt. will arrange for all Fanatis to be handed over to O.C. " D " Company, O.T.C. by 1700 on 5th April.

9. Transport to move Cooking utensils and Officers Kit to LUDD Station on day of entrainment, may be obtained but only the minimum number of camels will be provided. The Quartermaster Sgt. will report number of Camels required to the Orderly Room by 1100 on 5th April.
   This baggage must be kept down to a minimum.

10. The following permanent loading party till the Battalion embarks is detailed:-
   Lieut. D.L.Macintyre.
   2nd Lt.R.J.A. Cumming.
   10 Other Ranks per Coy.(To include 2 N.C.Os)
   These men should be detailed at once that they may be ready when called on to report.
   This party will be responsible for loading and unloading Battalion baggage on all trains and at port of embarkation.

11. O.C. Loading Party must at all times ensure that Battalion baggage is clear of train 30 minutes after arrival at station of detrainment.

12. All entrainments and embarkation must be carried out quickly and quietly.
No talking will be allowed except by Officers and N.C.Os when giving orders. Perfect discipline must be maintained.
Coy. Commanders will carefully think out their arrangements beforehand to ensure that all orders regarding entraining and embarkation are correctly carried out.

13. Acknowledge.

(signed) Patrick Bruce Capt.
Adjutant 1/6th H.L.I.

Issued at......1300...3/4/18.

```
Copy No 1 to O.C. A. Coy.
  "   "  2 "   "   B.  "
  "   "  3 "   "   C.  "
  "   "  4 "   "   D.  "
  "   "  5 "  Quartermaster.
  "   "  6 "  Transport Officer.
  "   "  7 "  C.O. & War Diary.
  "   "  8 "  Aders.
```

Appendix
3/4/18

WAR DIARY
1/6ᵗʰ H.L.I.
1ˢᵗ — 31ˢᵗ MAY 1918.

Volume III

Army Form C. 2118.

WAR DIARY
or
INTELLIGENCE SUMMARY.

(Erase heading not required.)

VOLUME NO 11   MAY 1918.
16 H.L.I.

Summary of Events and Information   Ref. Map. FRANCE 36(a)'
1/40000

Instructions regarding War Diaries and Intelligence Summaries are contained in F. S. Regs., Part II. and the Staff Manual respectively. Title pages will be prepared in manuscript.

Place	Date	Hour	Summary of Events and Information	Remarks and references to Appendices
LA LACQUE	1/5/18	0700	Physical Training — N.C.Os. under Regt¹ S¹ Major.	
		0930-1200	Specialists Training — Gas Training, all men wearing Box Helmets for two hours. — Route marches by Coys. — 2 Platoons bayonet fighting training under Brigade Instructors.	Yes.
		1400-1500	Musketry — Bombers Training under Battn. bombing officer.	
			C.O., Adj¹, D¹¹C Corp¹, various Sen¹ Officers reconnoitred line to be held by this battn. in event of enemy breaking through present front line. (see appendix)	Appendix 1/5/18
	2/5/18	1100	Lecture on "Bayonet Fighting" to whole battalion by G.H.Q. Instructor (Major Campbell) held by this Battn. Adjt, 2nd in command (BMr.), & Coy 2nd in command reconnoitred trenches to be held by this battn.	Yes
			Training as for yesterday.	
		2100	Capt J.N. McMURDO rejoined battn. from Brigade HdQrs. Sounds of heavy shelling. — Word received from Brigade re likelihood of enemy aeroplane attack during night.	
		1600	Enemy aeroplane observed chased by 3 of our machines.	
		2010	O.C. Coys with 50% Officers & N.C.Os reconnoitred route to trenches N¹ Bois D'AMONT.	
	3/5/18		Coys marched to Bois Damont reconnoitred trenches held. Relieve by a colm¹ 4 B.G.R.A. detailed by G.H.Q. on manoeuvres.	8
			Specialist bayonet fighting under Brigade Instructors. 15 officers attended. Capt MMURDO made outmost order to G33 d.1. Reid 13th Patterson attd rejoined from U.K.	
	4/5/18	0730	This batt. left camp and marched to G 33 d. 1 — moment through a Chlorine Gas Cloud. also attended a demonstration in the Projector, Livens Cylinder Flammenwerfer & Tear Gas.	P
			To comp at 1700 — A small party under L¹D.L. McIntyre left for Trenches.	

Army Form C. 2118.

WAR DIARY
or
INTELLIGENCE SUMMARY.
(Erase heading not required.)

Instructions regarding War Diaries and Intelligence Summaries are contained in F. S. Regs., Part II. and the Staff Manual respectively. Title pages will be prepared in manuscript.

Place	Date	Hour	Summary of Events and Information	Remarks and references to Appendices
LA LACQUE	5/3/18	0930	All troops by on ready for loading transporting to new area.	
		0930	Church parade.	
		1000	Inspection of billets by C.O.	
		1400	Inspection of Baths by C.O.	
			Advanced billeting party under Lt Cumming left for new area.	
		1100	Conference of O.C. Coys. under C.O.	

WAR DIARY
or
INTELLIGENCE SUMMARY.
(Erase heading not required.)

Army Form C. 2118.

Place	Date	Hour	Summary of Events and Information	Remarks and references to Appendices
LA LACQUE	6/5/18	0745	Bath paraded & proceeded to AIRE STATION & entrained for MAREUIL arrived MAREUIL about 1530 and marched to billets at NEUVILLE ST VAAST / on night of 7th May – Emelie (2 pn platoon 1/1st Cdn Hldrs) from 75th CANADIAN REGT reported remained one night. (see appendices)	appendices 6/5/18
NEUVILLE ST VAAST	7/5/18	0845	C.O. Adjt & OC Coys visited sector to be taken over	Q
		0930	Advanced parties left for new sector	
		1900	Bath paraded & proceeded to trenches to relieve 75th CANADIAN REGT – Relief completed at 0330 on 8/5/18.	
VIMY, 2nd LINE TRENCHES	8/5/18	0400	Stand to Arms – (Gas helmet drill immediately) Coys continued work in Trenches – LT D. McTAVISH appointed Bath works Officer.	Q
		1930	Stand to Arms. Fire positions checked.	
		2000	Enemies T.M. and fire heavy from right LENS direction.	
		2300	Work resumed & probable bombardment of enemy to resume & mines – all Coys notified.	
	9/5/18	0100	Stand to Arms – Usual work in trenches – All Enemies; SAA, Gas Plant material returned – Word received from Bde that enemy would probably open a Gas shell bombardment at 2230 till 0130 when his infantry would advance.	Q
		2130	600 Gas projectors successfully launched by 155th Bde on our right accompanied by a short bombardment. Enemy did not retaliate.	
			light passed quietly – LT LOCKHART to GAS COURSE.	
	10/5/18	0100	Stand to Arms – Enemy T.M. heavy must shew up early (actually morning then was scarcely any shelling by either side – all our Coys labelled with number of section, platoon, Coy, Coy etc, etc occupying them –	Q
	11/5/18		Occupy by NCOs visited Sector nightly 11/12, 12/13, 13/14, 14/15th May. – Orders received that 1/6 H.L.I would receive 1/5 A.P.S.M on night of 14/15th May. – leave to U.K. opened 1/N 52, 2 other N52 officer every 4 days, 10 officer every 4 days. – LT McINTYRE to hospital.	Q

WAR DIARY
or
INTELLIGENCE SUMMARY.
(Erase heading not required.)

Army Form C. 2118.

Place	Date	Hour	Summary of Events and Information	Remarks and references to Appendices
CHAUDIÈRE DEFENCES	12/3/18	0700	Stand to Arms — Orders for relief of 1/5 A.S.H. To be carried out on night 13th/14th May renewed, not 10th/11th.	
			6 Enemy observation balloons up in direction ARRAS, 9 of ours up.	
		1600	Enemy shelled 18 pdr. gun near battn. Hd Qrs with H.E.'s. no damage done.	
		2130	"B" Coy reported for own.	
			O.C. and Adj visited 1/5 A.S.H. sector — Orders received for relief (appendix 12/3/18) Advanced parties proceeded to movements.	(appendix 12/3/18)
	13/3/18	0920	Enemy aeroplane worked heavily shelled by our A.A. guns.	
		1500	C Coy relieved Coy 1/5 A.S.H. in battle reserve in new sector.	
		2030	Relief commenced by 2300 — Patrol under 2/Lt CURRIE 300706 in front of our own — nothing to report.	
	14/3/18	0330	Stand to Arms — C.O. visited Coy areas — work in trenches carried on as handed over by 1/5A.S.H. — Raid on our right by 1/7 H.L.I. Enemy trenches entered but no prisoners were taken + no Germans killed. Pt. Patrol under 2/DOBSON to near enemy wire, nothing to report.	
	15/3/18		Bty took over most of KEANE TRENCH from D Coy. A Coy took our new word TEDDIE SICKWOOD/MM B Coy. Enemy shelled DORIS DUMP — heavy shelling observed on our immediate right. 1 Sgt. killed in HAYTER TRENCH — work on trenches etc. as usual. Patrol under 1st MORRISON almost reached enemy wire found no gap then.	
	16/3/18		Preparations made for two attacks, but postponed owing to adverse winds. — Worse usual. — heavy shelling heard on right. Patrol under Lt MCINTOSH proceeded to enemy wire but owing to brightness of moon could not advance further.	

Army Form C. 2118.

WAR DIARY
or
INTELLIGENCE SUMMARY.
(Erase heading not required.)

Place	Date	Hour	Summary of Events and Information	Remarks and references to Appendices
CHAUDIERE DEFENCES (northern)	17/5/18		Stand to Arms from 0330 - 0800 every to a very that mist. Work as usual. C.O. returned on 1 day leave. Officers reduced to 20 (combatant) while Batt'n is in line, remainder sent to a Brigade Details Camp. All other ranks brought up from Brigade Details Camp to an far as possible to complete return to 1500 P. men apportioned under Lt D Hobbs naked sentry men but every opportunity of daylight did not succeed in entering enemy Trenches. — Defence scheme completed (see appendices)	appendix 17/5/18. P
	18/5/18	0330	Stand to Arms 0330 - 0430. Orders received for raid by 1/15 ArgSH on night 19/5/20 & Raid orders prepared for a raid on enemy Trench MERIC T.11.a.O/8 (informed)	appendix 18/5/18 Q
		2030	C.O. inspected all Platoons of B Coy in rapid manning of dugouts of apportion	
		2100	Enemy shelled two area between BETTY and VESTA TRLEY. No damage done.	
		1600	Conference 1 OC Coys.	
	19/5/18	0330	Stand to Arms. Work as usual. Preparations made for move. Relief completed by 1330 and 1/6 H.L.I moved into Brigade Reserve. (See Appendices)	appendix 19/5/18. P

WAR DIARY
or
INTELLIGENCE SUMMARY.
(Erase heading not required.)

Army Form C. 2118.

Place	Date	Hour	Summary of Events and Information	Remarks and references to Appendices
LA CHAUDIERE LINE. (Bde. RESERVE)	20/5/18	1000	Conference I.C.Os. at Brigade HdQrs to meet Corps Commander — all NCOs men in Baths. 1 rd S.A.A. — high material selected — Major W. ANDERSON rejoined battn from details camp to take over Temporarily during absence of Lt.Col. ANDERSON on leave to UK. Work on M.G. bays & Trenches carried on. New orders for Gas attack prepared (see appendix)	P
	21/5/18	0900	Lt.Col. ANDERSON proceeded on leave to UK. (14 days) — Extra personnel sent to Transport Section for cleaning harness, limbers etc. Two platoons daily to hot baths at NEUVILLE ST VAAST, & new underclothing supplied. 5 Rds. fired by enemy N.C.O. guns on the battn.	Appendix 20/5/18. P
		1000	Battn was in "PETIT VIMY" shelter both W.2 & S.9. Work on trenches carried on during night Major W.M. ANDERSON took over command (Amp) of battn. 5 Officers 158 N.C.Os. nominated for area.	
	22/5/18		All Officers reports from details camp rosters sent to replace — Two Lewis Guns sent to details Camp for training purposes. Reserve Ration dumps formed at CHAUDIERE and near Battn HdQrs. Lt.DOBSON on 14 days furlough to UK. Brick field working drilled between 0900-1100	S

Army Form C. 2118.

WAR DIARY
or
INTELLIGENCE SUMMARY.
(Erase heading not required.)

Instructions regarding War Diaries and Intelligence Summaries are contained in F. S. Regs., Part II. and the Staff Manual respectively. Title pages will be prepared in manuscript.

Place	Date	Hour	Summary of Events and Information	Remarks and references to Appendices
LA CHAUDIERE LINE. BRIGADE RESERVE	22/5/18		C.O. & Adjutant visited W/Army Line Section & Right 52nd Divn Sector.	P
	23/5/18	1100	Advanced Guard S and E.A.R. Advanced parties of relieving bn. (1/4 K.O.Y.L.I.) arrived.	
		1415	Camouflage received for our attack taking place tonight. All Rortn were inspected by the Commandt. The wagons were parked in Kranaston 50 yds in front of TOLEDO TRENCH, they arrived much by the slopes being slippery & horses few. Artillery Fire. At 0145 the Capts were fuzed & at that close of Column phosgen gas rolled towards the enemy line in a N.W. Easterly direction. No wind from the enemy trenches & then was no artillery fire on our front line Trenches. Round was heavy at 18 mile p.h. Porter returned to camp about 0400.	P
	24/5/18		All Reparations made for relief. Fused work carried on & party & 1 R.M. N.S.R. by all men. Both were relieved by the 1/4 K.O.Y.L.I. at 2300 & proceeded to FRASER CAMP, STEENWI in motor wagons from Junction of LA FOLIE, NEVILLE ST VAAST RD. become Divisional Reserve. All Coys reported in new area at 2430. See Appendix 24/5/18	P Appendix 24/5/18
ST ELOY	25/5/18		Medical officer inspected all Coys – Two companies bathed & received new clothing – Camp cleaned up etc.	P

Army Form C. 2118.

WAR DIARY
or
INTELLIGENCE SUMMARY.

(Erase heading not required.)

Instructions regarding War Diaries and Intelligence Summaries are contained in F. S. Regs., Part II. and the Staff Manual respectively. Title pages will be prepared in manuscript.

Place	Date	Hour	Summary of Events and Information	Remarks and references to Appendices
ST ELOY	26/5/18		Commanding Officer inspected billets — Church Parade — Two companies bathed — G.O.C. Division inspected Camps — C.O. 12 in Command reconnoitred route to rendezvous of Brigade in case of alarm — Intelligence Officer & 1 Officer per Coy reconnoitred route to Rifle Ranges and Training Ground.	8
	27/5/18	0900- 1200	Physical Training under a Staff Instructor attached — NCOs under R.S.M. — Coy, Platoon & Section Tactical Exercises — Specialist Training — Two companies Lewis Gun Teams fired on L.G. Range 1 mag per man, results were good — Two companies fired a pumping practice at 100 yds, application at 150 yd, 10 rds rapid with Two Respirators on at 150 at LA MOTTE range. Enemy long range guns fired a few rounds into ST ELOY during the day & all splashed in a field occupied by 2 of our F.A. Enemy aeroplanes were overhead at night & a few bombs were dropped. Lt HILL'S proceeded on leave to U.K.	8
	28/5/18		Training, Lewis Gun & Rifle Range Firing same as yesterday —	8
	29/5/18		The G.O.C. inspected some of the coys in tactical exercises — Training — Hostile aeroplanes flew overhead about 2100. Specialist	8

Place	Date	Hour	Summary of Events and Information	Remarks and references to Appendices
ST ELOY	30/5/18		All Employed putting a "Bunting Cross" Rownd Huts — Signallers demonstrated with Aeroplane New POPHAM PANEL — Sig N/L Col, & 2nd in command attended demonstration of Messrs Gwynns Rocket (Miniature rocket travelled one about 2200 yds. All Officers attended conference in Y.M.C.A. Hut when Bri. Gen. spoke on discipline of Troops.	P.
	31/5/18	11.30	Advanced Parties left for trenches — All men employed drying huts etc. covering Huts. Ammo dump moved to BERTHONVAL FARM.	g

G. Stuck Storms Capt
 ad. 16 H.L.I

1/6th Bn H.L.I.

To Headquarters,
157th Bde.

Herewith Sketch of Proposed Defences for the Sector of the 157th Bde. front allotted to this Battn.

Ernest Jours Captain
for Lieut. Col.
Commdg 1/6th H.L.I.

Date 30/4/18

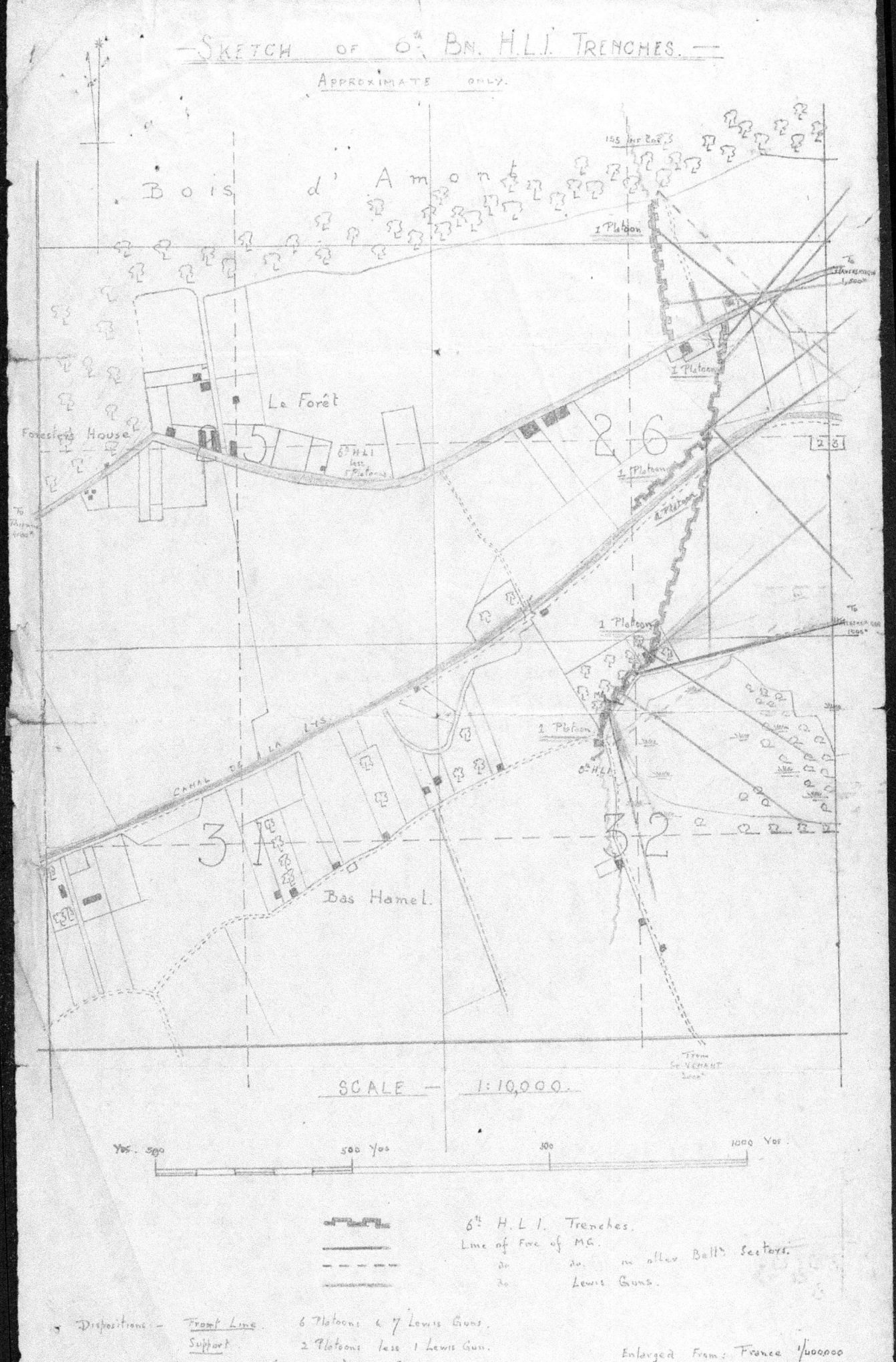

Copy No..8...

SECRET.

BATTALION ORDER NO. 2.
BY.
LIEUT COL. J. ANDERSON, C.M.G., D.S.O. Commdg. 1/6TH.BN.H.L.I.
            2nd May

REFERENCE MAP FRANCE, SHEET 36 A.1/40,000.

---

1 INFORMATION.

(a) The 157th Inf. Brigade will be prepared to occupy the BUSNES-STEENBECQUE Line from COURANT BRAYELLE River at P.2.c.4.7. (exclusive) to the SOUTHERN EDGE of the BOIS D'AMONT at J.20 d.2.2 (inclusive).

(b) The 1/6th Bn.H.L.I. will occupy the Left of the Brigade Line as follows -
    From Road Junction at J.32 a.8.5. (inclusive) to the
    Southern Edge of the BOIS D'AMONT at J.20 d. 2-2
The 5th H.L.I. will hold the Line on the RIGHT, the dividing line being the Road running parallel to, and about 300 yards SOUTH of the Lys Canal.
This road will be inclusive to the 1/6th Bn.H.L.I.
The position to be held is a rearward system in case of the front line system being penetrated.

The line will be occupied by a nucleus garrisons only, which must be in a position before penetration of the front line takes place.

The 7th Bn.H.L.I. and the 5th A.&.S.H. will be in Brigade Reserve.

1. DISPOSITIONS.

The line allotted to this Battalion will be held as under-
3 Platoons B.Coy from junction with 155th Bde at EDGE of BOIS D'AMONT (J.20 .d.2.2.) to the **NORTHERN** bank of the LYS Canal.
inclusive.
2.Platoons A.Coy. from SOUTHERN bank of LYS Canal to junction with 5th Bn.H.L.I. at Road Junction J.32 .a.8.5. (road running parallel to, and about 300 yards SOUTH of LYS canal inclusive.

3. STOKES GUNS.

4 Stokes Guns will be allotted to this Battalion and will be situated as under -
    2 Guns about J.26.b.3.4.   2 Guns about J.32 b. 2.9.

4. MEDICAL.

(a) 1 Section 2nd L.F.A. will furnish a MAIN DRESSING STATION on the present site of the billets at LA LACQUE with 2 Collecting Stations at.
    (1) The Road Junction near Footbridge in square O.5.d.10.9.
    (2) The Road Junction I.30 c.7.4.
(b) The Battalion Dressing Station will be situated at J.15 Central.

5. HEADQUARTERS.

(a) Brigade Hdqrs. will be situated WEST of CENSE A VI6 at house in square I 35 c 3.8.
(b) The Battalion Hdqrs. with the Battalion, less 3 platoons of B. Coy and 2 platoons A. Coy. will be situated at J.15 Central.

6. ORDERS TO TROOPS.

Troops will move to their positions on receipt of the order " Man Battle Positions"
In order to occupy line as early as possible after receipt of above order A.& B. Coys will each hold 1 platoon always in readiness to move at a few minutes notice.
On receipt of above order these platoons will march off independently without waiting for the Battalion to assemble and will take up their allotted positions.

The remainder of the Battalion on receipt of the Order " Man Battle Positions" will fall in, in Mass on Alarm Post ready to move.
(Dress and other orders same as Standing Orders for an Alarm.

7. ROUTE.

Troops will move to their Battle Positions as under
6th H.L.I. Via the TANNAY - LE FORREST Road.
5th Bn.H.L.I and 6th Bn.H.L.I. will have precedence on the roads.

8. BRIDGES.

The following bridges not shown on the map, now exist and should be marked on all maps and made known to runners.
(a) Pontoon Bridge over LYS Canal in square I 18.d. where marked Ferry.
(b) Fascine bridge over Lys Canal in square J.26 c. 5.2.
(c) Stone bridge over COURANT BRAYELLE RIVER at square P.2.c.4.7.

9. REPORTS.

Reports to Battalion Hdqrs at J.15 Central.

10. ACKNOWLEDGE.

Issued at 2030 8/5/18.

Capt.
Adjutant 1/6th Bn.H.L.I.

Copy No 1 TO O.C. A Coy.
"   " 2 "   "   B "
"   " 3 "   "   C "
"   " 4 "   "   D "
"   " 5 " Hdqrs Coy.
"   " 6 " Q.M. & T.B.
"   " 7 " R.S.M. & FILE.
"   " 8 " C.O. & File.

Secret.   Copy No. 6

BATTALION ORDER No 3.
By
LIEUT-COL. J. ANDERSON, C.M.G. D.S.O. COMMGD. 1/6th Bn. H.L.I.
5th May, 1918.

REF. MAP. – Sheets MAROEUIL & ST. NAZAIRE RIVER, Scale 1/20,000.

I. INFORMATION.
(a) The 52nd Division will move from the neighbourhood of AIRE on the 6th, 7th, & 8th inst., and take over the MARICOURT Sector of the Line from the 4th Canadian Division from HUDSON Trench in square T.29.a.8.4. to the present northern boundary of the Canadian Corps Line at T.3.6.4.0. — a frontage of about 4,500 yards.

(b) The 157th Brigade Group will relieve the 11th Canadian Infantry Brigade in the line on the night of 7/8th May.
The 156th Bde. Group will be in support about NEUVILLE ST. VAAST.
The 155th Bde. Group will be in reserve about ST. ELOY.

II. DISPOSITIONS.
(a) The 7th H.L.I. & 5th A. & S.H. will take over the front zone from the 87th Canadian Regiment and 102nd Canadian Regiment respectively. 7th H.L.I. being on the RIGHT & the 5th A. & S.H. on the LEFT.
The 6th H.L.I. will take over the 2nd Defensive Zone from the 75th Canadian Regiment.
The 5th H.L.I. will take over the 3rd Defensive Zone from the 54th Canadian Regiment, less 2 Coys.
The 185th L.T.M. Bty. (emb. attached 157th Brigade) will take over existing gun positions from the 11th Canadian L.T.M.B.

(b) Dispositions of Coys. later.

III. GUIDES.
Arrangements have been made for 2 Guides per Platoon from the 75th Canadian Regiment to meet this Battn. at NEUVILLE ST. VAAST Camp on the evening of 6th inst.
These guides will remain with Bn. for the night and following day, and will be available to guide Coys. up to the Line on the night of 7th inst.

IV. ROUTE.
The Battn. will proceed from AIRE in tactical trains on the 6th inst. to NEUVILLE ST. VAAST Camp and thence by Route March to new area on the night of 7/8th inst.

V. TRENCH & AREA STORES.
Defence Schemes, Trench Maps, existing communications, aeroplane photos, log books, trench and area stores will be taken over and receipts given for same. Duplicate copies of receipts given will be rendered to Orderly Room by 1200 on 8th inst.

VI. RELIEF.
The Battalion will not commence to cross the VIMY RIDGE until 2000 and relief must be complete by 0600 on the 8th inst.
Detailed Orders for Relief later.

VII REPORTS

(a) The completion of Relief will be reported by Priv. French Code to Battn. H.Qrs. by Priority wire (Priv. French Code will be explained to O.C. Coys. later.)

(b) Brigade H.Qrs. will be on the VIMY RIDGE in LA FOLIE COPSE, square 5030.

VIII ACKNOWLEDGE.

                                                    Signature
                                                         Captain.
                                        Adjt. 16th Bn. H.L.I.

Issued at 1630   5/5/18.

         Copy No 1 - to O.C. A Coy
                  " 2 - " " B "
                  " 3 - " " C "
                  " 4 - " " D "
                  " 5 - " " H.Q. "
                  " 6 - " " Q.M. & T.O.
                  " 7 - " " R.S.M & FILE
                  " 8 - " " CO & FILE

SECRET   BATTALION ORDER No 6   Copy No 6
                          By
            Lieut Col T Anderson, CMG, DSO, Comdg 16th H.L.I.
                                                    7th May, 1918

I. GENERAL INFORMATION
    The 16th Bn H.L.I. will take over 1st line Trenches from 75th Canadian Regt tonight

II. MOVE
    Guides have been allotted to each Coy who will meet Coys at the points to be taken over.
    Order of precedence will be :-   9th Bn H.L.I.   16th Bn H.L.I.
    Coys will proceed to the line via MORTER DUMP WEST of MT ST VAAST.
    Coys are not to move in bodies larger than 1 Platoon at 100 yds distance, and will not pass over VIMY RIDGE before 8.30 p.m.
    All Coys will parade on Coy Parade Grounds ready to move at 7.30 p.m. & will move without waiting on receiving orders from the Adjt.
    Dress:- Full Marching Order, greatcoats worn, blankets strapped onto back of packs, haversacks in usual position, Steel Helmets.

III. DISPOSITIONS
    A, B, C, D Coys 16th H.L.I. will take over from A, B, C, D Coys of the 75th Canadian Regt, respectively.
    A Coy on the Right, D Coy on the Left.

IV. LEWIS GUNS
    All Lewis Guns with 3 leather cases of tin boxes, each containing 6 loaded magazines per gun, & spare parts will be taken by Coys tonight. These will be taken up as far as possible on limbers, & then man-handled to the Trenches. All remaining Lewis Gun equipment will be sent to Transport lines tonight & will be sent to Coys along with the rations tomorrow night.

V. MOVEMENT
    (a) All ranks are cautioned that the slightest movement about the trenches to be taken over draws hostile artillery fire. It is also most important that the enemy should not know that a new Battn has taken over.
    (b) Coke only will be used for cookhouse fires and these will be placed in a suitable position. No smoke whatever must be visible by day, or glare of fires by night, as this draws artillery fire.

    NOTE. There will be no movement in the open - trenches only being used in the daylight. Any infringement of this order will be strictly dealt with.

VI. RATIONS & WATER
    (a) Rations are sent up nightly by light railway and Coys will send over, under C.Q.M.S., a small ration party to collect same. Coys will be notified later of the place where rations will be carried on the men tonight.
    (b) Water for C & D Coys & HQ is drawn in D Coys area by means of petrol tins. Only small parties will be sent to draw water at one time. There must be no congestion at the pipe line.
    Water for A & B Coys is drawn from a pipe near A Coys HQ.

VII. TRENCH STORES
    All reserve rations taken over tonight should be carefully checked. No broken boxes S.A.A. should be taken over.

VIII. WORKING PARTIES
    A statement of the work in hand will be taken over by Coys, & the work will be continued.

13. S O S SIGNAL is as follows:-

Given by a N° 32 Grenade bursting into Green over Red over Green. This is taken up from the front line by a post at Batt. HQ'rs, repeated by them to Bde HQ. The S.O.S. will at the same time be sent by phone.

Immediately on the S O S signal being sent up, Battle positions will immediately be taken up by all ranks.

This S.O.S. signal also holds good on our Right in the 13th Corps as far South as ARRAS DOUAI Railway.

On the Left however the S.O.S. signal is Green, Green, Green.

14. COMMUNICATIONS

There are to be no telephone conversations on anything tactical either backward or forward.

15. MEDICAL

There will be a main Dressing Station at AUX RIETZ (A.8.c). Advanced Dressing Stations of the 2nd L.F.A. will be at LA CHAUDIERE (S.18.c.9.2) and VIMY VILLAGE (T.25.d.9.4).

16. PERSONNEL TO REMAIN BEHIND

Personnel to remain behind, as detailed separately, will, till further orders, remain at Transport lines.

17. TRANSPORT

2 Limbers will be allotted to each Coy. including HQ's, to carry up all Lewis Guns & L.S. equipment, Officers Baggage and Rations. These limbers will proceed with the Coys as far as possible, when all baggage will be man handled to the trenches. Limbers returning to Transport lines.

18. GAS SENTRIES

(a) All Gas Sentry Posts will be taken over & sentries instructed that they are responsible for informing all personnel in the dugouts, immediately a Gas attack takes place.

(b) Gas Respirators will, at all times, be worn in the "Alert Position" day & night everywhere men are sleeping.

19. REPORTS

Relief completed will be reported to Batt. HQ by Priority wire as follows:- 316 (Followed by name of Coy Commander.)

20. ACKNOWLEDGE

ISSUED AT 1810 4/5/18

G Patrick Weir
A/Lt. 16th Batt.

COPY N° 1.- To OC A Coy.
2 - " B "
3 - " C "
4 - " D "
5 - " HQ "
6 - QM & TO
7 - RSM & FILE
8 - CO & FILE

SECRET   BATTALION ORDER Nº 5   COPY Nº 6
BY
LIEUT. COL. J. ANDERSON, C.M.G., D.S.O. Commdg. 1/6th Bn. H.L.I.

REF. MAP :- ST. NAZAIRE RIVER 1/20,000.   10TH MAY, 1918.

I INFORMATION

The 1/6th Bn. H.L.I. is responsible for the defence of the CHAUDIERE DEFENCES.

II DISPOSITIONS

The Battalion Sector has been divided into 5 defended localities. Localities are allotted to Coys. as under. Each Coy. is responsible for the defence of the locality allotted to it.

A Coy.

EAST Boundary	- T.15 central, thro' T.21.b.6/0	to T.21.c.6/0.
SOUTH "	- T.27.a.7/8 to T.26.b.9.9	thence to T.20.d.5.4
WEST "	- T.20.d.5.4	to T.15.d.3.7

B Coy.

EAST Boundary	- T.15.d.3.7	to T.20.d.5.4.
SOUTH "	- T.20.d.5.4	to T.19.b.8.4.
WEST "	- T.19.b.8.4	to T.14.b.2.5.
NORTH "	- T.14.b.2.5	to T.15.d.3.7.

C Coy.

WEST Boundary	- T.13.c.5.5 to S.12.d.4.5.	thence to T.1.c.2.3.
NORTH "	- T.1.c.2.3	to T.7.b.3.9.
EAST "	- T.7.b.3.9 thro' to T.7.b.9.4	and T.7.d.8/0 to T.13.c.5/5
SOUTH "		

D Coy.

NORTH Boundary	- T.7.b.3.9	to T.2.c.8.3
EAST "	- T.2.c.8.3 to T.8.c.2.7	thence to T.14.a.3.8.
SOUTH "	- T.14.a.3.8	to T.7.d.8.0.
WEST "	- T.7.d.8.0 to T.7.d.5.9	& T.7.b.8.4 to T.7.b.3.9.

H.Q'S. Coy.

NORTH Boundary	- T.7.d.8.0 to T.14.a.3.8	thence to T.14.b.2.5.
EAST "	- T.14.b.2.5	to T.19.b.8.4
SOUTH "	- T.19.b.8.4	to T.13.c.5.5.
WEST "	- T.13.c.5.5	to T.7.d.8.0.

III ORDERS TO TROOPS

(a). Special.

"A" Coy. will adhere to orders already issued in the event of enemy turning our RIGHT Flank & attacking from the SOUTH.

B Coy. In the event of enemy penetrating our Front Line Works, B Coy will be prepared to put a block on PEGGIE Trench. Should the enemy pass round our RIGHT Flank & attack from the SOUTH, B Coy must be prepared to put a block on PEGGIE Trench & also maintain KURTON Trench.

C Coy. Special precautions require to be taken for the security of the LEFT Flank at LENS - ARRAS Road.
C Coy. will be prepared to form a defensive flank in CENTRE Trench and BADDECK should the enemy succeed in passing round the LEFT flank. Particular attention will be paid to all Trenches leading to "C" Coys Sector from the direction of the enemy.
A forward position for a Lewis Gun firing NORTH and NORTH EAST should be selected about the AMHURST Trench.

D Coy – Particular attention should be paid to all Trenches leading to D Coy's Sector from the direction of the enemy also to the Railway Embankment. Attention is particularly drawn to the fact that D Coy is responsible for the defence of the entire Railway Embankment and very careful arrangements should be made for its security.

A forward position for a Lewis Gun and Escort should be selected in BLUE NOSE Trench NORTH of the Western end of DARTMOUTH.

(b) General

Full use of should be made of Coy Scouts to ensure early warning of the approach of the enemy being given.

There should be no hesitation on the part of Coy or Platoon Commanders in initiating counter attacks on any small bodies of the enemy to prevent them establishing themselves near our line.

IV REPORTS

During an attack O.C. Coys will render to Battn HQs at T 13 d. 5.9 hourly situation reports.

V COMMUNICATION

A Battn Chain is being arranged between Battn HQs & C & D Coys and Battn HQs & B & A Coys.

VI ACKNOWLEDGE

Patrick Shaw
Capt
Adjt 1/6th Bn H.L.I.

ISSUED AT 0100. 10/5/18

Copy No 1 – To O C A Coy
2 – " " B "
3 – " " C "
4 – " " D "
5 – " " HQ Coy
6 – " " CO + FILE

SECRET.   Copy N°

BATTALION ORDER NO 6
BY
LIEUT. COL. J. ANDERSON, C.M.G. D.S.O. COMMDG. 1/6TH BN H.L.I.

Reference Map - ST. NAZAIRE RIVER 1/10000.   13th May 1918.

INFORMATION.
   A Local 157th Brigade Relief takes place on the nights of 13th/14th and 14th/15th May, as under.
      5th H.L.I. relieves 7th H.L.I. on night of 14th/15th inst.
      6th H.L.I. relieves 5th A.& S.H. on night of 13th/14th inst.

1. RELIEF.
   (a) The 1/6th Bn H.L.I. will relieve the 1/5th A.& S.H. in the left sector of the 157th Bde. Sector. The 1/5th A.& S.H. when relieved will move into area presently occupied by this Battn.
   (b) Coys will relieve as under -

	1/6.H.L.I.	1/5 A& S.H.	
RIGHT FIRING LINE	A. Coy will relieve	C. Coy	in trenches VESTA TILLEY, LILY ELSIE & TEDDIE GERARD. Coy Hdqrs near junction of PEGGY & TEDDY GERRARD.
SUPPORT.	B. Coy " "	A. "	in trench TEDDIE GERRARD from KEANE to VESTA TILLEY. Coy Hdqrs in DORIS TRENCH
RESERVE.	C. Coy " "	B. "	in trenches HAYTER & GLADYS Coy H.Qrs in HAYTER (New H.Qrs to be selected by O.C. Coy).
LEFT FIRING LINE	D. Coy " "	D. "	in trenches KEANE, BETTY & unnamed trenches in T.8 b. H.Qrs. BETTY TRENCH near embankment.
	Battn H.Qrs. " "	Bn.H.Qrs.	in DORIS TRENCH.

Note.-
   On night of 13th/14th or early morning of the 14th May after completion of relief of 1/5th A.& S.H. the 1/7th H.L.I. will take over from 1/6th H.L.I. all trenches east of VESTA TILLEY, leaving VESTA TILLEY with this Battn. New dispositions for the platoons of A. Coy holding trenches taken over by 1/7th H.L.I. will be detailed later.

3. ADVANCED PARTIES.
   Advanced Parties from Coys and Battn.H.Qrs will be sent to take over on night of 13th May as ordered.

4. MOVE.
   (a) C. Coy will move from their present position at 1800 on 13th May and proceed to relieve Reserve Coy 1/5th A.& S.H. during daylight.
   Medical Officer and Medical personnel will also proceed at 1800 to relieve 1/5th A.& S.H. Medical personnel.
   Both of the above reliefs must be carried out by means of communication trenches and in small parties.
   (b) Remaining Coys and Battn H.Qrs will move from their present position at following hours.
      A.   1930   if sufficiently dark that movement cannot be seen
      B.   1940   "   "   "   "   "   "
      D.   1930   "   "   "   "   "   "
      Battn.Qrs 1940 "   "   "   "   "   "
   In the event of the night being misty the hour of relief may be put forward in orders sent by Orderly Room.

5. GUIDES.
   (a) The 1/5th A.& S.H. have arranged for 5 Guides per Coy (1 per platoon and 1 Coy H.Qrs) and 1 Battn. HdQrs to report to Coys at their present positions at 1500 on 13th. These guides will only be able to direct platoons on arriving at their Coy areas and do not know the routes from present Coy positions of 1/6th H.L.I. to Coy areas of 1/5th A.& S.H.

GUIDES (Cont).
   these routes must be thoroughly reconnoitred by O.C. Coys & Platoon Commanders during daylight tomorrow.
   (b) 1 Officer 1/5th A. & S.H. per Coy and Batn.H.Qrs will remain with this unit on night of 13/14 May to give any assistance required.

6. TRENCH STORES.
   (a) Coy and Battn Representatives from 1/5th A & S.H. will report tomorrow to take over all Trench and Area stores from this Sector.
   (b) Officers proceeding with advanced parties will take over all Trench and Area Stores in new area.
   Duplicates of receipts given and taken both for A and B to be rendered to Orderly Room by 1500 on 14th May.

7. SANITATION.
   (a) All Trenches and Coy areas presently occupied by this unit will be left scrupulously clean & receipts obtained on handing over that the area was taken over in a clean and sanitary condition.
   (b) Trenches to be taken over will be inspected & certificates given as to their sanitary condition.

8. RATIONS & WATER.
   (a) Commencing from night of 13th inst rations for the whole Battn will be sent via VICTORIA DUMP and transferred there into wagons which are pushed by a fatigue party detailed from Reserve Coy to dump near Battn Hdqrs where there they are unloaded by Reserve Coys Fatigue party and stored overnight.
   Rations will come up partly cooked and divided into Coy portions (platoon portions in each Coy Bag) Each Coy will send 1 man to meet wagons on arrival at Battn Dump and guard Coy Rations overnight.
   After Stand to Arms each morning all Coys will send a party consisting of C.Q.M.Sgts & 10 men to draw rations from Battn Dump.
   No more than 1 man per Coy from any of the Coys in the firing line and support is permitted to leave his Coy area after Stand to Arms at night.
   (b) Water.
      Water is obtained from water pipes situated as under -
      No 1 Pipe in DORIS TRENCH near Battn Hdqrs for use of Btn H.Qrs Coy and Reserve Coy.
      No 2 Pipe Near junction of Trenches PEGGY & TEDDIE GERRARD for use of A.& B. Coys (This pipe is in 1/7th H.L.I. Sector and permission has kindly been given to let this Battn have use of same)
      No 3 Pipe T.8 b.7.6. for use of D. Coy.
      Only small parties will draw water from any of the pipes at one time.
      Sentries will be posted at pipes by Coys as under-
      No 1 Pipe - C. Coy.   No 2 Pipe B. Coy.   No 3 Pipe D. Coy.

9. TRANSPORT.
      As much Coy Baggage as possible will be taken to new areas on night of 12th inst and during day of 13th May but all movement must be screened from view of the enemy. On Night of Move all remaining Coy Baggage will be man handled to new areas.

10. PATROL & SNIPERS.
    (a) There is an Observation Post by day, a listening post by night, in each of A. & D. Coys Sectors consisting of 1 N.C.O. & 6 men. These will be relieved on taking over.
    A post of 1 N.C.O. & 4 men in front of wire presently found by Right Firing Line Coy 1/5th A & S.H. will be taken over by 1/7th H.L.I. from A. Coy during 14th May.
    (b) Snipers will be pushed forward to natural positions in front of trenches under Coy arrangements.

11. MEDICAL.
    Battn Dressing Station is situated near junction of Trenches HAYTER & DORIS

12. STAND TO ARMS
    Stand to Arms will be at following hours-
        Morning 0345- 0445 or All Clear.
        Night. 2000- 2030 roll call and checking fire positions.

13 WORK IN HAND.
The Battn Works officer will arrange for all work in hand by 1/5th A & S.H. to be continued by this unit.

14 PASSWORD.

The Password for night of Relief 13/14th and up to 1800 on 14th will be "HAM"

15 REPORTS.
Completion of relief will be wired priority or sent by runner to Battn H.Qrs as under.

"316" followed by name of Coy Commander.

16 ACKNOWLEDGE.

(signature)
Capt.
Adjutant 1/6th H.L.I.

Issued at 2100. 13/5/18.

```
Copy No 1 To O.C. A. Coy
  "    " 2 "   "   B  "
  "    " 3 "   "   C  "
  "    " 4 "   "   D  "
  "    " 5 "   "   H.Qrs Coy & R.S.M.
  "    " 6 "  O.C. & File
  "    " 7 "  Q.M. & T.O.
  "    " 8 " 1/5th A.S. & H.
```

SECRET.

DEFENCE SCHEME of "BETTY" AREA.

Ref: maps. MARCOEUIL & ST.NAZAIRE RIVER 1/10,000 and Trench Map.

1. **ORGANIZATION OF BDE. SECTOR.**
   The Sector is divided into 4 areas in depth, composed of two front line areas and two second Line areas.

2. **BATTALION SECTOR.**
   The "BETTY" sector is one of the front line areas and lies to the NORTH WEST of the TOAST area, which is the other front line one.

3. **FIRST ZONE OF DEFENCE.**
   The TOAST & BETTY areas constitute the first zone of Defence consisting of -
   (a) An Outpost Line.
   (b) The main Line of Resistance.

4. **THE OUTPOST LINE.**
   The Outpost Line consists of VESTA TILLEY and BETTY trenches. The role of the Garrison of this line is to hang on as long as possible so as to break up the enemy's infantry attack and then to fall back on the main Line of Resistance.
   The Outpost Line is again covered by look-out posts in BILLY BURKE at its junction with VESTA TILLEY and BETTY.
   The role of these look-out posts is to give warning of the hostile infantry attack and then to fall back to the Outpost Line.
   In addition their instructions are to drive off enemy reconnoitring patrols.

5. **THE MAIN LINE OF RESISTANCE.**
   The BLUE line is the main line of resistance and consists of TEDDIE GERRARD, MEANE, & ACTRESS trenches. The Garrison of this line will fight to the last. There will be no retirement from it, nor will it be reinforced from the rear.

6. **PRINCIPLES OF DEFENCE.**
   1. The Battn. <u>area</u> is to be defended the trenches are regarded merely as the back bone of the defence and as covered communications, and areas are allotted to Hdqrs and Coys for which their respective commanders are responsible.
   2. Distribution in Depth.
   3. Local Counter Attack.

7. **COY. AREAS.**
   Three Coys have had sectors of the main line of resistance allotted to them, H.Qrs and 1 Coy are in rear in DORIS, HAYTER., and GLADYS. The Coy in GLADYS & HAYTER trenches is Battalion Reserve. In the event of this Coy being called on for counter attack, each platoon leaves 1 section as a nucleus garrison in platoon area, the whole under 1 Officer, and the Coy (less 1 Officer and 4 Sections) assembles in HAYTER.
   The centre Coy in front line has one platoon in Coy Reserve in DORIS, The left Coy has one platoon in Coy Reserve in BETTY, west of its junction with ACTRESS. Bays for flank defence to accommodate one platoon are being dug off PEGGIE. This platoon will then be in second line and will act as Coy Reserve.
   Coy Areas are as shown in Appendix Area A.

8. **LEWIS GUNS.**
   Each Coy has 7 Lewis Guns with it, 6 are retained at Battn. H.Qrs. Of these three are intended to be used as a mobile reserve and three are intended to replace any which may be damaged in action.

9. **GENERAL REMARKS ON TRENCHES.**
   In all cases with the exception of TEDDIE GERRARD & DORIS fire bays have been formed on both sides of trenches and the latter should have fire positions made in the parados. PEGGIE C.T. is insufficiently provided with fire bays and work has been started near its northern end to remedy this.
   On the left flank, the system is strong, as the WESTER

portion of BETTY, GLADYS, DORIS, & HAYTER make valuable switch lines. The right flank is not provided with switch lines but on the other hand, is fully covered by the Right Battn in TOAST Area and partially covered by RIGHT BATTN. in second line.

10. WIRE ENTANGLEMENTS.

The front of the main BLUE line is strongly wired, but much of it is old and in need of repair. Considerable stretches of this have been done, but a great deal is still required. Wire has also been put up perpendicular to trenches Trenches in rear of main line are well wired, but repairs are required here also and more perpendicular wire is required EAST of HAYTER. Gaps in front wire are indicated by boards within the trenches. Chevaux de frise and gooseberries are placed at points where a block may later be required.

11. TOPOGRAPHICAL

On the LEFT of the BETTY Sector is the CHAUDIERE spur, above which runs the embankment of the VIMY-CITE ST. ANTOINE railway This embankment is not included in the Battn. Sector, but is defended by left Battn. in second line. About 1000 yards EAST of the CHAUDIERE spur and separated from it by a valley with gentle slopes, is another and slightly lower spur, along the WESTERN side of which the Battn. Boundary runs. In consequence of the situation of the area the view to the flanks is very limited There are no natural difficulties in the Battn. Sector and a good field of fire is to be had almost everywhere. This is limited however, in front of TEDDY GERRARD but excellent cross fire can be had from VESTA TILLEY, KEANE and BETTY.

12. TACTICAL.

The principal weaknesses of the area are-
1. the absence of switch lines behind TEDDY GERRARD (?) the absence of flank defence in depth on right flank and (3) the railway embankment on the left, which renders very careful arrangements fp communication and mutual support necessary.

Penetration of the main line at the right Coy area by considerable numbers would be serious as a large portion of TEDDY GERRARD can be infiladed from the right. If the platoon in Coy Reserve should be unable to restore the situation, counter attack by the Coy in Battn Reserve or a portion of it would be made at once from HAYTER across the open, combined in certain circumstances with attack along TEDDIE GERRARD. Some covering fire for this movement could be given by Vickers or Lewis Guns of LEFT Battn in second line. The situation of the Battn. Reserve increases greatly the security of the centre and left flank. The trenches and wire however require careful study by O.C. Reserve Coy, as free movement is difficult in this locality on account of quantities of wire.

An enemy penetration near the centre or WESTERN end of TEDDIE GERRARD can be localised at DORIS & KEANE on one flank and at PIGGIE on the other while a crossing of TEDDIE GERRARD can be taken in flank from HAYTER and in REVERSE from DORIS.

If the Eastern end of BETTY is given up, a block is placed near its junction with KEANE and a Vickers and several LEWIS guns fire from main line along its flanks.
The Western end of BETTY gives protection to ACTRESS and ACCESS against enemy movement on the EAST of the embankment and as there is no wire on its Northern face counter attack is not difficult towards the north. Hayter, DORIS, and GLADYS combined make a strong inner line or "keep" for the Battn. area from which counter attack can be launched freely on many directions.

13. GARRISON.

1 Infantry Battalion.
1 Section M.G. Battalion.
1 Section (less 1 gun) L.T.M. Battery.

14. DISPOSITIONS IN DETAIL.
Right Firing Line is disposed as follows -
a) 1 Platoon in VESTA TILLEY TRENCH with F.O.P. of
1.Off. 1 .N.C.O. & 6 O.R.at junction of BILLIE BURKE
and VESTA TILLEY.
b) 1 Platoon in TEDDIE GERRARD from T.15.a.8.8. to T.15.b.1.7.
c) 1 Platoon in PATTIE TRENCH.
d) 1 Platoon in TEDDIE GERRARD from T.15.a.8.8. to T.9.c.4.5.
   Coy H.Grs at T.15.a. 9.8.
Centre Firing Line Coy is disposed as follows-
a) 1 Platoon in TEDDIE GERRARD from T.9.c. 4.5. to T.9.c.5.5.
b) 1 Platoon in TEDDIE GERRARD from T.9.c.5.5. to T.8.d.7.7.
c) 1 Platoon in KEANE TRENCH from T.8.d.7.7. to T.8.b.8.8.
d) 1 Platoon in DORIS TRENCH from T.8.d.7.7. to T.8.d.1.8.
   Coy. H.Grs at T.8.d.5.8.
Left Firing Line Coy.is didposed as follows -
a) 1 Platoon in KEANE TRENCH from T.8.b.8.5. to T.9.a.0.7.
b) 1 Platoon in BETTY from T. 9.a.0.7. to T.9.a.7.9. with
   F.O.P. of 1 OFF. 1.N.C.O. and 6 O.R. at junction of
   BETTY and BILLIE BURKE.
c) 1 Platoon in ACTRESS TRENCH from T.8.b.7.7. to T.7.c.0.5.
d) 1 Platoon in BETTY from T.8.b.7.7. to T.8.b.9.5.
   Coy H.Grs at T.8.b.8.5.
RESERVE Coy is disposed as follows -
a) 3 Platoons in Gladys Trench from T.8.a. 6.5. to T.8.d.0.8.
b) 1 Platoon in HAYTER TRENCH from T.8.d. 0.8. to T.14.a. 5.9.
Coy H.Grs at GLADYS.
Battn. H.Grs are situated in DORIS TRENCH at T.8.d.5.7.

15. MACHINE GUN DEFENCE.
Machine Gun Defence is organised by the Divisional
M.G.Battn. under Divisional Arrangements.
There are 4 M.Gs. within the area of defence allotted to
this sector. For position of these guns and lines of fire
see map attached Appendix "D".
C.9.C.10. AINTREE and KEANE .
Fire Orders -Direct Fire at visible targets.
In addition Machine Guns sited on flanks or in rear have orders
to deal with observed enemy targets to their flanks if it
is obvious that no enemy activityb is developing within theire
allotted zone.
All guns are sited for direct fire and have selected alternate
battle positions.
Communications - By Runner only.

16. T.M.BATTERY.
The attached Sketch Append. C. shows positions,
arcs of fire, Sect. H.Grs and Dump of Trench Mortars.Two
guns are kept in mobile reserve at Battery H.Grs at T.13.d.
5.9.
Communication by Runner only.

17. ARTILLERY.
a) Field Batteries 504 and 505 Batteries 65th Bde.R.F.A.
are in immediate support of this sector.
The S.O.S. signal on being fired is repeated by the Reserve Bt
H.Grs O.P.and taken up by Bde .H.Grs. S.13.c.1.4. and
Artillery F.O.P. 500 yards behind this latter point.
On this signal being received S.O.S. barrages are opened
as shown. On sketch (appendices E.& F.)
A liaison Officer is stationed with Battn.H.Grs in DORIS
TRENCH at T.8.d.5.6. Communication with Art.Bde H.Grs by phone.
F.O.P. is situated about 500 yrds W. of Bde. H.Grs
(S.13.c.1.4.) 2 or 3 guns are pushed forward about T.19.a
for sniping purposes.
b) Heavy Batteries. 18th H.Art.Bde.
Positions of batteries and Arcs of Fire are as follows-

Batty.No	Calibre.	Co-ordinate.	Arc.of Fire: grid:
79.Siege Bat.	9.2.(4 gns)	A.3.c.35.30.	45°-100° "
504 " "	6"how.(6)	A.18.b.55.55.	30°-130° "
534 " "	8" " (6)	A.11.d.65.90.	38°-180° "
580 " "	6" " (6)	A.17.b.30.70.	zero-180° "
13 Hev. "	60pdrs(6)	A.17.b.50-40	25°-130 d
146 "	" (6)	A.17.b.70.55	20°-125 "

ARTILLERY (Cont.)
Barrages in immediate support of this sector are as shown in in attached sketch. Append.
All F.O.Ps are situated at S.f3.c.8.4. Liason Officer is stationed at Infantry Bde. H.Qrs S.f3.c.1/4.
Communication by phone with Infantry Bde H.Qrs.
Any targets which require Heavy Art. which it is desired to be engaged are phoned with location to "LIAISON" R.A. Inf. Bde. H.Q" along with suggested spot for F.O.P. in front line or thereabouts and the target is taken on next day.
Method of Carrying out S.O.S. Signal - See Memo from Bde. Apend

18. GAS PROTECTION.
All dugouts are protected and in a good condition of defence against Gas. Blankets are periodically sprayed.
All appliances are maintained at various posts and alarms, are all in good working condition. In the event of a Gas bombardment fans are supplied for the purpose of clearing out all dugouts. Sentries are posted over all Gas Proof Dugouts, one at entrance and one at foot of dugout and are provided with whistles in order to warn all of a gas attack whether cloud or a bombardment.

19. SIGNAL COMMUNICATIONS.
As per attached diagram and explanation. Append.

20. SNIPING & PATROLLING.
Patrols are sent out as ordered by Battn. H.Qrs nightly to reconnoitre enemy's wire and No Man's Land. Movement near enemy's line is difficult on account of the large numbers of flares sent up. Nothing has yet been seen of his patrols at night.
Snipers take up positions by day, ? in front of gap at T.10.a.4.1.and ? in front of gap at T.3.d.6.1.
Battm. F.O.P. is situated at.
It is manned by Battn Intelligence section under Intelligence Officer. Reports are rendered.

21. ADMINISTRATIVE ARRANGEMENTS.
A. Trench Stores.
The following is the distribution of S.A.A. Grenades, and S.O.S. Rockets.

	S.A.A.	Gdes (Hd)	Grenades (Rd@)	S.O.S.Rockets.
Right. F.L.Coy	5000	480	480	?
Centre F.L.Coy	38.000	1500	84	?
Left. F.L.Coy	67000.	1375	636	5.
Reserve Coy	106000	348	480	?.
Battn.H.Qrs Reserve.				
No 1 Grenade St.	7000	168		
Local Store.	9000	600	54	4.
Vesta Tilley Store	16000	776		
Stand To Dp.	7000	135		5.

Coys draw from H.Qrs to replace ammunition used..
Battn. H rs. draws S.A.A. from PEGGY DUMP T.19b.65.60. Route TEDDIE GERRARD and PEGGIE TRENCH other S.A.A. Dumps are.
NANAIMO T.13.a.15.65.
COT DUA S.14.c.55.80.
CULVERT. T.50.c.50.30.

Rations and water.
Rations arrive daily by train at VICTORIA DUMP about 5100.
A Fatigue Party of 1 N.C.O. and 50 men supplied by the reserve Coy leaves DORIS DUMP (T.8.d.6.6.) with trolleys which are kept there when it is sufficiently dark and proceeds by Light Ry. to VICTORIA DUMP where the rations are transferred to the trolleys;

RATIONS.(Cont).

3.   and brought to DORIS DUMP where they are stored for the night and issued to all Coys next morning.

Water.
Water is drawn from Water Pipes situated as follows.
a) No 1 Pipe in DORIS TRENCH near Battn H.drs and Reserve Coy.
b) No 2 Pipe near junction of Trenches PEGGIE and TEDDIE GERRARD for use of Right and Centre F.L.Coys
(This pipe is in Right Sector Area.)
c) No 3 Pipe at T.S.b.5.5. for use of Left. F.L. Coy.
Sentries are posted to regulate size of parties drawing water as under.
No 1 Pipe Res.Coy No 2 Pipe Centre F.L.Coy No 3 Pipe L.F.Line Coy.

11. Reserve Supplies.
Two Reserves maintained by Bde Hdrs. each containing -
40 Tins of Biscuits.
40 " Preserved Meat.
24 " Water.
are situated at.
CHAUDIERE WOOD. T. d.8.3.
BLACKPOOL (in CANADA TRENCH) T. 20 b.

Cooking.
All rations requiring to be cooked are cooked under R.M. arrangements at Transport Lines before being sent up, and sent up cooked. Where cooking is necessary or food already cooked requires to be heated up this is done by using solidified alcohol under platoon or section arrangements at the discretion of the Coy Commander or in coke fires in deep dug-outs.

Medical.
1. The Regtl.Aid Post is situated in HAYTER trench at T.S.c.95.65.
A relay of 4 Stretcher bearers from the Field Amb. is stationed there. Other Regtl Aid Posts are situated as follows.
T. 13 d. 5 .5.
T. 13 c. 6. 9.
T. 15 a. 6 .9.
2. From Regtl Aid Post all sick or wounded are evacuated by Relay Posts to Adv. Dressing Station which are situated as under.
LA CHAUDIERE.   S. 18.c.9.3.
Route HAYTER TRENCH and WHITE TRAIL
Main Dressing Station is at AUX RIETZ   A.S.C.

SALVAGE.
A Brigade Salvage Dump has been formed at VICTORIA DUMP situated at T.13.b.5.7. All salved articles are taken down there under unit arrangements

BURIAL PARTIES.
Arrangements have been made with the Divl. Burial Party to collect all dead at PEGGY DUMP T.19 b.1.7. Units are responsible for notifying Bde when Burial Parties are required and also for handing over all dead to the burial party at above point.

POSTAL.
All letters are sent in to Battn Hdqrs by 1400 each day, whence they are sent down by Ration Train at night to the Transport and Details Camp, and stamped there by the postal staff.

Transport.
Transport is brigaded and parked at FORT GEORGE at F.1c.a.2.3 Transport is used to draw Rations and convey same from Ration Dump to XIVY station for loading on Ration Train.

R.E.DUMPS.
R.E. DUMPS are situated as follows-
VICTORIA DUMP.   T.13.b. 5.7.
PEGGY DUMP.   T. 19 b. 1.7.
NEW BRUNSWICK   T. 19 d.9.1.
CANADA DUMP.   T. 20 b. 3.5.

SECRET.
COPY NO. 6

OPERATION ORDER for RAID on ENEMY TRENCH MERIL
BY
LIEUT.COL. J. ANDERSON, C.M.G. D.S.O.

Reference Map- ST.NAZAIRE RIVER 1/20,000.   /5/18.

1. INFORMATION.

The garrison of the enemy trenches opposite BILLIE BURKE appear to be merely a holding one and is not likely to be aggressive. It is important therefore to secure identification. Patrols have examined the enemy wire opposite MERIL TRENCH and report that the wire is passable with the assistance of hand wire cutters.

2. INTENTION.

On night of   to raid enemy front and support line Trenches for 100 yards on either flank of MERIL in order to obtain enemy identifications, to take prisoners, and to inflict casualties. Troops to withdraw immediately identification or prisoners has been secured or failing to secure identification or prisoners 15 minutes from time of entry of enemy trench.

3. TROOPS FOR THE OPERATION.

A. Coy 1/6th H.L.I. will provide Troops as follows:-

O.C. RAIDING PARTY.
   Lieut. D.B. LOCKHART with 2 Runners.

ASSAULT PLATOON.

	OFFICERS.	N.C.Os.	MEN.
H.Qrs.	Lieut. H.G. SPENCE	1	2
No 1 Sect.		1	6.
2 "		1	6.
3. "		1	6.
4. "		1	6.
Total.	1.	5.	26.

SUPPORT PLATOON.

	OFFICERS	N.C.Os.	MEN.
H.Qrs		1.	2
No 1 Sect.		1	6.
2 "		1	6.
3 "		1	6.
4 "		1	6 with two Lewis Guns
	1.	5.	26.

| COMPANY CHAIN. | | 1. | 10. |
| STRETCHER BEARERS. | | | 4. with two stretchers |

4. OBJECTIVES.

1) MERIL TRENCH (T.11.a. 0.8. to T.11.a. 3.9.)
2) Enemy Front Line, 100 yards on either flank of MERIL
   T.11.a. 2.7. to T.10.b. 96.95.
3) Enemy Support Line 100 yards on either flank of MERIL
   T.11.a. 3.8. to T.11 a.1.10.

5. POSITION OF ASSEMBLY.

VESTA TILLEY TRENCH near junction with BILLIE BURKE (T.10.c.35.10

6. TIME OF ASSEMBLY.

Zero hour minus

7. ADVANCE TO ENEMY WIRE.

The Raiding Party will file out through our wire at BRANDON GAP ( ) at Zero Hour plus
The Assault Platoon will adopt a diamond formation followed closely by the SUPPORT PLATOON in a similar formation.
A screen of Scouts will be provided by the Support Platoon leaving the Assault Platoon intact to enter the enemy trenches. O.C. Assault Platoon will be responsible for direction and pointing out to the Scouts position of gap to be cut in enemy wire
Route from BRANDON GAP via HULL ROAD to T.10.b.85.45. thence to a point in enemy wire as near as possible opposite MERIL TRENCH (T.11.a.0.8.)

8. CUTTING OF ENEMY WIRE.

The Scouts will cut a gap through enemy wire at position pointed out by O.C. Assault Platoon by means of hand wire cutters.
After Assault Platoon has passed through the gap the scouts will improve the gap for the return journey.

9. ATTACK.

Immediately a gap has been cut in enemy wire the Raiding Party will proceed as follows -

a) ASSAULT PLATOON will pass through the gap in wire and enter enemy front line trench at junction with MERIL.
No 1 Section will proceed North West along enemy front line for a distance of 100 yards where a block will be established.
No 2 Section will proceed South East along enemy front line for a distance of 100 yards where a block will be established.
No 3 Section will push up MERIL Trench to the enemy Support Line then North West along the SUPPORT Line for a distance of 100 yards where a block will be established.
No 4. Section will push up MERIL Trench to enemy Support Line then South East along the Support Line for a distance of 100 yards where a block will be established.
Platoon H.Qrs will take up a position at junction of MERIL Trench and enemy SUPPORT Line T.11.a.3.9. In each Section men will previously be told off to hold blocks established and to mop up enemy trenches.

b) O.C. Raid with two runners will take up a position in enemy front line at junction with MERIL TRENCH.

10. PROTECTION TO ATTACK.

The Support Platoon with two Lewis Guns will take up a position outside the enemy wire at gap where it can cover the operations and withdrawal of the ASSAULT PLATOON, and deal with any enemy attack from outside. It will remain in position till the ASSAULT PLATOON has passed it on the return journey and will then follow it.

11. ESCORT TO PRISONERS.

One Section of the SUPPORT PLATOON will be detailed to act as escort to prisoners.

12 WITHDRAWAL.

The Signal for withdrawal will be three long blasts on the whistle. If prisoners or identification are secured the N.C.O. i/c Section securing same will immediately report to O.C. Raid or ASSAULT PLATOON with the prisoners or identification. O.C. Raid or O.C. ASSAULT Platoon will then immediately sound the withdrawal Signal which will be repeated by O.C. Assault Platoon or O.C. Raid as the case may be.

In the event of no identification or prisoners being secured within 15 minutes from the time of entry of enemy trenches, O.C. Raid will sound the withdrawal signal, which will be repeated by O.C. Assault Platoon.

On the withdrawal signal being sounded all sections of the Assault Platoon and platoon H.Qrs/

WITHDRAWAL. (Cont.).
----

will close on the gap in the enemy wire under cover of SUPPORT PLATOON.

The N.C.Os i/c of Each Section will be responsible that each man of his section passes him before leaving the enemy trench allotted to him, he will be the last of the Section to leave.

The N.C.Os i/c Sections detailed to raid Support Line will report to O.C. Assault Platoon who will remain in position until both N.C.Os report to him. Similarly the NCC.Os i/c Sections detailed to raid the enemy front line will report to O.C. Raid. O.C. Assault Platoon will also report to O.C. Raid prior to leaving enemy trenches.
O.C. Raid will remain in position on enemy front line at junction with MERIL till he has received the reports of O.C. Assault Platoon and N.C.Os i/c Sections which raided enemy front line.
O.C. Raid will then withdraw his entire party to a position due EAST of MERIL on EDMONTON ROAD where he will retain his party pending the lifting of the enemy barrage should there be one. If the enemy Artillery is silent then he will withdraw party direct to our lines by same route as on outward journey. The SUPPORT Platoon will find protection in rear during return journey.

13. SIGNAL COMMUNICATION.
----

a) O.C. A. Coy will arrange for 1 N.C.O and 10 men to form a chain between Support Platoon and BRANDON GAP. The N.C.O. and 10 men will be detailed from another platoon than those taking part in the raid and will accompany the Support Platoon across NO MAN'S LAND 2 men being dropped 200 yards from BRANDON GAP and 2 others every 200 yards thereafter until enemy wire is reached.

The chain will be used for passing any messages that may be necessary to Battn. H.Qrs. The N.C.O. i/c Chain will be responsible for the placing of the chain as the Support Platoon moves forward
b) Battalion Signalling Officer will arrange for a chain between BRANDON GAP and Hd.Qrs of Right Firing Line Coy from where all messages received will be communicated direct to Battn. H.Qrs by Fullerphone

14. ARTILLERY.

In order to secure surprise effect there will be no Artillery preparation prior to the Raid, but it will be prepared to open fire during the raid or to cover the withdrawal if called upon.

Signal for Artillery will be arranged later.

15. M.G. CO-OPERATION.

M.G. Cooperation and signal to same will be arranged later.

16. MEDICAL
----

4 Stretcher Bearers (to be detailed by A Coy) with 2 Stretchers each stretcher with 1 blanket to carry additional wounded if necessary will accompany the Raiding Party moving in the rear of the Support Platoon. The Medical Officer will arrange for a temporary Advanced Dressing Station to be situated in Dugout in VESTA TILLEY near junction with TEDDIE GERRARD and also for a relay of 4 Stretcher bearers with 2 Stretchers (taken from B. Coy) to be held in readiness at junction of VESTA TILLEY and BILLIE BURKE

17. DRESS.

Steel helmet, equipment without pack or haversack or Water bottle - Kilt and Apron- Tunic- Field Dressing sewn on to right lower corner of tunic.

On no account are letters, identity discs, maps, orders, private diaries, or other articles by which enemy might gain identification if they fell into his hands, to be taken by any Officer or man of the troops taking part in the operation.

Every Officer will wear a white armlet 3 inches wide on each arm, every N.C.O. and man of the Assault and Support platoons will wear a similar armlet on the same left arm care being taken that these armlets are so securely fastened that they will not fall off.

DRESS (Cont)

N.C.O. & men of Chain will wear a white band round their steel helmets.

The following articles will be carried by the Raiding party in addition to those already mentioned.

  O.C. Raid 1 Electric Torch - 1 Whistle fastened securely round neck
        2 Runners to carry 50 rds. S.A.A. each -bayonets fixed.

ASSAULT PLATOON.
1. Electric Torch to be carried by O.C. Platoon and if obtainable by each Section Commander.
2. Each N.C.O and man will carry 50 rds S.A.A.
3. 2 men per section will each carry 1 grenade Bucket containing 6 bombs. These men to carry rifles slung and act with parties detailed to block trenches.
4. Pocket knives will be taken by at least 2 men in every section.
5. O.C. Assault Platoon will carry revolver and whistle tied round neck.
6. Each N.C.O. and man to carry 2 grenades in pockets, less men carrying grenade buckets.
7. Bayonet Fixed.
8. 1 Felling axe to be carried by 1 man per section (rifle slung bayonet not fixed.)

SUPPORT PLATOON.

1. O.C. to carry 1 Very Pistol and 6 White Very Lights -Revolver.
2. 8 Sets hand wire cutters on Lanyard round neck.
3. Each N.C.O. & man will carry 50 rds S.A.A. except Nos 1 & 2 of Lewis Guns who will be armed with revolvers.
4. Bayonets Fixed.
5. Each N.C.O. & man to carry 2 hand grenades less men carrying rifle grenades.
6. Rifle Section to carry 4 Rifle grenades and 4 blank cartridges each.

CHAIN.

1. 50 rds S.A.A. per man.
2. Bayonets Fixed.

STRETCHER BEARERS.

1 Water Bottles filled.

18. SILENCE & SMOKING.

Absolute silence will be observed. There will be no smoking or lights.

19. PASSWORD.

Password will be "BULL DOG" - The Regtl. Whistle should also be used.

20. SYNCHRONISATION OF WATCHES. Will be carried out at 2000 under the arrangements of the Battalion Signalling Officer.

21. ZERO HOUR.

Zero hour will be notified later.

22 ROLL CALL

Rolls will be prepared beforehand and checked as each man leaves trench. All men of the Raiding Party will answer their names on return to the position of Assembly.

23. REPORTS.

All Reports from the Raiding Party will be transmitted by means of Chain to Battn. H.Qrs.

24. STAND TO.

The ~~Left~~ Right Firing Line Coy will Stand to Arms from the time the Raiding Party is due at Position of Assembly until Ordered to Stand Down.

25. ACKNOWLEDGE.

[signature] Capt.
Adjutant 1/6th H.L.I.

Issued at........18/5/18.

```
Copy No 1 )
         2 )    O.C. A. Coy.
         3 )
         4  157th Bde. H.Qrs.
         5. File
         6. War Diary.
```

BATTALION ORDER No 8
BY
Lieut-Col. J. ANDERSON, C.M.G., D.S.O. Commdg 1/6th Bn H.L.I.
18th MAY 1918.

REF: MAP ST. NAZAIRE 1/20,000

I. INFORMATION

A local 154th Bde. Relief takes place on the night of 19th/20th May as under:- 1/5th A. & S.H. relieve 1/6th H.L.I.

II. RELIEF

(a) The 1/6th H.L.I. will be relieved in the left sector of the 154 Bde. sector by the 1/5th A. & S.H. & when relieved will move into 1A CH & U DIEF area at present occupied by 1/5th A. & S.H.

(b) Coys will be relieved as under:-

1/6th H.L.I.	1/5th A. & S.H.
A Coy by	C Coy
B	D
C	B
D	A

when relieved

GLACE TR. A Coy 1/6th H.L.I. will take over area held by A Coy 5th A & S.H.
BROWN TR. B   "   do   do   do   B
RED TR. C   "   do   do   do   C
BOIS DE LA) D "   do   do   do   D   (Bois de
CHAUDERIE)   Chauderie)

Battn HQ. will be situated at PETIT VIMY (S.24.c.5.9)
A Coy will be relieved in daylight probably in the afternoon.
B, C, & D Coys & Battn HQ will be relieved after dusk.

III. ADVANCED PARTIES

Advanced Parties or nucleus garrisons consisting of

1 Officer per Coy   1 N.C.O. per Platoon
       do   1 Lewis Gunner per Platoon
2 Signallers do   1 Section per Platoon

will proceed to new areas, leaving here at 1500, and will take over new areas from Coys. of 5th A & S.H. presently there & will be responsible for the security of the areas taken over until the arrival of the remainder of the Coys. Battn H.Qs. will also send the following personnel to take over Battn HQ's area from the 1/5th A & S.H. leaving here at 1500.

LT. WILSON, 2 Runners, 2 Signallers, 2 Police, 1 Batman.
1/5th A & S.H. Advanced Parties will report here at 1400.

IV. GUIDES

Guides if required should be arranged mutually by O.C. Coys with O.C.s of relieving unit.

V. MOVEMENT

All movement by day must be carried out by small parties. Special care will be taken when moving baggage etc. that all movement is screened from enemy observation.
There must be no movement when hostile aeroplanes

VI. TRENCH STORES

All Trench Stores in new areas will be taken over by Officers proceeding with Advanced parties.

List of Trench & Area Stores here including all maps, defence sch. etc. will be prepared ready for handing over to relieving units.

Duplicates of lists of items taken will be forwarded to Orderly Room by 1100 on 20th May.

VII. SANITATION

All trenches & dug-outs occupied by this unit will be left in a clean & sanitary condition. Receipts will be obtained from relieving units and forwarded to Orderly Room by 1100 on 20/5/18, that areas were taken over in a clean & sanitary condition.

VIII. RATIONS AND WATER

A & B Coys at "CAYUGA" Dump.
C & D " " "VICTORIA" do.

IX. TRANSPORT

As much Coy baggage as possible will be taken to new areas during daylight on 20th May. In addition "C" Coy will have one G.S. wagon to take any remaining baggage to VICTORIA DUMP from DORIS DUMP but these wagons will not be used on any account before dark. Wagons used will be left at VICTORIA DUMP and there handed over to an officer 1/5th A.&S.H. O.C. Coys will detail an officer to hand the wagons over.

Coys should arrange mutually with Coy of Relieving Unit for sending down of Lewis Gun magazines during daylight.

No magazines will be sent away from the firing line until a similar number has arrived from relieving Coy. 1/5th A.&S.H.

X. DUTIES

All sentries and other Coy duties will be taken over from Coy 1/5 A.S.H.

XI. STAND-TO-ARMS

MORNING — 0330 to 0430 or till clear.
NIGHT — 2030 to 2130

XII. REPORTS

Completion of Relief will be wired in Code Priority or sent by Runner to Batln H.Q. as under:—

"314" followed by name of O.C. Coy.

XIII. ACKNOWLEDGE

Signed by [signature]
Adjt. 1/6th Bn. H.L.I. Capt.

Issued at 18/5/18.

Copy No. 1 To O.C. A Coy   Copy No. 5 To HQ & RSM
    "   2 " " B "   "   6 " C.O. & FILE
    "   3 " " C "   "   7 " 1/5th A.&S.H.
    "   4 " " D "   "   8 " FILE

HEADQUARTERS 157TH INFANTRY BRIGADE

No. ...
Date ...

Addendum G.S. to 157th Brigade O. 2/138 dated Jan. 19th 1916.

1. On the arrival of the first train at the discharge point, the O.C. detachment with R.E. will arrange for a few sentry groups to be posted immediately on the enemy's side of the discharge point to afford local protection, while the preparations for the discharge of the gas are being made. These sentry groups must be withdrawn to a place of safety shortly before zero hour.

2. Men of the 6th R.W.F. detachment must conform to all the orders, re. the wearing of Box Respirators of being ready to cut them off, as issued to the men actually holding the trenches.

Walker Major.
Brigade Major. 157th Infantry Brigade.

19th Jan.

P.T.O.

All Officers in charge of pushing parties
should reconnoitre the route between
Dewar Nek and Maharajpi point before dark.
but great care must be taken that they do not
show themselves to the enemy as it may give
the show away.

A.W. Dawson Capt
Staff Capt 157 Bde

SECRET.

BATTALION ORDER NO 9.
BY
MAJOR W.M.ANDERSON, COMMDG., 1/6th

Map. Ref. ST. NAZAIRE RIVER 1/20,000.   rd May 1918.

1 INTENTION.

(a) The 157th Inf. Brigade will be relieved in the LEFT Section of the 52nd Divisional Sector by the 155th Inf. Brigade on the night of 24/25th May 1918.
(b) After relief the 157th Inf. Brigade will take over billets and dispositions of the 155th Inf. Brigade in Divisional Reserve.

2. RELIEF.

(a) The 1/6th BN.H.L.I. will be relieved in the LA CHAUDIERE Sector by the 4th Bn. K.O.S.B. and when relieved will move into the Billets vacated by that unit at MONT ST.ELOI (Fraser Camp)
(b) Coys when relieved will move off independently to the Barrier on the NEUVILLE ST. VAAST - LA FOLIE Road where they will be met by busses.
   Dress - Full Marching Order, waterproof sheet inside pack. Blanket neatly folded and strapped on the pack below Cross Straps. Nothing must be left hanging on to the pack. Steel Helmets. Box Respirator - Alert. Greatcoats will be worn.

3. GUIDES.

(a) The following Guides from each Coy will report to Orderly Room at Battn. HQrs. at 1900 on 24th May.
   1 Officer per Coy. 1 Junior N.C.O. per platoon.
A guide will be supplied by Battn. HQrs. to direct Coy Guides to debussing point of the 4th K.O.S.B. and from there Coy Guides will direct the respective Coys of the relieving unit to their Coy Sectors.
Probable hour of relief - 2130.
(b) Guides sent to direct 4th K.O.S.B. will after relief of 1/6th H.L.I. Coys, direct their Coys to the embussing point (i.e. the same place as that where the 4th K.O.S.B. debussed.
(c) On arrival in New Area guides provided from Details Camp will meet Coys and direct them to their billets.

4. ALARM.

(a) In the event of an Alarm during relief troops will halt and send Officer to report at the Battn. H.Q. of the Battn. in whose area they happen to be.
(b) In the event of the approach of hostile aircraft parties will clear off the road and remain still until the danger is passed.

5. TRENCH AND AREA STORES ETC.

Greatest care must be taken to hand over all details concerning orders re S.O.S., trench discipline, gas orders, work in hand, and especially projected work, to the incoming unit.
A receipt will be taken for all trench and area stores, trench maps, and defence schemes handed over and duplicate rendered to Orderly Room by 1000 on 25th May.

6. TRANSPORT.

(a) 2 limbered wagons per Coy will be available to convey all Coy. baggage and Lewis Gun Equipment from the LENS - ARRAS Road to the New billeting area on the night of 24th May.
1 reliable guide per Coy in addition to those already detailed will report to Adjutant at Battn. H.Q. at 2000 on 24th May to direct wagons to the most suitable place on the LENS - ARRAS Road.
(b)

...s will proceed to the barrier on the LA FOLIE
Road and will be conveyed to their billeting
areas.
...., Assistant Staff Capt. will be embussing Officer
Lieut. ...... will be for allocating busses to units.
Each bus will hold 1 platoon and men must be warned to get into
the busses quickly when ordered to do so, as a second trip will be
necessary.
Platoon Commanders must ensure that all men of their platoons
are present prior to arrival at the embussing point, that there
may be no occasion for delay.
(c) Each party will be drawn up at the embussing point on the right
side of the road facing direction in which the convoy is proceeding.

7. SALVAGE PARTIES.

The Salvage party of 1 N.C.O and 6 men found by D Coy S.H.L.I.
at VICTORIA DUMP will rejoin Company at 1800 on 14th inst.

8. SUPPLIES.

(a) Water is laid on in New Camp. Strict supervision
must be exercised to prevent wastage.
(b) The extra days rations issued to Coys on the night
15/16th May will be collected by Coys and handed over in bulk
to the relieving unit. A special receipt being obtained
which will be forwarded to Orderly Room.

9. REPORTS.

O.C. Coys will report personally to the Adjutant at Battn. H.Q.
when their Coys have passed Battn. Hdrs after having been relieved.

10. ACKNOWLEDGE.

Patrick ......
Capt.
Adjutant 1/6th H.L.I.

Issued at 1500. 13/5/18.

Copy No 1 TO O.C. A Coy.
"   " 2 " " B "
"   " 3 " " C "
"   " 4 " " D "
"   " 5 " C.O. R.S.M. & Hdrs Coy.
"   " 6 " Q.M. & T.O.

SECRET.

O.C.

Reference 2/696 of 16th May.

From ZERO plus 2 hours to ZERO plus 8 hours.
Harassing fire will be vigorously carried out by the
R.A.

SM/b/18.
                                                    Major.
                            Brigade Major, 187th Inf. Brigade.

O. C.,

Addendum No. 1 to 157th Bde. No. Z/896 dated 16th May, 1918

1. In continuation of para 8. Arrangements must be made for every man to have a label fixed on the front of his Box Respirator bearing the number of the party to which he belongs.

2. In continuation of para 9. All men must be carefully warned that there must be no noise of any sort. The Trucks must be moved as silently as possible and there must be no talking or laughing. All orders must be whispered.

3. In continuation of para 13. All troops eastwards of a line drawn through T.15. - T.21. and T.27. centrals, not ordered to wear Box Respirators should be ordered to be ready to adjust them at a moments notice from midnight onwards.

4. Reference para 14. the Blankets or Curtains of all protected Dugouts forward of the line through T.17. - T.18. and T.1 Centrals should not be rolled up until the trench system is reported clear.

5. The O.C., 4th H.L.I., will arrange for a Lewis Gun under an Officer to be posted in LILY ELSIE near the junction of this trench with VESTA TILLEY. The Officer will, if he hears any noise made by the Trucks being moved, order a few short bursts of fire to cover same. Care must be taken that these bursts are not too long in case it may draw the enemy's attention to the fact that something unusual is on.

6. The O.C., 2nd L.F.A., Adv. D.S.,will arrange for an Officer with the necessary personnel and appliances for treating Gas cases to report to the O.C., Detachment R.E., at DORIS DUMP and accompany the party until latter has finished its task.

7. Separate instructions are being issued to the O.C., Detachment as to procedure to be adopted in case of an enemy attack.

Major,
Brigade Major, 157th Infantry Brigade.

16th May, 1918.

SECRET.

O.C. 6/H.L.I.

Reference Z/696 of 16th May.

From ZERO plus 2 hours to ZERO plus 5 hours harassing fire will be vigorously carried out by the R.A.

23/5/18.

Major,
Brigade Major, 157th Infantry Brigade.

SECRET.

O. O. 64/42/1

Z/696

1. A "Gas beam" attack will be carried out on the XVIIIth Corps Front from T.9.b., to N .25.b., on the night of May. 16/17th, or the first night after upon which the wind is favourable.

2. In the 187th Infantry Brigade area there will be a Power Head situated at DORIS Dump, T.9.d.80.95., and a discharge point squares T.9.b.45.60., to T.5.d.20.07.

3. A total of 4725 cylinders will be discharged of which 1875 will be discharged from the Brigade area.

4. Infantry parties will be required to assist in the arrangements for discharging the Gas. These parties will be found from the 5th A. & S. H., as many as possible being taken from that portion of the RED LINE held by the 5th A. & S. H., and the remainder from their portion of the BROWN LINE.

5. The cylinders will be transported to the Power Head (DORIS Dump square T.9.d.80.95.) on the Light Railway in 75 trucks made up into trains as follows:-

    7 Trains of 10 Trucks &
    1 Train of 5 Trucks.

6. From the Power Head (square T.9.d.80.95.) trucks will be pushed up by the parties furnished by the 5th A. & S. H., to the discharge point (squares T.9.b.45.60. to T.5.d.20.07.)

7. The 5th A. & S. H., will furnish a detachment of 300 Men exclusive of Officers and N.C.Os. These men will be organised into 15 parties each of 20 men plus a Senior N.C.O. in charge of each party.

Every 2 parties will be under 1 Officer and the odd party will be also under an Officer.

The acting Second in Command will be in charge of the whole/-

P. T. O.

whole.

The total strength of the party to be furnished will therefore be:-

9 Officers (including the 2nd in Command.) 15 Senior N.C.Os and 300 O.R.

These parties will parade at the Power Head (DORIS Dump square I.8.d.80.9a) at 10 p.m. on the night of the discharge.

8. This party must be very carefully organised into the separate 15 parties of 1 N.C.O. and 20 Men, with 1 Officer to each 2 Parties, and 1 Officer to the 15th Party.

Parties must be paraded beforehand, told off and numbered, and steps taken to ensure that every N.C.O. and man knows to which party he belongs, the parties being numbered 1 to 15.

9. From the Power Station each party will push a group of 5 trucks up to the discharge point. Parties 1 to 14 will dispose of the 70 trucks comprising the first 7 trains, and party No. 15, will push up the last 5 Trucks of the last train.

Pushing and other parties will observe silence and the former must be careful on decline to check the pace of trucks.

1 O.R. special Coy. R.E., will proceed with every truck.

In the event of a cylinder being hit by hostile fire, all ranks will adjust Respirators but will not sound Klaxon Horns. The danger will, in any case be very local.

10. After unloading at the discharge point, parties will withdraw to a suitable trench in the vicinity and await there. The Divisional Gas Officer will be asked to advise the O.C., Detachment how far away he should take his party.

11. After the discharge of the gas the same parties as before will push the trucks back to the Power Head. The O.C., Detachment, 5th A.S.H., will ask the Officer i/c Special R.E. Party, for instructions as to when he will march his party away after their work is completed.

12. The/-

2.

12. The Outpost Line between VESTA TILLEY Trench in square T.10.c., and N.20.a.0.4., also the troops in VESTA TILLEY TRENCH itself will be withdrawn by 12 mid-night on the night of the discharge till after the discharge; and will return to their positions when the trenches and dug-outs are reported to be free from gas.

13. Troops forward of a line through T.11.c.0.0. - T.15.b.0.7.- T.1.b.9.9., will wear Box Respirators from 12 mid-night on the night of the discharge until the orders for their removal is given by an Officer. This order should in no case be given until Zero plus 30, and then only if the trench system is reported clear of gas.

14. The Divnl., Gas Officer has been instructed by the Division to assist the Anti-Gas Personnel of Units to make arrangements for
    (a) Clearing Dug-outs, by means of fires etc., immediately after completion of discharge.
    (b) Clearing Trenches, Saps etc., by means of Flappers etc.
    (c) Troops should not re-occupy trenches etc., until qualified Anti-Gas personnel have declared them to be safe.
These points require most careful attention and C.Os., must satisfy themselves that the arrangements made by their Anti-Gas personnel are satisfactory and issue orders that any instructions issued by the latter are to be carried out. Special care must be taken to see that all blankets of protected Dug-outs are let down prior to the discharge, and that every dug-out in the danger area is carefully cleared of gas after the discharge. Company Commanders must work in co-operation with the Anti-Gas personnel, so that they may know when to give the orders for the removal of Box Respirators.

15. A decision will be given at 1 p.m. daily as to whether the operations will be carried out.
    Code words will be used as follows:-
"Gas Beam attack will take place to-night"   ASTI.

    No message will be sent at 1 P.M. if no attack is to take place.
    Two/-

P.T.O.

to cancel has been previously ordered the word "CHIANTI" will be sent.

16. Zero hour will be at 12 mid-night and, or as soon after as the trucks are reported to be in position.

17. All technical details regarding the discharge of Gas are being arranged by a Special Unit R.E.

18. The O.C., 6th H.L.I., will arrange to keep the Brigade informed of the situation. An Officer should be detailed to be at the discharging point and he should have a few runners to take messages back to the nearest Fuller Phone.

19. The O.C., 5th H.L.I., and 6th H.L.I., will arrange to re-occupy the lines of resistance and outpost on the first available oppurtunity reporting by Priority wire when this is done.

                                                 Major,
                            Brigade Major, 157th Infantry Brigade.

16th May, 1918.

O.C. 6 HLI

For your own information. Please do not pass out to [illegible] yet -

O.C., 6th H.L.I.

Addendum No.1 to 157th Bde. No. Z/696 dated 16th May, 1918.

1. In continuation of para 9. Arrangements must be made for every man to have a label fixed on to the front of his Box Respirator bearing the number of the party to which he belongs.

2. In continuation of para 9. All men must be carefully warned that there must be no noise of any sort. The Trucks must be moved as silently as possible and there must be no talking or laughing. All orders must be whispered.

3. In continuation of para 13. All troops eastwards of a line drawn through T.15. - T.21 and T.27. centrals, not ordered to wear Box Respirators should be ordered to be ready to adjust them at a moments notice from midnight onwards.

4. Reference para 14, the Blankets or Curtains of all protected Dugouts forward of the line through T.17. - T.13. and T.1 Centrals should not be rolled up until the trench system is reported clear.

5. The O.C., 5th H.L.I., will arrange for a Lewis Gun under an Officer to be posted in LILY ELSIE near the junction of this trench with VESTA TILLEY. The Officer will, if he hears any noise made by the Trucks being moved, order a few short bursts of fire to cover same. Care must be taken that these bursts are not too long in case it may draw the enemy's attention to the fact that something unusual is on.

6. The O.C., Adv.D.S., 2nd L.F.A., will arrange for an Officer with the necessary personnel and appliances for treating Gas cases to report to the O.C., Detachment 5th A. & S. H., at DORIS DUMP and accompany the party until the latter has finished its task.

7. Separate instructions are being issued to the O.C., Detachment as to procedure to be adopted in case of an enemy attack.

A Williams
Major,
Brigade Major, 157th Infantry Brigade.

16th May, 1918.

You already have copy of Z/696 per the
Div Gas Officer today
A Williams Major
B.M. 157 Bde.

SECRET.

To: O.C. HQ; C.O. RSM + File

1. A "Gas Beam" attack will be carried out on the 18th Corps Front from T.9.b. to N.15.b. on the night of May 16/17th or the first night after upon which the wind is favourable.

2. In the 157th Brigade area there will be a Power Head situated at DORIS Dump T.8.d. 80.95, and a discharge point, squares T.9.b. 45.60. to T.3.d.30.07.

3. A total of 4715 cylinders will be discharged of which 1575 will be discharged from the Brigade area.

4. Infantry parties will be required to assist in the arrangements for discharging the Gas. These parties will be found from the 6th Bn.H.L.I. as under.

5. The Cylinders will be transported to the Power Head (DORIS DUMP square T.8.d.80.95.) on the Light Railway in 75 Trucks made up into trains as follows.
   7. Trains of 10 Trucks each.
   1. Train of 5 Trucks.

6. From the Power Head (T.8.d.20.95) trucks will be pushed up by the parties furnished by the 6th H.L.I. to the Discharge Point (T.9.b. 45.60. to T.3.d.30.0.7.)

7. The 6th H.L.I. will furnish a detachment of 300 men exclusive of Officers and N.C.Os. These men will be organised in 15 parties each of 20 men plus a Senior N.C.O. – each party
   Every 2 parties will be under 1 Officer and the odd party will be also under an officer.
   Major J.C. Coats will be incharge of the whole.
   The total strength of the party to be furnished will therefore be –
       9 Officers (Includg. the Second in Command) 15 Senior N.COs and 300 Other Ranks, detailed from Coys as per attached table.
   These parties will parade at VICTORIA DUMP in parties by Coys at 1000 and proceed to the Power Head (DORIS DUMP T.8.d. 80.95.) when orders are received from the Adjutant on the night of the discharge. Each N.C.O. i/c Party will have a Nominal Roll of all men in his party.

8. This party must be very carefully organised into the separate 15 parties of 1 N.C.O. and 20 men with 1 Officer to each 2 parties and 1 Officer to the 15th Party.
   Parties must be paraded beforehand, told off and numbered, and steps taken to ensure that every N.C.O. and man knows to which party he belongs, the parties being numbered 1 to 15.
   All parties will be inspected by the C.O. and Adjutant (tomorrow) at a date to be notified later.

9. From the power station each party will push a group of 5 trucks up to the Discharge Point. Parties 1 to 14 will dispose of the 70 trucks comprising the first 7 trains, and party No 15 will push up the 5 trucks of the last train.
   Pushing and other parties will observe silence, and the former must be careful on the decline to slacken the pace of trucks.
   1.O.R. Special Coy R.E. will proceed with every truck.
   In the event of the cylinders being hit by hostile fire, all ranks will adjust respirators but will not sound Klaxon Horns.
   The danger will in any case be very local.

10. After unloading at the Discharge Point, parties will withdraw to a suitable trench in the vicinity and await there. The Divisional Gas Officer will be asked to advise the O.C. detachment how far away he should take his party.

11. After the Discharge of Gas the same parties as before will push the trucks back to the Power Head. The O.C. Detachment 1/6th Bn. H.L.I. will ask the Officer i/c R.E. Party for instructions as to when he will march his party away after their work is completed.

12. A decision will be given at 1 p.m. daily as to whether the operations will be carried out.
    Code Words will be used as follows -
    "Gas Beam attack will take place to-night" ASTI.
    No message will be sent at 1 p.m. if no attack is to take place.
    To cancel Gas Beam Attack previously ordered the word "CHIANTI" will be sent.

13. Zero hour will be at 12 mid-night or as soon after as the trucks are reported in position.

14. All technical details regarding the Discharge of Gas are being arranged by a special unit R.E.

15. There must be no noise.
    There must be no talking.
    Each Officer N.C.O. and man will have clearly written in chalk in front of his Box Respirator the number of the party to which he belongs. Rock chalk which is to be found in quantities in the trenches should be used for this purpose. All Box respirators to be chalked by 1200 on the 22nd May.

    Example -

    15

    or whatever the number is of the party as per table.

16. Dress:-
    Skeleton Order with Rifle slung.
    Steel Helmet - Box Respirator (Alert)

O.C. Party Major J.C.Coats.

Party No.	Supplied by.	N.C.O. i/c.	Coy Finding Off.i/c.		Remarks.
1.	D. Coy.	D. Coy	)	D.	
2.	D. "	D. "	)		
3.	D "	D. "	)	D.	50 men in each
4.	D "	D. "	)		party in charge
5.	C "	C. "	)	C.	of an N.C.O.
6.	C "	C. "	)		
7.	C "	C. "	)	C.	One Officer in
8.	C "	C. "	)		charge of these
9.	B. "	B. "	)	A.	parties except
10.	A. "	A. "	)		No 12 which is
11.	A. "	A. "	)	A.	in charge of
12.	A. "	A. "	)		1 Officer itself.
13.	B "	B. "	)	B.	
14.	B "	B. "	)		
15.	B "	B. "	)	B.	

21/5/18.

Capt.
Adjutant 1/6th H.L.I.

Op. H.
56 sheets

CONFIDENTIAL

1/6 HLI
9/SC 3

On His Majesty's Service.

CONFIDENTIAL

D.A.G.
3rd Echelon.

War Diary
June 1918.

Army Form C. 2118.

WAR DIARY
or
INTELLIGENCE SUMMARY. 1/6 H.L.I. JUNE 1918
(Erase heading not required.)

Instructions regarding War Diaries and Intelligence Summaries are contained in F.S. Regs., Part II. and the Staff Manual respectively. Title pages will be prepared in manuscript.

REF MAPS MAROEUIL 20000

Place	Date	Hour	Summary of Events and Information	Remarks and references to Appendices
ST ELOY	1/6/18		Scheme of "Bursting Crust" embraced recommendation in H.Q. ring of S.O.S. projects attended by all Coys.	
		1130	Advanced party left for the trenches	
		1520	Orders received for relief of 11/12 Royal Scots by the battn.	
			Q.M & Transport lines transferred to BERTHONVAL FARM.	
TRENCHES	2/6/18	0930	Battn. proceeded in m.t.s. sections to CANADIAN monument, thence via MERSEY ALLEY	Appendix 2/6/18
HUDSON TRENCH			To trenches relieved 11/12 Royal Scots (See appendix)	
			Battalion. A Coy Right Front line Coy, B Coy Centre front line Coy, C Coy Left Front line	
			Coy. Baths resumed.	
		1430	Relief completed	
			CASUALTIES. 1 man wounded by shell (for divisional wound L.G.B.)	
		2300	Gas projectors put over by us on to left artillery group / not ours / machine guns. Nil.	
	3/6/18	0300	Stand to arms	
			Enemy N.C.O. & man found 3 Res SA Coy No.7 lost & only practice	
			took no trouble over to the trenches wire & surrendered.	
			American Offrs attached for instruction.	
			Started under Lt Johnston - wasted many & wire & brought lot useful information as to	
			manning of enemy posts.	
			Wiring of new proposed front line - New Brunswick - HUDSON - OTTAWA.	
		2200	CASUALTIES. 2 killed 3 wounded.	

Army Form C. 2118.

WAR DIARY
or
INTELLIGENCE SUMMARY.
(Erase heading not required.)

Instructions regarding War Diaries and Intelligence Summaries are contained in F.S. Regs., Part II. and the Staff Manual respectively. Title pages will be prepared in manuscript.

Place	Date	Hour	Summary of Events and Information	Remarks and references to Appendices
FIRING LINE HUDSON TR. ETC.	4/6/18		Making of daily list in new proposed front line commenced. — Proposed Raid orders submitted to Brigade (see Appendix)	Appendix 4/6/18
		1700	Misty afternoon as yesterday — Draft of 40 O.R. arrived from Base. —	P
		2300	Our artillery bombarded enemy trenches. Enemy artillery became very active & shelled our outpost line.	
	5/6/18	0230	NCO & Queen (Bn. Scouts) took up a position in a shellhole in no man's land near enemy wire at HUDSON TRENCH. Stayed out all day returning about 2230. Nothing unusual carried on.	P
	6/6/18	0600	Enemy put a few shells over into MONTREAL Trench. Work & normal.	P
	7/6/18	0200	A day post of 1 NCO & 2 men took up a position in NO MANS LAND near HUDSON Trench & remained in observation till evening E.D. 2200. Information gained was not enough. Pte J Anderson wounded from bomb to UK. - Bugler W Anderson proceeded to trench school, camp.	P
		1030	Cokonnet failed him 1/RSH arrived	O
	8/6/18		All trench work promptly suspended. Made ready for leaving on —	Appendix 8/6/18
		1630	Relief completed 9/6 Hrs. moved into "Brigade Reserve" (see Appendix 8/6/18) getting into position at 1910.	
	9/6/18	1300	CO visited D. Coy. in CANADA Trench. — Bn moved from HANSON CAMP, THELOS POST. Bathe arranged for companies. —	P

Major F.M. ANDERSON attached to M.C.
M.N.I.F. DALY (? illegible) (?) acting adjt DSO (?)

A/7921. Wt. W12539/Mr29. 750,000. 1/17. D. D. & L., Ltd. Forms/C.2118/4.

Army Form C. 2118.

WAR DIARY
or
INTELLIGENCE SUMMARY.
(Erase heading not required.)

Instructions regarding War Diaries and Intelligence Summaries are contained in F. S. Regs., Part II. and the Staff Manual respectively. Title pages will be prepared in manuscript.

Place	Date	Hour	Summary of Events and Information	Remarks and references to Appendices
THELUS POST	10/6/16	10.30	C.O. visited all coy. during forenoon at THELUS POST. C.O. inspected billets & dispositions of B Coy succeeding to Coy's behind in relieving days at NEUVILLE ST VAAST. Improvements being made by Coy CO AMMINGTON to MORT=UK,ZIDRIAN trenches (between samps?)	S/L
		21.00	Intense of bombs fired of various kinds on enemy line for 3 mins ending at Retaliation for Canadians Book carried on as usual Copy of Report & & appendices to VIII Corps H.Q.	
	11/6/16		C.O. visited B, C & D Coy in BROWN LINE PRESSING 1 Platoon A Coy proceeded to Corps SCHOOL, HESDIN for 1 week course Work carried on as usual. Baths arranged for all coy.	BLW
	12/6/16	13.00	C.O. visited all Coy during forenoon at BROWN LINE and THELUS POST Units proceeded with — BROWN LINE and THELUS POST Intense bombardment of various points in enemy line opposite the sector carried out. 1. Burst each of 2 mins duration	BLW
	13/6/16	15.00	Advanced Party (1 Off. and 4 O.R. per Coy) left for Fire Trenches All others remained working in the trenches during the day Work carried on as above. Baths arranged for all coy. Raid carried out by 5th A.S.H. against ARLEUX sector of enemys defences.	BLW
	14/6/16	23.00		
		14.30	Bath. proceeded to Firing line via MERSEY ALLEY and GRAND TRUNK and relieved 16th A&S.H. (See Appendix) Disposition — A Coy & left Firing line Coy; B Coy; Right Reserve Coy; C Coy left Centre Firing line Coy; & relieved D Coy; Centre Firing line Coy.	Appendix 14/6/16 BLW

Army Form C. 2118.

WAR DIARY
or
INTELLIGENCE SUMMARY.
(Erase heading not required.)

Instructions regarding War Diaries and Intelligence Summaries are contained in F. S. Regs., Part II. and the Staff Manual respectively. Title pages will be prepared in manuscript.

Place	Date	Hour	Summary of Events and Information	Remarks and references to Appendices
FIRING LINE HUDSON AND OTTAWA TR. ETC	14/6/18 (contd)	1730 2400	Relief completed. Front of 1 offr (2/Lt D. FRASER) + 1 Plat. + left on outlook of a difference both at T.29 d 9/7. Enemy quiet at 0215. No enemy movement.	
	15/6/18	0300- 0400	Stand to arms.— Enemy M.G. + rifleman fire & Bn S.A.A. daily. Considerable movement all day and around CHALK QUARRY (U20c) and ULSTER TR. Further Cos served on wiring in front of HUDSON + NEW BRUNSWICK TRENCHES. Res. Coy + Bn HQrs making 'CUBBY HOLES' for BABY ELEPHANTS. O. Offensive Patrol of 1 Plgtoon under Lieut CARMICHAEL reached T29 d 1.8 from where	BLM
		2230	spot was returned Trench at this point was occupied by the enemy's but returned at 0240 on 16 th	
	16/6/18	0300- 0400	Stand to arms.— Day O.P. kept all tracks established in HUDSON TRENCH. has works. and wiring Sharned at ARLEUX LOOP. Usual work carried out Harassing fire by M.Gs on ARLEUX LOOP from 1800 to 2400	BLM
		1800 2100- 2150 2200	Stand to arms. Defensive Patrol 8/1 Officer (Lieut DOBSON) and Platoon reached T23 d 2/3. Sent to which got no enemy one at T29 b 7/7 M.G. sported at latter point. 116. scouts in one minute of wood about 3 ft high, however wounded 6 entered. returned at 0220	

WAR DIARY
or
INTELLIGENCE SUMMARY.
(Erase heading not required.)

Army Form C. 2118.

Place	Date	Hour	Summary of Events and Information	Remarks and references to Appendices
FIRING LINE HUDSON TR ETC	17/6/18	0300-0400	Stand to Arms. — Day O.P. & wiring party of 4 O.R. established in HUDSON SAP from O.Lu.S hill 0730.	Blh.
		0900	Conference of O.C. Coys at Bn H.Qrs. Work carried on as usual.	
		1800	Heavy artillery cutting wire at T29 B6/8 and T23 d7/6. M.Gs keep up harassing fire till 2400. Lulls and considerable movement observed during day at CHALK QUARRY (U20c). Stand to Arms. —	
		2100-2130 2315	Test S.O.S. carried out in WILLERVAL Section. Twice Twice Defensive Patrol of 7 Platoon under Lt J.W. FINGLAND took up position at T29 b1/8 sent reading as far as T23 d7/1. Enemy wire appears down to keen wire at the front. Bombing party under Lieut P.A.E. McCRACKEN (5 O.R.) bombed enemy sap in HUDSON TRENCH. Roughly grid after 9 bombs were thrown all of which landed in sap.	
	18/6/18	0330 0400	Stand to Arms. — C.O washed line. Day O.P. in HUDSON SAP established Manual work done. Wiring and wiring of Baby Elephants.	Blh.
		1800	Considerable movement during day at CHALK QUARRY (U20c). Destructive Artillery shoot on enemy wire at HUDSON SAP. Harassing M.G. fire kept up 2400 till 0230 on 19th.	
		2100-2130	Stand to Arms. —	

WAR DIARY or INTELLIGENCE SUMMARY.

Army Form C. 2118.

(Erase heading not required.)

Instructions regarding War Diaries and Intelligence Summaries are contained in F. S. Regs., Part II. and the Staff Manual respectively. Title pages will be prepared in manuscript.

Place	Date	Hour	Summary of Events and Information	Remarks and references to Appendices
	18/9/18 (cont)	2000	2 Bombing Parties in 2 Relief of "3" Coy each took up defensive position outside HUDSON SAP east of Block. No enemy encountered. Patrol of 7 OR and 30 OR sighted about 100 yds distant, sounds of the enemy heard from direction of enemy block in HUDSON SAP.	
	19/9/18	0300-0400	Stand to arms 2nd 1/c N.W. sector front line.	
		0900	Conference of O.C. Coys at Bn HQ. 1300. Enemy parties of 1 W 5 OR 1 W 8 OR. Visibility bad all day owing to driggling rain and slight mist. 4th R.S.F. arrived in Strathrie.	MONT ST ELOI
		2100-2130	Strathrie to Arras.– Advanced Parties of R.S.F arrived in Strathrie.	
		2130	Heavy reciprocal Artillery fire.	
		2130	Defensive Patrol of 1 Platoon under Lieut BRUCE took up position outside HUDSON TRENCH about 20 yds East of MANITOBA RD. Scouts were sent forward for about 30 yds. No enemy wire. Patrol worked in 2 Reliefs returning at 0230. No enemy patrols were encountered.	
	20/9/18	0300-0415	Stand to arms.– C.O visited line.	Appendix 20/9/18
		1100	4th R.S.F. arrive at Funighue and at commence relief. Relief completed.	
		1500	Battn proceeded by Motor Wagon from CANADIAN MONUMENT. to FRASER and LANCASTER CAMP. (see appendix)	

Army Form C. 2118.

WAR DIARY
or
INTELLIGENCE SUMMARY.
(Erase heading not required.)

Instructions regarding War Diaries and Intelligence Summaries are contained in F. S. Regs., Part II. and the Staff Manual respectively. Title pages will be prepared in manuscript.

Place	Date	Hour	Summary of Events and Information	Remarks and references to Appendices
ST. ELOI.	21/6/18	0600	Reveille. Btn on duty	Bhn
		0700	Orderly Room.	
		0800- 1700	1½ Coys ## Camp Construction Party under R.E. A & E Coy.	
		and 1300- 1700	B Coy D Coy	
		2100	Baths arranged for B, D & H.Q's at BERTHONVAL FARM Guards & Piquets mounted as required by Btn in ST ELOI Area. Lights out.	
	22/6/18	0600	Reveille	Bhn
		0700	Log Training C & D Coys — Arms Drill, Lecture, Drill and Tactical Handling of Platoons.	
		0630 - 0700	Physical Training	
		0900- 1200		
		1300- 1700	A Coy 1000 — 1100 B Coy 1100 — 1200 All S.B.R. tested at Gas Hut St ELOI. Baths at ST ELOI allotted to Battn and take arranged for all Coys	
		0900	B.O. Inspection of A Coy 0930 B Coy 1630 Conference of O.C. Coys.	
		1800	B.O. Inspection of C Coy 1830 D Coy 1430 O.C. Division meets Battn	
		2130	Lights out. Platoon of A Coy return from Corps School.	
	23/6/18	0630	Reveille	Bhn
		0900	Church Parade at Y.M.C.A. Hut OTTAWA CAMP.	
		1000	B.O Inspection — C Coy — 1100 B.g.C inspects No 2 Platoon & A Coy returned from CORPS SCHOOL. C.O inspection A Coy 1130 — B, 1145 — H.Q. 1200 — Transport, 1400 — D Coy 1800.	
		1500	Conference for all officers with B.g.C in Y.M.C.A Hut LANCASTER CAMP.	
		1800	Conference of O.C. Coys at Btn H.Q	

Army Form C. 2118.

WAR DIARY
or
INTELLIGENCE SUMMARY.
(Erase heading not required.)

Instructions regarding War Diaries and Intelligence Summaries are contained in F. S. Regs., Part II. and the Staff Manual respectively. Title pages will be prepared in manuscript.

Place	Date	Hour	Summary of Events and Information	Remarks and references to Appendices
MONT ST ELOI	24/6/18	0600	"Reveille" — Bns on duty	
		0800-1200, 1300-1700 } 1900	Camp Construction Party under R.E. in PRASER CAMP. 'B' Coy + ½ D Coy. Fatigues. ½ Platoon showing + 1 Platoon in afternoon at Tilsit fort burial grounds and all recruits not attested by Bde. Retreat 2130 Lights out	BHn
	25/6/18	0600	Reveille	
		0630-0700	Physical Training - Small arms.	
		0900-1100	A + B Coys — Bayonet Fighting, musketry, saluting, arm Drill, Tactics, Handling of [Platoons	
			C + D Coys — All S.B.Rs tested at Gun Hut, ST ELOI.	
		1130-1230	Batt parade under Capt K.G. TODD for demonstration by Platoon from Corps School.	BHn
		0700	Major W.H. ANDERSON M.C. left for a visit to CORPS SCHOOL, FRESSIN returning at 1900.	
	26/6/18	0600	Reveille.	
		0700-1200	All Coys. tennis Gymnen returning from Range "FOREST RANGE". Each man fired 4 complete magazine.	
		0900-1200	Specialists Training — Lewis guns (B + D). at ABBEY RANGE Tactical Training.	BHn
			All Coys — musketry, saluting, arm Drill and tactical Schemes. Corps Commander (Lt.Genl. HUNTER-WESTON) visited the Batln during training.	

Army Form C. 2118.

WAR DIARY
or
INTELLIGENCE SUMMARY.
(Erase heading not required.)

Place	Date	Hour	Summary of Events and Information	Remarks and references to Appendices
MONT ST. ELOI.	27/6/18	0600	Reveille — Btn on duty	
		0800–1200	Camp Construction Party under R.E. at FRASER CAMP — C Coy + 2 Dry	Blm
		1300–1700	1 Platoon B Coy and 1 Platoon of D Platoon in afternoon at the Transport Lines.	
			Lunch, Bisquits etc administered by Batt.	
		19.00	Retreat 21.30 Lights out	
	28/6/18	0600	Reveille —	
		0700–1200	All ranks of C & D Coy attended Baths at ST ELOI	
		1400–1600	" " A & B Coy attended " at ST ELOI.	
		0900–1300	Musketry Parade — A & B Coy practicing of 48,64 etc	Blm
		1300–1700	" " — C & D Coy " " " "	
		1500–1700	Working Party of 100 O.R. at WINNIPEG CAMP preparing ground for visit of Duke of Connaught	
		21.30	Demonstration by representative from Divion in firing of S.O.S Rocket. Lights out.	
		14.30	Advance Parties of 7 Officers & 10 O.R per Coy proceed to Ersy Line.	

Army Form C. 2118.

WAR DIARY
or
INTELLIGENCE SUMMARY.
(Erase heading not required.)

Instructions regarding War Diaries and Intelligence
Summaries are contained in F. S. Regs., Part II.
and the Staff Manual respectively. Title pages
will be prepared in manuscript.

Place	Date	Hour	Summary of Events and Information	Remarks and references to Appendices
MONT ST ELOI	29/6/18	0330	Reveille -	
		0800	Inspection of camp by C.O.	
		0845	Batt. parade in Column Post in threes.	
		0900	Bat'n commenced advance and proceeded by bn to Nepes to CAMPBELL ROAD (S27a3/9) and thence via BLIGHTY and GLACE tunnels and relieved the 1/7th Royal Scots (see in the CHAUDIÈRE SECTOR (see Appendix) Disposition - A Coy, Right Firing line Coy - B, Right Centre - C, Left Centre - D, Left Firing line Coy.	Appendix 29/6/18 RDh
		1730	Relief completed.	
		2100-2130	Stand to arms (Area HQrs Coy)	
		2030-0130	Intense bombardment of enemy trench line system at MÉRICOURT carried out by R.A. in conjunction being raid that Bdes (Guards) Division was being relieved by ##th Divn SAg DA g	
		2230	2 Defensive Patrols of 1 Officer (Lieut CRAIG) and 1 section and 1 Sergt + 1 section took up defensive positions at T 10 a 7/8 & T 4 c 5/1 respectively ho enemy were by letter of patrol met enemy patrol estimated at 70 which detected presence of our patrol became off before it could be engaged	
LA CHAUDIÈRE SECTOR (FRONT LINE)	28/6/18	0830- 0415	Stand to arms - C.O. made his tried 6 Rds, this being daily practice (Work is taken over from 1/7th R.S. continued C.O visited that F. Firing line Coy.	
		0900 13:00		

Army Form C. 2118.

WAR DIARY
or
INTELLIGENCE SUMMARY.
(Erase heading not required.)

Place	Date	Hour	Summary of Events and Information	Remarks and references to Appendices
LA CHAUDIERE SECTOR	30/4/18 (contd)	1400	Liaison with 20th Divn on left flank arranged	BWh
		1700-2000	C.O. visited left & left centre Firing line Coys.	
		2100-2130	Stand to Arms.	
		1700-22.00	Day O.P. established so to have had between BETTY and VESTA TILEY. Very little movement detected	

TABLE SHOWING INCREASES & DECREASES
IN STRENGTH OF BATTN DURING
THE MONTH OF JUNE 1918

	Off	O.R
STRENGTH AS AT 21-5-18	46	869
DECREASES		
Hospital over 7 Days	1	26
Commission	–	8
Killed	–	2
Wounded	–	1
Absentees	–	1
	45	831
INCREASES		
From Hosp	–	6
Draft	–	40
Taken on Egypt	–	1
STRENGTH AS AT 8-6-18	45	878
DECREASES		
Hospital over 7 Days	–	20
Wounded	–	2
	45	856
INCREASES		
From Hosp	–	9
Draft	–	1
Egypt	–	20
From N.R. Base	–	1
STRENGTH AS AT 15-6-18	45	887

	Off	O.R
Brought forward	45	887
DECREASES		
Hospital over 7 Days	–	24
D.C. Regt Depot	1	1
Commission	–	2
Wounded	–	1
To U.K.	–	2
	44	857
INCREASES		
From Hosp	–	11
Draft	–	14
STRENGTH AS AT 22-6-18	44	882
DECREASES		
Hospital over 7 Days	–	18
Left for L.Bde	–	1
Staff Corps	–	6
Leave on U.K.	–	1
	44	856
INCREASES		
Draft	–	22
Hospital	–	15
STRENGTH AS AT 30-6-18	44	893

SECRET.   Appendix 2/6/18   Copy. No 6
                BATTALION ORDER. No 9
                        BY.
            MAJOR. W.M. ANDERSON. COMMDG. 1/6th H.L.I.

REF. MAPS. – MAROEUIL & LA TARGETTE. 1/20.000.   1st JUNE '18

1 INFORMATION.
(a) The 157th Inf. Brigade will relieve the 156th Inf. Bde. in the Right (WILLERVAL) Section of the Divisional Sector on 2nd June.
The WILLERVAL Section is divided into 2 Sub-Sections of which the Boundaries are as follows:-
Right Boundary. TIRED ALLEY. – SPUR POST (B.14.a central) BORDER POST (B.13.a.) all inclusive.
Inter Sub-Section Boundary. WESTERN ROAD (inclusive to Right Sub-Section)
Left Boundary. ACHEVILLE – NEW BRUNSWICK Road (both inclusive) as far as the junction of the GRAND TRUNK (6.9) with the BROWN LINE (exclusive) thence to the CEMETERY (T.25.d.) inclusive thence to Bois du Goulot at T.25.c.00.00. and thence due W. along the grid line.
The actual method of holding the line is to be changed shortly, but units will take over as it stands at present.

(b) The 6th H.L.I will relieve the 7th Royal Scots in the Left Sub-Section, Front System.
The 5th H.L.I will be in the Right Sub-Section, Front System.
  7th H.L.I. – Right Reserve.
  5th A.S.H. – Left Reserve.

2 DISPOSITIONS OF COYS.
Dispositions are as follows:-
  A. Coy – Right Firing Line Coy.
  B. " – Centre Firing Line Coy.
  C. " – Left Firing Line Coy.
  D. " – Battalion Reserve.

3 ADVANCED PARTIES.
Advanced Parties as already detailed proceed on 1st June.

4 RELIEF.
(a) The Battalion will proceed from MONT. ST. ELOI, to the debussing point on the NEUVILLE ST. VAAST – THELUS Road about 1000 yards WEST of LES TILLEUS cross roads in Motor Busses. The first platoon arriving about 1000.
Details re embussing will be issued later.

RELIEF (Cont)

(b). All movement EAST of NEUVILLE ST. VAAST will be by Sections at 100 to 150 yds distance. Every precaution must be taken to avoid movement being observed by the enemy.

5. GUIDES

(a). A chain of piquets will be provided by the 156th Brigade from the debussing point to the WEST End of MERSEY ALLEY. (Avoiding Canadian monument)

At the WEST end of MERSEY ALLEY, the 7th Royal Scots will have guides waiting as follows.

1 Guide per Platoon
1 Guide for Battn H.Qrs.

6. TRENCH STORES.

(a) All Trench and Area Stores, maps, defence schemes etc. should be taken over by the Officers proceeding with Advanced Parties.

Copies of Receipts given will be rendered to Orderly Room by 1000 on 3rd June.

(b) Coy Gas NCOs. will be responsible for taking over all protective curtains and anti-gas appliances.

7. LEWIS GUNS.

The following Lewis Gun baggage will be man handled all the way

8 Lewis Guns and spare parts per Coy.
(Chests to be left behind)
70 Lewis Gun Magazines loaded (4 @ 10 per gun less A.A. Gun contained in 18 Brown canvas buckets.

All other Lewis Gun equipment will be left at Q.M's Store.

On arrival in new area each Coy should take over from 7th Royal Scots 240 Magazines (loaded) contained in 60 Brown Canvas buckets.

HdQrs Coy will carry up 2 Guns and spare parts, without any magazines.

The Battalion Lewis Gun Officer will arrange to take over 120 Lewis Gun Magazines contained in 30 Brown Canvas buckets; in addition to those taken over by Coys.

A similar number of Lewis Gun Magazines (loaded) and Canvas Buckets will be handed over here to the 7th Royal Scots by the Battn Lewis Gun Officer. All magazines taken and handed over should be thoroughly cleaned and in good condition.

B.O. No. 9. Sh. 2.

8. TRANSPORT
(a) No transport will be provided for Coy baggage.
(b) 5 Dixies per Coy will be taken and manhandled by Coys.
(c) Medical Stores, Officers Mess Stores, and Battn HQ baggage will be left with the Transport Officer who will arrange to transport it to the Battn at night along with rations.
(d) The Transport Officer will arrange with the Q.M. for the transfer of all Battn stores and baggage from the present Q.M. Dump to the new one at BERTHONVAL FARM. On 1st and 2nd June.

9. PATROLS, SENTRY POSTS ETC.
O.C. Coys must be careful to see that all S.O.S. Observation, and Listening Posts, Gas Sentries, etc. and information about Patrols are taken over in a correct manner.

10. DRESS
(a) Dress for Battn. proceeding to trenches will be Fighting Order; Steel Helmet, Box Respirator at the "Alert" Waterproof sheet neatly rolled and strapped to Haversack. Iron Rations will be carried inside the Haversack, Water bottles filled. Greatcoats will be neatly rolled and tied on to the waist belt at the back. Mess Tins should be securely tied to the Haversack and not allowed to hang from it.
(b) All orders re wearing of equipment, and Box Respirators, Fixing of Bayonets, etc, while in the trenches, must be strictly adhered to.
(c) As already ordered, blankets and packs will be left at Q.M. Dump. All headgear other than the steel Helmet will be left in the packs.

11. WORK IN HAND
The Battn Works Officer (Lieut Cumming) will arrange for all work in hand by the 7th Royal Scots to be continued by this Unit.

12. SUPPLIES & WATER
Rations will be brought up nightly in bulk by pack transport; less Left Firing line Coy, to which rations will be sent direct. The R.Q.M.S. will issue rations for 3 Coys at Cookhouse. (Further orders later).
Water:- The Battn in Left Reserve will fill all Petrol tins from the tanks at Morrison Dump and will carry them to Left Firing line Battn Cookhouse where it will be issued to 3 Coys. The Left Firing line Coy will draw water direct from place to be notified later.

13. PERSONNEL TO BE LEFT BEHIND.

The following Officers (with servants) will not proceed with the Battn. to the Firing Line but will proceed to RESPIN CAMP. (X 19.c.90/80) on 2nd June arriving there before 1800. Lieut J. Todd will report to the Commandant of this Camp by 1000 on 2nd June for instructions as to accommodation.

Lieut Todd will act as Adjutant for 1/6th N.L.I. Details.

LIEUTS. J. TODD, C. BRUCE, W.D. THOMPSON.

14. SANITARY.
(a) Usual certificates re cleanliness of lines will be given and taken.

Areas vacated must be left scrupulously clean.

15. REPORTS.
Completion of Relief will be wired or sent by runner to Battn. HQrs by the code word (NEBI) followed by the name of O.C. Company

16. ACKNOWLEDGE

Jas P. Wilson Lieut
Capt.
Adj- 1/6th Bn N.L.I.

ISSUED AT. 1700. 1/6/18.

Copy No 1. To O.C. A Coy.
" " 2 " " B "
" " 3 " " C "
" " 4 " " D "
" " 5 C.O. R.S.M & HQrs.
" " 6 T.O. & QM.

T/d/O.C. 6th H.L.I.   Secret

(1) The relief takes place on the 2nd June by
daylight. Battalions at MONT ST ELOY will
move up in order - 6th H.L.I. 5th H.L.I.
7th H.L.I. 6th H.L.I. starting off about 0900
(others at about 2 hours interval) Orders follow ~~tomorrow morning~~ tonight

(2) Advanced parties as under will go into ✱
the line tomorrow as detailed below:-
Advanced Parties:-
    1 Officer per Battalion (Intelligence officer
        in case of 5th 6th H.L.I.)
    4 Scouts or Observers
    1 N.C.O. & 4 O.R. (1 per platoon) per company
Party from 7th H.L.I. to be at 156th Bde H.Q. at 1400
    "   "   5th H.L.I. " " "   "   " "   " 1415.
    "   "   6th H.L.I. " " "   "   " "   " 1430.
    "   "   5th A.&S.H. to arrange guide and time
             direct with C/O concerned

156th Brigade H.Q. is situated on the
MERSEY duck boards about the mile square
A 6 a 50.00.

31st May 1918   Alwth.   Major
                      Brigade Major, 157th Inf Brigade

SECRET. Copy No. 2

157th Infantry Brigade Order No. 102.

31st May, 1918.

Reference Maps MAROEUIL & LA TARGETTE 1/20,000

1. (a) The 157th Infantry Brigade (less 157th L.T.M.Bty) will relieve the 156th Infantry Brigade (less 156th L.T.M.Bty) in the Right (WILLERVAL) Section of the Divisional Sector on the 2nd June.

(b) The WILLERVAL Section is divided into 2 Sub-Sections of which the Boundaries are as follows:-

Right Boundary. TIRED ALLEY - SPUR POST (B.14.a.central) BORDER Post (B.13.a.) all inclusive.

Inter Sub-Section Boundary. WESTERN ROAD (inclusive to Right Sub-Section)

Left Boundary. ACHEVILLE - NEW BRUNSWICK Road (both inclusive) as far as the junction of the GRAND TRUNK with the BROWN LINE (exclusive) thence to CEMETRY (T.25.d.6.9.) inclusive thence to BOIS du GOULOT at T.25.c.00.00, and thence due W. along the grid line.

2. The actual method of holding the line is to be changed shortly, but Units will take over as it stands at present.

3. Battalions will relieve as follows:-

5th H. L. I. relieve 4th R.S. in the Right Sub-Section (Front system)
6th H. L. I. " 7th R.S. " " Left " " " "
7th H. L. I. " 7th S.R. Right Reserve.
5th A.& S. H. " 8th S.R. Left Reserve.

4. Advanced Parties will be sent into the line on the 1st June, as already detailed.

5. (a) 5th, 6th, & 7th H. L. I. will proceed from MT. ST. ELOI to the debussing point on the NEUVILLE St. VAAST - THELUS road about 1,000 yds WEST of LES TILLEUS Cross Roads, in Motor Busses in the order 6th H.L.I., 5th H.L.I., 7th H.L.I. - the leading platoon of 6th H.L.I., arriving about 1000. 5th & 7th H.L.I., will follow 6th H.L.I., at intervals of about 2 hours.
Details re. embussing will be issued separately.

(b) The 2 forward Coys - THELUS POST Platoon, 5th A.& S. H. will proceed the whole way by route march. The CANADA Trench Coy., leaving NEUVILLE ST. VAAST in sufficient time to arrive at the debussing point about 1400.

(c) All movement EAST of NEUVILLE ST. VAAST will be by Sections at 100 to 150 yds distance.

(d) (i) 7th S.R. are providing two chains of picquets.
Upper Chain From the Debussing point to the WEST end of MERSEY ALLEY (avoiding CANADIAN Monument)
Lower Chain. From the Debussing point to the junction of TIRED ALLEY and THELUS Ridge Line (avoiding CANADIAN Monument).
(ii) Forward of these points and for all Posts W. of the BROWN Line guides will be arranged by O.Cs. concerned.

(e) Units will be directed as follows:-
5th H.L.I. by Lower Chain and
TIRED ALLEY.

P.T.O.

- 2 -

5. (e) Contd.

7th H.L.I. advanced Coy and Coy for THELUS RIDGE Post by the Lower Chain.

That portion of the former which is to be located in VANCOUVER Road can not carry out its relief until after dark, unless the visibility is very bad. It will therfore be necessary for them to be kept back under cover until the relief can take place. (The Post Line is suggested as a good place to put them).

7th H.L.I. BROWN LINE Coys., by Upper Chain and MERSEY ALLEY
6th H.L.I. by Upper Chain and MERSEY ALLEY.
5th A & S. H. Forward Coy and. BROWN LINE Coy, by Upper Chain and MERSEY ALLEY.

(f) O.C. Battn. must be careful to see that all S.O.S. Posts in their sub-sections are taken over.

The B.S.O., will arrange that all runner relay posts are taken over.

(g) Lewis Gun magazines with the exception of 10 per gun, which 10 must be carried up with the team, may be exchanged by mutual arrangement.

6. The 157th L.T.M. Bty. will relieve the 156th L.T.M.Bty on the 3rd. June, details of relief being arranged mutually between the C.Os. concerned.

7. Completion of relief will be wired to Headquarters, 156th Brigade by the Code word "NEBI".

8. Battns. will go into the line with 22 Officers only. The 2nd in Command and 2 Coy. Commanders will be left behind.

Sections will be of the strength of 1 N.C.O. and 6 Men.

Battn., Coy. and Platoon Hqrs., approximately as laid down in S.S. 143, Training of Platoons, 1918, but less that personnel especially detailed to remain out in accordance with S.S. 135. (Viz:- 2 O.R.Ms., 1 Sergt., 1 Cpl., & 1 L/Cpl. per Coy, and instructors).

Personnel in excess of this will proceed to MAPLE CAMP, (X.19.c.90.80) on the 2nd June, arriving there before 1800.

An Officer from each Unit will report to the Commandant by 1000 for instructions as to accomodation.

9. Administrative arrangements will be issued separately.

10. Brigade Hqrs. will close at ST. ELOI at 0830 on 3rd. June, and will re-open at the same hour at A.6.c.50.20.

The Command of the WILLERVAL Section will pass to the G.O.C. 157th Infantry Brigade at 0900, June 3rd.

From the time their relief is complete, until this hour, Battns will be under orders of G.O.C. 156th Infantry Brigade.

11. ACKNOWLEDGE.

A.Williams
Major,
Brigade Major, 157th Infantry Brigade.

31st May.   Issued at 2100

Copies No. 1 to 5th H.L.I.   Copy No. 7 to H.Q. 52nd Divn.
       2   6th H.L.I.   8   52nd M.G. Battn.
       3   7th H.L.I.   9
       4   5th A & S.H.   10   War Diary
       5   157th L.T.M. Bty.   11   File
       6   H.Q. 156th Bde.

SECRET   Copy No ...2......

            Administrative Order No. 11, issued with
            Reference to Brigade Order No. 102.
            =================

                                                    1st June, 1918.

Reference Map MAROEUIL 1/20,000

1. <u>Transport</u>. The Brigade less 5th A & S. H., and L.T.M. Bty., will be conveyed on June 2nd from Mont St. ELOI to a point on the road about 1000 yards short of A.11.a.9.9. by Motor Lorries.
    Sixteen motor lorries, one per platoon, will be parked on the Main road at FRAZER Camp at 0900 on the 2nd inst.

        First Journey   6th H. L. I.   0930
        Second   "   5th H. L. I.   1130
        Third   "   7th H. L. I. &   1330.
                         Bde. Hqrs.
    5th A & S. H. will proceed by march route.

    Lorries will move off immediately they are loaded up.

2. <u>Transport</u>. Will be brigaded at BERTHONVAL Farm (F.4.d.3.7) All Units transport and Q.M. Parties will move to the Brigade Transport Lines on the 2nd. Move to be completed by 1400. Any baggage which is to be sent up on the night of the 2nd should be loaded separately.

3. <u>Rations</u>. Commencing on 2nd inst.
    (a) Rations will be drawn at 0900 daily from R.P. (A.3.c.3.9.) and taken by the Divnl. Train to the Transport Camp at (F.4.d.3.7.)
    (b) The method of forwarding to Units is as follows:-

Right Sub-Section   Bn. Front Line.   By Pack Ponies) To be arranged
Left   "   "   "   "   "   "   "   ") by Bde. T.O.
Right Reserve Bn.   2 Coys.   ) By Light Ry from ZIVVY to
) Longwood (B.15.a.2.8.)
                    7 Platoons   ) By Light Ry. from ZIVVY to
                    (in Posts)   ) Farbus Junctn. (B.7.d.5.6.)
bn. Hqrs.   1 Platoon   By Limber to Hqrs.
Left Reserve Battn. 2 Coys.   ) By Light Ry. from ZIVVY to
) Morrison (T.26.c.2.4.)
                    1 Platoon at   ) Railway from ZIVVY to Farbus
                    Thelus Post   ) Junction.
                    Bn. Hqrs. &   ) By Limber to Camp.
                    7 Platoons.
Brigade Hqrs.   By Limber.
L.T.M.Bty.   By Limber to Bty. Hqrs. thence
                                           by carrying parties to line

    Rations forwarded by Light Railway must be loaded in trucks at ZIVVY Station not later than 1930.
    Coy. Q.M.S. will accompany the train from ZIVVY.

4. <u>Water</u>.
    <u>Right Sub-Section Battn. Front Line</u>.
    Is drawn from Pipe line or tanks at Longwood B.15.a.2.8., by means of petrol tins conveyed by trolleys to WILLERVAL, thence by carrying parties, provided by Right Reserve Bn.
    <u>Left Sub-Section Battn</u>.
    From 4 Tanks at Morrison by means of petrol tins, carrying parties provided by Left Reserve Battn.
    <u>Right Reserve Battn</u>.
    2 Coys (BROWN LINE) From Longwood in Petrol Tins.
    7 Platoons (in Posts) From 4 Tanks at Farbus.
    Battn. Hqrs.   Tank at A.6.c.8.6 (Bde. Hqrs.)
        Both by Carrying parties.

                                                    P. T. O.

4. **Water (Contd.)**
   Left Reserve Battn.
   2 Coys. Tanks at Morrison by Petrol Tins.
   1 Platoon Thelus Post. Tanks at Farbus Junctn.
   Battn. hqrs. & 7 Platoons Vicinity of Camp.
   All done by Carrying parties.
   L.T.M. Battery.
   From tanks at Longwood and Morrison.
   Battery hqrs. from A.5.b.6.6.
   Brigade hqrs.
   From 400 gallon tank at A.6.c.8.6. which is filled each morning from pipe line.
   Transport.
   At Transport Camp.
   Note:- All tanks are refilled nightly.
   The following petrol tins will be handed over.

   Right Battn. ... ...
   Left Battn. ... ...
   Right Res. Bn. ... ...
   Left " " ... ...
   L.T.M. Bty. ... ...
   Brigade Hqrs ... ...
   Brigade Reserve
   at Bde. Dump. ... ...
   T.?.6.d.3.2.

5. **Ammunition.**
   The Bde. Ammunition dumps are situated at following points

   Bde. hqrs.   A.6.c.6.5.
   Longwood   B.15.a.3.8.
   Farbus   B.2.d.3.1.
   MERSEY   B.2.a.7.7.
   Red Brick Stack T.36.d.3.2.

6. **Reserve Rations.**
   Two tins biscuits (50 lbs) and 56 tins preserved meat are held at the following points.

CANADA	T.22.c.6.3.	Suburb	B.9.b.9.8.
SHEFFIELD	T.21.d.3.0.	Durham	B.9.b.1.4.
Beehive	T.27.b.1.1.	Spur	B.14.a.5.6.
Wakefield	T.27.d.7.8.	Border	B.13.a.4.0.
Barnsley	T.27.d.7.1.	Tape	A.17.d.9.1.
Torant	B.3.c.5.8.	Farbus	B.7.d.7.7.
		Thelus	B.7.a.5.7.

   The above rations will be carefully checked and taken over by Battn., occupying the post.
   Brigade Reserve.
   122 tins biscuits and 63 cases preserved meat at FARBUS B.2.d.3.1. Under Brigade charge.
   These rations will be shown on the monthly Reserve Ration Return.

7. **R.E. Material.**
   R.E. material will be supplied on demand through Brigade from the main R.E. Dump at ZIVVY (A.10.a.4.7.) and will be sent up by Light Ry., to Longwood, Morrison, and Farbus.

8. **Medical.** **Right Battn.**
   (a) R.A.P. (B.15.a.0.8.) evacuated through the A.D.S. of Division/

3.

8. **Medical (Contd)**
Division on the Right.
   (b) Left Battn.
     R.A.P. (T.38.a.4.1.) with a relay post at T.26.a.3.9. evacuated through A.D.S. VIMY (T.26.a.9.4.).
   (c) Supplementary R.A.P. (B.2.a.9.8.) with relay post at A.11.b.3.9.
     The Main Dressing Station for (b) & (c) is at AUX RIETZ (A.8.c.5.5.)

9. **Burial.**
     Bodies are conveyed by units to the collecting station at the junction of MERSEY Trench and Morrison Valley, Brown Line (B.2.b.2.8.).
     Cemetries are at Thelus A.5.c.8.5.
               AUX RIETZ A.8.c.5.9.
     The former is used normally.
     Units wire Divnl. Burial Officer who will collect bodies at collecting station.

10. **Stragglers Posts.**
     First line stragglers posts are established at:-

     Commandant's house.   B.7.d.5.2.
     MERSEY Alley.   B.1.b.8.7.
     VIMY   T.25.b.5.8.

11. Each Battn will detail a party to clear up the camp area after the Battn has left.
     All huts must be left scrupously clean.
     The E.G.C. will inspect the area after Battns. have left.
     Each Battn will obtain a clearance certificate from the Town Major, before leaving.

12. ACKNOWLEDGE.

                               HMHewison
                                          Captain,
                    Staff Captain, 157th Infantry Brigade.
     Issued at 1800........

Copies No. 1 to   5th H.L.I.
            2   6th H.L.I.
            3   7th H.L.I.
            4   5th A & S.H.
            5   157th L.T.M. Bty.
            6   157th bde. T.O.
            7   2nd L.F.A.
            8   413th Field Coy. R.E.
            9   (
           10   (War Diary.
           11   (File.

1/6th H.L.I.

To
Headquarters,
154th Brigade.

PROPOSED RAID SCHEME ORDERS.

MAP REF. MAROEUIL 1/20,000.

I INTENTION
To raid HUDSON Trench from junction with WINNIPEG Trench to junction with BRANDON Trench.

II OBJECT
To obtain enemy identifications - take prisoners - inflict casualties - do all possible damage.

III TROOPS FOR OPERATION
1). O.C. Raid with 2 Runners.
2). Two Platoons each consisting of 1 Officer, 5 N.C.O.s & 26 men.
3). One Grenadier Section 1 N.C.O. & 6 men.
4). Four Stretcher Bearers.
5). One N.C.O. & 10 men Communication Chain.

IV OBJECTIVES
1). Post at junction of HUDSON and WINNIPEG Trenches.
2). HUDSON Trench between WINNIPEG & BRANDON Trenches.
3). Post in HUDSON Trench about point T 29. b. 65/80.

V POSITION OF ASSEMBLY
(a). For whole party, less 1 Grenade Section - MONTREAL Trench at point T 23 c. 90/75.
(b). For 1 Grenade Section - Junction of HUDSON Trench & MONTREAL Trench.

VI TIME OF ASSEMBLY
ZERO - 60.

VII CUTTING OF ENEMY WIRE
(a). Gaps to be cut by Artillery & Trench Mortars on X Day.
  T 23 d. 44/52.
  T 23 d. 45/35.
  T 29 b. 65/80.
  T 29 b. 60/45.
(b). Scouts to improve gaps T 23 d. 45/35.
(c). 1 Additional Grenade Section to improve Gaps T. 29. b. 65/80.

VIII. ATTACK - AT ZERO HOUR.

(a) Assault Platoon.

No 1 Sect. Establish Block in WINNIPEG Trench T.23.d.15/43.
" 2 "   do   HUDSON Trench T.23.d.85/28.
" 3 " Raid Post in HUDSON Trench at T.29.b.75/80.
" 4 " Establish Block in BRANDON Trench T.29.b.75/75.
Platoon HQrs proceed with No 3 Section.

(b) Support Platoon.

1 Lewis Gun Section, with Guns & 3 Grenadiers as Escort, take up a position on enemy parapet at T.23.d.75/35 & prevent any enemy approach along HUDSON Trench from TRIUMPH Trench. The 3 grenadiers will also, from the parapet, assist in preventing any enemy approach along WINNIPEG Trench from the North.
Remainder of Platoon take up a position at entrance Gap and outside enemy wire & cover the operations.

(c) Additional Grenade Section.

Attract enemy attention at point T.29.b.65/83 by throwing bombs into enemy Post there at ZERO - 1 and afterwards improve gap. report to O.C. Assault Platoon on arrival at T.29.b.65/83 & guide Nos 3 & 4 Sections out of Gap at T.29.b.65/80.

IX. WITHDRAWAL.

Signal - Repeated long blasts on whistle.
Nos 1 & 2 Sections Support Platoon via Gap at T.23.d.45/35 & thence across No MANS LAND to position of Assembly.
Nos 3 & 4 Sections via Gap T.29.b.65/80 & thence across No MANS LAND to our lines at point T.23.c.4/1.
Withdrawal Signal to be given immediately identification is secured or at ZERO + 15.

X. SIGNAL COMMUNICATION.

Chain of 2 Runners every 300 yards between Support Platoon & position of Assembly.
Phone communication between position of assembly & Battn. HQrs.

XI. MEDICAL

(a). 4 Stretcher Bearers with 2 Stretchers, each Stretcher with 1 Blanket to carry additional wounded if necessary - to remain with Support Platoon.

(b). Relay Stretcher Post at Position of Assembly.

(c). Advanced Aid Post in HUDSON Trench about T.23.c. 1/2.

5/6/18.

McKenzie Anderson
Major,
Commdg. 1/6th Bn. H.L.I.

46th Bn. A.I.F.   Appendix 4/6/18

To Headquarter,
   15th Brigade

ALTERNATIVE RAID SCHEME

I. MAP REF. — MARCEUIL 1/20,000

II. INTENTION.

To raid BRANDON TRENCH and scuffle or capture enemy post in HUDSON TRENCH at T.29.b.65.85.

III. OBJECT.

To obtain enemy identifications — take prisoners — inflict casualties — do all possible damage.

III. TROOPS FOR OPERATION

(1) O.C. Raid with 2 Runners.
(2) Two platoons each consisting of 1 Officer, 5 N.C.Os & 26 men
(3) 4 Stretcher Bearers
(4) 1 N.C.O & 10 men communication chain.

IV. OBJECTIVES

(1) BRANDON TRENCH immediately South of junction with HUDSON TRENCH.
(2) Post in HUDSON TRENCH about point T.29.b.65.85.

V. POSITION OF ASSEMBLY

MONTREAL TRENCH at point T.29.a.4.9.

VI. TIME OF ASSEMBLY.

ZERO HOUR MINUS 45

VII. CUTTING OF ENEMY WIRE

(a) Gaps to be cut by Artillery on X day
T.23.d.7.52 — T.23.d.75.35 — T.29.b.6.8.
T.29.b.6.18 — T.29.b.6.7.
(b) Scouts on arrival at enemy wire to improve gap at T.29.b.6.7.

VIII. ATTACK AT ZERO HOUR

(a) Assault Platoon

Enter BRANDON TRENCH immediately South of junction with HUDSON TRENCH.
No 1 Section establishes block in Brandon Trench at T.29.b.62.70.
No 2 Section will rush post T.29.b.65.
No 3 Section establishes block in Hudson Trench T.29.b.7.9
No 4 Section available to assist any section in difficulty — to do as much damage as possible to Brandon Trench.
PLATOON HQRS will proceed with No 3 Section.
O.C. Raid will remain in Brandon Trench at entrance point

IX. SUPPORT PLATOON

Will take up a position outside the enemy wire at point T.29.b.6.7. and cover the operations and withdrawal of the assault platoons.

X. WITHDRAWAL

SIGNAL – Repeated long blasts on whistle

Withdrawal Signal to be given immediately identification has been secured or at ZERO + 10. Withdrawal to be effected through gap at T.29.b.6.7. across "No Man's Land" to position of assembly.

XI. SIGNAL COMMUNICATION

Chain of Runners every 200 yards between Support Platoon and Position of Assembly.

Telephone communication between Position of Assembly and Batt. HQrs.

XII. MEDICAL

(a) 4 Stretcher bearers with 2 stretchers, each stretcher with 1 blanket to carry additional wounded.
(b) Relay Stretcher Post at Position of Assembly.
(c) Advanced Aid Post in HUDSON TRENCH about T.23.c.1.2.

Menzie Andrew
Major.
Commdg 1/6 Bn. H.L.I.

5-6-18.

Appendix 8/6/18

157th Infantry Brigade Order No. 103.

1. The following reliefs will be carried out on 8th June, 1918.
    (a) 7th H.L.I., will relieve 5th H.L.I.
    (b) 5th A & S. H. "   "   6th H.L.I.

   After relief 5th H.L.I., and 6th H.L.I., will take over same dispositions as 7th H.L.I., and 5th A & S.H., respectively.

2. As much of relief as possible will take place during daylight. Not more than 2 Platoons of each Company of the relieving Battalions should be on the move at the same time (this does not apply to Companies at NEUVILLE ST. VAAST.)
   Companies moving from NEUVILLE ST. VAAST to the Eastern foot of VIMY ridge and vice versa will do so in sections at not less than 100 yards interval.

3. Relief will be completed by 2300.

4. Details of relief will be arranged by Os. C. concerned. A percentage of observers, scouts etc., of reserve battalions should proceed to the line 24 hours in advance.

5. All trench maps, stores, etc., will be handed over.

6. Completion of relief will be wired "Priority" to Brigade Headquarters, using the code word "GUM".

7. ACKNOWLEDGE.

Brigade Major, 157th Infantry Brigade.

6th June, 1918.

File   1/6th H.L.I

Reference Battn Order No 10 para II posts are as under:-

I. 3 S.O.S Relay Posts - 1 N.C.O. & 4 men each. co-ordinates are as under
   (a) T.26.d.2.3 W. of Breck. store.
       3 S.O.S. Grenades, Green, Green, Green - 1 Rifle.
   (b) B.2.b.1.2 - Railway Line
       3 S.O.S. Grenades, Green, Green, Green - 1 Rifle.
   (c) A.6.b.8.4.
       6 S.O.S Grenades, Green, Green, Green

II. 3 Stragglers Posts - 1 N.C.O. & 3 men each.
   (a) LA TARGET Corner.
   (b) AUX RIETZ   "
   (c) Refilling Point.
   These posts will remain in camp selected from 1 Platoon & be ready to man posts at very short notice.

III. Water Point Duties - 1 man at each post - 6 A.M. till 9 P.M. daily.
        Locations A.2.c.4.9.
                   A.2.c.3.9.
                   A.2.d.7.5.
                   A.3.a.3.3.
                   A.10.a.6.7.

IV. Supply Guard - 1 N.C.O & 3 men.

                                Patrick Jones
7/6/18   Capt.
                                Adjt. 1/6th H.L.I

SECRET.   BATTALION ORDER No 11. Appendix 14/6/18 Copy No. 5
                              By
        Major W. M. ANDERSON, M.C. COMMDG. 1/6TH BN. H.L.I.
                                              13TH JUNE, 1918.

REF. MAPS — MAROEUIL & LA TARGETTE.   1/20,000.

I. INFORMATION.

(a) There will be a local Brigade Relief on the 14th June as follows:—
   5TH H.L.I. will relieve 7TH H.L.I.
   6TH H.L.I. will relieve 5TH A. & S.H.
Relief will be completed by 2300.
Battalion Boundaries are as follows:—
RIGHT BOUNDARY — Western Road (exclusive)
LEFT BOUNDARY — New Brunswick – Acheville Road.
(both inclusive) as far as the junction with the Grand Trunk with the Brown Line (exclusive)

(b) A. Coy 1/6th H.L.I. will relieve A. Coy 5th A & S.H.
    D.   "   "   "   "   B   "   "
    C.   "   "   "   "   D   "   "
    B.   "   "   "   "   C   "   "

II. DISPOSITIONS OF COYS.

A. Coy with 1 Platoon B. Coy attached — Right Firing Line Coy.
    3 Platoons in OTTAWA TRENCH.
    1   "   in HUDSON TRENCH.

D. Coy — Centre Firing Line Coy.
    1 Platoon in HUDSON from junction with NEW BRUNSWICK, to T.28.b.5.9.
    1 Platoon T.28.b.5.9. to T.28.b.2.8.
    1 Platoon T.28.b.2.8. to junction with OTTAWA.
    1 Platoon in CANADA TRENCH.

C. Coy — Left Firing Line Coy.
    3 Platoons in NEW BRUNSWICK TRENCH from junction with HUDSON to ACHEVILLE.
    (less 1 Section from each platoon)
    3 Sections MONTREAL TRENCH
    1 Platoon CANADA TRENCH from T.22.d.2.1 to its junction with OTTAWA.

B. Coy — Reserve Company
(less 1 Platoon)   BEEHIVE TRENCH.

BATTN. H.Qrs. — T.27.d.4.5.
These dispositions will probably be slightly altered shortly.

III. ADVANCED PARTIES.

(a) Advanced Parties as already detailed proceed on 13th June.

(b) Advanced Parties from 1/5th A & S.H. will report to respective Coys, being relieved on morning of 14th June to take over all Trench & Area Stores, Maps, etc.

RELIEF

(a) Coys. will move in the following order:—

A. Coy. NEUVILLE St VAAST platoons at 1200.
THELUS POST platoons at 1330.
B. Coys platoon att. A. Coy. at 1330.
ROUTE:— MERSEY ALLEY, C.P.R TRENCH.

C. Coy. – at 1430.
ROUTE:— GRAND TRUNK, CANADA TRENCH.

D. Coy. – at 1515.
ROUTE:— MERSEY ALLEY, C.P.R. TRENCH.

B. Coy. – (less 1 Platoon) at 1600.

BATTN. H.Q's at 1600.

(b) NEUVILLE St VAAST. platoons will move by sections at not less than 100 yards interval, to the (Eastern) foot of VIMY RIDGE.
Remainder of Coys. will move by platoons at not less than 200 yards interval.

V. TRANSPORT

(a) No Transport will be provided for Coy and H.Qs. baggage.

(b) Medical Stores, Officers Mess Stores, Battn H.Q's baggage will be man handled during the forenoon.

VI PATROLS, SENTRY POSTS ETC.

O.C. Coys. must be careful to see that all S.O.S., Observation and Listening Posts, Gas Sentries etc., and information about patrols is taken over in a correct manner.

VII DRESS

(a) Dress for Battalion proceeding to the trenches will be:—
Fighting Order, Steel Helmet, Box Respirator (Alert) Waterproof Sheet, neatly rolled & strapped to Haversack, Iron Rations will be carried in the Haversack, Water bottle filled. Great Coat will be neatly rolled & tied to the belt. at the back. Mess Tins will be securely tied to the Haversack.

(b) All orders re wearing of Equipment, Box Respirator, fixing of bayonets etc, while in the trenches must be strictly adhered to.

VIII TRENCH STORES.

(a) All Trench & Area Stores, Maps, Defence Schemes etc, will be taken over by the Officer proceeding with Advanced Party
Copies of Receipts given will be rendered to Orderly Room, by 1000, on 15th June.

(b) Coy & H.Q's Gas N.C.O. will be responsible for taking over all protective curtains, and Anti-Gas appliances.

IX. LEWIS GUNS.

All Lewis Guns & Equipment will be man handled.
The following Lewis Gun Equipment will be handed over to 5th A. & S.H. and a similar quantity taken over from them.
Each Coy. 240 Magazines (loaded) without buckets.
Battn. Lewis Gun Officer will arrange to hand over, and take over 80 (loaded) Magazines less buckets for HQrs Coy.
All Magazines taken and handed over should be thoroughly cleaned & in good condition.

X. WORK IN HAND.

Battalion Works Officer will arrange for all Work in hand by the 5th A. & S.H. to be continued by this unit.

XI. STAND-TO-ARMS.

Morning   0300 till "All Clear."
Evening   2100 till 2130 – All Coys (less HQrs Coy)

XII. SUPPLIES & WATER.

Rations for the Firing Line Coys. will be brought up by Pack Transport to VANCOUVER DUMP and issued in the morning.
Reserve Coy & Batt. HQrs Rations come to to Battn HQrs on Pack Transport.

Water.
(a) Water is brought up from MORRISON DUMP to all Coys. in Petrol Tins.
(b) Coys. will arrange mutually with those of 5th A.&S.H. for exchange of Petrol Tins with sufficient water for evening meal on day of relief.

XIII. MEDICAL.

R.A.P. is situated at junction of HUDSON Tr. and VANCOUVER ROAD.

XIV. SANITARY.

Usual certificate re cleanliness of lines will be given & taken. Certificates to be handed to Orderly Room by 1000 on 15th June. Areas vacated to be left scrupulously clean.

XV. REPORTS.

Completion of Relief will be wired or sent by Runner "PRIORITY" to Battn H.Qrs using code word "MAUD" followed by name of the O.C. Company.

XVI. ACKNOWLEDGE

David M Macintyre Lieut
A/Adjt 1/6 H.L.I.

(P.T.O)

Issued at _ _ _ _ _ _ 13/6/18.

Copy No 1 To O.C. A. Coy
" 2 - " B. "
" 3 - " C "
" 4 - " D "
" 5 - C.O. R.S.M. H.Qs Coy & File
" 6 - Q.M. & T.O.
" 7 - C.O. 1/5 A & S.H.

SECRET.   No. 2.

157th Infantry Brigade Order No. 105.

12th June, 1918.

1. The following reliefs will be carried out on 14th June, 1918.

    (a) 5th H.L.I. will relieve 7th H.L.I.
    (b) 6th H.L.I.   "   "   5th A & S. H.

After relief 7th H.L.I. & 5th A & S. H. will take over same dispositions as 5th H.L.I. and 6th H.L.I. respectively.

2. As much of relief as possible will take place during day light. Not more than 2 Platoons of each Coy of the relieving Battns should be on the move at the same time.
(This does not apply to Platoons at NEUVILLE ST VAAST.)
Platoons moving from NEUVILLE ST VAAST to the Eastern foot of VIMY Ridge and vice versa will do so in Sections at not less than 100 yards interval.

3. Relief will be completed by 2300.

4. Details of relief will be arranged by Os.C. concerned. A percentage of observers, scouts etc., of reserve battns should proceed to the line 24 hours in advance.

5. All trench maps, stores, etc., will be handed over.

6. Completion of relief will be wired "Priority" to Bde Hqrs. using the code word "Pemberton".

7. ACKNOWLEDGE.

                                                                   Major,
Brigade Major, 157th Infantry Brigade.

Issued at ....

Copies No. 1 to 5th H.L.I.
         2   6th H.L.I.
         3   7th H.L.I.
         4   5th A & S. H.
         5   157th L.T.M. Bty.
         6   Hqrs. 52nd Division.
         7   Hqrs. 156th Inf. Bde.
         8   Hqrs. 153rd Inf. Bde.
         9   Artillery Hqrs.
        10   )
        11   ) War Diary.
        12   File.

SECRET   Copy No. 2

BATTALION ORDER No 12
By
Major W.M. Anderson M.C. Comdg 1/6th Bn K.L.I.

REF MAP – MARŒUIL 1/20,000   19th June 18

1. INFORMATION

(a) 154th Inf Brigade will be relieved by 155th Inf Brigade in the present sector on the 20th June.

(b) The 6th Bn K.L.I. will be relieved by 5th Royal Scots Fusiliers in the present area.
    Relief will be carried out by daylight.

(c) A Coy 6th K.L.I. will be relieved by A Coy R.S.F.
    B   do   do   do   B   do
    C   do   do   do   C   do
    D   do   do   do   D   do
    Relief to be completed by 6 a.m. on 21st June.

2. ADVANCED PARTIES

Advanced Parties provided to-day as per separate instructions issued.

3. EMBUSSING POINT

Coys when relieved will proceed independently to the embussing point on the MAROEUIL–ST VAAST road.
On leaving communication trenches will move by sections at not less than 100 yards distance apart.
Lieut D.B. LOCKHART 155th Brigade will be in charge of embussing arrangements.
From debussing point coys will proceed and take over billets vacated by 1/5 K.S.F. at Fraser Camp ST ELOI where guides to coy areas will be provided.

4. TRENCH & AREA STORES

(a) Soyer Stoves, Food containers, Petrol tins and all Trench Stores will be handed over and receipts obtained.
Communications, French Maps, Maps of No Mans Land, Defence Schemes, Log Books and notes on Work in Progress will also be handed over.
In addition the following complement of Lewis Gun magazines will be exchanged and receipts obtained.
    240 Lewis Gun Magazines (loaded) per Coy
        (two buckets)
    60 L.G. Magazines (loaded) two buckets H.Q.
        Coy
Receipts for above as per above forms issued to coys will be rendered to Orderly Room by noon on 20th June.

5. SANITATION

Greatest care will be taken that trenches are handed over in a thoroughly clean and sanitary condition and certificate to this effect obtained.

6. DETAILS.

Details at RISPIN Camp will rejoin Battalion at Fraser Camp on 20th inst.

7. TRANSPORT

Under Orders of Brigade Transport Officer Battn Transport and details (less Orderly Room) will move from the present area to that of relieving Battalion.

Relief will be completed by 11.00 on 20th inst

8. SUPPLIES

From 20th inst (inclusive) Rations will be drawn from BLACKPOOL SIDING A.4 d 4.8.

Water is laid on in the camp. Strictest supervision must be exercised to prevent wastage.

9. REPORTS.

Completion of Relief and Arrival in Camp will be reported by the Code words "DORIS" and "KENNE" respectively followed by name of Company Commander.

10. ACKNOWLEDGE.

David Mackintosh
Lieut.
a/Adjutant 4th H.L.I.

ISSUED AT 18.30 19/6/18

Copy No 1. to O.C. A Coy
" 2 " B "
" 3 " C "
" 4 " D "
" 5 C.O. R.S.M. HQrs Coy & FILE
" 6 Q.M. & T.O

Amendment to Brigade Administrative Instructions No. 103.
===

Para 3 Supplies is cancelled and the following substituted:-

3. <u>Supplies</u>.

From 20th June inclusive, rations for all Units of the Bde. will be drawn from BLACKPOOL SIDING A.7.d.4.8.

(signed) H M Hewison
Captain,
Staff Captain, 157th Infantry Brigade.

(signed) QM

18th June,

O/C 5 HLI

Handing Over of Communications

4th R.S.F.   Issued with Bde Orders No 107
FRASER CAMP   of 17-6-18.

1. Each Battn of relieving Bde will send in advance Bn. Hdqrs & Coy Signallers to take over communications in the Bn Area.

2. Bttns of 157 Bde will arrange to send early on day of relief 2 men to Bn Hdqrs of their opposite numbers to take over any existing communications and instruments that are being handed over.

3. O/C Regt 5 HLI will arrange for his function to be shown over all test boxes & lines and to get all information regarding his role under Divnl Defence Scheme. Communication from HILL'S CAMP (5 HLI) to Bde will be thro' TETER by phone.

4. Each Bttn of this Bde will detail 1 linesman

2

to remain 24 hours with relieving Bn.
This liaison man must have a thorough knowledge
of all lanes in the Bn area & the various methods
of water comm. to Bde and to flanks.

5. The following equipment will be handed over
to relieving unit and a receipt obtained:

Unit	Fullers	Bivouac tents	Magneto	M/083	Power Buzzers
5 HLI	2	1	1	1	1
6 HLI	2	1	1	1	1
7 HLI	2	1	-	-	-
5 ASH	2	1	-	-	-

These receipts will be sent in to Bde after
arrival at billets.

D.III's and other articles of equipment will
NOT be handed over or exchanged.

6. Power Buzzer personnel will be placed with
Bn Signallers to whom they are attached & will
travel to rest billets with them. Power Buzzer
personnel presently with 5 HLI will be attached
to them during period in rest.

3.

7. Signal Offices will be handed over in a condition with all lines and leads clearly labelled. Accurate diagrams will be handed to O/C by relieving Bde. also line diagrams & Route Records supplied by Brigade.

8. All damaged or stray lines in the trenches will be pointed out to O/C relieving Bde. so that the recovery may be proceeded with.

9. The system of Runners, Relay Posts, Pigeon Service and Power Buzzer working will be made clear, & position of tunnel stations and method of exchange signals employed.

18-6-18   [signature] Bde Major
                 157 Inf Bde.

"C" FORM.		**MESSAGES AND SIGNALS.**	Army Form C. 2123. (In books of 100.) No. of Message..........

Prefix........Code......Words..24 Received. From PEDU By Mloo
Charges to Collect
Service Instructions PEDU
Sent, or sent out. At............m. To............ By............
Office Stamp. PEFA 19/6/18

Handed in at...Bde...........Office 1147 m. Received 1184 m.

TO PEFA

Sender's Number.	Day of Month.	In reply to Number.	AAA
SE 205	19		

ref	BDE	ADMIN	instr
no	103	part	8 duties
read	batln	on	duty
20 th	peta	next	for
duty	pefa		

FROM PLACE & TIME PEDU

"C" FORM.   Army Form C. 2123.
MESSAGES AND SIGNALS.   (In books of 100.)

Prefix...... Code...... Words 20 | Received. From Pefa By Bakery D | Sent, or sent out. At......m. To...... By...... | Office Stamp. Pefa 19/6/18

Charges to Collect

Service Instructions PEDU

Handed in at............Office.........m. Received 1747 m.

TO   PEFA

*Sender's Number.	Day of Month.	In reply to Number.	AAA
SC 208	19	—	

Ref Bde admin instru no 103 party for chaff cutting will not be required.

Para f (7) At no 103.
2 Reg'tl Police   1745
4 Orderlies
2 Fatigue men   0830

FROM PLACE & TIME   PEDU

*This line should be erased if not required.

SECRET.   Copy No. 3...

157th Infantry Brigade Order No. 107.
= = = = = = = = = = = = = = = = = = =

Appendix 20/6/18

Reference map MAROEUIL 1/20,000

1.   157th Infantry Brigade will be relieved by 155th Infantry Brigade in the WILLERVAL Section on the 20th & 21st June.

2.   Reliefs will be carried out in day light and will be as follows:-

   June 20th.   5th H.L.I. will be relieved by 5th R.S.F. in YUKON Area.
                6th H.L.I. will be relieved by 4th R.S.F. in OTTAWA Area.
                7th H.L.I. will be relieved by 5th K.O.S.B. in FARBUS Area.
                5th A.& S.H. will be relieved by 4th K.O.S.B. in MERSEY Area.
                Relief to be completed by 6 a.m. on 21st June.
   June 21st.   157th L.T.M.Bty will be relieved by 155th L.T.M. Bty, relief to be completed by 6 a.m. on 22nd June.

3.   Details of relief will be arranged between Os.C. concerned.

4.   Communications, Trench Maps, Maps of No Man's Land, Defence Schemes, Log Books and Notes on Work on Progress and Trench Stores will be handed over.
     Lewis Gun Magazines may be exchanged by mutual arrangement.

5.   Advance parties from 155th Inf. Bde., are going into the line on the 19th June. Guides will be arranged as follows:-

   5th H.L.I.   1 Guide to take party to Battn Hqrs at 2 p.m. at 157th Bde. Hqrs.
   6th H.L.I.   1 Guide to take party to Battn Hqrs at 2-15 p.m. at 157th Bde. Hqrs.
   7th H.L.I.   Guides for all Posts and Companies at Bde. Hqrs at 2-45 p.m.
   5th A.& S.H. Guides for all Posts and Companies at 3 p.m. at 157th Bde. Hqrs.

6.   Relieving troops for the BROWN LINE and EAST thereof will be guided to the point at which the Railway crosses TIRED ALLEY and MERSEY ALLEY, respectively, under Brigade Arrangements as shewn below. Beyond these two points and for the Posts WEST of the BROWN LINE arrangements will be made between Os. C. concerned.
     The relieving troops will arrive by Bus. Debussing point will be on NEUVILLE ST. VAAST - LES TILLEULS Road at a point which will be notified later.
     7th H.L.I., will provide a chain of picquets under an Officer (who will be stationed at debussing point) along the tracks from the NEUVILLE ST VAAST - LES TILLEULS Road to the junction TIRED ALLEY - FARBUS Ridge Line. 5th A.& S.H. will provide a similar chain under an Officer along the tracks from NEUVILLE ST VAAST - LES TILLEULS Road to the end of MERSEY ALLEY, thus avoiding CANADIAN Monument. These chains will be in position by 9-30 a.m. and will remain till all relieving troops have passed up.
     Units of 155th Infantry Brigade will be directed as follows:-

       5th R.S.F.   by TIRED ALLEY.
       4th R.S.F.   by MERSEY ALLEY.
       5th K.O.S.B. by TIRED ALLEY.
       4th K.O.S.B. by MERSEY ALLEY.

2.

7. Outgoing troops on leaving the communication trenches will move in sections at not less than 100 yards interval.

8. On relief Units will move into Camps as follows:-

    5th H.L.I.   HILLS Camp, NEUVILLE ST VAAST.
    6th H.L.I.   FRASER Camp, MONT ST. ELOI.
    7th H.L.I.   OTTAWA CAMP.   "   "   "
    5th A & S.H.   LE PENDU Camp   "   "   "
    157 LTMB   CUBITT CAMP NEUVILLE ST. VAAST

9. Units may send in advance a party of not more than 5 Officers in all and 10 O.R. per Coy., to take over Camps.

10. Details at RISPIN Camp will rejoin their Units at the Camps shewn above on day of relief.

11. Completion of relief and arrival in Camp will be reported by the code words "DORIS" and "KEANE" respectively.

12. The time at which Command will pass will be notified later. At this hour Brigade Headquarters will close at THELUS MILL and re-open at MONT ST ELOI at the same hour. 0900 21st.

13. Acknowledge.

                                              Major,
                Brigade Major, 157th Infantry Brigade.

        Issued at 3 p.m. 19/9/18.

    Copies No. 1 to 5th H.L.I.   No. 8 to Artillery Hqrs.
            2   6th H.L.I.   9   Hqrs. 156th Bde.
            3   7th H.L.I.   10   Hqrs 154th Bde.
            4   5th A.& S.H.   11   G.O.C.
            5   157th L.T.M. Bty.   12)
            6   Hqrs. 52nd Division.   13) War Diary.
            7   155th Inf. Brigade.   14   File.

Conference.

SECRET.   Copy No. ......

157th Infantry Brigade Administrative Instructions No. 103.

Issued with reference to Brigade Order No. 107 of 17/6/18.

Reference Sheet 51c. N.E.

1. **Relief.**

    5th H. L. I. relieved by 5th R. S. F. Will proceed to HILLS CAMP,
                                                           NEUVILLE ST. VAAST.
    6th H. L. I.   "   " 4th R. S. F. Will proceed to FRASER CAMP.
    7th H. L. I.   "   " 5th K. O. S. B.   "   " OTTAWA CAMP.
    5th A & S. H.   "   " 4th K. O. S. B.   "   " LE PENDU.
    157th L.T.M. Bty, "   " 155th L.T.M. Bty   "   " CUBITT CAMP.

2. **Transport.**

    Under Orders of the Brigade Transport Officer Transport will move from the present lines to lines occupied by the relieving Battns. Relief will be completed by 1400 on 20th inst. Arrangements will be made direct between Brigade Transport Officers.
    Relief of Duties. Battns will arrange to hand over to relieving Battns the water point duties furnished in this area.

3. **Supplies.**

    Rations for 21st will be drawn as at present from LEADLEY SIDING and sent to the camps which Units are to occupy.
    Rations for consumption from 22nd. From BLACKPOOL SIDING for Units in ST. ELOI Camps.
    From LEADLEY SIDING for 5th H. L. I., & L. T. M. Battery. The 5th H. L. I. will provide transport for L.T.M. Bty.

4. **Water.**

    Water is laid on in the camps. Strict supervision must be exercised to prevent wastage.

5. **Lorries.**

    The motor lorries which bring up the relieving Battns will be available to convey the Battns of this Brigade to ST. ELOI.
    Embussing Officer Lt. D.B. LOCKHART.

6. **Area and Trench Stores.**

    Soyers stoves, Food Containers, Petrol Tins and all Trench stores will be handed over and receipts obtained.
    The pro-forma issued with Q.198/5 will be used and the instructions laid down carefully complied with. The duplicate will be sent to Brigade Headquarters by 1800 on 21st. This will be returned if required

7. **Billet Improvements.**

    Units of the 155th Brigade will hand over to the relieving Units their scheme of work for billet sanitation and minor improvements and a schedule of the work in progress. This will include the construction of ovens, anti-aircraft protection etc.

8. **Duties.**

    Battn on duty 21st, 7th H. L. I.
    Next for Duty 6th H. L. I.
    The following Guards and Picquets will be furnished by Battn on Duty/

2.

8. Duties (Contd)

duty and will mount as shown:-

No.	Duty	Strength	Location	Time
(1)	Bde. Hqrs Guard.	1 N.C.O., 6 Men	Brigade Hqrs.	1700.
(2)	Picquet.	1 N.C.O. 3 men 3 men	F.15.a.0.7. F.14.a.0.5.	1500 - 2130.
(3)	Picquet.	1 Officer 2 N.C.O. & 12 Men.	F.13.b.8.6.	1500 - 2130.
(4)	Picquet.	1 N.C.O. 3 Men	F.13.a.2.7.	1500 - 2130.
(5)	Picquet.	1 N.C.O. 3 Men	F.1.a.4.2.	1500 - 2130.
(6)	To be held in readiness if called on. Officer will report at Bde hqrs.	1 Platoon.		1800 - 2200.
(7)	Divnl. Canteen.	1 Sergt.	OTTAWA Camp	1715 - 2030.
(8)	Camp construction Party.	120 Men exclusive of Offrs. & N.C.Os. ½ Picks, & ½ shovels	R.E. Dump FRASER Camp.	0800 - 1200 1300 - 1700.

9. Duties to be furnished by Battalions.

by 5th R. L. I.

No.	Duty.	Strength	Location	Time to report.
(9)	F.P. Compound.	1 Sgt. 1 L/Cpl. 6 Men.	AUX RIETZ Caves A.8.c.6.8. (Ref. MAROEUIL Map)	N.C.O. i/c Compound at 0900 on 20th & daily thereafter.
(10)	Ammunition Dump.	1 N.C.O. & 3 Men	HILLS Camp.	0900 on 20th
(11)	Forward battle Stragglers station.	1 N.C.O. & 5 men	A.11.b.1.8.	When called on see A.I. No. A.F.9 of 25/5/18
(12)	Prisoners of War Cage.	1 N.C.O. & 12 Men.	A.8.c.3.7.	When called on See A.I. No. A.F.9 of 25/5/18

The names of men detailed for 11 and 12 will be sent direct to A.P.M.

13)	Water Picquets.	1	(A.8.a.1.5. (A.8.a.3.6.	horses. "
		1	A.8.a.3.8.	Drinking.
		1	A.8.b.0.5.	horses.
			(F.11.b.1.2. (F.11.b.6.3.	" "
		1	(F.12.a.1.4. (F.12.a.2.1.	" Drinking.
		1	(F.12.a.6.2.	horses.
			(F.12.a.4.6.	Taps.
		1	(F.12.a.3.6. (F.12.a.6.9.	" "
		1	(A.8.c.7.6. (A.8.d.9.2.	Tank, horses.

Men detailed for Water Duty will report at 0900 on 20th to Battn Hqrs of Battn which is to be relieved.

3.

9. (Contd)

By 6th H.L.I.

No.	Duty	Strength	Location	
(14)	Water Picquet	1 Man	(F.8.a.8.2. (F.8.b.3.1.	Drinking. Horses.
		1 Man.	(F.9.c.9.1. (F.9.d.4.3.	Horses. Drinking.
		1 Man.	(F.9.c.9.4. (F.9.c.9.5.	" ~~Drinking~~ Horses

Men detailed for duty will report at 0900 on 20th to Battn Hqrs of Battn which is to be relieved.

By 7th H.L.I.

No.	Duty	Strength	Location	
(15)	Water Picquet.	1 Man	F.3.a.28.	Drinking.
		1 Man	F.2.c.14.	"

Men detailed for duty will report at 0900 on 20th to Battn Hqrs of Battn which is to be relieved.

By 5th A.& S.H.

No.	Duty	Strength	Location	
(16)	Water Picquet.	1 Man	(F.8.c.5.9. (F.8.c.5.6.	Tank. Drinking.
		1 Man.	(F.4.d.1-2. (F.4.d.2-1.	Horses. Drinking.
		1 Man.	(F.10.d.1-4. (F.10.d.1-8.	Tank. Horses.

Men detailed for duty will report at 0900 on 20th to Battn Hqrs of Battn which is to be relieved.

Divisional Chaff Cutting Depot. To be furnished by Battn on Duty each day.

No.	Duty	Strength	Location	Time
(17)	Chaff Cutting.	1st Shift 2 Sections	Blackpool Sdg.	0730 – 1130
		2nd Shift 2 Sections.	A.7.d.4.8.	1400 – 1800

Men detailed will report to N.C.O. i/c Divisional Chaff-Cutting Depot five minutes before their shift is due to start.

Water Picquets.

(a) Chloride of Lime is required for all water tanks and is provided by the M.O. of the unit finding the water picquet.
(b) The duties of water picquets are detailed in 52nd Divnl Circular Administrative Instructions No. 7 dated 24/5/18.

Orders in writing will be handed over by all picquets being relieved.

The Brigade Transport Officer will detail one Water Cart daily for the Signalling School, VILLERS AU BOIS. The cart will be left at the Camp.

10. **Discipline.**

N.C.Os and Men are forbidden to leave the Divisional Area.

ECOIVRES and other villages in the 51st Divn Area (i.e. South of an East and West Line through Cross Roads F.14.b.10.6.) are strictly out of bounds for all units of the Brigade.

11. **Bounds.**

The bounds for the Brigade are marked by 52nd Divnl Boards at the following points.

F.15.a.1.7.
F.14.a.8.7.
F.13.b.8.6.
F.13.a.9.9.
F.1.d.5.2.

No N.C.O. or man is allowed outside these Points without a pass signed by his Commanding Officer and bearing the office stamp.

Battalion bounds will be marked by Battn Boards which have been issued.

No man will leave the area of the three camps at ST. ELOI or the Camp area at NEUVILLE ST VAAST without a belt.

It must be impressed on all men that they must be properly dressed and tidely dressed when going out of camp area.

Steps will be taken to see that this carried out.

12. **Baths.**

Baths are allotted to Units as under:-

NEUVILLE ST VAAST, Baths.
60 men each half hour.

21st	5th H.L.I.	0900 to 1200	=	360 men.
"	"	1300 to 1600	=	480 "
				840

22nd L.T.M. Bty.	0900 to 1000	=	120 Men.

Berthonval Baths.

60 men each half hour.

21st	6th H.L.I.	0800 tp 1200	=	480
"	"	1300 to 1700	=	480
				960

ST. ELOI, Baths.

40 men each half hour.

21st	5th A & S.H.	0800 to 1200	=	320
"	"	1300 to 1700	=	320
22nd	"	0800 to 0900	=	80
				780
22nd	Brigade Hqrs.	0900 to 1030	=	120.

VILLER AU BOIS Baths.

40 men each half hour.

21st	7th H.L.I.	0800 to 1200	=	320
"	"	1300 to 1700	=	320
				640

13. **Area Stores.**

Area stores taken over should be carefully checked and a copy of/

13. Area Stores (Contd)

of the receipt sent to Brigade Hqrs by 1800 on 21st.

14. ACKNOWLEDGE.

H M Hewison
Captain,
Staff Captain, 157th Infantry Brigade.

Issued at ..3p.m. 18/6/18..

Copies No. 1 to 5th H. L. I.
        2   6th H. L. I.
        3   7th H. L. I.
        4   5th A.& S. H.
        5   157th L. T. M. Bty.
        6   Bde. Transport Officer.
        7   Hqrs. 155th Inf. Bde.
        8   Hqrs. 52nd Division.
        9   G.O.C.
       10   (War Diary.
       11   (
       12   File.

SECRET.   BATTALION ORDER No 13.   Appendix Copy No. 5
                By   29/6/18
MAJOR W. M. ANDERSON, M.C. COMMDG. 1/6TH BN H.L.I.
                                   28TH JUNE. 1918.

REF. MAP. - MAROEUIL. 1/20,000.

1. INFORMATION.
   (a) The 157th Bde. will relieve the 156th Bde. in the LEFT (CHAUDIERE) Section of the Divisional Sector.
   (b) The 6th H.L.I. will relieve the 7th Royal Scots in the front line, LEFT Sub Section.
       The 7th H.L.I. will be in the front line, RIGHT Sub Section.
       The 5th H.L.I. will be in Reserve. Units will take over dispositions from Battalion to be relieved as they stand at present.

2. DISPOSITIONS OF COYS.
       Dispositions are as follows:-
       "A" Coy ---------- Right Firing Line Coy.
       "B" " ---------- Right Centre Firing Line Coy.
       "C" " ---------- Left Centre Firing Line Coy.
       "D" " ---------- Left Firing Line Coy.

3. ADVANCED PARTIES.
       Advanced Parties as already detailed proceed on 28th June.

4. MOVE.
   (a) Battalion will move by Motor Lorry from ST. ELOI as under:-
       Via the ARRAS - SOUCHEZ Road - CAMPBELL Road to S.28.a.3.8. starting at 9 a.m.
       The Motor Lorries will be parked on Main Road at 0900.
       Lorries for this Battalion will be at the entrance to FRASER CAMP.
       Orders re Embussing & Debussing will be issued later.

5. GUIDES.
       1 Officer & 1 O.R. per Battalion H.Qrs. 1 Officer per Coy & 1 O.R. per Platoon will meet Battalion at S.28.a.3.8. on CAMPBELL ROAD at 0915.
       From Debussing Point Coys will move by BLIGHTY, GLACE, and HAYTER trenches.
       Up to the VIMY RIDGE, movement will be by Platoons at 200 yards distance, after that it will be by groups of 2 Sections at 100 yards distance.
       Every precaution must be taken to avoid movement being observed by the enemy.

6. TRENCH STORES
   (a) All communications, trench maps, Defence Schemes, Log Books, Trench & Area Stores, etc, will be taken over by Officers proceeding with Advanced Parties.
       Copies of receipts given, signed by Officer handing & Officer taking over, will be rendered on pro-forma issued to Coys. to reach Orderly Room by 1200 on 30th June.

6. TRENCH STORES. (CONTD)

(d) Coy. Gas N.C.Os. and Battalion Gas N.C.O. will be responsible for taking over all protective curtains, and Anti-gas appliances.

7. LEWIS GUNS.

The following Lewis Gun Baggage will be man-handled all the way.

8 Lewis Guns and Spare Parts per Coy.
(Chests to be left behind)

80 Lewis Gun Magazines per Coy (loaded) ie. 10 per gun, in 20 Canvas Buckets. All remaining Buckets will be carried up empty.

On arrival in new area each Coy will take over from 7th Royal Scots, 240 Lewis Gun Magazines (loaded) less Buckets.

A similar number of Lewis Gun Magazines (loaded) less Canvas Buckets will be handed over here to relieving Coys. of the 7th Royal Scots.

Battalion HQr will carry up 2 Lewis Guns and Spare parts (less chests) and 20 Magazines in 5 Buckets.

All remaining Buckets for these 2 Guns will be carried up empty.

On arrival in new area, H.Q. Coy. will take over 60 Magazines (loaded) less Buckets.

A similar number of L.G. Magazines (loaded) will be handed over here to H.Q. of the 7th Royal Scots.

All other Lewis Gun Equipment will be left at Q.M. Dump by 0700 on 29/6/18.

Receipts will be given and taken for above and sent in with Trench Store Receipts, to Orderly Room.

All magazines taken and handed over should be thoroughly cleaned and in good condition.

8. TRANSPORT.

(a) No Transport will be provided for Coy. baggage.
(b) 5 Dixies per Coy will be taken and man-handled by Coys.
(c) Medical Stores, Officers Mess Stores, Battn HQ Baggage etc, will be left with the Transport Officer who will arrange to Transport it to the Battalion at night along with rations.
(d) The T.O. will arrange with the Q.M. for the transfer of all Battalion Stores & Baggage from the present QMs. Dump to the new one at ROSE and DALY CAMPS on the 29th.

9. PATROLS, SENTRY POSTS ETC.

O.C. Coys must be careful to see that all S.O.S. observations and listening posts, Gas Sentries etc. and information about patrols are taken over in a correct manner.

10. DRESS.

Dress for Battalion proceeding to Trenches will be "Fighting Order" Steel Helmet S.B.R. at the Alert. W.P. Sheet neatly rolled & strapped to the Haversack.

— BATTN. ORDER No. 13. SHEET 2 —

10. DRESS. (CONTD).

Iron Rations will be carried inside the Haversack, Water Bottles filled.

Greatcoat neatly rolled and tied on to Waist Belt at the back. Mess tins will be securely tied to the Haversack.

All orders re wearing of equipment and S.B.R. Fixing of Bayonets while in Trenches must be rigidly adhered to.

All blankets & packs will be stacked at QM's Dump by Coys. by 0700 without fail. All Head gear other than the Steel Helmet will be left in the Packs.

All Officers Kits, valises etc. will be stacked at QM's Dump by 0700 on 29th inst. without fail.

11. WORK IN HAND.

Capt. K.G. TIDD will arrange all details re work in hand by 7th Royal Scots to be taken over and continued by this unit.

12. SUPPLIES & WATER.

(a) Rations will be brought up by Light Railway to VICTORIA DUMP, T.13.b.3.3. nightly. (Further detailed orders will be issued later)

(b) Water supply is situated as under:–

    T.8.a.0.0. .... 1-400 Gallon Tank.
    T.8.a.7.8. .... 4-400 Gallon Tanks.
    T.8.d.5.6. .... 4-400 Gallon Tanks.

(c) OC 'C' Coy will furnish a picquet of 1 N.C.O. and 2 men over water Supply mentioned in (b) to relieve those found by 7th Royal Scots, by 1400 on 29th.

(d) <u>Reserve Rations</u> are situated as under:–

    T.8.d.3.7   BISCUITS 750.   MEAT 768.

13. R.E. MATERIAL & SALVAGE

(a) All indents for R.E. Material must reach Battn. HQrs by 0830 each morning and will be sent up by Light Railway from ZIVY DUMP.

(b) All salvage will be collected in Coy. Areas & sent in to Salvage Dump at VICTORIA DUMP.

14. MEDICAL.

Battn. Aid Post is in HAYTER TRENCH.

Main Dressing Station, AUX REITZ – A.8.c.5.5.

A.D.S. – LA CHAUDIERE – S.18.c.9.5.

15. BURIAL.

An Advanced Collecting Post is situated at T.19.b.8.4.

Coys will wire to Battn. HQrs when the services of the Divnl. Burial Officer are required & arrangements will be made for removal & burial.

16. BILLETS.

All Billets and Camps must be left scrupulously clean and be ready for Commanding Officers inspection by 0730 on 29th inst.

17. PERSONNEL REMAINING BEHIND.

The following Officers (with Servants) and O.R.s will not proceed with the Battalion to the front line, but will proceed to Divnl. Details Camp on 29th June, arriving there by 1500. 2/Lieut K A MacIntosh will report to Camp Commandant of this Camp by 1000 on 29th for instructions as to accommodation.

2/Lieuts. Morrison, Macintosh & Fraser and Other Ranks as already detailed (Less L/Cpl Griffin who will proceed to Transport Lines as L.G. Instructor)

All O.R.s awaiting leave & courses will proceed to Transport Lines & remain there till due to depart.

18. SANITARY.

Usual certificates re cleanliness of lines will be given and taken.

19. ALARM.

In the event of alarm during relief, Coy or other units will send an Officer to the nearest Battn. H.Q. to report their position to the Battn H.Q.s in whose area they happen to be and also to Bde H.Q.s

20. PIPE BAND.

Pipe Band will proceed to the Transport Lines along with Q.M. Party

21. REPORTS.

Completion of Relief will be wired or sent by runner (priority) to Battn. H.Q.s using the Code word "CERTIE" followed by name of O.C. Coy. concerned.

22. ACKNOWLEDGE.

David Macintosh Lieut
A/Adjt 1/6 H.L.I.

Issued at 1500 28/6/18

Copy No. 1 To O.C. A Coy
      2 - " B "
      3 - " C "
      4 - " D "
      5 - C.O. H.Q.s By R.S.M. & file
      6 - Q.M.T.O.

17. PERSONNEL REMAINING BEHIND.

The following Officers (with Servants) and O.R's will not proceed with the Battalion to the front line, but will proceed to Divnl Details Camp on 29th June, arriving there by 1500. 2/Lieut K A MacIntosh will report to Camp Commandant of this Camp by 1000 on 29th for instructions as to accommodation.

2/Lieuts. Morrison, Macintosh & Fraser and Other Ranks as already detailed (less L/Cpl Griffin who will proceed to Transport Lines as L.G. Instructor)

All O.R's awaiting leave & courses will proceed to Transport Lines & remain there till due to depart.

18. SANITARY

Usual certificates re cleanliness of lines will be given and taken.

19. ALARM

In the event of alarm during relief, Lewy or other units will send an Officer to the nearest Battn. H.Q. to report their position to the Battn H.Q's in whose area they happen to be and also to Bde H.Q's

20. PIPE BAND

Pipe Band will proceed to the Transport Lines along with Q.M. Party

21. REPORTS.

Completion of Relief will be wired or sent by runner (priority) to Battn H.Q's using the Code word "CERTIE" followed by name of O.C. Coy. concerned

22. ACKNOWLEDGE.

David MacIntyre Lieut
A/Adjt 1/6 H.L.I.

Issued at 1500 28/6/18

Copy No 1 To O.C. A Coy
  2 - " B "
  3 - " C "
  4 - " D "
  5 - C.O. H.Q's Coy R.S.M & File
  6 - Q.M. T.O.

SECRET.   Copy No. 2.....

157th Infantry Brigade Order No. 108.
= = = = = = = = = = = = = = = = = = = =

27th June, 1918.

Ref. Map MARCEUIL 1/20,000

1.   The 157th Infantry Brigade will relieve the 156th Infantry
   Brigade in the LEFT (CANADIAN) Section on the 29th - 30th June
   as under:-

   29th June.
      7th A.L.I. relieve 4th R.S. in front line RIGHT SUB-SECTION
      6th A.L.I.   "   7th R.S.   in front line LEFT SUB-SECTION
      5th A.L.I.   "   7th S.R.   in RESERVE.
   30th June.
      157th L.T.M.B. relieve 156th L.T.M.B.

2.   (a) Battns billetted at MONT ST. ELOI will move by Motor Lorry
   as follows:-

      7th A.L.I. to Barrier on LA FOLIE FARM Road at S.28.d.8.8.
         starting at 9 a.m.
      6th A.L.I. via the ARRAS - SOUCHEZ Road - CAMPBELL Road to
         S.28.a.3.8. starting at 9 a.m.
   (b) (i) H.Q. & 2 Coys 5th A.L.I. will proceed by route march from
   MILLS Camp to the Barrier on the LA FOLIE Farm Road the leading
   platoon arriving there at 1215 p.m.
      (ii) 2 Coys will proceed via the ARRAS - SOUCHEZ Road -
   CAMPBELL Road to S.28.a.3.8. leading platoon arriving at 1215 p.m.

3.   (a) Guides, 1 Officer and 1 O.R. per battn Hqrs. 1 Officer per
   Coy and 1 O.R. per platoon will meet units as follows:-
      6th A.L.I. on CAMPBELL Road, S.28.a.3.8. at 9.15 a.m.
      7th A.L.I. at Barrier, S.28.d.8.8. at 9.15 a.m.
      5th A.L.I. for 2 Coys & Hqrs at Barrier S.28.d.8.8. at 1215 p.m.
         &   for 2 Coys on CAMPBELL Road. S.28.a.3.8. at 1215 p.m.

4.   (a) 7th A.L.I. & H.Q. & 2 Coys 5th A.L.I. will move by BUMPER,
      PEGGY, & TOAST Trenches.
      6th A.L.I. & 2 Coys 5th A.L.I. will move by BLIGHTY, CLACE
      & RATION Trenches (latter for 6th A.L.I. only).
   (b) Up to the VIMY Ridge movement will be by Platoons at 200 yards
      distance, after that it will be by Groups of 2 Sections at
      100 yards distance.

5.   (a) 7th A.L.I. & 6th A.L.I. will arrange for their own debussing
      Officers.
   (b) An Officer of the Brigade Staff will superintend the enbussing
      at MONT ST. ELOI.

6.   (a) Advanced parties consisting of Battn Intelligence Officer, &
      1 Officer per Coy., 1 N.C.O. per platoon, Coy Gas N.C.Os.
      & a proportion of Lewis Gunners, Signallers, Scouts and
      runners will go into the line on 28th June.
      3 Motor Lorries have been arranged for, to take above up.
      Busses will be at MONT ST. ELOI (entrance to FRASER Camp)
      at 3 p.m. and are allotted 1½ to each of 6th & 7th A.L.I.
      5th A.L.I. advanced party will march up.
   (b) Guides for advance parties have been arranged as follows:-
      5th & 7th A.L.I. at Barrier S.28.d.8.8. at 3 p.m.
      6th A.L.I. on CAMPBELL Road at S.28.a.3.8 at 3 p.m.

7. 157th L.T.M.B. will proceed up to the line on 30th June by route march. O.C., L.T.M.Bty will make his own arrangements re routes & guides.

8. Communications, trench maps, maps of No Man's Land, Defence Scheme, Log Books, and Trench Stores will be taken over.

9. All other details re, relief will be arranged between C.Os. concerned.

10. In the event of Alarm during relief, Units will send an Officer to the nearest Battn Hqrs. to report their position to the Battn H.Q. in whose area they happen to be and also to Bde H.Q.

11. Personnel of units to be left out of the line will proceed to Divisional Details Camp arriving there by 3 p.m. 29th June.

12. Between the completion of the Infantry and L.T.M. Bty relief, the 157th L.T.M.Bty will come under the orders of G.O.C. 156th Infantry Brigade.

13. Completion of reliefs will be reported to Bde. Hqrs by the code word "CHAUDIERE".

14. Command will pass on completion of the Infantry Relief. Brigade Headquarters will close at MONT ST. ELOI at 4.30 p.m. on 29th June, and open at S.27.b. 0.5. at same time.

15. ACKNOWLEDGE.

A.Williams
Major,
Brigade Major, 157th Infantry Brigade.

```
Copies No. 1 to 4th K.O.S.B.
         2    6th K.O.S.B.
         3    7th K.O.S.B.
         4    157th L.T.M. Bty.
         5    Hqrs. 52nd Division.
         6    Hqrs. 156th Inf. Bde.
         7    Hqrs  155th Inf. Bde.
         8    52nd M.G. Battn.
         9    C.R.A. 52nd Divnl. Artillery.
        10    B.G.C.
        11   (
        12   ( War Diary.
        13    File.
```

SECRET.   Copy No. 2......

157th Infantry Brigade Administrative Instructions
No. 105.
Issued with reference to Brigade Order No. 108 of 27th June. 1918.
= = = = = = = = = = = = = =

27th June, 1918.

Ref. Map MAROEUIL. 1/20,000

1. MOVE.

The Brigade less 5th H.L.I. and L.T.M.B. will be conveyed on June 29th by motor lorries from MONT ST. ELOI to relieve the 156th Bde.

7th H.L.I. to Barrier at LA FOLIE FARM. S.28.d.8.8.
6th H.L.I. by CAMPBELL ROAD to S.28.a.3.8.

The motor lorries will be parked on the main road at 0900.
Lorries for 6th H.L.I. will be at the entrance to FRASER CAMP.
Lorries for 7th H.L.I. at entrance to OTTAWA CAMP.

2. RELIEF.

5th H.L.I. will relieve 4th R.S.,
6th H.L.I. will relieve 7th R.S.
7th H.L.I. will relieve 7th S.R.

3. TRANSPORT.

Transport will be brigaded in ROSS & DALLY CAMPS.
Units will take over the lines of the battalions which they relieve.
Arrangements for the move will be made between the Brigade Transport Officers.
The move will be completed by 1400 on 29th.

4. RATIONS.

Refilling point from 29th June inclusive will be LEADLEY SIDING
Rations will be drawn at 0730 daily.   (A.2.c.5.9.)
Rations are forwarded to units from the Transport lines as follows:-

Right Line Battalion.
  For 4 Companies.   By Light Railway to CANADA DUMP, T.20.b.6.3.
  Battn. Hqrs.   NEW BRUNSWICK, T.19.d.8.2.
  LEFT LINE BATTALION SUPPORT   VICTORIA DUMP. (T.13.6.33)
Left Line Battalion.
  2 Companies.   By Light Railway to CAYUGA DUMP S.24.c.6.8.
  1 Company.   NEW BRUNSWICK   T.19.d.8.3.
  1 Company.   BORDER   T.25.a.4.8.
  Battn Hqrs.   By rail to CAYUGA or by Limber.

L.T.M. Bty.   VICTORIA DUMP.

5. WATER SUPPLY.

MONT FOREST System.

T.15.b.7.8.   3   400 Gallon Tanks.
T.16.c.6.8.   3   "   "   "
T.16.c.9.2.   1   "   "   "
T.16.d.2.7.   3   "   "   "
T.16.b.9.1.   3   "   "   "

GIVENCHY MAIN.

S.12.b.9.6.   1   W.B.F. 12 Taps.
S.12.b.8.5.   3   400 Gallon Tanks.
T.8.a.0.0.   1   "   "   "
T.8.a.7.8.   4   "   "   "
T.8.d.5.6.   4   "   "   "

VIMY.

S.18.c.9.3.   2   S.P.
S.24.b.2.9.   2   200 Gallon Tanks.
T.20.c.3.1.   2   "   "   "

2.

6. **WATER PICQUETS.**
   The following picquets will relieve those found by the 156th Bde by 1400 on 29th.

   Right Line Battn.
   1 N.C.O. & 5 men for MONT FOREST System.

   Left Line Battn.
   1 N.C.O. & 9 men for GIVENCHY.
   T.8.a.00.   T.8.a.7.8.   T.8.d.5.6.

   Reserve Battn.
   1 N.C.O. & 4 men for GOODMAN MAIN & VIMY (T.20.c.3.1.)
   1 N.C.O. & 3 men for GIVENCHY (S.5.b.9.6.) (S.12.b.8.5.)
   & VIMY (S.18.c.9.3.) (S.24.b.3.9.)

7. **AMMUNITION SUPPLY**
   The Brigade ammunition dumps are situated as follows:-

Main Dump	Cayuga	S.24.c.8.5.
Forward Dumps.	Culvert	T.20.c.3.1.
	PEGGIE	T.19.b.7.8.
	NANAIMO	T.13.a.2.4.

8. **RESERVE RATIONS.**
   Reserve rations will be taken over by Battalions as follows:-

		Biscuits	Meat
Right Line Battn.	T.16.c.9.5.	700	690
Left Line Battn.	T.8.d.3.7.	760	768
Support Battn.	S.24.d.1.2.	750	756
	T.7.d.9.5.	1,350	1,336
	T.21.a.3.3.	600	576

9. **R.E. MATERIAL**
   Will be supplied on demand through Brigade from ZIVY Dump and will be sent up by Light Railway.

10. **SALVAGE.**
    All salvage will be collected and sent to VICTORIA, CAYUGA or PEGGY Dump.
    The Reserve Battn will detail 2 Sections to report at 1000 on 30th at VICTORIA Dump for salvage duty.

11. **MEDICAL.**
    Main Dressing Station, AUX RIETZ. A.8.c.5.5.
    A.D.S.   LA CHAUDIERE   S.18.c.9.5.

12. **BURIAL.**
    An advanced collecting post is established at T.19.b.8.4.
    Units will send bodies there and will wire to Divnl Burial Officer who will remove these and arrange for burial.

13. **STRAGGLER'S POSTS.**
    Stragglers posts are established at following points and are manned by personnel found by A.P.M.
    S.11.d.4.2.   S.18.c.9.2.   S.24.b.4.6.   T.19.c.3.5.

14. **BILLETS.**
    (a) All billets and Camps must be left scrupulously clean.
    (b) A list of Area Stores handed over to incoming units will be forwarded to Brigade Hqrs., on 30th June by 12 noon.
    (c) Certificates will be obtained from the Area Commandant that there are no outstanding claims for damage to Government property.

15. **TRENCH STORES.**
    List of Trench Stores taken over will be furnished as per schedule to reach Bde Hqrs, not later than 1200 on 1st July.

16. ACKNOWLEDGE.

H M Hewison
Captain,
Staff Captain, 157th Infantry Brigade.

Issued at ....20.30....29/6/18.

Copy No. 1 to   5th H. L. I.
       2   6th H. L. I.
       3   7th H. L. I.
       4   Bde. Transport Officer.
       5   Area Commandant.
       6   Hqrs. 156th Inf. Bde.
       7.   Hqrs. 52nd Divn.
       8.   157th L.T.M.Bty.
       9.   2nd Lowland Field Amb.
      10.   B.G.C.
      11.   (
      12.   (War Diary.
      13.   File.

6 HLI (BS/19)

COMMUNICATIONS

Issued with Bde Order No 108
27 June/18.

1. Each Btn of 157 Bde will send in advance on arrival of 23rd inst 1 Signaller per coy & 2 from Bn HQdrs to take over and get all necessary information regarding existing communications.

2. Bns of the 156 Bde will hand over to relieving Btn the following equipment.

9 R.S. — 7 HLI 3 Fullers, 16 eq, 1 Buzzer/tel, 1 Power Buzzer
7 R.S. — 6 HLI 3 " 1 " 1 " 1 "
7 S.R. — 5 HLI 2 " — 1 " 1 P.B. ampl.

Any Telephones No 108 in possession of 156 Btn will also be taken over.

5 HLI will hand over to 7 S.R. 1 Chatty from and magneto Telephone.

3. Receipt for equipment taken over handed over will be forwarded to Bde Sig officer by evening of 30th.

4.

4. Power Buzzer Stations in the line will be manned by Signallers detailed from Bde. The 5th HLI will man the Power Buzzer and amplifier station at Stone River Ndugu with trained personnel presently attached to them. One of these 4 men should be sent with advanced party on 29th to note present system of working. (Accumulators for Power Buzzers are sent up as reqd by ration train from IVY DUMP, marked with name of unit to which they are destined. O i/c Btn Sigs will be advised of their arrival & should arrange to meet train & draw them. "Dud" accumulators will be sent down by the same method.

5. Lamp & telephone will be manned by 2 Signallers from the Brown Line Btn (Partially trained Signaller and Buffer). Each Btn will find one orderly for duty there from those normally left at Siors.

6. Each Btn will detail the following men to report to Bde Hdqrs at 1500 on 28th.
   5 HLI 1 Visual Sig. 3 Runners
   6 HLI 1   "   2   "   (All Bde Pool trans
   7 HLI 1   "   3   "   (presently with Btns

7. Bde Visual Station is situated near o/d Bde Hdqrs at LA FOLIE copse & will be manned by

(3)

Bde Section assisted by Bns Visual Signallers previously detailed.

(i) At least 2 messages will be sent by visual by Bns each 24 hours. The DD method will be employed & no notification of message coming will be given by Bn. RD will be sent by Phone.

2 (i) The following relay posts will be taken over & established.
Post No 1. At Old Bde Hdqrs in La Folie Copse
 (S 23 c 2 2) 6 men from 5 HLI
 " No 2 " Bn Hdqrs in Sunken Road
 { 2 men from 5 HLI
 { 2 "   "   6 HLI
 { 2 "   "   9 HLI

(ii) 2 Post will link to Right & Left Line Bn Hdqrs & Back to 5/1st Post.

(iii) The following are the times allowed for runners between Relay Posts
 Bde Hq to No 1 Post 20 min.
 No 1 Post - No 2 17 "
 No 2 - to Left Bn. 25 "
 No 2 - Rt Bn 25 "

(iv) There will be four runs daily leaving Bde

(4)

at 0630
1100
1530
2030

Pigeons should leave Bttn in time for up & down runners to meet at N° 2 post.

(v) Sealed Packets for units outside Bde & transport leave Bde HQrs at
0700
1000
1300
1900

9. The Brim Inn Bttn will detail pigeoneer to report at Bde HQrs each morning at 1200 to take up pigeons to N° 2 post. Kemmel Inn Bttn sending their pigeoneer to meet him at N° 5 post at 1100.

10. Any enemy rocket stations & supplies of rockets will be taken over by units in whose area they are. Arrangements as to procedure to be adopted will be notified later.

11. Every effort should be made by Bttn to

salve - ground cable, of which a large
quantity is lying dis... in the sector
is to be taken over. Cable picked up & if
not required by Sigs Btn should be sent
to Salvage dump & Bde Sig. Officer
notified of approx mileage recovered.

12. OCs Btns will please ensure that the
requisite numbers of messages are sent
by alternative methods of Communication
     1. 4 per day by Power Buzzer
     2. " " Visual
     1. " " Pigeon
These messages should be ordinary
routine messages but should not be left
to O i/c Btn Sigs to send practice ones.

If the alternative methods are regularly
employed both the officers writing the messages
and the signallers sending them will gain
confidence in their reliability & come to
regard them as a normal means of
communication.

27-6-18

Bellchay
157 Inf Bde.

Instructors presently at Villers-au-Bois Signalling
School will return to their units on evening of 28 June.

1/16th Bn. H.L.I.

War Diary.

Volume III

July. 1918.

Army Form C. 2118.

WAR DIARY
or
INTELLIGENCE SUMMARY. 1/6 H.L.I. JULY 1918 VOLUME III
(Erase heading not required.)

Instructions regarding War Diaries and Intelligence Summaries are contained in F. S. Regs., Part II. and the Staff Manual respectively. Title pages will be prepared in manuscript.

1/6 H.L.I. JULY 1918 VOLUME III
Neufchâtel MAROEUIL 1/20000.

Place	Date	Hour	Summary of Events and Information	Remarks and references to Appendices
LA CHAUDIÈRE SECTOR (FRONT LINE)	1/7/18	0300-0415	Defensive Patrols of 1 Officer (2/Lt D. HOGG) and 12 Sections and 1 Sergt and 14 Sections took up positions at T.4.C 7/4 and T.10 b 5/5 respectively. No enemy was encountered. At 0130 sounds of wiring overheard. Patrols returned at 0130.	Appendix 1/7/18.
		1000	Stand to Arms — G.O. visited the line. Work carried on as usual. Wiring of Black Line, digging of Cable Holes etc.	
		2100-2130	G.O. visited left & left centre Coy.	
		2215	Stand to Arms.	
	※		Defensive patrol of 1 Platoon under 2/Lt HOGG & backed up 2/Lt PATERSON took up a position at T.10 a 9/4. No hostile patrols encountered. Patrol withdrew at 0130. Proposed Raid scheme found F.R.U. (See appendix)	
do	2/7/18	0300-0415	Stand to Arms — 5 Rds Fancy practice carried out each morning. Usual programme of work carried out.	
		1030	C.O. visited Right & Right Centre Coys. Patrols of 1 Lt Section under Lieut W.O. THOMPSON and 1 Lt Sections under Sgt Connell at T.10 B 7/7 and T.10 C 4/0 respectively from 2215-0145. No enemy seen to hand.	
		2100-2130	Stand to Arms. —	

Army Form C. 2118.

WAR DIARY
or
INTELLIGENCE SUMMARY.
(Erase heading not required.)

Instructions regarding War Diaries and Intelligence Summaries are contained in F. S. Regs., Part II. and the Staff Manual respectively. Title pages will be prepared in manuscript.

Place	Date	Hour	Summary of Events and Information	Remarks and references to Appendices
do.	3/7/18	0300-0415	Stand to Arms. — C.O. visited line.	
		1000	C.O. at Left Coy. — Work carried on as per programme.	
		1600	Lt/Col J. ANDERSON CMG, DSO. rejoined from 157 Bde H.Q. & assumed command of Bn.	SLh
		2100-2130	Stand to Arms.	
		2200	Very heavy shelling of Left Coy Area till 2230 — Casualties 1 Officer (Lieut TODD) killed, 3 O.R. killed and 5 O.R. wounded.	
		2215	Patrol of 1 Officer (2/Lt J.V. STEWART) and 1 Platoon worked T.10 B.6/4. Officer & scout crawled forward to reconnoitre enemy's wire. Bomb were thrown & bursts away & Rifle fire opened on Patrol by hostile patrol estimated at 20-30. Officer wounded at 2300. Scout failed to return.	
do.	4/7/18	0300-0415	Stand to Arms. — C.O. visited line	
		1000	C.O. went round line accompanied with Left Coy.	
		1600	Advance parties 5th KRI arrived. Officers reconnoitred the Battn lines occupied by 5 KRI during the day.	SLh
		2150-2130	Stand to Arms	
		2300	Patrol of 1 Officer (Lieut BRUCE) and 1 Platoon proceeded by HULL RD to T.10 B.8/9. returning at 0300. No enemy were encountered	

WAR DIARY or INTELLIGENCE SUMMARY

Army Form C. 2118.

Place	Date	Hour	Summary of Events and Information	Remarks and references to Appendices
	5/7/18	0300-0415	March to Annex. C.O. visited line.	Alexander 15/7/18. DHm
		1100	Relief completed (see Appendix). Bnys after relieved moved to Bn. Batt Area. – Disposition: A Coy – Right, B – Right Centre, D – Left Centre and C – Left Coy, B.H.H.Q. at PETIT VIMY.	
		2130-2130	March to Annex. 1 section per Platoon began with ANDERSON M.C. preceding draft to U.K. (14 days)	
VIMY SECTOR (RESERVE LINE)	6/7/18	0300-0415	March to Annex – 1 section per Platoon Work carried on – Wiring, Improvement of Trenches etc. Baths arranged allotted to Coys as under – 1 Platoon per day	DHm
			A Coy 1000-1030 ; B 1130-1200 ; C 1330-1400 , and D 1600-1630.	
		2100-2130	March to Annex – 1 section per Platoon	
	7/7/18	0300-0415	March to Annex – 1 section per Platoon Baths arranged allotted as at 6th.	DHm
		0900-1030	Conference of O.C. Coys at Bn. H.Q. – Work carried on as per programme.	
		1030	C.O. visited C Coy Sector. 1130 D Coy Sector.	
		1400	C.O. inspected Transport & Q.M. Lines at DALY CAMP.	
		2100-2130	March to Annex – 1 Platoon per Coy. CASUALTIES: 1 O.R. killed and 1 O.R. wounded.	

Army Form C. 2118.

WAR DIARY
or
INTELLIGENCE SUMMARY.
(Erase heading not required.)

Instructions regarding War Diaries and Intelligence Summaries are contained in F. S. Regs., Part II. and the Staff Manual respectively. Title pages will be prepared in manuscript.

Place	Date	Hour	Summary of Events and Information	Remarks and references to Appendices
	7/7/18 (contd)	2100	Enemy plane tried to land within Batt: area. Searchlights taken forward & machine guns fired into flames & destroyed. Lieut J.F. KENNEDY rejoined from GHQ Course.	
	8/7/18	0300-0415	Stand to arms — 1 Section per Platoon	F.h.h.
		1000	C.O. visited B Coy area 1100. A Coy area Batths arranged & allotted as under. — 1 Platoon per Coy per day B Coy 0930-1000 ; C 1130-1200 ; D 1330-1400 ; A 1600-1630. M.O. inspection - A Coy — Work carried out as per programme	
		1000		
		2100-2130	Stand to Arms — 1 Section per Platoon	
	9/7/18	0300-0415	Stand to Arms — 1 Section per Platoon L.O. visited C Coy area 1430 ; D Coy 1130. Batths arranged & allotted as under — 1 Platoon per Coy. C Coy 0930-1000 ; D Coy 1130-1200 ; A Coy 1330-1400 ; B Coy 1630-1630. Hostile plane driven down by m.g. own patrols at WILLERVAL area.	F.h.h.
		1000		
		1130	Medical inspection — B Coy.	
		1000	Work continued as per programme	
		2100	Stand to Arms — 1 Section per Platoon	
		2130	F.C.S.WEST Lt.Hol. Course (Infantry) FRESSIN. Capt M.D. MACRAE N.Z.C. transferred from Leave to HQ OC.	

A7091. Wt. w12839/M1297. 750,000. 1/17. D.D & L., Ltd. Forms/C2118/14.

WAR DIARY
or
INTELLIGENCE SUMMARY.

Army Form C. 2118.

Place	Date	Hour	Summary of Events and Information	Remarks and references to Appendices
	10/7/18	03.00-04.15	Stand to arms - 1 Section per platoon. Baths arranged, toilet/tables amended - 1 Platoon per Coy. D Coy 0730-1000; A Coy 1130-1200; B Coy 1330-1400; C Coy 1600-1630	
		10.20	Brigade Inspection - C Coy	10/7/18 D.Ch
		16.00	Advance Parties 1/9th Highrs. 1 NCO + 1 L.G. per platoon B/Lt L.O. Lenfesty proceed to Front line preparatory to relief in Right Subsector. Bde. Order A....	
		21.00-21.30	Stand to arms. 1 Section per platoon.	
		21.00	Officer [unclear] to Front Line per 8.7)	
TOAST SECTOR (FRONT LINE)	11/7/18	03.00-04.15	Stand to arms - 1 Section per platoon. Batt. proceeded to relieve 1/5 H.H.L.I. in "TOAST" area (see Appendix). Disposition A Coy - Right; B Coy - Right Centre; D Coy - Left Centre; C Coy - Left Coy	Appendix 11/7/18 D.Ch
		07.30	Relief Complete.	
		13.00	Work per tenders commenced.	
		19.00-19.30	Stand to arms - all Coys (from H.Q.)	
		19.45	C.O. visits all Coys in the Line.	
		21.00-21.30		
		21.30-24.00	Patrol 2/Lt Spiers (10/14 D Jamieson) sent Instructions to keep position at The C 3/5 from 22.30 - 02.00 the enemy spleen.	
			Word received that Capt K. Gridd seriously unwell went sick June on 12th Capt K. Gridd proceeded on leave to U.K. (14 days)	

Army Form C. 2118.

WAR DIARY
or
INTELLIGENCE SUMMARY.
(Erase heading not required.)

Instructions regarding War Diaries and Intelligence Summaries are contained in F. S. Regs., Part II. and the Staff Manual respectively. Title pages will be prepared in manuscript.

Place	Date	Hour	Summary of Events and Information	Remarks and references to Appendices
	12/7/18	0300 - 0430	Stand to Arms - Rest men fired 5 Rds S.A.A.	
		1100	Work in Trenches. Wing its carried out safe programme. Corps & made cominal work at B.C. Sector Informer reached BM.	
		2100 - 2130	Stand to Arms. Capt. I. F. KING left for Lewis Gun School LE TOQUET. Lieut A. MARTIN left for Musketry Course MATRINGHEM	
	13/7/18	0200	Gas Shell Attack carried out from the 13th Area, being part of a major operation on the Lys front. (See Appendix.) All troops withdrawn from front line from 0030 to 0245; Gas Achieves rendezvous from 0200 - 0230. Enemy did not retaliate after discharge was complete. Usual bombardment of enemy's communications & flanks of gas attack	Appendix 13/7/18 K.W.
			from 0230 - 0330	
		0300 - 0415	Stand to Arms - Work in trenches. Wiring to Coy front. Salvage Parties organized collecting salvage in 13th Area during the day.	
		2100 - 2130	Stand to Arms -	
		2200	Patrol of 7 Officer (2/Lt SMITH) and 1/2 trench reached T 18 a 1/1. Returning at 0130. No enemy were seen or heard.	

Army Form C. 2118.

WAR DIARY
or
INTELLIGENCE SUMMARY.
(Erase heading not required.)

Instructions regarding War Diaries and Intelligence Summaries are contained in F. S. Regs., Part II and the Staff Manual respectively. Title pages will be prepared in manuscript.

Place	Date	Hour	Summary of Events and Information	Remarks and references to Appendices
	14/7/18	0300-0420	Stand to Arms – L.O. visited the line.	Appendix 14/7/18 BN.
			Work at Trenches & Barrage continued throughout the day.	
		2100-2130	Stand to Arms –	
			(Patrol 1 Officer (Lieut I.E. DOBSON) and 20 O.R. left at 2230 and reached T10 b 8/3 returning from lines at 0220. No sign of the enemy were seen on Rear Defence Scheme patrol for sector (see Appendix)	
	15/7/18	0300-0420	Stand to Arms – 0700 Lts Potter left for HANSOM CAMP NEVILLE ST VAAST. Word received that H.Q. R.S. would relieve Bn in TOAST AREA on 16th	Appendix 15/7/18 BN.
			(Warning Order)	
			Work on Trench Wiring, Salvage & clearing of lines continued.	
		1430-1600	L.O. inspected all trenches occupied with "B" Coy.	
		1430.	Advance parties of 1/4 R.S. arrived	
	16/7/18	0150	Relief Completed. Bath moved independently by bivy to HANSOM CAMP (Neuville) (See Appendix)	
		0600	Baths arranged for all Coys at Bths NEUVILLE -ST-VAAST – A Coy 0900-1030 B Coy 1030-1130, C Coy 1130-1200 & 1330-1330, D Coy 1400-1530.	
		0900		

Army Form C. 2118.

WAR DIARY
or
INTELLIGENCE SUMMARY.
(Erase heading not required.)

Instructions regarding War Diaries and Intelligence Summaries are contained in F.S. Regs., Part II. and the Staff Manual respectively. Title pages will be prepared in manuscript.

Place	Date	Hour	Summary of Events and Information	Remarks and references to Appendices
NEUVILLE ST VAAST	16/7/18 (Cont)	1100	Washing of equipment, kit & Gunners etc during the day. Inspection of Bays by the Company Officer.	Appendix 16/7/17 B.Ch.
		1800	Conference of all Officers at Bn.H.Q. Lieut. I.W. FINGLAND M.E. reported Unit from leave to U.K.	
	17/7/18	0600	Ecurie. 0800 Boy Inspection.	
		0900–1100	Drift Training under R.S.M. Handling of Arms. Drill etc. Boy Training–	
		1115	Inspection of Billets etc. Handling of Arms. Inspection of Drifts by Company Officer. Technical Inspection of Drafts.	B.Ch.
		1315	A.M.O. Inspection of Drafts by handling officers.	
		1400	Brts pushed & marched to OTTAWA & DURHAM CAMPS, ST ELOI arriving there at 1600. Lieut A. MACINTYRE and 2/Lt W.B. CURRIE reported from 8 Lnt Canadian Coved	B.Ch.
MONT ST ELOI	18/7/18	0630 0800	Ecurie – Bts on duty, Guards, Piquets, Working Parties etc provided as required by O.C. Baths at ST ELOI allotted A Boy 0800–0900 B Boy ! 0900–1000 C Boy 1000–1100 D Boy	
			0900–1200 Drift Training under R.S.M. — A O.C. Inspection B Boy 0730–0735 D Boy 1000–1100 A Boy 1100–1200 B Boy 1100–1200 C Boy 1400–1500 Reading of Standing Orders. Army Act, K.R. Form 463 etc to all the s/c arrived since 2/6/18 by Orderly Officer.	

Army Form C. 2118.

WAR DIARY
or
INTELLIGENCE SUMMARY.
(Erase heading not required.)

Instructions regarding War Diaries and Intelligence Summaries are contained in F. S. Regs., Part II. and the Staff Manual respectively. Title pages will be prepared in manuscript.

Place	Date	Hour	Summary of Events and Information	Remarks and references to Appendices
MONT ST ELOI	15/7/18	1800	Sorting of Equipment, Cleaning of Kits, Arms etc throughout the day. Inspection of all Officers at Bttn H.Q.	Appendix 15/7/18 BLu
		1400	C.O. + 2nd C: Coys on Reconnaissance in CARENCY AREA.	
		1500	B.C. visited and inspected Camp. Capt W.D. MACRAE M.C. to HQRS 15th Bde as Acting Staff Capt (Bttn Orders were issued. See Appendix)	
	19/7/18	0630	Marville. 1000 Billeting Party, 1/1 Officer + 30 O.R. left for RAIMBERT.	
		0830 – 1030	Draft Training under R.S.M. and instructors. Coy Training Lecture of 2nd Platoon in Handling of Arms, Drill, Turnout and in General ["at"] Tactical Scheme. Warning Orders received that Division would be relieved by 9th Divn.	BLu
		on 20d		
		1010	G.O.C. VIII & both Bdes inspected Baths during training. Scrubbing of Equipment, Washing of Kits, Aprons & general cleaning up carried out during day.	
		1800	Lectn by Brigade Major to all Officers from LIEUT A. MACINTYRE proceeded on leave to U.K. (14 days)	
	20/7/18	0500	Reveille	Appendix Appendix(5) 20/7/18
		0630	Advance party 9th Divn arrived.	
		0700	Inspection Baths by Sanitary Officer.	
		0830	Bttn marched to ST. ELOI Stn. Hereafter by Moving and left ST. ELOI Stn at 1550 (See Appendix)(5)	BLu
		1400	Arriving at CHOCQUES R/COURT at 1550	

Army Form C. 2118.

WAR DIARY
or
INTELLIGENCE SUMMARY.

(Erase heading not required.)

Instructions regarding War Diaries and Intelligence Summaries are contained in F. S. Regs., Part II and the Staff Manual respectively. Title pages will be prepared in manuscript.

Summary of Events and Information Ref Map 36.B. 1/40000

Place	Date	Hour	Summary of Events and Information	Remarks and references to Appendices
	20/7/18 (contd)		Batt detrained at CALONNE RICOUART and marched to RAIMBERT arriving there at 1700. Billets allotted to Coys. Lt Col J Andrew Adjt DSO. proceeded 157 Bde hqrs W.h. being pte assuming command of Batta Brig.r W.h. ANDERSON M.C. reported from leave to U.K. Draft of 170.R. joined and Other Standing Orders (see Appendix A)	
RAIMBERT	21/7/18	0630	Reveille	
		1000	0800. Coy Inspection. Church Parade. All Training Grounds & Ranges reconnoitred.	Ich
		1700	Conference of O.C. Coys at Btn H.Q. Draft of 2/23 O.R. joined Batt.	
	22/7/18	0600	Reveille. 0730 Coy Inspection	
		0830-}	Drill Practice Schemes of Best Method in Handling of Ammo Turnout	
		1200 }	Coy Training. Bayonet Fighting. Lewis Gun & Rifle Training Inspection of Btn Lewis Gun Officer.	
		0830-} 1000 }	Draft Training under R.S.M. and Launcher	Th
			During intervals an Officer Competition, all Coy carry on less 2 n.c.o.	
			3 O.R. Officers on Musketry, & Ficks on training	
		1700	Conference of O.C. Coys at Btn H.Q.	

Army Form C. 2118.

WAR DIARY
or
INTELLIGENCE SUMMARY.
(Erase heading not required.)

Instructions regarding War Diaries and Intelligence Summaries are contained in F. S. Regs., Part II. and the Staff Manual respectively. Title pages will be prepared in manuscript.

Place	Date	Hour	Summary of Events and Information	Remarks and references to Appendices
RAIMBERT	23/7/8	0600	Reveille — 0730 Coy Inspection	
		0830–1200	Bn Training under R.S.M. & Instructors. Bayonet Fighting, Musketry, Bayonet Fighting, Lecture of Best Platoon Handling of Arms, Training Stealing Drill Company Officers	F.h.h.
		0830–1200	Lewis Gun training under Bn Lewis Gun Officer. 2nd (1 pr Platoon) " Intelligence Officer. Training cancelled owing to heavy rain. Conference of O.C. Coys & Bn H.Q. Lt Col. J. ANDERSON C.M.G. D.S.O. rejoined unit from Bde H.Q. assumes Command Draft of 37 O.R. joined unit	
		1445		
		1700		
	24/7/8	0600	Reveille — 0730 Coy Inspection	
		0830–1200	Inspection of all men not below the standard for 12 months for T.A.B. Coy Training as above — Selection of Best Platoon in Tactical Scheme by Company Officers. — Selection Best L.G. Section by O.C. Coys — Musketry and Bayonet Fighting Drafts Inspection and Squad Training under R.S.M. and Specialist Officers respectively.	F.h.h.
		1500	Regimental Tour for all Officers under L.O. on Training Ground. Capt. SIEKING attached from language LE TOQUET School joined unit who being appt. Bn Lewis H.G. officer vice <s>Lt Braids</s> who on bn 2 Oct 23rd filled by Orderly Officer.	

A7093. Wt. w2859/M1297 750,000. 1/17. D.D & L., Ltd. Forms/C2118/14.

Army Form C. 2118.

WAR DIARY
or
INTELLIGENCE SUMMARY.
(Erase heading not required.)

Place	Date	Hour	Summary of Events and Information	Remarks and references to Appendices
RAIMBERT	25/7/18	0600	Reveille. 0730 Coy Inspection & Inspection of Billets.	
		0830-1200	Range Practice – Selection of Lead Platoon – Practice fired 3 Rds Application and 15 Rds Rapid.	Appendix 25/7/18. K.h.
			Musketry – Bayonet Fighting and Close Order Drill – Draft Training. Specialists – Stack + Lyddites under L.O. + Ly. M.s respectively. Training cancelled at 10:45 owing to very heavy rain.	
		1400	Reconnaissance – C.M.Goves – Lillers hve 1/A + B Coy Officers under Coundy Officer.	
		1830	Lecture by Coundy Officer to all Officers on "Village + Wood Fighting". 2/Lt D. JOHNSTON proceeded on leave U.K. (14 days). Preliminary Emergency move orders issued (See Appendix).	
26/7/18		0600	Reveille. 0730 Coy Inspection & Inspection of Billets.	
		0830-1200	Range Practice – as on 25/7/18. Musketry – Bayonet Fighting – Attack Formation – Bombing Competitions. Selection of Lead Platoon on Bombing. Draft Training. Specialist Training – Lyddites + Scouts under Ly. M. + L.O.	K.h.
		1400	Tactical Tour for all Coy Officers NCOs under O.C. Coy. M.O's inspection of Battⁿ with Battⁿ blueprint – Re-inspection of all water bottles.	

Capt. K. G. TIDD reported unfit from leave to U.K.

Army Form C. 2118.

WAR DIARY
or
INTELLIGENCE SUMMARY.
(Erase heading not required.)

Instructions regarding War Diaries and Intelligence Summaries are contained in F.S. Regs., Part II. and the Staff Manual respectively. Title pages will be prepared in manuscript.

Place	Date	Hour	Summary of Events and Information	Remarks and references to Appendices
RAIMBERT	27/7/18	06.00	Reveille	
		0830-1200	0730 Coy Inspection & Inspection of Billets. Range Practice. — as for 26/7/18. Musketry — Bayonet Fighting and Attack on a wood & villages. Bombing & Bomb hitting — selection of Best Platoon in Bomb Throwing. Draft Training. Specialists — Lewis Gunners & Signallers & Scouts' Training. Training cancelled at 1100 owing to heavy rain.	Shm
		1400-1530	Range Practice — to last [?] by Coy. Lecture to Coy Officers & NCOs under O.C. Coy.	
		1830	Conference of O.C. Coys at Bn H.Q. on Programme for ensuing week.	
	28/7/18	0630	Reveille — 0800 Inspection of Billets.	
		0930	Inspection of Bn. by Command Officer — A.D.Os — A, B, C & D Coys.	Shm
		1015	Church Parade.	
		1100	Inspection of Coy Cookhouses by Command Officer.	
		1400	Reconnaissance by 2/Lt ... for Coy of Choques Billers [?] line under Major W.L. Andrew M.C.	

Army Form C. 2118.

WAR DIARY
or
INTELLIGENCE SUMMARY.
(Erase heading not required.)

Ref Sheet 36 B 1/40000

Place	Date	Hour	Summary of Events and Information	Remarks and references to Appendices
RAIMBERT	29/7/18	0600	Reveille	
		0730	Bags Inspection & Inspection of Billets.	
		0830-1200	Range Practice - Bombing Competition. Cattack formations by Platoons - Attack practices on a Village	
			(a) Work - Mutual Support - Communication in the attack - Draft Training - Musketry, Bayonet Fighting & Lewis Gun Drill. Specialists - Lewis Gunners, Signallers & Scouts S.B.'s room for ½ an hour at any clock time during above training by S.M. All ranks why were not actually training 1000-1015.	
		1400-1500	All NCOs with RSM and instructors. Bayonet Fighting flag drill Drill & Commanding Drill.	
		1500	Batt. Sports held in RAIMBERT. Draft of 5 O.R. joined Unit from 14 IBD.	
		1000	Warning order received that Btn wound move on 30th to BARLIN	
		1300	Advance Parties 1 Officer & 3 NCO's left for BARLIN	
	30/7/18	0500	Reveille 07.15 Inspection of all billets by Coy. Commdr.	Appendix 35/7/18 Ditto
		0500	Batt. proceeded by route march to BARLIN (See Appendix) arriving there at 16.00	
		0900	Advance party 1 Off. & 3 NCOs left for ARRAS	
		2030	Foot inspection 2130 Lights out. Batt. warned for the trenches.	

Army Form C. 2118.

WAR DIARY
or
INTELLIGENCE SUMMARY.

(Erase heading not required.) Ref Sheets 36 B. 1/40000 and MAROEUIL 1/20000

Instructions regarding War Diaries and Intelligence Summaries are contained in F. S. Regs., Part II. and the Staff Manual respectively. Title pages will be prepared in manuscript.

Place	Date	Hour	Summary of Events and Information	Remarks and references to Appendices
BARLIN.	3/7/18	0630	Reveille	
		0900	Bn. Inspection.	
		0930	Conference of O.C. Coys at Bn. H.Q.	
		1130	O.C. Coys proceeded in advance to reconnoitre the line and make necessary arrangements re relief.	Appendix
		1245	Batt. proceeded by route march (See Appendix) to MADAGASCAR CAMP. arriving thereat Shts A 27 d & A 26 c (near ARRAS) arriving there at 2000.	3/7/18 Shts.
		2100	Fort Inspection 2130 lights out	
			Lieut. P.A.E. McCRACKEN and 2/Lt MACINTOSH rejoined from S.O.S. and P.& B.T. Courses respectively.	

WAR DIARY or INTELLIGENCE SUMMARY

Army Form 2118

TABLE SHEWING INCREASES & DECREASES IN BATTN. CAMP STRENGTH DURING MONTH OF JULY, 1918.

Place	Date	Hour	Summary of Events and Information			Remarks and references to Appendices
				Off	O.R.	
			Camp Strength as at 1st July 1918	28	724	
			Decreases Killed — 1 Off, 3 OR			
			Wounded — 1, 16			
			Prisoners — 1, 25			
			To Hosp (Sick) — , 6			
			On Leave — , 3			
			To Rest Camp			
			" Batd Baty	3	57	
				25	667	
			Increases From Hosp (Sick) — 10 OR			
			" Leave — 1 Off, 14			
			" Courses — 1, 5			
			" Batd Baty — 3, 3	5	32	
			Camp Strength as at 2400 on 7/7/18	30	699	
			Decreases Killed — 1 Off, 1 OR			
			Wounded — , 8			
			Died of Wounds — , 21			
			To Hosp (Sick) — 1, —			
			On Leave — , 11			
			" Batd Baty			
			" Courses of Instr — 5, 11	7	43	
				23	656	
			Increases From Hosp (Sick) — 1 Off, 8 OR			
			" Leave — , 22			
			" Courses — , 8			
			" Batd Baty — , 4			
			Recruits from attached			
			Medical Officer	2	78	
			Camp Strength as at 2400 on 14/7/18	25	734	
			Decreases To Hosp (Sick) — 1 Off, 12 OR			
			On Leave — , 23			
			To Rest Camp — , 5			
			" Batd Baty — 2, 4	4	53	
				21	681	
			Increases From Hosp (Sick) — , 19 OR			
			" Egypt (RAF) — , 2			
			" Leave — 2, 18			
			" Courses — , 14			
			" Batd Baty — , 21			
			" 137th Pioneers by Drafts from other Units — , 24	4	103	
				25	784	
			Camp Strength as at 2400 on 21/7/18			
			Decreases To Hosp (Sick) — 1 Off, 13 OR			
			On Leave — , 18			
			To Batd Baty — , 7	1	38	
				24	746	
			Increases From Hosp (Sick) — , 16 OR			
			" Egypt R/Temp — 1 Off, 16			
			" R.A.F. Egypt — 1, —			
			" Leave — , 22			
			" Rest Camp — , 6			
			" Batd Baty — , 14			
			" Courses of Instr — 1, 3			
			Drafts from other Units — , 50	5	133	
				29	879	
			Camp Strength as at 2400 on 28/7/18			
			Decreases To Hosp (Sick) — , 16 OR			
			On Leave — , 8			
			To Batd Baty — , 1	—	27	
				29	852	
			Increases From Hosp (Sick) — , 1 OR			
			" Leave — , 5	—	13	TOTAL NET INCREASE FOR THE MONTH 1 Off & 141 OR
				29	865	
			Camp Strength as at 2400 on 31/7/18			

File

SECRET.   Copy No. 2

157th Infantry Brigade Order No. 100.

2nd July, 1918.

1.   The 5th H. L. I., will relieve the 6th H. L. I. in the Left sub-Section of the Brigade Section, on 5th July 1918.
     After relief 6th H.L.I. will take over same-pack dispositions as 5th H. L. I.

2.   The relief will take place during daylight and in view of special operation, should commence immediately after breakfast and must be completed by 2 p.m.
     Not more than 2 Platoons of each Company of relieving Battalion should be on the move in the open at the same time. Platoons will move in sections at not less than 100 yards interval.

3.   Details of relief will be arranged by O.Cs. concerned. The usual observers, scouts etc., of reserve Battn should proceed to the line 24 hours in advance.

4.   All Trench Maps, Stores, Log books, etc will be handed over.

5.   Completion of relief will be wired "priority" to Brigade Headquarters, using the code word GLADYS.

6.   Acknowledge.

                                              [signature]
                                                    Captain,
                              A/Brigade Major, 157th Infantry Brigade.

     Issued at ....

     Copy No. 1 to 5th H. L. I.
          2   6th H. L. I.
          3   7th H. L. I.
          4   157th L.T.M.Bty.
          5   52nd M.G. Battn.
          6   Hqrs Artillery.
          7   2nd Lowland Field Amb.
          8   Hqrs 52nd Division.
          9   Hqrs 155th Infantry Brigade.
         10)
         11)   War Diary.
         12   File.

SECRET   Copy No. 5

BATTALION ORDERS No 17
BY
LIEUT. COL. J. ANDERSON C.M.G. D.S.O. Commdg 1/6th Bn H.L.I.

REF MAPS VIMY AND ROUVROY - 1/10,000   10TH JULY 1918

(1) A Gas beam attack will be carried out on the night of 5/6TH July or on 1st night after upon which the wind is favourable. "O" Special Coy. R.E. will be in charge of the Operations on the Divisional Front. The Cylinders can be discharged in any wind between W.N.W. and S.W. of velocity not less than 6 miles per hour. Simultaneously Flank Divisions will carry out similar operations.

(2) On the Battn. Sector Gas will be discharged from T16.C.3.6.

(3) The trucks will be pushed up by parties furnished by 7th H.L.I.

(4) In the event of a cylinder being hit by hostile fire all ranks will adjust Respirators, but will not ring bells or sound alarm Horns — the danger will in any case be very local.

(5) (a) Artillery action which might cause retaliation will be avoided, otherwise Artillery and M.G. fire will be normal.
(b) OC "B" Coy will detail a Lewis Gun under an Officer to be at the Discharge Position to cover the noise of the Discharge. The Gun will be in position at 11 P.M. and fire occasional short bursts of fire.
If the Officer hears any noise being made by the trucks moving he will order short bursts of fire to cover the noise. Care must be taken not to draw the enemy's attention to the fact that anything unusual is going on.
The Gun will be withdrawn one hour after the trucks have left the discharge point.

(6) Troops occupying the Observation Line and Blue Line will be disposed as follows
"A" Coy. All Observation posts and troops in Blue Line will be withdrawn & disposed in TOAST TRENCH not less than 300 yards S.W of junction of TOAST - McDERMID. S B Rs will be worn
"B" Coy All Observation posts and troops in Blue Line will be withdrawn and disposed in TOAST beyond (1c) S.W of "A" Coy. S B Rs will be worn
"D" Coy. All Observation posts and troops in Blue line will be withdrawn & disposed in TOMMY, not less than 200 yds. South of junction of TOMMY & GERRARD. S B Rs will be worn

"C" Coy All Observation posts will be withdrawn and troops in Blue Line will be disposed in TEDDY GERRARD not less than 200 yards W. of junction of TOMMY-TEDDY GERRARD S.B.Rs will be worn.

All Lewis Guns & 4 Magazines per Gun & spare parts will be withdrawn with the troops. Other L.G. Magazines will be placed in protected Dugouts.

Orders will be sent out by Runner for the time at which troops above will be withdrawn — and when they are to reoccupy the trenches.

(7) Each Coy will supply 2 runners to report to C.O. in Tunnel, at 2360 & will also detail the following parties to report to NCOs in Tunnel by 2400, for work with Gas NCOs in clearing Trenches etc after the discharge

(8) "A" Coy. 10.O.Rs "D" Coy 9 ORs "B" 9 ORs C Coy 8 ORs. Orders have been given to Battn & Coy Gas NCOs who will be in Tunnel. They will ensure that blankets on all protected Dugouts in Blue line and forward thereof are lowered

(9) S.B.Rs will be worn by all ranks in areas stated in para 6 above from Zero – 2 minutes, until orders are given by an Officer for their removal. This order will not be given till zero plus 30 minutes, and then only if Trench System is reported clear of Gas. Coy Officers will work in co-operation with Gas NCOs and will ensure that instructions given by the latter are carried out.

(10) The following Code will be used:—
Operation will take place tonight ---- JAPAN
Operation Postponed ---------- SPAIN
Cancel Operation previously Ordered --- RUSSIA

(11) Zero hour will be 12.30 A.M. or as soon after as the Trucks are reported to be in position.

(12) The extra days rations sent up last night are for consumption on the day following the Gas attack. Should the attack be postponed Rations will be sent up from the Transport Lines as usual. The Code word RATIONS will be sent, and the extra days rations now in hand will be retained at Coy. Headquarters, & will be kept for the day following the attack.

(13) A Medical Officer detailed by O.C. 2nd L.F.A. for treating Gas Cases will accompany the pushing parties of the 4th H.L.I. from POWER HEAD at T21a.3.9. until Operation is completed.

(14) ACKNOWLEDGE.

David MacIntyre
A/Adjt 1/6th H.L.I. Lieut &

Issued at 2300 10/7/18
Copy No 1 To OC "A" Coy
"   " 2 — " "B" "
"   " 3 — " "C" "
"   " 4 — " "D" "

Reference B.O. No 17. para 8. - of 10th July. 1918.

The following parties are detailed to work under Gas N.C.O's

1. 1 Coy Gas N.C.O, 1 N.C.O & 8 men of "C" Coy (with 2 fans to each party) to clear trenches - TEDDIE GERARD from junction with TOAST - TOMMY - LILY ELSIE & QUEBEC.
One party will clear from TOAST along TEDDIE GERARD to VESTA TILLEY & then up TOMMY & LILY ELSIE.
  The other party will clear up TOAST, QUEBEC & LILY ELSIE & will meet the first party.

2. Two Parties from D Coy.
 (1) Gas N.C.O & 6 men (with 3 fans) to clear NEW BRUNSWICK from TUNNEL - TOAST - McDERMID to meet No 2 Party.
 (2) 1 N.C.O & 6 men with 3 fans to clear McDERMID - TOAST - meet No 1 Party

3. (1) Bn Gas N.C.O. & 6 men of 'A' Coy (with 3 fans) - to clear TEASER - TOPER - MONTREAL - QUEBEC - to meet 2.
 (2) Gas NCO & 6 men of 'C' Coy. with 3 fans to clear QUEBEC - TOPER - to meet 1.

4. Gas N.C.O. & 4 men of 'A' Coy. (with 2 fans) to clear NEW BRUNSWICK from junction with TOAST to TOPER

    David McIntosh Lieut.
    & A/Adjt
    1/6 H.L.I.

10/7/18.

HEADQUARTERS
No. BM 4/25
Date 3/7/15
157th INFANTRY BRIGADE

O. of C.,

1. Similtaneously with the operation order by Brigade Order No. 110, the flank Division will carry out similar operation.

2. The danger area on the Right does not affect this Brigade.

3. The danger area on the Left is shewn on the Map attached to Brigade Order No 110.

A/Brigade Major,
157th Infantry Brigade.

3rd. July, 1915.

File.

G.R.4/4/2.
6/7/18.

H.Q.
157th INFANTRY
BRIGADE.
No ....
Date 6/7/18

S.O.S. LIFT SECTOR.
----

1. Reference Divisional Order No. 113 of 2nd inst. from zero plus one hour to zero plus 5 hours heavy artillery will carry out increased harassing fire.

2. This will be repeated on the night following the discharge, from zero plus 5 hours to zero plus 5 hours.

(sd) T. Henderson, Capt.
for Lt. Colonel, G.S.,
52nd Division.

6th July, 1918.

O.C. ....

Forwarded for information with reference to 157th Infantry Brigade Order No. 110 of 3rd inst.

6th July, 1918.

Kirkpatrick
Captain.

SECRET   Copy No. 2

                                      110
               157th Infantry Brigade Order No. ~~107~~.

Ref (Map 1/20,000 MAROEUIL.   3rd. July, 1918.
    (Attached Sketch.

1.   A Gas Beam attack will be carried out on the First Army
Front on the night 5th/6th July, or on the first night after upon
which the wind is favourable. 'O' Special Coy. R.E., will be in
charge of the operation on the Divisional Front.
        The cylinders can be discharged in any wind between N.N.W.
and S.W. of velocity not less than 6 m.p.h.

2.   On the Divisional Front Gas will be discharged from Nos. 5
and 6 Railheads, (shown on attached Map) on the Mont Foret and
Caribou Lines as follows.-

Line.	Base	Power Heads	Discharge Points.	Trucks.	Cylinders
5.	TERRITORIAL. (N. of ROUAIN).	T.21.a.3.9.	T.16.a.c 3/6	30	1050
6.	TERRITORIAL.	T.14.b.1.9.	T.9.b.	50	1050

3.   (a) The Infantry pushing parties will be furnished by 6th H.L.I.
Four hundred men (exclusive of Officers and N.C.Os.) will be required.

        (b) This personnel will be divided into 2 parties i.e.,
Detachment A and Detachment B, both Detachments to be employed in
pushing trucks from the POWER HEADS to the DISCHARGE POINTS and in
pulling them back again after the discharge.

        (c) Both Detachment A and Detachment B will each be organized
into 10 pushing parties numbered 1 to 10, each of 20 men exclusive
of N.C.Os. with a senior N.C.O. in charge of each of the 10
parties. One Officer will be in charge of every 2 parties and a
Senior Officer in charge of Detachment A and of Detachment B.
        Number of personnel required therefore will be:-

                1 Senior Officer
                5 Officers.
                10 Senior N.C.Os.
                200 Men.
        Total, 6 Officers, 10 N.C.Os., 200 men for each Detachment.
        Total for both Detachments,
                12 Officers, 20 N.C.Os., 400 men.

        (d) These parties must be very carefully organized, paraded
beforehand, numbered and steps taken to ensure that every N.C.O.
and man knows to which party he belongs and what his duties are.
        Each man should have a label tied on to his Box Respirator
bearing the number of the party to which he belongs or else the
Box Respirator should have the number chalked on to it.
        Strict discipline must be maintained, there must be no
noise of any sort made by the men. All orders must be given in a
low voice.
        The trucks must be moved as silently as possible and their
pace checked on declines

        (e) One O.R. of "O" Special Coy R.E., will proceed and return
with every truck.

4. Detachment A will work on line No.5, and Detachment B on line No.6.

From the two Power Leads trucks will be pushed up to the Discharge Points, each party of 20 men pushing a train of 5 trucks.

After pushing the trucks to the Discharge Points pushing parties will be withdrawn to a suitable trench system in the vicinity and there await the completion of the Discharge.

The O.C., 6th D.L.I. will have these places reconnoitred beforehand and made known to all Officers in charge of parties.

After completion of Discharge the parties organized as before will pull (not push) the trucks containing the empty cylinders back to the Power Heads. They will wear their Box Respirators on the return journey.

The men of the Special Coy R.E., have been warned that they are not to give orders or advice to the Infantry pushing parties as to removing their Respirators.

5. Detachments A & B will report to Officers of "O" Special Coy., R.E. at their respective Power Leads (vide para 2), at 1045 p.m. on the night of the operation.

The trains will arrive at 11 p.m.

6. In the event of a cylinder being hit by hostile fire, all ranks will adjust Respirators but will not ring bells or sound Klaxon Horns. The danger will in any case be very local.

7. (a) Artillery action which might cause retaliation will be avoided otherwise artillery and M.G. fire will be normal.

(b) The O.C., 5th and 7th D.L.I., will each arrange for a Lewis Gun under an Officer to be at the Discharge Point in each of the areas to cover the noise of the Discharge.

These guns should be in position at 11 p.m. and fire occasional short bursts. They will be withdrawn one hour after the trucks have left the Discharge Point.

If the Officer hears any noise being made by the trucks moving he will order short bursts of fire to cover the noise.

Care must be taken not to draw the enemy's attention to the fact that anything unusual is going on.

(c) On the arrival of the first trucks at the Discharge Points the O.C. A and B Detachments will each arrange for a few sentry groups to be posted immediately on the enemy's side of the Discharge Point to afford local protection while the preparations for the discharge of the Gas are being made.

These sentry groups must be withdrawn to a place of safety just before ZERO Hour. They will be withdrawn under orders of the O.C. A & B Detachments respectively.

8. (a) The areas which must be clear of troops before Zero are marked RED on attached map. Those in which the Box Respirator must be worn are marked GREEN. Box Respirators should be worn from Zero - 2 minutes until orders for their removal are given by an Officer. This should not be given until Zero plus 30 minutes and then only if the trench system is reported clear of Gas.

(b) The Divisional Gas Officer assisted by the anti-gas personnel of Brigade and Battalions should make arrangements for:

(i) Clearing Dug-outs and Cellars by means of fires etc., immediately after completion of Discharge.
(ii) Clearing trenches, saps etc., by means of Flappers etc immediately after completion of Discharge.
(iii) Troops should not reoccupy Trenches etc., until qualified anti-gas personnel have declared them to be safe.

These orders require most careful attention and C.Os. must satisfy themselves that the arrangements made by their Anti-Gas personnel/

3.

personnel are satisfactory and issue orders that any instructions issued by the latter are to be carried out.

Special care must be taken to see that all Blankets of protected dugouts are let down prior to the discharge and that every dugout in the danger area is carefully cleared of gas after the discharge.

Company Commanders must work in cooperation with Anti-Gas personnel so that they may know when to give orders for the removal of Respirators and when to re-occupy trenches dugouts, etc

9. (a) A decision will be made by higher authority at 1 p.m. on 5th July (or succeeding days) as to whether the operation shall take place and all concerned will be notified as early as possible.

(b) The following code will be used:-

Operation will take place to-night. ... ... JAPAN.
Operation postponed. ... ... SPAIN.
Cancel operation previously ordered ... ... RUSSIA.

10. Zero Hour will be at 12.30 a.m. or as soon after as the trucks are reported to be in position.

The order for discharge will be given by O.C., Special Coys., R.E., First Army from Corps Heavy Artillery Exchange, NEUVILLE ST. VAAST, A.3.d.4.8. (51.B.N.W.)

He will be in telephonic communication with the Discharge Points

Battalions in the line in the Left Section will keep Left Section Hqrs., informed of the progress of the operation. These reports will be forwarded to Divisional Hqrs.

Frequent reports will be sent in by Battalions after 11 p.m. until the Discharge takes place.

11. The Brigade Signalling Officer will arrange to send out Signal time to O.C. Battalions at 7 p.m. on July 5th (and daily thereafter if required)

12. The O.C., 2nd L.F.A., will arrange for an Officer with the necessary personnel and appliances for treating Gas cases to report to the O.C., A and B Parties at their respective Power Stations, and to accompany them until the completion of the operation, i.e. on returning to the Power Station again.

13. On the day fixed for the operation, the Light Railways will be closed to ammunition and supplies from 12 noon unless information is received that the operation is postponed. 2 days ammunition and supplies will therefore be taken up on 4th July. There will thus be 1 days supply in and for use on the day following the night of the operation. Only normal transport will be employed on the night of the operation in distributing supplies.

14. ACKNOWLEDGE.

Captain,
A/Brigade Major, 157th Infantry Brigade.

Issued at ....

Copies No. 1 to 5th H.L.I.   Copy No. 8 O.C., 2nd L.F.A.
        2   6th H.L.I.   9 Signalling Officer
        3   7th H.L.I.   10 Divnl. G.O.
        4   157th L.T.M. Bty.   11 Bde Gas Officer.
        5   R.E.   12 Staff Captain.
        6   155th Inf. Bde.   13)
        7   Hqrs. 60th Inf. Bde.   14) War Diary.
                                           15   File.

SECRET. Copy No. 2

157th Infantry Brigade Administrative Instructions No. 106.

3rd, July, 1918.

1. Reference 157th Brigade Order No. 110 dated 3rd. July.

   Two days rations will be ~~issued~~ sent up to the Brigade on the night of 4/5th July, in preparation for the Gas beam Attack on the night 5/6th July.

2. The extra days rations thus sent up will accordingly be consumed during the 24 hours following the Gas Attack.

3. Should the attack be postponed, however, rations will be sent up nightly from transport lines as usual, until the night of attack, and the extra days rations will be kept for the day following the attack.

4. Rations will be issued daily as usual and taken to the Transport lines so that in the event of any postponment, rations will be available to be sent up at short notice.

5. Battalions and Transport Officers, will be notified by Brigade each day if, owing to postponment rations are to be sent up as usual.
   The code word "RATIONS" will be used?

6. ACKNOWLEDGE.

H.M.Hewison
Captain,
Staff Captain, 157th Infantry Brigade.

Issued at 15.30 on 3/7/18

```
Copies No. 1 to  5th H. L. I.
         2       6th H. L. I.
         3       7th H. L. I.
         4       157th L. T. M. Bty.
         5       52nd M.G. Battn.
         6       2nd L. F. A.
         7       B.G.C.
         8  )
         9  )    War Diary.
        10       File.
```

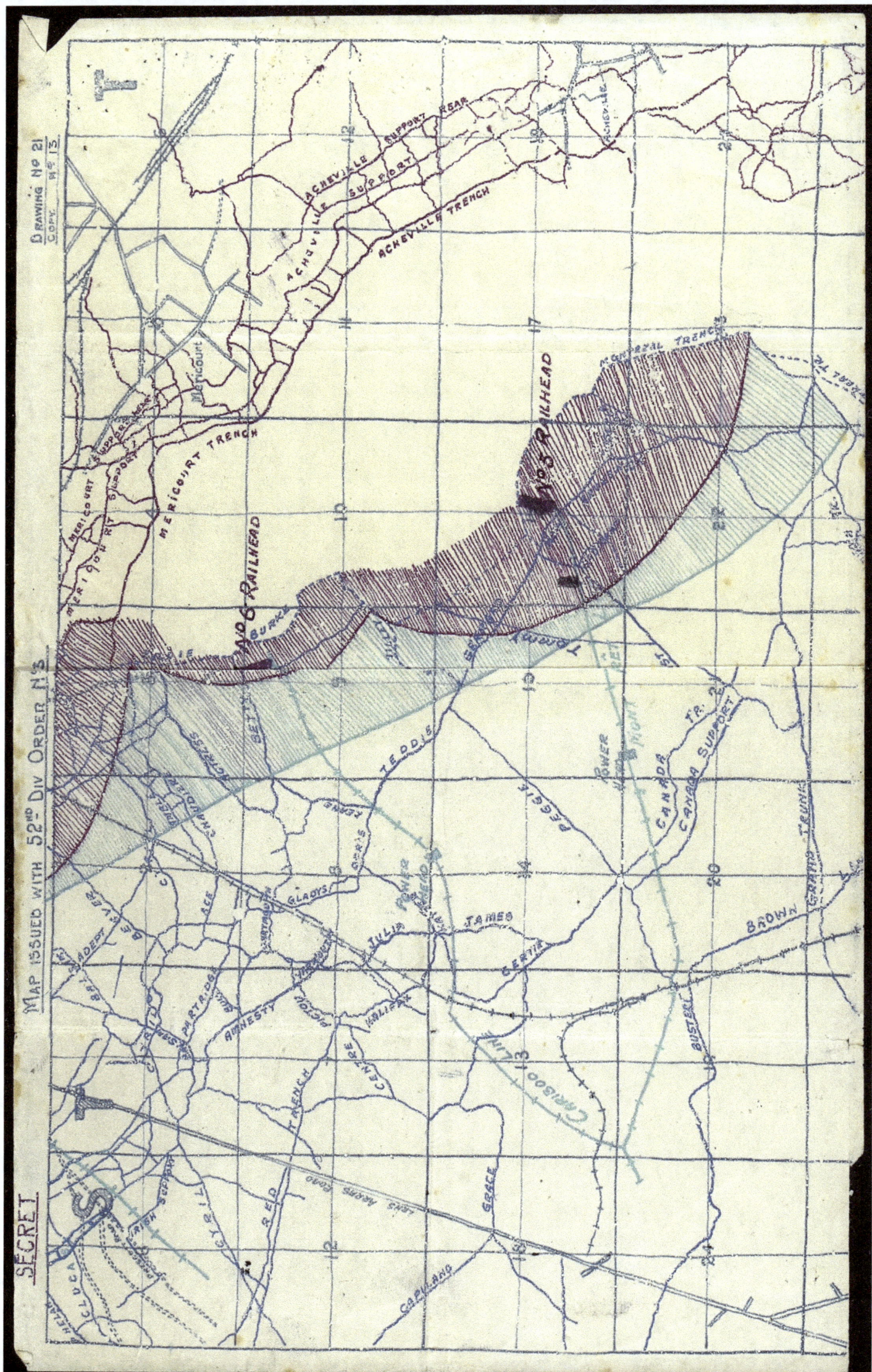

Mine Actions Rd & Tue
Light and heavy 1015
time required in yds total
1:30 - 4:30 and 5 first

NCO given when time
up been on sentry duty
during night both then
0830 - 12:30 Relieved not
Sunday P during
night relieved also for
2-4. NCO's men off duty
for duty. I am off also
to march during afterno
to him which shall furnish
guards in 5 P during

Succeeding night, work
1:30 - 3:30.
By day the sentries
and the corporal in
NCO's on duty the duty
all relieved between
the times relieved
every

SECRET.   BATTALION ORDER No. 14.   Copy No. 6
By
LIEUT-COL. J. ANDERSON, C.M.G. D.20. COMMDG. 1/6TH BN H.L.I.
3RD JULY, 1918.

REF. MAP. VIMY – 1/10,000.

1. **INFORMATION.**
   (a) There will be a Local Brigade Relief in the LEFT SUB
   SECTION on 5th July, 1918.
   The Relief will take place during daylight, and in
   view of special operations will commence immediately
   after Breakfast and must be completed by 1400.
   (b) 5th H.L.I. will relieve the 6th H.L.I.
   (c) "D" Coy, 5th H.L.I. will relieve "A" Coy. 6th H.L.I., who will take
   over dispositions of "D" Coy, 5th H.L.I.
   "C" Coy, 5th H.L.I. will relieve "B" Coy 6th H.L.I., who will take
   over dispositions of "C" Coy 5th H.L.I.
   "A" Coy, 5th H.L.I. will relieve "C" Coy 6th H.L.I. who will take
   over dispositions of "B" Coy. 5th H.L.I.
   "B" Coy 5th H.L.I. will relieve "D" Coy 6th H.L.I. who will take
   over dispositions of "A" Coy 5th H.L.I.
   Battalion Headquarters - PETIT VIMY.
   After relief Coys. will take over same dispositions
   as presently made by 5th H.L.I.

2. **ADVANCED PARTIES.**
   (a) 5th H.L.I. advanced parties of 1 Officer per Coy., 1 N.C.O. per
   platoon and 1 Lewis Gunner per platoon, and proportion
   of signallers and Scouts will arrive on afternoon of 4th
   inst.
   (b) 1 Officer per Coy. & 1 Section per Platoon, as nucleus garrison
   (including H.Q. Coy) will proceed on morning of 5th inst. to
   areas to be taken over from 5th H.L.I. arriving there by 0630.
   (c) All Area & Trench Stores etc., will be taken and handed
   over, receipts being given and taken for same.
   Duplicate receipts will be sent to reach Orderly
   Room not later than 1800 on 6th inst.

3. **RECONNAISSANCE.**
   O.C. Coys. will arrange for reconnaissance of line
   held by 5th H.L.I. to be made during 4th inst. by all Officers.

4. **GUIDES.**
   Guides for 5th H.L.I. will be supplied by Coys. to be
   at points as under by 0800 on 5th inst:-
   1 Officer per Coy., 1 N.C.O. per platoon;
   1 N.C.O. from H.Q. Coy.
   "C & D" Coys. where GLACE TRENCH crosses NANIAMO ROAD,
   (T.13.a.3.2.)
   "A & B" Coys. at junction of GERTIE & PEGGIE T[RENC]HES,
   (T.14.d.0.0.)
   Routes to be taken are as under:-
   "A" Coy. 2 Platoons GERTIE, JAMES.
   2 Platoons by PEGGIE to TEDDIE.
   "B" Coy. 2 Platoons by PEGGIE to TEDDIE.
   2 Platoons by PEGGIE, GERTIE, JAMES, & HAYTER.

B.O. No. 14. Sheet 2.

4. GUIDES. (CONT'D.)

"C" Coy. - GLACE, CENTRE, HALIFAX, JULIA & HAYTER.
"D" Coy. - GLACE, CENTRE, PICTOU, DARTMOUTH, BETTY to KEANE.

5. LEWIS GUNS.

240 L.G. Magazines (loaded) per Coy. and 60 per H.Qrs. Coy. will be handed over and receipts taken. A similar number taken over from 5th H.L.I., receipts being given for same.
All other L.G. equipment, ~~~~, will be retained.

6. S.O.S. POSTS.

O.C. Coys. will ensure that all orders re S.O.S. Posts, also Sentries &c., are carefully taken over, also a full statement of Work in hand.

7. DUTIES.

(a) Bde Headquarters O.P. will be manned by 1 N.C.O. & 3 Scouts plus additional personnel laid down in B.R.O. No. 74 d/ 3-7-18.

(b) Relay Posts. - Officer i/c Signallers will arrange for relay posts as under to be relieved by 0800 on 5th inst.
(i) 1 N.C.O. & 3 men at LA FOLIE COPSE (Old Bde. H.Qrs.)
    NOTE:- This post also takes over an Ammunition Dump.
(ii) 2 O.R. at 5th H.L.I. Bn. H.Qrs.

(c) Reserve Ration Guard. - O.C. "B" Coy. will detail guard of 1 N.C.O. & 3 men over above Dump at VIMY (S.24.d.1.2)

(d) Water Piquet:- 1 N.C.O. & 4 men. - GOODMAN & VIMY SUPPLY - (T.20.c.3.1.)
1 N.C.O. & 3 men - GIVENCHY SUPPLY - (S.12.b.9.6. & S.12.b.8.3.)
& VIMY SUPPLY - (S.18.c.9.3. & S.24.b.2.9.)
O.C. "A" & "C" Coys. will detail above piquet, to report at H.Q. 45th H.L.I. (S.24.u.2.0) by 0630 on 5th inst.

8. SUPPLIES.

Rations for consumption on 5th and 6th will be brought up to 5th H.L.I. Area on night of 4/5th inst.
These rations will be unloaded and taken to Coy. areas by Ration Parties of 5th H.L.I.
Each Coy. will detail a party consisting of C.Q.M.S. & 2 O.Rs. to report to relieving Coys. of 5th H.L.I. by 2000 on 4th inst. to take over rations arriving that night.
Similarly, rations for 5th H.L.I. will be sent up to VICTORIA DUMP on night of 4/5th and transported to Coy. Areas where they will be taken over by advanced parties of 5th H.L.I.
Rations arrive as under:-
"A" Coy. - By rail to NEW BRUNSWICK DUMP.
"B" " - By rail to BORDEN DUMP.
"D" " - By Limber to Coy. H.Q. on LENS-ARRAS ROAD.
"C" " - By Limber to West end of SUNKEN RD. passing Battalion H.Q.
Bn. H.Qrs. - By Limber to Bn. H.Qrs. (PETIT VIMY)

Water is drawn from Coy. Areas - Coys. will take over all details re water arrangements.

9. SALVAGE.

Salvage Dump is at CAYUGA DUMP. All Coy. salvage will be brought to this dump and receipts obtained for same.

B.O. No 14. Sheet 3.-

10. **SANITATION.** Usual clearance certificates will be given and taken.

11. **COMPLETION OF RELIEF.**
Completion of Relief and Arrival in new area will be wired or sent by Runner "priority" to Battn. H.Qrs using code words "SULTAN" and "AHMED" respectively.

12. **ACKNOWLEDGE.**

Donald M Macintyre
Lieut.
a/Adjt. 1/6th Bn H.L.I.

Issued at 0300 4-7-18.

Copy No 1 To OC "A" Coy
" 2 — " "B" "
" 3 — " "C" "
" 4 — " "D" "
" 5 — CO. "H.Qrs" " R.S.M. & File
" 6 — Q.M. & T.O.

S E C R E T.

O. C.,
    5th H. L. I.
    7th H. L. I.

    Reference Brigade Order No. 110 para 10. The following is a Code for use on the night in question. The G.O.C., wishes, in addition to any information which you may think it advisable to communicate, a message sent when each or any of the undernoted events take place.

O.C. Special Coys, R.E. First Army	ATK
Officer i/c No. 5 Railhead	BOO
" " 8	BOR
Special Coy Officer Arrived	SCOA
First Train arrived	ADA
Last Train arrived	TDA
Reay for Discharge	BON
Track broken	DUD
Trucks derailed	HAD
Wind favourable	MAT
Wind unfavourable	PSP
Wind right direction but too weak	TST
Discharge Complete	ABD
Trains clear of Discharge Point	MPS

NUMBERS.

    1 KA. 2 KB. 3 KC. 4 KD. 5 KF.
    6 KG. 7 KH. 8 KP. 9 KS. 0 KT.

    Datum Hour will be Mid-night.

    When Railheads have reported "ready for discharge" Zero hour will be indicated by means of code showing the number of minutes to be added on to Datum hour.

    e.g., KC., K.T.   12.30 a.m.
           KS., KT.,   1.30 a.m.

    Acknowledged BAT.

    Please acknowledge receipt.

                                        Captain,
            A/Brigade Major, 157th Infantry Brigade.

3rd. July, 1918.

Copy to O.C., 6th H. L. I. for information.

SECRET.   BATTALION ORDER No. 16.   COPY No. 6
          BY
    LIEUT- COL. T. ANDERSON, C.M.G. D.S.O. COMMDG 1/6TH BN H.L.I.

REF. MAPS. VIMY AND ROUVROY - 1/10,000.   10TH JULY 1918.

1. INFORMATION.
(a) 6TH H.L.I. will relieve 7TH H.L.I. in RIGHT SUB SECTION on 11TH inst. Relief to be completed by 1400.
(b) "A" Coy. 6TH H.L.I. will relieve "A" Coy 7TH H.L.I. who will take over present dispositions of "A" Coy 6TH H.L.I.
"B" Coy. 6TH H.L.I. will relieve "C" Coy 7TH H.L.I. who will take over present dispositions of "B" Coy. 6TH H.L.I.
"D" Coy 6TH H.L.I. will relieve "B" Coy 7TH H.L.I. who will take over present dispositions of "D" Coy 6TH H.L.I.
"C" Coy. 6TH H.L.I. will relieve "D" Coy 7TH H.L.I. who will take over present dispositions of "C" Coy 6TH H.L.I.

2. DISPOSITIONS OF COYS.
"A" Coy — 2 Platoons — NEW BRUNSWICK from ACHEVILLE RD (exclusive) to point 150 yds NORTH of TEASER.
2 Platoons in CANADA from NEW BRUNSWICK RD. (exclusive) to T.21.a.2.5.
Coy H.Q.s — CANADA TR.

"B" Coy — 2 Platoons — NEW BRUNSWICK from LEFT OF "A" Coy to junction with TOAST (exclusive).
2 Platoons in CANADA & KURTON from LEFT of "A" Coy to MERICOURT RD (inclusive).
Coy H.Q.s — CANADA TR. (Old Dressing Station)

"D" Coy — 2 Platoons in GERRARD from junction with TOAST (inclusive) to TOMMY (inclusive).
2 Platoons in CANADA from MERICOURT RD (exclusive) to PEGGIE TR (inclusive).
Coy H.Q.s — at junction of CANADA - GERTIE.

"C" Coy — 2 Platoons in TEDDIE GERARD from TOMMY (inclusive) to VESTA TILLEY (exclusive).
2 Platoons — CANADA from junction with PEGGIE (exclusive) to junction of JAMES & GERTIE.
Coy. H.Q.s — junction of CANADA - GERTIE.

In addition to above dispositions Coys will take over all details re S.O.S. & Observation Posts on Outpost Line.

BN H.Q.s — T.25.b.4.9.
R.A.P. — KURTON TR.

3. ADVANCED PARTIES
(a) Advanced Parties proceeded as per separate instructions today 10TH inst.
(b) All trench & area stores, Maps, Log Books etc will be taken & handed over, receipts being given & taken for same. Duplicate receipts will be sent to reach Orderly Room not later than 1800 on 12TH inst.

4. GUIDES.
(a) Guides will be supplied by 1TH H.L.I. of 1 N.C.O. per platoon to be at points as under at 0800 on 11TH inst. (H.Q. x 1 - 1 N.C.O.)

4. GUIDES (CONT'D)
   "A" Coy — Junction of GRAND TRUNK & TOAST TR.
   "B" " — Junction of CANADA & PEGGIE.
   "C" " —   do.   do.
   "D" " — Junction of FAMES & GERTIE.
   "HQ's" Coy — VIMY. T.19.c.1.5.

   (b) Each Coy 6th H.L.I (less HQ's) will have 1 guide per Coy at above points at 0600 on 11th to guide nucleus garrisons 7th H.L.I to reserve area.

   (c) Each Coy will leave guides of 1 N.C.O. per Platoon (HQs Coy - 1 N.C.O) as they pass above points to guide Coys. of 7th H.L.I to reserve areas.

   (d) Routes to be followed are as under:—
   "A" Coy — GRAND TRUNK & TOAST.
   "B" " — BROWN LINE — PEGGIE.
   "C" " — BROWN LINE — PEGGIE.
   "D" " — BROWN LINE — GLACE, HAYTER TUNNEL & GERTIE

   (e) Coys will move off from reserve area starting at 0730. — Movement will be by Platoons at 100 yds. interval — 50 yds lateral between sections.

5. LEWIS GUNS.
   240 L.G. Magazines (loaded) per Coy and 60 per HQs Coy will be handed over & receipts taken. A similar number taken over from 7th H.L.I receipts being given for same.
   All other L.G. equipment will be retained.
   The greatest care will be taken that these are handed over in a thoroughly clean & serviceable condition.

6. S.O.S. POSTS.
   OC Coys will ensure that all orders re S.O.S. Posts, Gas sentries etc. are carefully taken over also a full statement of work in hand.

7. RESERVE RATIONS.
   OC "A" Coy will take over Reserve Rations situated as under:—

	Biscuits	Preserved meat
T.21.a.5.3	600 lbs.	576 tins.

8. SALVAGE.
   All salvage will be taken to CANADA Dump by Coys & receipts obtained for same.
   H.Q.S. to NEW BRUNSWICK.

9. SUPPLIES.
   Rations are brought up by rail nightly to CANADA DUMP. Each Coy will send ration parties of 1 N.C.O & 10 men to reach there at 2130.
   H.Qs — NEW BRUNSWICK DUMP by rail.
   OC HQs Coy will detail ration party to meet this train at 2130.

   Water Supply is as under:—
T.15.b.7.6.	3	400 gall TANKS.
T.16.a.6.8.	3	do do
T.16.c.9.2.	1	do do
T.16.d.2.7.	3	do do
T.16.b.9.1.	3	do do

10. **STAND-TO-ARMS**

    0300 - All Clear. (morning)
    2100 - 2130 - (evening)

    O.C. Coys. will ensure that 5 rds. per day are fired by each N.C.O. & Man in Coy.

11. **REPORTS ETC.**

    Reports will be rendered as in LEFT SUB-SECTION

    R.E. Indents as follows for following day must reach Orderly Room 0830.

    Weekly & Daily Work Reports will be rendered to reach Orderly Room by 1700 on 17th and 0830 daily respectively.

12. **SANITATION**

    O.C. Coys. will ensure that areas are left scrupulously clean & sanitary.

    Usual clearance certificates will be taken & given.

13. **WORK**

    Work in hand will be taken over & continued at earliest opportunity.

14. **COMPLETION OF RELIEF**

    Completion of Relief will be wired or sent by runner "PRIORITY" using code word "MAFEESH" followed by name of Company Commander.

15. **ACKNOWLEDGE.**

David MacIntyre
Lieut.
A/Adjt 1/6th Bn. H.L.I.

Issued at 1900. 10.7.18.

Copy to 1. To O.C. 'A' Coy.
          2. " " 'B' "
          3. " " 'C' "
          4. " " 'D' "
          5. - C.O. H.Qs. R.S.M. & FILE.
          6. - Q.M. & T.O.

ORDERS FOR SCOUTS

The following scouts will man O.P. in the Right Sector.

Pte ANDREWS	No 2 PLATOON
" HAMILTON	" 5 "
" SHORE	" 11 "
" BEATTIE	" 12 "
" SCOTT	" 13 "
" DYKES	H.Qrs

L/CPL McPHERSON, Pte ANDREWS and Pte SHORE will parade at 1400 on the 10th inst at Bn H.Qrs & proceed to new line with advance party, 24 hours rations to be carried.

Remainder will report to I.O. in QUARRY off N. BRUNSWICK TR on arriving in area.

Scouts will ~~spend night~~ live with their platoons reporting each night to their platoon sergeants & are always available for Company or Battalion patrols.

BDE. O.P

This O.P. will be handed over to 5th H.L.I. by L/Cpl SCOTT & receipts obtained for stores & a certificate certifying that billets & O.P. are clean. Scouts manning O.P. will rejoin their Coys in new area.

INTELLIGENCE

Each platoon scout is responsible for reporting enemy shelling in his platoon area, any flashes & enemy flares seen at night by sentries. Reporting of night shelling is important, giving when possible, bearing of sound on flash, a scout not on duty will collect reports from platoon scouts & compile Coy intelligence report. Support line will render separate reports from firing line in order to save time & unnecessary walking.

A H.Q scout will collect these reports immediately after stand down.

MAP.

A map of NO MANS LAND & enemy line giving information of enemy's posts will be issued to each Coy. These should be given to scouts & kept up to date by them. In order that this can be done a HQrs scout will go round Coys daily with a map giving latest intelligence. This intelligence should be passed on to men of platoons.

H.Q.,
157TH INFANTRY
BRIGADE.
No. BM 726
Date 9-7-18

SECRET.

O.C. 6th Bn. H.L.I.
&th Bn. H.L.I.

Warning order

1. The 5th H.L.I. will relieve the 7th H.L.I. in the RIGHT sub-section on the 11th July, 1918. Relief to be completed by 2 p.m.

2. Ref. Bde. Order No.110, of 3rd. inst.
O.C. 7th H.L.I. will get in touch with O.C. 6th H.L.I. at once in order to have all arrangements with reference to the "Gas Beam Attack" complete as early as possible after the relief.
O.C. 6th H.L.I. will hand over all orders and instructions regarding this same to O.C.7th H.L.I.

Acknowledge.

S. Mickey-Cooper
Captain,
Brigade Major, 157th Infantry Brigade.

9th July, 1918.

Copy to 5th H.L.I. for information.

SECRET.   Copy No. 2

                          Brigade Order No.111.   10/7/18.

1.   The 6th H.L.I. will relieve the 7th H.L.I. in the RIGHT Sub-
     sector on 11th July, 1918.   On relief, the 7th H.L.I. will
     take over the same dispositions as those at present held by the
     6th H.L.I.

2.   In view of the "Gas Beam Attack" which is ordered to take place,
     the Relief will commence immediately after breakfast and be
     completed by 2 p.m.

3.   All orders and instructions with reference to the "GAS BEAM
     ATTACK" will be handed over to O.C. 7th H.L.I. who will be prepared
     to furnish the "pushing parties" from the 11th July.

4.   Details of Relief will be arranged between the C.O.s concerned.

5.   Trench stores, log books, special maps and plans will be handed
     over.

6.   Completion of Relief will be wired to Brigade H.Q. by the code
     word "PLANET".

7.   ACKNOWLEDGE.

                                                    Captain,
                                                    Brigade Major.

Issued at 10 a.m.

Copy No. 1 to 5th H.L.I.   Copy No. 8 to Left Group M.G. Bn.
        2   6th H.L.I.   9   156th Inf. Bde.
        3   7th H.L.I.   10   60th Brigade.
        4   157th L.T.M.B.   11)
        5   2nd L.F.A.   12) War Diary.
        6   Divn. H.Q.   13   File.
        7   Left Group Arty.

Copy No. 2.

1/6th Bn H.L.I. Defence Scheme.

Toast Area.

- Index -

Para	1.	Organisation of Brigade Sector	Para. 7.	Trench Mortars.
"	2.	Boundaries.	" 8.	Machine Guns.
"	3.	Description of the Area	" 9.	Anti-Tank Guns
"	4.	Probable Line of Enemy Approach	" 10.	Anti-Aircraft Defence.
"	5.	Organisation of Area for Defence	" 11.	S.O.S.
"	6.	Artillery	" 12.	Communications.

Para 13. Administrative Arrangements.

Appendices.

Appendix I. List of Co-ordinates.
" II. Company Boundaries.
" III. Communications.

Maps & Diagrams:-

Map. A Disposition of Troops — Map. C. Lewis & Machine Guns
" B Artillery & T.M. — Diagram D. Communications.

1/6TH Bn H.L.I.   Copy No 2

SECRET.   — DEFENCE SCHEME —
                   — TOAST AREA. —
                — First Zone of Defence —

REF. MAPS:— LA TARGETTE & MAROEUIL, 1/20,000.

1. ORGANISATION OF BRIGADE SECTOR.

    The 157th Infantry Brigade holds the LEFT SECTION of the 52nd DIVISIONAL SECTOR.   This sector is divided into three Areas:— TOAST, BETTY, and VIMY-CHAUDIÈRE, each of which is held by one Battalion.   TOAST and BETTY Areas comprise the first Zone of Defence, and the VIMY-CHAUDIÈRE Area the second.
    The First Zone of Defence is composed of:—
 (a) An Observation and S.O.S. Line, very lightly held:— MONTREAL, QUEBEC, LILY ELSIE, VESTA TILLEY, TOLEDO, and BETTY TRENCHES.
 (b) The Outpost (BLUE) LINE, held by half the strength of the Battalions:— NEW BRUNSWICK, TEDDIE GERARD, KEANE and ACTRESS TRENCHES.
 (c) The BLACK LINE, main line of resistance, held by half the strength of the Battalions:— CANADA, GERTIE, JAMES, HAYTER, GLADYS and PARTMOUTH TRENCHES.

2. BOUNDARIES

    The TOAST Area is bounded:—
    On the South.— By the ACHEVILLE and NEW BRUNSWICK ROADS (both exclusive) to T.21.c.7.6.
    On the West.— By a line joining T.21.c.7.6 — T.20.a.8.6 — Junction of the EMBANKMENT and PEGGY TRENCH (inclusive) — T.13.d.3.3.
    On the North.—
                    By a line joining T.13.d.3.3. — EMBANKMENT JUNCTION (exclusive) — Junction of JAMES and GERTIE TRENCHES, T.14.c.05.70. — T.15.a.00 — Junction of VESTA TILLEY and TEDDIE GERRARD (inclusive) and thence along VESTA TILLEY (exclusive)   (see Map A.)
                    Patrols operate between the SOUTHERN BOUNDARY and the HULL ROAD (inclusive).

3. DESCRIPTION OF THE AREA

    The most noticeable feature in the area is the NOVA SCOTIA SPUR running E. from VIMY through T.20., and then swinging N. through T.15.
    It is most important that this spur should be held as it affords splendid observation over the trench systems both north & south, and its occupation by the enemy would render these difficult and costly to retain.   The NEW BRUNSWICK RD. on the extreme RIGHT flank follows a reentrant, and affords an approach to CANADA TRENCH which is only under aerial observation.
    Important features in No Man's Land are:—
 (a) Our old trench systems and wire EAST of the present observation line.
 (b) The Light Railway Track running through T.19.a. and b.
 (c) The various roads crossing No Man's Land.
    (b) & (c) afford valuable guiding marks to patrols and raiding parties, and it has been observed that the enemy use them for this purpose.

4. PROBABLE LINE OF ENEMY APPROACH.
 (a) It is improbable that the enemy will make a direct frontal attack on VIMY RIDGE, but should he obtain an initial success either to the NORTH or SOUTH of the Ridge, he would probably try to confirm his success by pushing in against this front.
 (b) As far as the TOAST AREA is concerned, a possible line of advance exists in the low ground about NEW BRUNSWICK ROAD.   The object of this would be to circumvent the strong points on the high ground, and to cut them off from the rear.

5. ORGANISATION OF THE AREA FOR DEFENCE
    The main defensive line is the BLACK LINE system of trenches, the first Battle line.   In front of this is the OUTPOST LINE, which is held by half the strength of the Battalion, less 8 sections pushed

5. ORGANISATION OF THE AREA FOR DEFENCE (CONTD.)

pushed forward into the Observation and S.O.S. Line. In case of attack these sections withdraw to the OUTPOST LINE as soon as they have fired the S.O.S. The duty of the garrison of the OUTPOST LINE is to hold out at all costs, but to conform to movement on flanks, it may be ordered by higher command to fall back and to join the garrison of BLACK LINE. The BLACK LINE must be defended to the last, and the garrison can expect no reinforcements from the rear, save only if the line is penetrated by a large raid or minor attack.

In this situation the G.O.C. Bde. may order one company and one platoon from the garrison of the VIMY-CHAUDIÈRE Area to counter-attack in the First Zone of Defense.

Companies are organised in depth for the defence. (See Map A and APPENDIX II.)

Battalion Headquarters are at T.25.b.5.9.
Approximate Length of Front 2000 yards - Approximate No. of Rifles - 500.
(Yds per rifle - 4 yds.)
No of Vickers and Lewis Guns - 38.
(Yds. per V.M.G. & L.G. 53 yds.)

6. ARTILLERY.

On the S.O.S. being fired, the Artillery put down the "OUTPOST BARRAGE", which is strengthened by the addition of M.G. Barrage. Should the OUTPOST LINE be evacuated and S.O.S. BLACK be called for, the OUTPOST BARRAGE is withdrawn and a barrage put down in front of the BLACK LINE. This Barrage is further strengthened by the addition of Newton and Stokes Trench Mortars. (See Map B.)

COMMUNICATION (a) By Artillery Liaison Officer who lives at Battalion HQrs, who has direct telephone communication to Artillery Brigade (D.mkIII)
(b) Through Infantry Brigade.

7. TRENCH MORTARS.

Six guns of Y Battery 6" Newton T.Ms. are available for defence and 3 guns of 157th L.T.M.B. (For positions etc. see Map B.)
Communication with N.T.M. through Infantry Brigade. With L.T.M.B. through LEFT FRONT LINE BATTALION.

8. MACHINE GUNS.

Machine Gun Coy. Headquarters are situated at T.26.a.7.3.
For positions of guns etc. (See Map. C)
Communication is by runner only.

9. ANTI-TANK GUNS.

Anti-Tank Guns for the defence of the TOAST AREA are situated as follows:-
Communication is through Infantry Brigade and Artillery Brigade.

10. ANTI AIRCRAFT DEFENCE

A.A. Lewis Gun Posts are established at:-

T.16.d.6.1	found by.	RIGHT COY
T.16.c.9.2	do:	RIGHT CENTRE COY
T.20.a.8.9	do:	LEFT CENTRE COY.
T.15.b.6.5	do:	LEFT COY.
T.25.b.5.9	do:	HEADQUARTERS COY.

(See Map. C.)

11. S.O.S.

The S.O.S. Signal is a No.32 RIFLE GRENADE, GREEN over GREEN over GREEN. The Posts in the Observation line are S.O.S. Posts.
S.O.S Grenade Relay Posts are established as follows:-

11. S.O.S. (CONTD)
   follows:-

   T.16.d.55.20.   T.16.a.1.2. ⎫
   T.16.d.1.5.   T.15.b.8.4. ⎬ --- OUTPOST LINE.
   T.16.c.5.9.   T.15.b.5.6. ⎪
   T.16.a.4.0.   T.15.b.1.7. ⎭
   T.21.a.6.1.   T.20.b.0.9. ⎫
   T.20.b.50.45.   T.14.c.8.1. ⎬ --- BLACK LINE.
   T.20.b.2.8.

12. COMMUNICATION.
   See Appendix III and "Diagram D."

13. ADMINISTRATIVE ARRANGEMENTS.
   (a) S.A.A.   Ammunition and Bombs are drawn from the Brigade.
        Dumps:- CULVERT DUMP, T.20.c.2.1.; PEGGY DUMP, T.19.b.7.8.
   (b) SUPPLIES. Rations and other supplies are brought up nightly
        by Light Railway as follows:-
            BATTN. H.Qs   to   CULVERT DUMP   T.20.c.2.1.
            COMPANIES   to   CANADA DUMP   T.20.b.3.5.
        There is a Reserve Ration Dump at T.21.a.5.3. containing
        600 lbs. biscuits, 576 tins preserved meat.
   (c) WATER.   Water is drawn from Tanks on the pipe line situated as
        follows:-
            3 - 400 gallon Tanks -------- T.15.b.7.6.
            3 --- do. --- do. ----------- T.16.c.6.8.
            1 --- do. --- do. ----------- T.16.c.9.2.
            3 --- do. --- do. ----------- T.16.d.2.7.
            3 --- do. --- do. ----------- T.16.b.9.1.
   (d) TRANSPORT. The Battalion Transport Lines and Base Orderly Room
        are at DALY CAMP, F.11.b.5.2.
   (e) SALVAGE.   Company Salvage is taken to CANADA DUMP, Battalion
        Headquarters to CULVERT DUMP where receipts are taken for
        salvage handed in.
   (f) MEDICAL.
        The R.A.P. is situated at T.20.b.1.5. in KURTON TRENCH.
        The Ad.D.S. is at T.25.a.9.4. whence casualties are evacuated
        to the M.D.S. at A.8.c.5.5. by motor.
   (g) ANTI-GAS MEASURES.
        All occupied dugouts are provided with at least two
        gas proof curtains. The following stores are in the area:-

Coy etc.	Strombos Horns	Strombos Cylinders	Location	Battalion & Company HQrs.						Area			
				Chloride of Lime lbs.	Hypo lb.	Soda lbs.	Vermorel Sprayers	Vacuum Bulbs	Gopher Suits	Gas Fans		Ayrton Fans	Perm. Tins
H.Q.	1	2	T.25.b.5.9	180	-	-	1	-	-	4	7	5	2
A.	1	2	T.16.d.5.2.	150	-	-	-	-	8	8	3	10	-
B.	2	{2 / 3}	T.16.d.1.5. / T.21.a.6.1.	180	7	7	1	1	4	4	8	13	-
C.	1	2	T.15.b.5.6.	60	-	-	1	-	8	8	8	10	-
D.	2	{2 / 3}	T.15.b.8.4. / T.14.c.8.1.	45	-	-	1	-	6	6	8	14	4

   (h) R.E.
        413th Field Company R.E. advanced H.Q. are in HUMBER TRENCH.
        An Officer of this unit visits the Battalion area daily.

   Copy No. 1 To C.O.
           2   - WAR DIARY
           3   - FILE

                                              David Macintyre
                                              a/adjt 1/6 H.L.I.

Appendix T

List of Co-ordinates

157th Infantry Brigade HQs	S.27.b.0.5.
Battalion Headquarters	T.25.b.5.9.
Company Headquarters	
"A" Coy (R)	T.21.a.6.1.
"B" " (R.C.)	T.16.c.9.3.
"C" " (L) ⎫ Together	T.14.c.8.1.
"D" " (L.C) ⎭	
Transport Lines	F.11.b.5.2.
R.A.P.	T.20.b.1.5.
1/5th H.L.I.	T.13.b.5.3.
1/7th H.L.I.	S.24.a.2.0.
M.G. Coy. HQs	T.26.a.7.3.
157th L.T.M.B.	T.13.b.5.1.
R.F.A. Bde	S.27.b.0.5.

APPENDIX II.

COMPANY BOUNDARIES.

RIGHT COMPANY
2 Platoons NEW BRUNSWICK from ACHEVILLE Rd. (exclusive) to T.16.d.3.3.
2 Platoons and Coy. H.Qs. CANADA from NEW BRUNSWICK ROAD (exclusive) to T.21.a.2.5.

RIGHT CENTRE Coy.
2 Platoons, NEW BRUNSWICK from T.16.d.3.3. to junction of TOAST (exclusive)
2 Platoons, CANADA & KURTON from T.21.a.2.5. to MERICOURT ROAD (inclusive)
Coy. H.Qs. – T.16.c.9.3.

LEFT CENTRE Coy.
2 Platoons – TEDDIE GERARD from junction with TOAST (inclusive) to junction with TOMMY (exclusive)
2 Platoons in CANADA from MERICOURT ROAD (exclusive) to PEGGY TRENCH (inclusive)
Coy. H.Qs. in GERTIE TRENCH – T.14.c.8.1.

LEFT COMPANY.
2 Platoons in TEDDIE GERARD from TOMMY (inclusive) to VESTA TILLEY (exclusive)
2 Platoons in GERTIE from junction with PEGGY (exclusive) to junction of JAMES and GERTIE (exclusive)
Coy. H.Qs. in GERTIE. – T.14.c.8.1.

APPENDIX III.

Communications

From	To	Service
BATTALION H.Q	(a) BRIGADE H.Qs	(1) Fullerphone
		(2) Magneto
		(3) Visual (Lucas Lamp)
		(4) Runner
		(5) Cyclist
		(6) Rocket (very unreliable)
		(7) Power Buzzer
do	(b) BRIGADE R.F.A.	(1) Through Bde H.Qs
		(2) Liaison Officer has a direct D.III Line
do	(c) M.G. Coy. H.Q	Runner
do	(d) L.T.M.B. HdQrs	Through Left Battn H.Qs
do	(e) Left Bn - Left Bde Sector	(1) Fullerphone
		(2) Runner
		(3) Cyclist
		(4) Power Buzzer
do	(f) Reserve Bn. — do —	(1) Fullerphone
		(2) Runner
		(3) Cyclist
		(4) Power Buzzer
do	(g) Left Bn. Right Bde Sector	(1) Fullerphone
		(2) Power Buzzer
do	(h) "A" Coy. H.Qs	(1) Fullerphone
		(2) Runner (Relay System)
do	(i) "B" Coy. H.Qs	(1) Fullerphone
		(2) Runner (Relay System)
do	(j) "C" & "D" Coys H.Qs	(1) Runner
		(2) D.III 'phone (emergency only)
"A" Coy H.Qs	"B" Coy H.Qs	(1) Fullerphone
		(2) Runner (Relay System)
do	"C" & "D" Coys H.Qs	(1) Runner
		(2) D.III 'phone (emergency only)
"B" Coy. H.Qs	do	(1) Runner
		(2) D.III 'phone (emergency only)

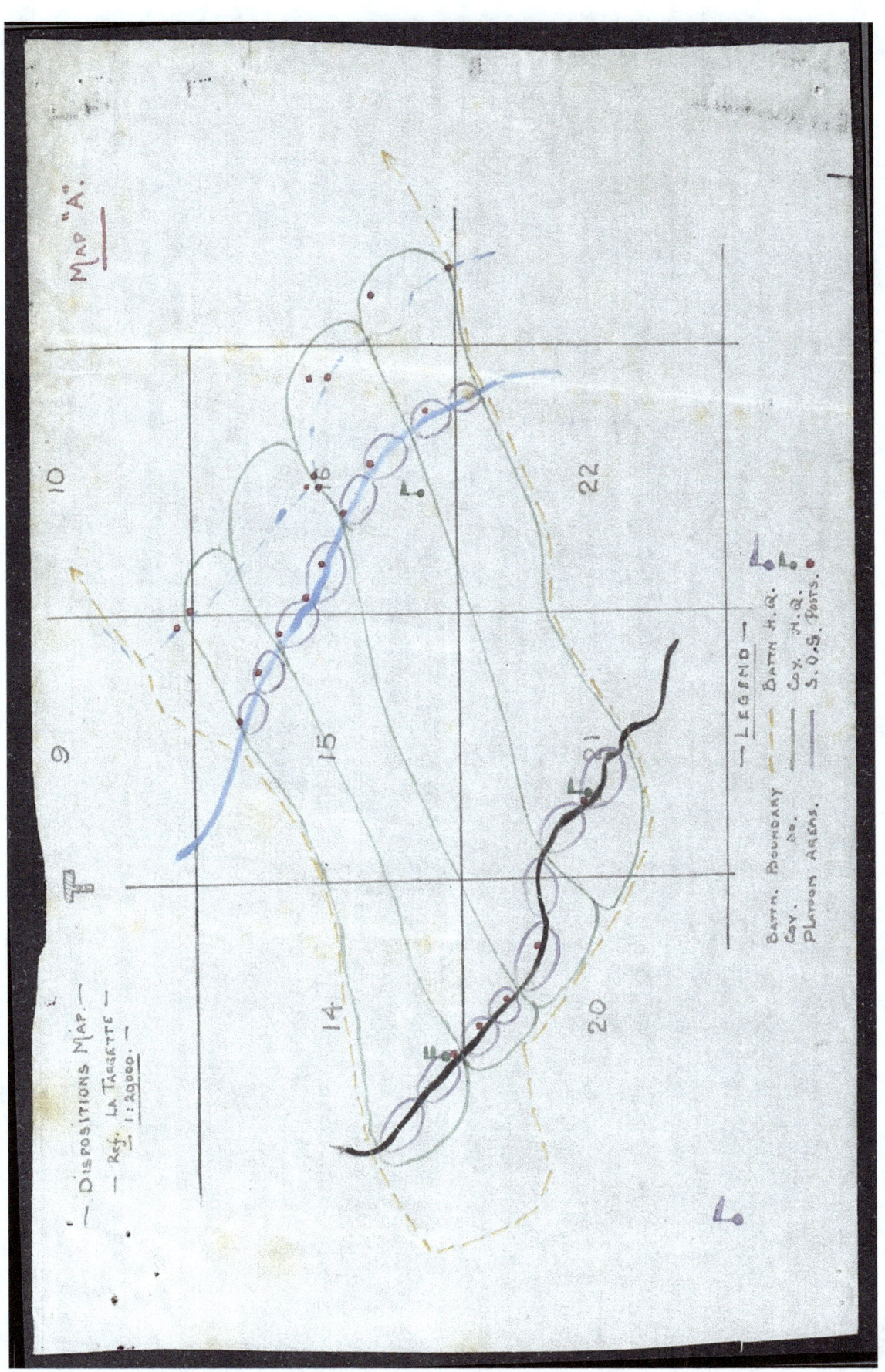

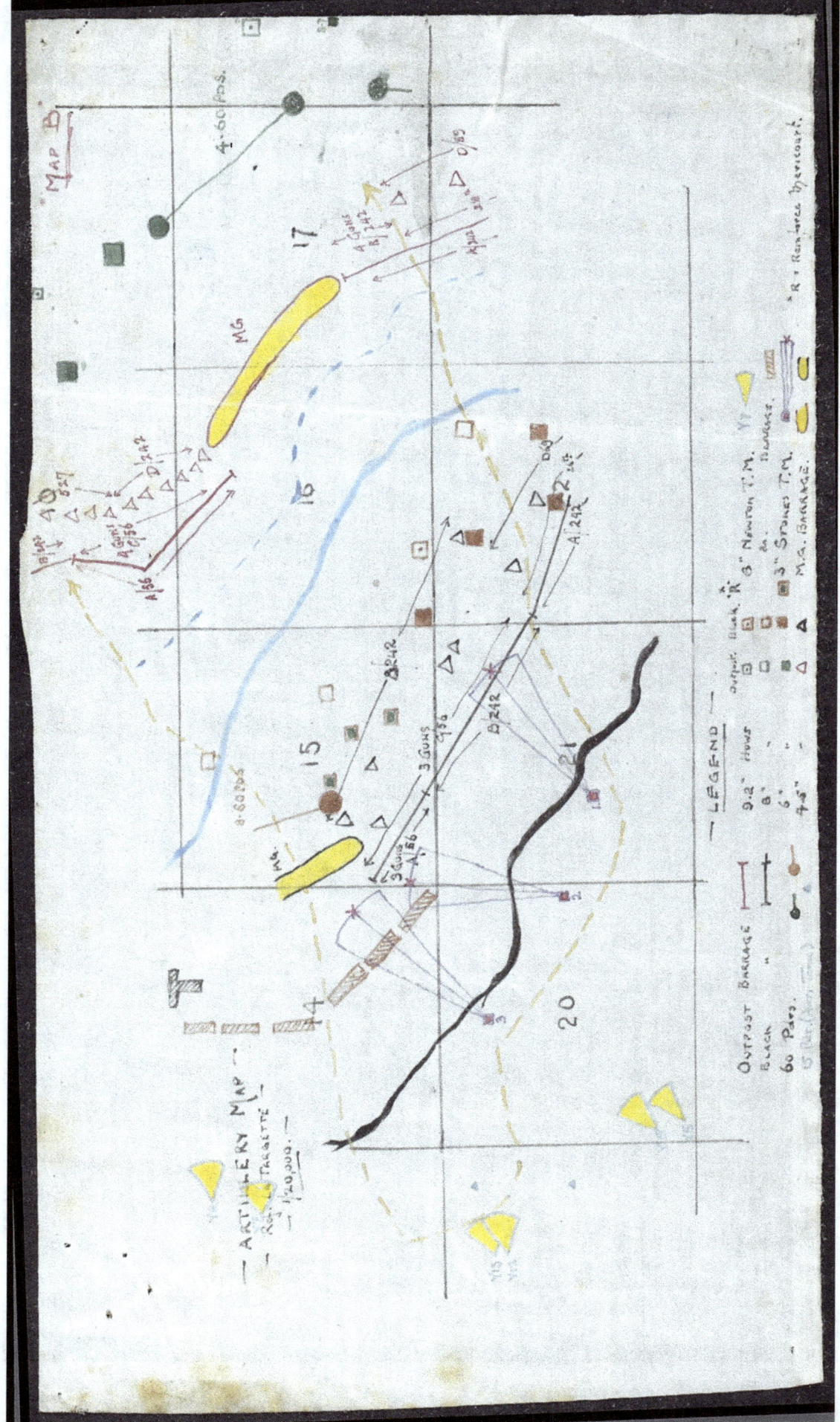

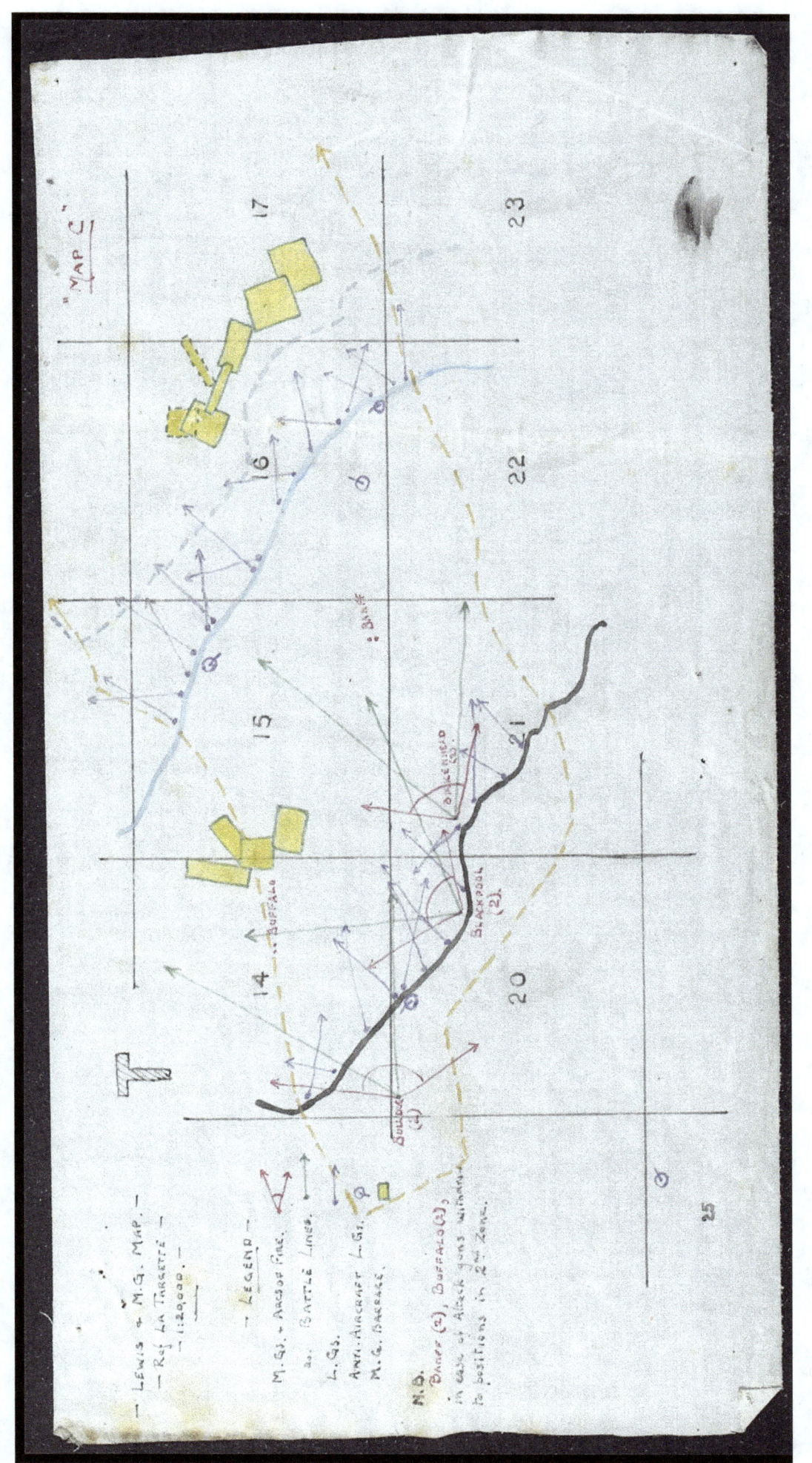

SECRET. COPY No. 5

BATTALION ORDER No 18.
By
Lieut-Col. J. Anderson, C.M.G. D.S.O. Commdg 1/6th Bn H.L.I.

14th July, 1918.

1. INFORMATION
(a) 1/6th H.L.I. will be relieved in the TOAST AREA of the Brigade Section on the 15th July: relief to be completed by 0600 on 16th.

(b) "A" Coy. 6th H.L.I. will be relieved by "A" Coy. 4th Royal Scots.
"B" — do: — do: — do: — "C" " — do: — do: —
"D" — do: — do: — do: — "B" " — do: — do: —
"C" — do: — do: — do: — "D" " — do: — do: —

On relief, Coys will move independently by Coys to HANSON CAMP, NEUVILLE ST. VAAST where they will be met by 1 Guide per Coy.

(c) Alarm — In the event of an alarm or enemy attack during the relief, troops will halt and man the nearest trenches reporting their dispositions at once to Battalion or Brigade Headquarters.

2. MOVEMENT.
(a) If relief is completed by daylight, movement will be by sections as far as HUMBER TRENCH & LA FOLIE TRACK at which point each platoon will close.

(b) If relief is not completed till dark, Companies will move by Platoons at 100 yards interval.
Strict march Discipline will be maintained, all sections & platoons will be well closed up.

3. ROUTES
"C & D" Coys:— GERTIE - HAYTER TUNNEL - LA CHAUDIÈRE, LENS ARRAS ROAD, HUMBER TRENCH, LA FOLIE ROAD.

"A & B" Coys:—
(a) If relief is completed by daylight - PEGGIE, RED TRAIL - LENS ARRAS ROAD - HUMBER TRENCH - LA FOLIE ROAD.

(b) If relief is not completed till after dark and night is quiet, NEW BRUNSWICK RD. - VIMY. - LENS ARRAS ROAD - HUMBER TRENCH. LA FOLIE ROAD.

All Officers who are not acquainted with above routes for respective Coys will make a careful reconnaissance of same on 15th inst.

4. GUIDES
Guides of 1 N.C.O. per Platoon will be at junction of TOAST and CANADA TRENCHES, times stated as under:—

"C" Coy. .... 1600.
"D" " .... 1630.
"A & B" " .... 1730.

NOTE:— It is pointed out that Coy. 4th Royal Scots may not arrive at times stated above as they have to be relieved by another Battn. before leaving their present area but guides will be in position at times as stated and await arrival of relieving companies.

5. TRENCH STORES.
Trench Stores will be handed over as per instructions already issued and receipts obtained. Duplicate receipts will be rendered to Orderly Room by 1200 on 16th inst.
All details of S.O.S. Posts, Gas Sentries, Observation Posts; work in hand and work projected will be carefully handed over.

6. LEWIS GUNS.
There will be no exchange of Lewis Gun Magazines or Equipment etc.

(P.T.O.)

6. LEWIS GUNS (CONTD.)

(a) "C & D" Coys. will manhandle all guns & equipment to junction of WHITE TRAIL AND LENS ARRAS RD, where 1 Limber per Coy. will arrive as soon as possible after dark.

(b) "A & B" Coys. will manhandle all guns & equipment to point where NEW BRUNSWICK ROAD crosses TOAST TRENCH, where 1 Limber per Coy. will arrive as soon as possible after dark.

(c) If any Coy. is relieved before dark, above equipment & Baggage will be left in Trenches as near above points as possible under charge of L.G N.C.O & 4 Lewis Gunners (1 per section)

7. SALVAGE.

Each N.C.O. of rank of Cpl. & under & each man will bring with him on coming out of the line some salved article — Picks, Shovels, (surplus to reasonable trench requirements) Petrol Tins (unserviceable) Equipment, Barbed wire, Spools etc will be taken.

Lewis Gunners carrying Guns or Ammunition & any N.C.Os or men carrying regimental equipment (such as degchies, signal equipment etc) will not be given any salved article.

"C & D" Coys will hand salved articles to N.C.O i/c VICTORIA DUMP receipts being obtained.

"A & B" Coys will collect salved articles at point where NEW BRUNS-WICK ROAD crosses TOAST TRENCH from which point it will be taken by Limber to Divisional Salvage Dump. O.C. "A" Coy will have 1 N.C.O i/c who will be responsible for making an inventory of "A & B" Coys salvage & obtaining receipts from Divisional Salvage Dump.

OC Coys will issue such orders as will ensure that no crowding is allowed to take place when salvage is being handed in.

8. SANITATION.

All Trenches, Shelters, deep dugouts Cookhouses, latrines & grease traps will be thoroughly cleaned and dumps closed.

OC Coys will make a careful inspection of these before handing over.

The usual clearance certificates will be taken before area is evacuated, and forwarded to Orderly Room by 1200 on 16th inst.

9. SUPPLIES.

(a) Supplies will be drawn at LEADLEY SIDING as at present.

(b) Water is laid on in the Camp.

The strictest supervision must be exercised to prevent wastage.

10. COMPLETION OF RELIEF.

Completion of relief and arrival in new area will be wired or sent by runner "priority" to Battalion H.Q. using Code words "ANNIE" and "LAURIE" respectively.

11. ACKNOWLEDGE.

Issued at 2300   14-7-18.

Copy No. 1 To O.C. A Coy
"   "   2 - "   B "
"   "   3 - "   C "
"   "   4 - "   D "
"   "   5 - C.O. HQ. Coy. R.S.M. & FILE.
"   "   6 - QM & T.O.

a/adjt 1/6 H.L.I.

ALARM ORDERS
BY
Lieut-Col. J. Anderson, C.M.G. D.S.O., Commdg. 1/6th Bn. H.L.I.

18th JULY, 1918.

Copy No. 5

While Battn is in Divsl. Reserve.

I. The Alarm will be communicated to Coys. by "Priority" wire & by runner.

II. An Officer (Battn S.O.) accompanied by an Orderly will proceed immediately to Bde. HQs for orders. The S.O. & runner will make themselves acquainted with the route to Bde. HQs both by day & by night.

III. Troops, fully armed & equipped as detailed for "Fighting Order" except as laid down in para VI of these orders, will fall in on Coy. Alarm Posts & report to Adjutant, by runner, when ready to move off.

IV. (i) OC "C" Coy will detail a Guard of 1 N.C.O. & 3 men to remain behind i/c Camp & Baggage OTTAWA CAMP.
(ii) The Quarter-Guard will remain behind i/c Battn HQs & Stores.

V. On receipt of alarm all working parties, range parties, etc. provided by coys will be immediately recalled.

VI. 120 rounds S.A.A. at present carried by N.C.Os & men will be increased to 200 rounds per man under arrangements by R.S.M.

VII. G.S. Limbered wagons & Maltese cart will be loaded, animals will be harnessed but will not be hooked in. Field-cookers & water-cart animals will be harnessed but will not be hooked in. All pack animals & riders will be saddled & loads for the former will be laid out but not put on.
Filled feed-bags will be attached in all cases.
All animals will be leg-haltered to prevent them breaking loose.

VIII. All water-bottles will be immediately filled.

IX. Strict silence will be enforced at night. The minimum number of lights will be used & then only for the shortest period necessary.

David McAnly Lieut
A/Adjt 1/6th Bn H.L.I.

Issued at 1600 18/7/18.

Copy No 1 — To OC "A" Coy
     2 —   "   " "B" "
     3 —   "   " "C" "
     4 —   "   " "D" "
     5 —   " CO, HQ Coy, R.S.M & File
     6 —   " Q.M. T.O. & File

COPY No. 5

BATTALION ORDER No 19
By
LIEUT COL J. ANDERSON. CMG. DSO. COMNDG. 1/6th H.L.I.
19th July 18.

———

0500 ... Reveille
0530 ... Breakfast A, C, & H.Qrs Coys
0600 ... Breakfast B & D Coys
0630 ... All huts will be evacuated by 0630. Coys will fall in at points already indicated and pile arms. Camp Cleaning Parties will be detailed and all huts, lines, etc ready for Commanding Officer inspection by 0700.
0700 ... All L.G. Baggage will be loaded up and limbers ready to move.
Lewis Guns, Equipment, etc will be stacked on Alarm Post near the main road.
0800 ... All Officers Baggage and Stores etc. will be loaded and Motor Wagon ready to move off at this hour. All Officers Baggage must be ready for loading by 0730.
0730 ... Transport, including Field Kitchens and Water Carts, will move by road, the head of column passing Winnipeg Camp at 0730.
0830 ... Battalion will parade en Masse facing N.W. on football ground on S. Side of ST. ELOI - CHAMBLAIN L'ABBÉ Road ready to move off at 0830.
 DRESS — Steel Helmet, Jacket Kilt Kilt Apron, Hosetops, Puttees, Full Marching Order, Water Bottles filled. Gas Helmets in ready position. Blanket and Greatcoat will be carried by the man. The former strapped to pack, the latter carried over the arm.
 Cooks, Sanitary men, etc will parade with their Coys.
 Each Coy will carry sufficient tea, sugar, dixies etc. for Midday Meal of tea.

Train Orders.
 Battalion Standing Orders for movement by train are issued herewith. O.C. Coys will ensure that these orders are made known to all ranks and strictly adhered to in every respect. These Orders should be returned to Orderly Room for safe custody by 1800 on 20/7/18.

FURTHER ORDERS WILL BE ISSUED LATER.

D. Macaulay
Lieut
A/Adjt 1/6th Bn H.L.I.

Issued at 2330 19-7-18.
 Copy No.1. To O.C. "A" Coy.
  "   " 2 " " B "
  "   " 3 " " C "
  "   " 4 " " D "
  "   " 5 " C.O. R.S.M. HQrs Coy & File
  "   " 6 " Q.M. & T.O.

BILLET STANDING ORDERS
BY
Major W. M. Anderson, M.C. Commdg 1/6th Bn H.L.I.

Copy No. 5

20th July, 1918.

I. BILLETS.
Once a Coy. has been allotted billets, it must not change or take up extra billets without first consulting the Adjutant.
Before a formation or unit leaves, the Town Major must be informed.

II. CARE OF PROPERTY.
O.C. Coys. are held responsible that billets are kept clean and in good order and left clean on departure. This includes the grounds and streets surrounding the billets. A full report to be made to the Orderly Room of any damage done by the troops. Animals if picketted in fields must be kept clear of trees.

III. SANITATION.
The Town Major has authority to :—
(1) To enter & inspect the sanitary arrangements in all billets.
(2) To make units responsible for the cleanliness of roads, drains, etc., in their vicinity, and to demand from the nearest units sufficient working parties up to one per cent (1%) of the strength of the units, for cleaning unoccupied areas, for the erection of extra incinerators and latrines where required, and for road mending where necessary.
He will notify the unit of the work he requires carried out, which will be done under the control of the unit officers.

IV. LATRINES.
Civilian latrines will be used only where permitted. Latrines which are constructed for military use in various parts of the town are to be kept in a sanitary condition by the units using same. Troops are forbidden from using any improper place as a urinal.

V. MANURE.
The Transport Officer will arrange to collect from the horse lines all manure and convey it to the manure dump situated at C.14.d.3.2.

VI. REFUSE.
Each unit will collect its own refuse and deposit it at Incinerator situated at C.14.b.8.4.; no refuse shall be buried. Headquarters will arrange with Transport Officers of units during occupation, for the supply of 1 limber or G.S. Wagon, 2 horses and driver to work in conjunction with Town Major's Sanitary Section for the cleanliness of streets in their area.

VII. GAS ALERT.
O.C. Coys & N.C.Os. in charge of detachments stationed in the district will give orders for the Gas Alert on the signal which will consist of :—
(1) Successive blasts from the Mine Sirens at Fosse No. 4
(2) Violent ringing of the Church Bells.

VIII. DRESS.
No N.C.O. or man is to be permitted to leave the immediate area of his quarters without wearing puttees and belt and Box Respirators.

IX. ESTAMINETS.

Cafés and Estaminets are open to the troops only between the hours of :-

1030 to 1330.
1800 to 2100.

All ranks are forbidden to enter Estaminets at any other than time stated. No whisky, cognac, gin, rum or other spirits may be purchased or accepted as gifts either at Cafés, Estaminets, wine Shops, or private Houses.

Gambling in Cafés or Estaminets is prohibited.

X. ROLL-CALL & LIGHTS-OUT.

All N.C.Os & Men unless on duty, are to be in their billets by 2100, Roll-call to be held under Coy. arrangements at this hour.

Lights out at 2130.

XI. LIGHTS.

All lights are to be extinguished or completely shaded one hour after sunset.

XII. FIRE ORDERS.

(1) In case of Fire, the French Official in charge of Water Supply will be sent to turn on the water.

Each Company will detail a Fire Picquet of 1 Officer & 16 O.Rs daily to be held in readiness in case of fire. In the event of fire breaking out, the Coy. concerned will immediately report to Orderly Room who will notify Town Major at once.

XIII. MILITARY POLICE.

The Military Police have orders to forward charges against any N.C.O. or man who does not strictly comply where concerned, with the foregoing orders.

XIV. INFECTIOUS DISEASES.

In case of any infectious disease, the Town Major must be notified at once, through the Orderly Room.

XII. FIRE ORDERS (CONTD.)

(2) The following orders are repeated for information and must be strictly observed :-

"Striking of matches, kindling of fires, smoking & the use of naked lights, even in candlesticks, in or near buildings containing straw, hay or similar inflammable material is strictly forbidden.

No candle will be lighted in any building or room unless it is stuck in a lantern or improvised candlestick. No lighted brazier is to be used in any building where there is any straw, hay or other inflammable material. The indiscriminate erection or use of extemporized fireplaces in or near barns or other buildings occupied by troops is forbidden.

XV. RANGES.

The Rifle range is situated at C.15.b.3.3. and units are responsible for the care and cleanliness of the range while using same.

- SHEET 2 -

XVI. WATER.
Water may be drawn from the stand pipes situated in several parts of the town. Os. C. Coys. will instruct water details to guard against any wastage and to see that cleanliness is maintained in all cases where water is concerned.

XVII. TRAINING GROUND.
The training grounds are situated at C.14.d 5.5. and C.15.b.3.3.

XVIII. ALARM POST.
Coys. will select their own Alarm Posts. Battalion Alarm Post is situated on vacant football ground on NORTH side of main road immediately opposite Orderly Room.

XIX. ALARM.
Companies will be ready to turn out at 1 hours notice. Water-bottles will be kept filled overnight and inspected nightly by an Officer.
Equipments to be made up each night and kept near at hand ready to put on.

XX. ANTI-AIRCRAFT POST.
Coy on duty will daily provide an Anti-Aircraft Lewis Gun Post, mounting at 0500 & dismounting at 2030. Position of Post will be selected and pointed out by Battalion Lewis Gun Officer.

XXI. AID POST.
The Regimental Aid Post is situated at No. 2 CHEMIN-DU-BOIS.

D.L.Macintyre Lieut
A/adjt 1/6 H.L.I.

Issued at 2330 20/7/18.

Copy No 1. To OC "A" Coy.
    2 -   " "B" "
    3 -   " "C" "
    4 -   " "D" "
    5 - CO "HQs" R.S.M & File
    6 - Q.M. & T.O

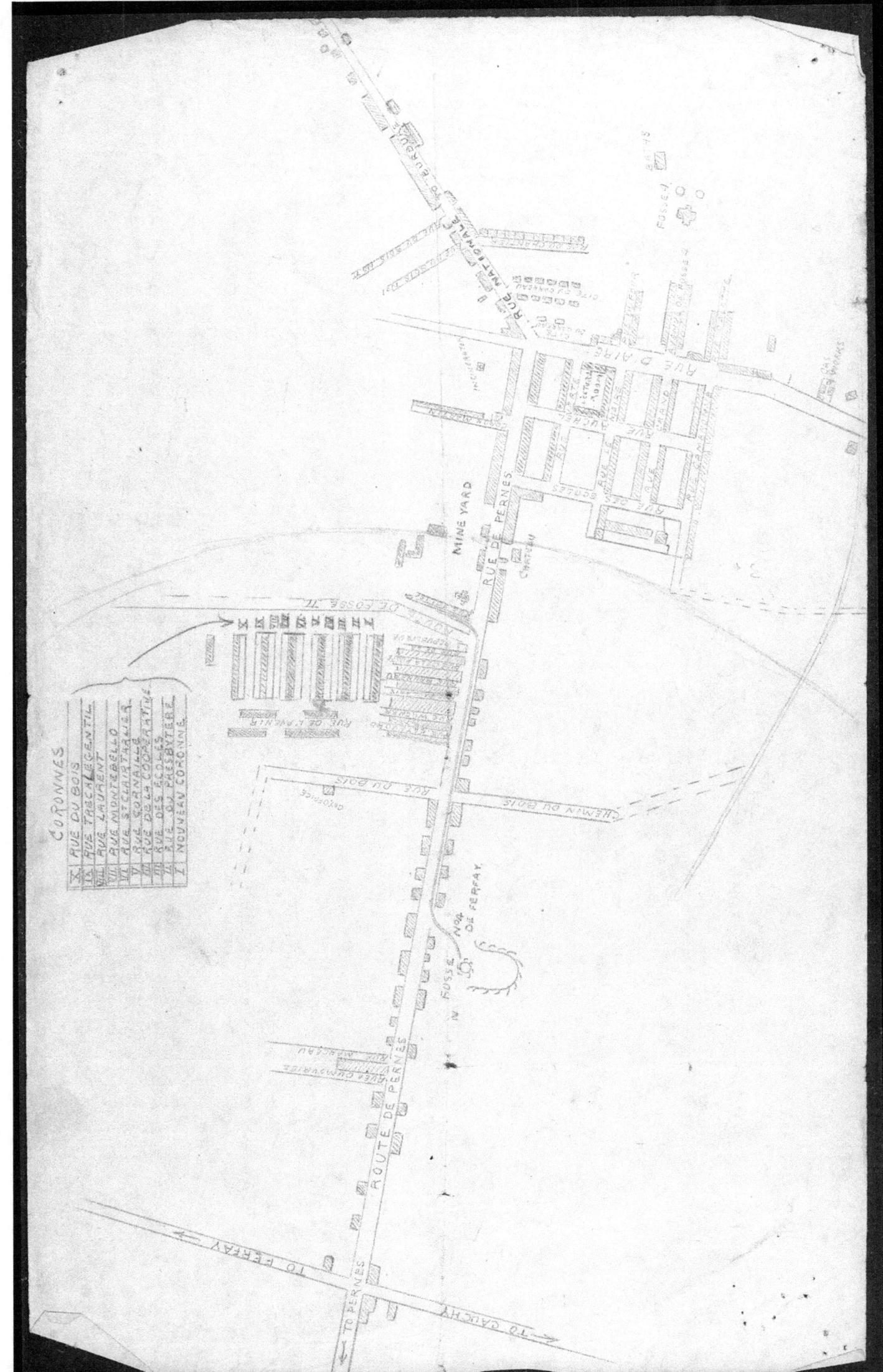

SECRET. BATTALION PRELIMINARY MOVE ORDERS Copy No. 8
BY
Lieut-Col. J. ANDERSON. C.M.G. D.S.O. Commdg 1/6th Bn. H.L.I.

Ref. Map. - LENS (II) - HAZEBROUCK (SA). - 1/100,000.   25th July. 1918.

1. INFORMATION.
   (a) The 52nd Division is now in G.H.Q. Reserve.
   (b) 157th Brigade Group will be ready to move by bus or Tactical Train at 6 hours notice.

2. MOVE BY TACTICAL TRAIN.
   (a) Entraining Station will be PERNES.
   (b) All Transport, with the exception of certain wagons as detailed in attached Tables A & B. will proceed by road.

MOVE BY BUS.
   (a) Head of Embussing Point at Y in CAUCHY LA TOUR.
   (b) If moving by bus, all Lewis Guns and at least 24 Magazines (filled) per gun and one days rations will be taken on the man.
   (c) A bus takes 1 Officer and 25 Other Ranks.
       A Lorry takes 1 Officer and 20 Other Ranks.
   (d) Battalion will arrive at the embussing Point ¼ hour before the time ordered for Embussing to start.
       Companies will embuss in the following order:-
           H.Qrs, A, B, C, & D. Coys.
   (e) Arrangements are being made to place Notice Boards at each end of the Embussing Point.

3. RECONNAISSANCE.
   The Embussing and Entraining Points will be reconnoitred by all Officers by day and night, and also roads leading to them.

4. TRANSPORT.

Issued at 2030   25/7/18

                    Lieut.
                    A/Adjt. 1/6th Bn H.L.I.

           Copy No 1 - To OC A. Coy
               2 - " B. "
               3 - " C. "
               4 - " D. "
               5 - " H.Qrs ", R.S.M & FILE
               6 - QM & T.O.
               7 - CO & FILE
               8 - WAR DIARY.

1/6th H.L.I.

Headquarters
15th Brigade.

PROPOSED RAID SCHEME

MAP REF VIMY & ROUVROY 1/10000.

I INTENTION.

To raid Front & Support lines for 100 yds on either side of MERIL TRENCH and MERIL TRENCH itself between front and support lines.

II OBJECT.

To obtain enemy identifications, take prisoners, inflict casualties, do all possible damage.

III TROOPS FOR OPERATION.

(1) O.C. Raid & 2 Runners.
(2) 1 Platoon consisting of 1 Officer & 25 O.R.s divided thus,
   (a) 1½ Sections & 1 Officer.
   (b) 1½ Sections including 1 Sergeant.
(3) 1 Section Scouts. 2 N.C.Os & 6 men to cut wire & put on blocks.
(4) Communication Chain. 2 N.C.O's & 12 men (2 Sections)
(5) 4 Stretcher Bearers.

IV OBJECTIVE

Enemy Front & Support line for 100 yards on each side of MERIL TRENCH & MERIL TRENCH itself between Front line & Support line.

V POSITION OF ASSEMBLY

VESTA TILLEY TRENCH near junction with BILLIE BURKE

VI TIME OF ASSEMBLY

ZERO - 60

VII CUTTING OF ENEMY WIRE

(a) The enemy wire will be cut with hand wire cutters at 2 points, each 100 yards outwards from MERIL TRENCH.

SHEET No 2.

VII. ATTACK AT ZERO HOUR.

(a) 2 men establish block at T.11.a. 20/80.
(b) 2 men establish block at T.5.c 00/00.
(c) 1½ sections each move inwards along front line trench from gaps where wire is cut till they reach MERIL TRENCH, they will then proceed along MERIL C.T. to the Support line preceded by Bombers. On reaching Support line each party of 1½ sections will turn outwards & search Support line for 100 yards on either flank of MERIL.

IX. WITHDRAWAL

Signal - Repeated long blasts on whistle, withdraw inwards along support line back through MERIL C.T. and make their exit from the front line by the gaps through which they entered.

X. MEDICAL.

(a) 4 Stretcher bearers with 2 stretchers, each with 1 blanket to carry additional wounded if necessary, to remain with O.C. raid at the gaps in wire.
(b) Relay Stretcher Posts at the position of assembly.
(c) Advanced Aid Post in DORIS TRENCH at T.8.d.60/40.

1st July 1918.

W Mackenzie Anderson
Major
Commanding 1/6th Batt H.L.I.

SECRET.   BATTALION ORDER Nº 20.   Copy Nº 5

BY

LIEUT- COL. J. ANDERSON, C.M.G. D.S.O. COMMDG. 1/6TH BN. H.L.I.

29TH JULY, 1918.

1. INFORMATION.

(a) The 6th H.L.I. will move by road to Billets in BARLIN on 30th July 1918.

(b) While on the march, the usual precautions against hostile aircraft will be taken, when & if necessary.

2. PARADE.

~~Companies will parade on Alarm posts, ready to move off at 0745 prompt~~

Order Companies will parade in Column of Route facing S.W. on main PERNES – RAIMBERT ROAD in the following order:– HQrs. B.D.C & A. ready to move off at 0745 prompt.

Position of Assembly. The head of the Column will rest on the Crossroads at C.19.d.5.5.

Dress:– Kilt & Apron, Tam o'Shanter Skeleton Order with haversack in centre of back. Steel helmets securely tied to Haversacks, Water bottles filled, S.B.Rs. at Ready Position.

A ration of Biscuits or Bread & Cheese will be carried on the man.

3. TRANSPORT.

All Greatcoats will be neatly rolled in bundles of 10 and labelled & stacked at QM Stores by Coys ready for loading by 0630.

Lewis Gun Limbers (1 per Coy) will be sent to Coy HQrs at 0700. Nothing except L.G. equipment will be loaded on these limbers.

Transport will move in rear of Battalion. 100 yards distance will be maintained between Transport & Battalion.

4. MARCH ORDERS.

100 yards will be maintained between Coys.
50 "   – do –   Pldtoons.

Medical Officer will bring up the rear of the Battn.

Any man unable to keep up will be given a card by an Officer marching in rear of his Coy & must not fall out unless in possession of this card.

No water will be drunk from water bottles without permission of an Officer.

5. SUPPLIES

Rations for the Bde Group for the 31st will be delivered direct to Units in their new area by Train Wagons.

Location of Railhead & Refilling Point will be notified later.

6. SANITATION

All billets Stores etc will be left scrupulously clean & will be thoroughly inspected by Platoon Commanders & OC Coys, & certificates rendered that Billets have been left in a thoroughly clean & sanitary condition by 0730, to Orderly Room. Certificates will also state that no equipment clothing or ammn has been left in billets.

Lieut
a/Adjt 1/6 H.L.I.

Issued at 2050 29.7.18

Copy No 1 to OC A Coy
2 - " B "
3 - " C "
4 - " D "
5 - HQs Coy. CO. & file
6 - QM. TO
7 - R.S.M.

SECRET. BATTALION ORDER No 21.   COPY No. 7
By
LIEUT-COL. J. ANDERSON, C.M.G. & D.S.O. COMMDG 1/6th Bn. H.L.I.

REF. MAPS - IENS 11. 1/100,000 & 51B. 1/20,000.   31st JULY, 1918.

1. The 1/6th Battn H.L.I. will proceed by route march today 31st July 1918, to camps in MADAGASCAR Area. A.26 d and A.27.c. Time at which head of Battalion will pass starting point at VEDREL village – 1.10 p.m.

2. Companies will parade on Alarm Posts, ready to move off at an hour to be notified. Late
    Dress:- Kilt & Apron, Tam o'Shanter, Skeleton Order with haversack in centre of back, Steel Helmet securely tied to Haversack, Water bottle filled, S.B.R. at ready position.
    A ration of Biscuits or Bread & Cheese will be carried on the man.
    Waterproof Sheet will be carried on the man.
    Battalion will march in 3s instead of 4s.
    Route – Camp. – VEDREL, GRAND SERVINS, VILLERS AU BOIS, LE PENDU, MT. ST. ELOI, ANZIN ST AUBIN, thence in an E direction to camps situated at junction of SOUCHEZ – ARRAS and ECURIE – ANZIN ST AUBIN RDS.

3. One horse Ambulance will follow in rear of Battalion. One lorry will accompany the march of the Transport of Brigade Group. This lorry will deal with breakdowns, stragglers etc. No man will be allowed on this lorry without written permission from an Officer.

4. 100 yards will be maintained between Coys.
   5 yards will be maintained between Platoons
    Medical Officer will bring up the rear of the Battalion.
    Any man unable to keep up will be given a card by an Officer marching in rear of his Coy. & must not fall out unless in possession of this card.
    No water will be drunk from water bottles without permission of an Officer.

5. All Greatcoats will be neatly rolled in bundles of 10 and labelled & stacked at Q.M. stores by Coys., ready for loading by 1100
    Transport will move in rear of Battalion – 100 yards distance will be maintained between Transport & Battalion.

6. At 3.30 p.m. Battalion will halt for 1 hour. During this halt the strictest discipline will be maintained.
    All Platoon Commanders will be with their Platoons. Men will not be allowed to wander about.
    All wagons will be pulled well in to the side of the road.

D. Chambers Lieut
Adjt. 1/6 H.L.I.

Issued at 1015 - 31/7/18

Copy No 1 — To O.C. A Coy
      2 — "   "   B "
      3 — "   "   C "
      4 — "   "   D "
      5 — HQ RSM & FILE
      6 — Q.M. & T.O.
      7 — C.O. & FILE.

Army Form C. 2118.

WAR DIARY
or
INTELLIGENCE SUMMARY.
(Erase heading not required)

Instructions regarding War Diaries and Intelligence Summaries are contained in F.S. Regs. Part II and the Staff Manual respectively. Title pages will be prepared in manuscript.

6. H.L.I. Volume 3 August 1918.   REF MAP MARQUEIL 1/20000

Place	Date	Hour	Summary of Events and Information	Remarks and references to Appendices
ROCLINCOURT	1/8/18	0600	Reveille — Daily Inspection.	
		0800	Advanced Parties for the Trenches left on Motor Buses.	
		0810	C + D Coy preceded by HHrs 1800 hrs from ROCLINCOURT & thence by M.L. march to the line. A + B Coy followed at 1200 Hrs Horses relieving the HHH Bn a dawn the latter relg by M.L. (See Appendix)	Appendix 4/8/18 Ebh.
		1730	Relief complete. Dispositions were:— Front line 'C' Coy on Right 'D' Coy on Left. 'A' Coy in supports B'lion left Bk. H.Q. B 21 a 7/4.	
			Lieut P.A.E. McCRACKEN and 2/Lt K= MACINTOSH rejoined from Courses (S.D.S. & R.F.B.T. respectively).	
		2100–2130	Stand to Arms.	
		0030	Patrol of 1 Officer (2nd Lt J.R. BUCHANAN) and (½ section proceeded to B15a 3/4 returning at 0030. A large working party (B30 – 1030 hrs had been behind enemy lines. Three enemy seemed to be everywhere watching my advance from B15a b/7 +DUKE STREET trenches.	
FRONT LINE	4/8/18	0330	Stand to Arms — Usual 5 Rds S.A.A. Practice fired.	
OPP. SECTOR		0430 – 0030	Patrol of 1 Officer and (2/Lieut D.M. FRASER) and 1½ Section B17c 6/8 and took up a defensive position about 3000 yds in advance of this. Lewis was sent on to act as a Base. Working Party will assisting party returned into trenches. Patrol returned at 0230.	

(1534201) W1.W8300/P713 750,000 3/15 E.2088 Forms/C2115/6   D. D. & L., London, E.C.

WAR DIARY
INTELLIGENCE SUMMARY

(Erase heading not required.)

Army Form C. 2118.

Place	Date	Hour	Summary of Events and Information	Remarks and references to Appendices
	2/8/18 (contd)	1530	C.O. visited the line. Work policy action on from 1/7 R.S. carried out. Stand to Arms.	Ibh.
		2100-2130		
		2200	A Patrol of 1 Officer (Lieut. J.F. KENNEDY) and 1½ Sections took up a defensive position about 200 yds. in front of B17 c 5/1. No enemy were seen or heard. Patrol returned at 0040.	
	3/8/18	0030	A Defensive Patrol of 1 Officer (2/Lt M.B. CURRIE) and 1½ Sections took up a defensive position as above returning at 0330 to B17 d 6/7. None of working party heard on right flank of patrol.	Ibh.
		0330-0445	Stand to Arms. C.O. visited the line. Work continued as above – Wiring, Safety Holes, Improvement of Fire positions & Reserve & foreground, Drainage & laying of Duck boards. C.O. visited I Front line fire bays during the day. G.O.C. Division visited the line. Stand to Arms.	
		2100-2130		
		2200	A Defensive Patrol of 1 Officer (Lieut. T. CRAIG) and 2½ Sections took up a defensive position at B17c returning at 0030. No signs of enemy seen or heard.	

WAR DIARY
or
INTELLIGENCE SUMMARY

Army Form C. 2118.

Place	Date	Hour	Summary of Events and Information	Remarks and references to Appendices
	4/8/18	0030	2 Patrols each of 1 Officer (2/Lt MORRISON and PATERSON) and 1½ Sections each left B17c7/5 at 0030 and took up a defensive position at B17d central. Found in front unreconnoitred for about 300 yds. taking the enemy low entrenchments, enemy were seen or heard. Both patrols returned at 0330.	
		0330-0435	Stood to Arms – L.O. visited the line. Used 5 Rds Pracher S.A.A.	
		0920	Tried 0920. Defence P.O.C. Coy at Bn HQ. W/K on Section duties carried out.	
			L.O. visited 2 Support Coys during forenoon. Brig-C maxim line Stand to Arms.	Etched
		2100-2130	2 Defensive patrols, one of 1 Officer (Lt W.D. THOMPSON) + 1½ Sections and one of 1 Sergt (Sergt W. REILLY) and 1½ Sections left at 2130. Taking up defensive positions at B17.b.3/3 and B17.d.4/3 at same respectively staying at 0030. No sign of enemy seen or heard. No lying Parties heard.	
			Lieut F.B. JOHNSTON left this for leave to U.K. 157 Bde Piano Coy organised 35 O.R. left Unit to compose same competition at 1st Army contest. 2/Lt K. MACINTOSH and 10 O.R. left this to take part in a Rifle Competition at 1st Army contest. Lieut A. MACINTYRE rejoined unit from leave to U.K.	
	5/8/18	0030	2 Patrols, one of 1 Officer (Lieut BRUCE) and 1½ Sections and one of 1 Sergt (Sergt MATHIESON) and 1½ Sections left at 0030 0030 and took up a defensive position at B17.d.4/3 and B17.b.3/3 respectively returning at 0330. No sign of the enemy seen or heard	

Army Form C. 2118.

WAR DIARY
or
INTELLIGENCE SUMMARY.
(Erase heading not required.)

Instructions regarding War Diaries and Intelligence Summaries are contained in F. S. Regs., Part II. and the Staff Manual respectively. Title pages will be prepared in manuscript.

Place	Date	Hour	Summary of Events and Information	Remarks and references to Appendices
	5/8/16 (contd)	0330-0440	Stand to Arms — Adjt visited the line	
			C.O. President of F.G.C.M. at ROCLINCOURT assembling at 0730.	
			Work etc carried on as usual in accordance with programme	
		2000-2130	Stand to Arms —	
		2130	Defensive Patrols of 1½ sections under an Officer each (2/Lt FRASER and Sgt LAURISTON respectively) to B17d (central) and B17d 2/3. No signs of enemy seen on found. Patrols returned 0015.	Ekh.
			Capt H. J. FARQUHAR rejoined Unit from course at 1st Army School	
	6/8/16		Defensive Patrols (2/Lt SMITH and 1½ sections and L/Sgt WEIR + 1½ sections) left to B17d 2/3 and B17d (central) returning at 0330. Saw or heard no	Appendix 6/8/16. Ekh.
			sign of enemy or hostile working parties	
			Stand to Arms — C.O. visited the line	
		0330-0445	Bn HQ organized the line ready to support him in B. Sec 6	
		0930	Battn HQ diaries (Army withdrawn from Front Line & Coy in reserve & coy in Coy HQ 1/7th H.R.S. (the Appendix)	
		1600	Relief complete — Dispositions — OUTPOST COY "C" COY BOW TRENCH & Bow Support — Post Line Coys. A & Right. B Centre and Left. D. POST LINE	
		2000-2130	Stand to Arms.	
		2400	"C" Coy withdrawn from front line in preparation for enfm Bon attack. Operation set out at 0218. unit in line no occurrences	

WAR DIARY
INTELLIGENCE SUMMARY

(Erase heading not required)

Army Form C. 2118.

Place	Date	Hour	Summary of Events and Information	Remarks and references to Appendices
	6/8/18 (contd)	2130	Defensive patrols of 1/4 W.B. (2/Lt W.B. CORRIE and Serjt PALLOCK + 1/2 section) each to B17 d 2/3 and B17 d (central). Saw or heard nothing of the enemy. Patrols returned at 0030.	
	7/8/18	0330-0445	No new patrols sent out from 0230 till dawn. Stand to arms. — Usual S.B. SAA fired.	
		0700	Advanced parties of 1/9 R INCO + 1 L.Y proceeded to BROWN LINE to take over 5/4 + 1 gun.	Appendix 7/8/18 Ehh
		0900	Batts relieved in this area by 1/5 HLI (See appendix)	
		13.00	Relief complete. After relief Batts took over 1/5 HLI disposition in BROWN LINE viz Shipertina + Right Coy. A Coy, Centre Coy. 2/14 B Coy Reserve D Coy.	
		1400	Conference of O.C. Coys at Bn HQ. hay'n W.M. ANDERSON M.C. arrived from Huclin. Lt Col J. ANDERSON CMG, DSO, and Major J.G. COATS proceeded to Huclin.	
		2100-2130	Stand to arms — Rations for platoons.	
			Lieut Col. J. ANDERSON C.M.G, D.S.O. to London and 11.7.18–12.8.18 in temp command of Bn — Major W.M. ANDERSON returns command of the Bn. Ehh	

WAR DIARY
or
INTELLIGENCE SUMMARY.

Army Form C. 2118.

(Erase heading not required.)

Place	Date	Hour	Summary of Events and Information	Remarks and references to Appendices
SUPPORT LINE OPPY SECTOR	5/8/18	0330–0440	Stand to Arms — 1 Section per Platoon — 0330 Coy Inspection — 0440. Reveille (for remainder). Bn. allotted to boys a rate at ROCLINCOURT. A Coy 2 Plat. B Coy 0930–1030, 'B' Coy 2 Plat. 1400–1500. Shower Baths arranged for C + D Coys at Bn. HdQrs and B 157 c S/2 respectively.	
			Holden Cleaning of Foreground etc. Wiring: Digging of Gullys.	B.H.
		1400–1630	Training.— 1 Lewis Gunner per Section under Bn. L.G.O. 4 NCOs per Coy under R.S.M. commanding Drill. Bn. k NCOs Musketry + Bayonet Fighting (Raising NCO.) 1 N.C.O per Coy under L/Cpl Brooke (Raising NCO.)	
		2140–2130	Stand to Arms — 1 Section per Platoon. Lieut. W.H. AIKMAN left Unit by leave to U.K. (14 days) Lieut. H. MARTIN attached Unit from Course (MUSKETRY)	
	4/8/18	0330–0430	Stand to Arms — 1 Section per Platoon — 0330 Coy Inspection Baths allotted as above — C Coy 0930–1030, D Coy 1400–1500. Shower Bath arranged for A + B Coys 17 H.Q.m.	B.H.
		1400–1630	Specialists Training — as before Lewis Gunner, 1 NCO per under R.S.M. 1 NCO's Raising Bonnac. Stand to Arms — 1 Section per Platoon	
		2130–2230		

Lieut Col. J. ANDERSON CMG. D.S.O. to command 157.th Bn. w/o W.M.

ANDERSON. resume command of the Batln.

Army Form C. 2118.

WAR DIARY
or
INTELLIGENCE SUMMARY.
(Erase heading not required.)

Instructions regarding War Diaries and Intelligence
Summaries are contained in F.S. Regs., Part II.
and the Staff Manual respectively. Title pages
will be prepared in manuscript.

Place	Date	Hour	Summary of Events and Information	Remarks and references to Appendices
	9/5/18 (contd)	2100-0300	"A" Coy - Work on new localities - 5" H.L.I. sector - OPPY FRONT LINE. "D" Coy ditto. 7 H.L.I. sector	
	10/5/18	0330-0445	Stand to Arms - Inspection for Platoon - 0530 by Inspection. Baths allotted as above to Coys. "B" Coy 0930-1030. "A" Coy 1400-1500. Shower Baths arranged for "C" & "D" Coy as above. "B" & "C" Coy - Work on Trenches "BROWN LINE" Wiring and Improvement Etc.	
			of fire position	
		1400-1630	Training - as above - Lewis Gunners NCO's - Lewis Gunners NCO's under R.S.M.L.; NCO's (Railway Corps)	
		2100-2130	# Stand to Arms - Inspection for Platoon	
			2/Lt D. JOHNSTON rejoined unit from leave to U.K.	
		2100-0305	"A" & "D" Coy - Work on new localities in front line as above.	
	11/5/18	0245-	Intense Hostile Bombardment on right of our Divisional Sector. S.O.S. Flares put up & responded to by our Artillery. Returned to Arms - 0315 Stand down.	
		0330		
		0330-0445	Stand to Arms - Inspection for Platoon - 0530 by Inspection. Baths allotted as above to Coys. "D" Coy 0930-1030. "C" Coy 1400-1500. Shower Baths arranged for "A" & "B" Coy as above.	

Army Form C. 2118.

WAR DIARY
or
INTELLIGENCE SUMMARY.
(Erase heading not required.)

Instructions regarding War Diaries and Intelligence Summaries are contained in F. S. Regs., Part II. and the Staff Manual respectively. Title pages will be prepared in manuscript.

Place	Date	Hour	Summary of Events and Information	Remarks and references to Appendices
	11/5/18 (contd)	1400–1630	Specialist Training – Lewis Gunners & NCO's classes as above	DHh
		1900–2130	Stand to Arms – 1 section per Platoon	
			Capt. J. FARQUHAR proceeded on leave to U.K.	
		0100–0300	'A' Coy + 'D' Coy W O/C on our Front Line Locality as above	
	12/5/18	0330–0430	Stand to Arms – 1 section per Platoon	
			Baths allotted to the Div. Baye 0730–1030 and 1400–1500	
		1000–1200	Specialist Training – Lewis Gunners & NCO's classes as above	Ahh
		1600	B.G.C. visited the line	
		2000–2130	Stand to Arms	
		1930	Advance parties – 1 Off. per Coy, 1 NCO per Platoon, 1 Lewis Gunner per Section = & H.Q. 2 NCO's + 4 Sig'rs TOTAL for Front Line OPPY SECTOR (see Appendix)	
			Provisional Defence Scheme issued	
			Stand to Arms – 1 section per Platoon	
	13/5/18	0230–0430	Stand to Arms – 1 section per Platoon 0700 Bny dispatchm.	
			Bath relieved 7KRRL in Rgt Subsector OPPY SECTOR	
			Dispositions – Outpost Coy – A Coy ; Right Post Line Coy – B Coy	
			Left Post Line Coy – D Coy	

WAR DIARY or INTELLIGENCE SUMMARY

Army Form C. 2118.

Place	Date	Hour	Summary of Events and Information	Remarks and references to Appendices
	13/8/18 (contd)		Disposition (notes): Bn Reserve Coy – 'C' Coy; Bn HdQrs B15c 6/4 ; R.A.P. B15 c 5/1. (See appendices)	Appendix (a) 13/8/18 (b) 13/8/18
		1445	Relief complete	
		1400–1600	Lip under Training – Training of H&Qrs Lip under O/C Lip. Work on trenches continued. – Wiring. Improvement of fire position. Dug outs & Sentry Holes etc.	
		1600	Warning Order received that 3.2nd Div. would be relieved by 51st Div. R.J.A. CUMMING rejoined unit from Course (signalling) appendices.	
			Stand to Arms – All fire positions checked	
		2100–2130	2/Lt I. CRAIG Rhd	
		2200	Patrol of 1 officer (A/Lt E.L. SMITH) and 11 Platoon took up defensive position at B5d 1/1 returning at 0030. No signs of enemy seen or heard. 2/Lt R J A CUMMING (signalling)	
	14/8/18	0330–0445	Stand to Arms – C.O. visited the line – 3 Rds (Practice) S.A.A. fired by all men.	D.H.W
			Work on Trenches – Wiring. Improvement of fire positions etc. continued. Training – H&Qrs Signallers 1000–1200 ; All Coys 1000–1200 ; Lewis	
		1000–1600	Gun Training and musketry. C.O. visited the outpost & Post line Coys	
		2100–2130	Stand to Arms. –	

WAR DIARY or INTELLIGENCE SUMMARY.

Army Form C. 2118.

(Erase heading not required.)

Place	Date	Hour	Summary of Events and Information	Remarks and references to Appendices
OPPY SECTOR. (FRONT LINE)	14/8/18	2130	A Patrol of 1 Officer and 1 Platoon left for B11a 3/5 returning at 0030. Nothing seen or heard of the enemy	
	15/8/18	0030	Patrol of 1 Officer (2/Lt D JOHNSTON) took up a defensive position at B11a 3/5 returning at 0330. No signs of enemy patrol activity.	
			Patrol of 1 Officer (Lt C BRUCE) and 17 O.R. took up a defensive position at B11c 2/7 returning at 0330. No signs of enemy seen or heard.	
		0330–04.30	Stand to Arms – B.O. visited line –	
		11.00	Move & Training carried out.	
		12.00–18.00	L.O.'s of coy's visited O.P.'s. B.O. visited the line.	
		18.00	1/B + 3 Sank (Adv. Party) 1st Worc. Regt. arrived.	
		21.00–21.30	Stand to Arms.	
	16/8/18	0330–04.30	Stand to Arms – B.O. visited the line	
		0900	Adv. Patrol (10M & 10 O.R. per Coy) 1st Worc. Regt. arrived in the line. Trenches cleaned and Trench Stores etc. stowed away for handing over.	
		1400	B.O. held Conference for O.C. Coys at 'B' Coys Hd.Qrs	

Army Form C. 2118.

WAR DIARY
or
INTELLIGENCE SUMMARY
(Erase heading not required.) Ref. Maps 44B 1/40000 & LENS 11 1/10000.

Instructions regarding War Diaries and Intelligence Summaries are contained in F. S. Regs., Part II. and the Staff Manual respectively. Title pages will be prepared in manuscript.

Place	Date	Hour	Summary of Events and Information	Remarks and references to Appendices
	16/8/18 (contd)	1900	Relief commenced	
		2030	Relief complete — Other Relief Coys moved independently to the Entraining load at ROCLINCOURT and thence by 'bus to MONT ST ELOI. (See appendix) Batt. arriving in by 2 am. 17th.	Appendix 16/8/18 thin
MONT ST ELOI	17/8/18	0630	Reveille	
		0930	Conference Y/O.C. Coys at Bn HQrs.	
		14.15	Batt. proceeded by route march to CHATEAU-DE-LA-HAIE (see appendix) arriving there by 1600.	
		2100	Roll call 2130 Lights out Capt STANSFELD M.C. R.A.M.C. (attached) admitted to Hosp.	Appendix 17/8/18 thin
CHATEAU-DE-LA-HAIE	18/8/18	0600	Reveille	
		0900	L.O. proceeded on reconnaissance with Brigade, known on returning at 1800.	
		0900-12.00 & 13.00-16.00	Weekly Monthly of equipment. Inspection of Regimental equipment & Coy Clays. Overhaul of Boots, Socks & clothing.	thin
		18.30	Church Parade on Bn. Alarm Post	
		21.00	Roll call 2130 Lights out — Lieut WILLIS M.A.C.C. U.S.R. joined unit for duty as M.O.	

WAR DIARY
or
INTELLIGENCE SUMMARY.
(Erase heading not required.)

Army Form C. 2118.

Place	Date	Hour	Summary of Events and Information	Remarks and references to Appendices
	19/5/18	0600	Reveille — 0730 Coy inspection	
		0900-1200	B Coy Range Practices — Range: W.17.B. 5 Rds Grouping; 5 Rds Application and 10 Rds. Rapid with S.B.R's on. A.C & D Coys — Coy Training — Musketty; Physical Drill & Bayonet Fighting, Attack Huts in Training. Specialists Training — Bomb, Lewis Gunners & Signallers under respective Specialist Officers.	Ahn.
		1400-1600	Training as above	
		2000-2100	Conference for O.C. Coys at R.B. Hd. Qrs. 2030 Roll Call, Lights out	
			Lieut. F.B. JOHNSTON rejoined Unit from leave to U.K. Lieut. P.A.E. McCRACKEN proceeded on — —	
	20/5/18	0600	Reveille — 0730— Coy Inspection	
		0900-1300	Coy Training — on CARENCY TRAINING AREA — Physical Drill — Bayonet Fighting — Huts in Training — Formal Formation for the attack — Artillery Formations in the attack	unfinished 25/5/18 BH
		1400-1500	Normal Formation for the attack	
		1500-1600	Battalion Sports — all day	
			Specialists Training 0900-1200 & as above	
		1500	Warning Order received by Phone that Bath would probably move	

WAR DIARY
or
INTELLIGENCE SUMMARY
(Erase heading not required.)

Army Form C. 2118.

Instructions regarding War Diaries and Intelligence Summaries are contained in F. S. Regs., Part II. and the Staff Manual respectively. Title pages will be prepared in manuscript.

Place	Date	Hour	Summary of Events and Information	Remarks and references to Appendices
	20/8/18	2015	Orders received to be ready to move off at 23.45.	
		2345	Batt. proceeded by route march to AGNES-LES-DUISANS, arriving there at 02.30. (See appendix)	
AGNES-LES-DUISANS	21/8/18	0700	Reveille	
		0900	Boot, Foot & Socks Inspection	
			Washing up. Bleaning &c. the Orders received that the men all day.	Appx
		1200	Warning Orders received that Batt. would not receive in the evening.	
		1900	Batt. ready to move 2200 not receive that any move might could be highly improbable.	
		2100	Lights out —	
	22/8/18	0630	Reveille	
		0900	Lecture for all Officers by S.O.2. Training Tanks at DUISANS.	
		1430	Warning Orders that Batt. will move about 5 pm. in the evening. Received Orders & made arrangements	Appendix 22/8/18
			Batt. ready to move off. Haversacks packed under Batt. arrangements	
		1900	Batt. moved off by route march to BELLACOURT arriving there at 0230 (See appendix)	
		1345	2/4 E.C.S. WEST rejoined unit from Signalling course	
	23/8/18	0700	Reveille	
		0900	Day Inspection	
		1200	Orders received to stand by ready to move at 2 hours notice. Orders recd.	
			To take up line from 59th Div. Shortly later	Appendix 23/8/18
		1900	Batt. moved by route march to BRICKWORKS S2 d & 3c arriving there at 2130 (See Appendix)	
			Batt. moved Lewis Guns, Tools etc. ready to dug preparatory to the attack	

WAR DIARY
or
INTELLIGENCE SUMMARY

Army Form C. 2118.

Instructions regarding War Diaries and Intelligence Summaries are contained in F.S. Regs., Part II. and the Staff Manual respectively. Title pages will be prepared in manuscript.

(Erase heading not required) Ref. Maps LENS II 1/10000 and 51B SW 1/20000

Place	Date	Hour	Summary of Events and Information	Remarks and references to Appendices
BRICKSTACKS S2.d & 3.c	24/9/18	0520	Advance on Hindenburg Line commenced - Objective Hindenburg Line between T5.a and N34.d. Disposition - C & D Coys Firing Line ; A & B Support. (See appendix (a))	Appendix (a) 24/9/18 (b) 24/9/18
		0700	BOIRY reserve trench (jumping off point) crossed. 0715 Firi[n]g opened by Enemy M.Gs from T3.b 0730 this was about T3 b.0/6 Light M.G. fire still advancing 0745. We held up by own barrage on line T5c 2/6 to T4a 3/7 - Tank operating on our right flank.	
		1130	Artillery lengthened range by 500 yds and then came fire. Depth of wire and width of it much heavier and M.G. fire make passage of wire impossible without Artillery covering.	
			Artillery Barrage on HINDENBURG LINE arranged 4 to 1545 but failed to come	
		1530	Bn. A further attempt made to penetrate enemy lines without Artillery support but front ineffectual owing to heavy casualties from M.G. fire	
		1600	Advanced posts withdrawn and line established and consolidated from T5c 2/6 to T4a 3/7. (See Appendix (b)	
		1830	Minor readjustment of area T4c with 7/8 Henry Shell	
	2000 / 2030	Defensive patrols sent out during the night towards HINDENBURG LINE.	
			Casualties: Killed 1 Officer (2/LT K.A. MACINTOSH) + 16 O.R. ; D. of W. 4 O.R. ; Wounded 9 Officers (Lt Col J. ANDERSON, C.M.G. D.S.O. ; Capt K.G. TIDD ; Lieut J.W. FINGLAND M.C. ; Lieut J.P. WILSON, 2/Lieuts E.C.S. WEST, D. JOHNSTON, D. HOGG, D.M. FRASER and J.A. MORRISON * / At duty ; Missing 9 O.R. ; N.Y.D.N. 1 O.R. Wounded 137 O.R.	
			Captures 7 prisoners and 2 M.Gs and Parts (unable) of arms to M.G. B.B.	

Army Form C. 2118.

WAR DIARY
or
INTELLIGENCE SUMMARY.
(Erase heading not required.)

Instructions regarding War Diaries and Intelligence Summaries are contained in F. S. Regs., Part II. and the Staff Manual respectively. Title pages will be prepared in manuscript.

Place	Date	Hour	Summary of Events and Information	Remarks and references to Appendices
ATTACK ON HINDENBURG LINE.	24/8/18	0330-0450	Ref. Map 57B. S.W. 1/20000. Stand to Arms – Intense shelling of area T4.c with gas & heavy shell. Enemy occasionally patrols pushed forward towards HINDENBURG LINE which were driven strongly held by the enemy M.G.s. Major W.M. ANDERSON M.C. rejoined unit and assumed command. Major J. G. COATS proceeded to trenches.	Appendix 25/8/18
		1140		
		1900	Dispositions altered over line established (see Appendix) A Coy – Outpost line. B, C, D Coys – main line of resistance Bn. H.Q. Tga 3/9. Strong patrols rushed from out post line towards FAT TRENCH & HINDENBURG LINE. Disposition complete.	
		2130	Casualties. Killed 1 O.R. 2 O.R. N.Y.D.N. 1 O.R.	
		2130-0300	Heavy bombardment of SUMMIT, FAT TRENCHES and HINDENBURG LINE by our Artillery with a view to cutting the enemy wire. Wounded 1 Officer (Lieut W.D. THOMPSON) & 19 O.R. D.of W.	
HINDENBURG LINE	25/8/18	03.00	An account of alterations in strategical plans and bombardment of the main line of resistance, M.A. outpost line (A Coy) withdrawn by 3 a.m. helichuis. Stand to Arms –	
CROISILLES		0330-0505	from N. and N.W. Contact Patrol & Counter Attack Aeroplanes flew over units at Zero + 2 hrs, Zero + 3 hrs and Zero + 5 hrs Zero hrg 0330	
		1210	Word received that Canadians had taken MONCHY and reported E. of BOIS DU SART and BOIS DE VERT.	

Army Form C. 2118.

WAR DIARY
or
INTELLIGENCE SUMMARY.
(Erase heading not required.)

Instructions regarding War Diaries and Intelligence Summaries are contained in F.S. Regs., Part II. and the Staff Manual respectively. Title pages will be prepared in manuscript.

Place	Date	Hour	Summary of Events and Information	Remarks and references to Appendices
	26/8/18 (cont'd)	1330	Officers patrol (Lieut J CRAIG) and 1 Platoon to recce the direction of the HINDENBURG LINE and watch for the approach of the 153'Bde who had entered the line up at N 34 b and d and not getting in up as they advanced S. & thro' E. Patrol returned at 1600. having seen no sign of 153'Bde.	Appendix 26/8/18 B.Schm 2
		1600	Officers patrol (2/Lt R. PATERSON) and 1 Platoon left with same object. As above returned at 2030. 153'Bde seen in N34a & line at last formed touch with 7th H.L.I.	
		1830	Officers observation post established in SUMMIT Trench with same object. As above encountered heavy M.G. and Artillery fire from both flanks. 7th H.L.I. patrol reported to be in touch with 153'Bde at N 34 d 7/1 at which point their advance was checked. heavy Phillips G/bn in charge of Observation Post (2/Lieut F.G SMITH) reported at 1930 that N.E. flanks had ceased fire withdrawn at 2030 at which time there was considerable M.G fire from flanks and sniper fire.	
		1910	Orders received to by pursued tomorrow at T4a and T36 n d on receipt of orders from Bde HQrs. Cancelled at 2130 (See Appendix)	
			Losses this Killed 1 O.R. Wounded 9 O.R. D. of W. 2 O.R. missing 10 R. N.Y.D.N. 2 O.R.	
	27/8/18	0010	2 Patrols (Lieut T CRAIG and 2/Lt R PATERSON) and 1 Platoon each proceeded to SUMMIT and FAT TRENCHES respectively, were subjected to heavy M.G. fire from both flanks and not FOSLEY TRENCH which was reported to be held by the enemy. SUMMIT and FAT SWITCH were reported clear of the enemy. Patrols returned at 0300	

Army Form C. 2118.

WAR DIARY
or
INTELLIGENCE SUMMARY.
(Erase heading not required.)

Instructions regarding War Diaries and Intelligence
Summaries are contained in F. S. Regs. Part II.
and the Staff Manual respectively. Title pages
will be prepared in manuscript.

Place	Date	Hour	Summary of Events and Information	Remarks and references to Appendices
ATTACK ON FONTAINE CROISILLES	27/5/16 (contd)	0600	Warning Order received to take up position along line 74.d.6/10 to 75.c.3/9. by	
		0900	Batt in position as above ready to move off	
		0930	Advance on FONTAINE CROISILLE'S commenced under heavy artillery Barrage. Disposition "D" Coy right Firing Line, "A" Coy left Firing Line, "C" Coy Right Support "B" Coy left Support. Barrage swinging to left at 0936. (See Appendix) Touch maintained with 7th H.L.I. on left flank but right flank was opened from the start owing to the failure of the 3.6 G.R. to advance from their jumping off trench "I" Point in FOLEY TRENCH thereby causing murderous cross M.G. fire from own right flank out near ___	Appdx 27/5/16 J. Ellis
		1200	1st Objective reached and brethren taken up in HUMBER TRENCH (U7 A). It was decided to suspend the advance due to the final objective owing to (a) the artillery barrage having ceased (b) Right flank completely exposed thereby inducing severe casualties from M.G. fire from flank and rear (c) Touch lost with 7th N.F. and 15th Bde on our left flank.) and (c) Shortage of Ammunition, grenades and tools position attacked by enemy bypass and also army must for Armes which was delivered to him later by an aeroplane	
		1400	HUMBER REDOUBT consolidated and prepared ready to meet counter attack	
		1430	Orders received to continue advance to final Objective (see Appendix) at 1530 with a Barrage of Artillery from field line running	

WAR DIARY or INTELLIGENCE SUMMARY

Army Form C. 2118.

(Erase heading not required)

Place	Date	Hour	Summary of Events and Information	Remarks and references to Appendices
	27/5/18		Known to be within U8 c 1.1 for a distance of 1500 yds. Footpoint advance	
		1630	hill 9600 and again hill 1630. Batty ready to advance at 1630 but arty no barrage was laid down the advance was postponed indefinitely.	
		2100	Word received that Btn would be relieved by 172 Bde during the night and that the Btn would not be relieved by another Battn of this Bde but would join the other Battns of the Bde had been relieved.	1, Appx
		2330	Enemy attack on HUMBER REDOUBT by a party of Germans with Bombs & Machine Guns. Repulsed by "A" Coy. Casualties Killed 2 Other Ranks (Lieut R.T.A. CUMMING and 2/Lieut F.G. SMITH) and 14 O.R., D.O.W. 1 ; Wounded 1 Officer (Lieut C. BRUCE) and 132 O.R. N.Y.D.N. 9 O.R. Captured 70 Prisoners (approximately) 12 M.G's; 1 Field Gun; large numbers of S&A Ammunition Telephonic apparatus etc.	
	28/5/18	0205	Battn moved off from HUMBER REDOUBT by route march via HINDENBURG line to T.H.C. where a halt was made at 0500 for tea and return to be resumed. At 0730 march was resumed and arriving HENIN to MERCATEL arriving there about 0930 where Baths, hair-cut ect in the Bgt.	
		1000-1200	Bathing, clean up of equipment, clothes, feet etc.	
		1200-1400	Rgtl. Sergt-Major's parade and dinner.	…
		1400-1800	Checking of equipment.	
			Strength of Battn on coming out of action 6 Officers and 223 O.R. Congratulatory Telegram received from Gen. on congratulating the B.W. B.Dei & Brig. on their 5 days splendid work in the defence.	
			1 O.R. Wounded.	

WAR DIARY
INTELLIGENCE SUMMARY.
(Erase heading not required.)

Army Form C. 2118.

Place	Date	Hour	Summary of Events and Information	Remarks and references to Appendices
NEUCHATEL	29/8/16	0700	Reveille — 0900 Coy Inspection	
		1000	1000 - 1200 Checking of Regtl Equipment Shoes etc. Casualties nominal Rolldocks	
		1400	1400 - 1700 Reorganisation of Lewis gun sections and coys Capt J.G. Coats, Capt S.F. Picke and Lieut W.H. Aikman reported unit from 9th Nucleus	
		1800	Inspection of Baths by C.O.	
		2100	Lights out — 2/Lts MARTIN, BAIRD and WELSH joined unit for duty	
	30/8/16	0700	Reveille — 0700 Coy Inspection	
			1000 - 1200 Preparation of Coys and Platoons	
			1 Coy ordinary work in area	
		1400	1400 - 1600 Checking of Regtl Equipment, Stores and by nominal rolls.	
		1500	1500 Inspection of Baths by C.O. Baths inspected into 4 Coys of 2 Platoons each	
		2130	2130 Warning order received of move on 1st prox to new area.	
	31/8/16	0700	Reveille — 0930 Coy Inspection	
			1015 - 1200 Checking of men equipped me clothing of Baths.	
			1 Coy on Leiturge Book in Area.	

Army Form C. 2118.

WAR DIARY
or
INTELLIGENCE SUMMARY.
(Erase heading not required.)

Instructions regarding War Diaries and Intelligence Summaries are contained in F. S. Regs., Part II. and the Staff Manual respectively. Title pages will be prepared in manuscript.

Place	Date	Hour	Summary of Events and Information	Remarks and references to Appendices
	3/9/14	1400	1400 – 1700 – Preparation to move – following our All supplies &c advanced the road to a Central Brigade Dump at T1 d 4/2. 1800 Inspection of Rifles by C.O. Each man served with 2 pair trenches found socks & in extra 100 Rounds S.A.A. 2100 Lights out.	DLL

D. D. & L., London, L.C.
(10340) Wt W3500/P713 750,000 3/15 E 2688 Forms/C2118/16

Army Form C. 2118.

WAR DIARY
or
INTELLIGENCE SUMMARY.
(Erase heading not required.)

Instructions regarding War Diaries and Intelligence Summaries are contained in F. S. Regs., Part II. and the Staff Manual respectively. Title pages will be prepared in manuscript.

Place	Date	Hour	Summary of Events and Information	Remarks and references to Appendices
TABLE SHEWING INCREASES & DECREASES IN Batt^n CAMP STRENGTH DURING MONTH OF AUGUST 1918				

Camp Strength as at 1st Aug 1918 → Off 39, OR 865

Decreases
- Wounded – Off 4 OR
- Sick to Hosp 1 " 10 "
- Det Duties – 10
- Leave 1 " 20 "
- Sch of Instr^n 1 " 11 "
- Cadet Sch – " 2 "
- Pioneer Coy – " 34 "
- Rest Camp – " 3 "

Total: 3, 94 → 26, 771

Increases
- From Hosp (Sick) – Off 4 OR
- " Det Duties – " 3 "
- " Leave 1 " 25 "
- " Schools 4 " 9 "
- " Reinf Camp – " 1 "
- " Rest Camp 1 " 5 "

Total: 6, 50

Camp Strength as at 2400 on 7/8/18 → 32, 821

Decreases
- Died of wounds – Off 1 OR
- Killed – " 1 "
- Wounded – " 2 "
- Sick – " 12 "
- Det. Duties 2 " 9 "
- Leave 2 " 20 "
- Schools – " 4 "
- Rest Camp
- Hosp. NYDN. – " 1

Total: 4, 50 → 28, 771

Increases
- From Hosp (S) – Off 10 OR
- " " (W) – " 1 "
- " Det Duty – " 9 "
- " Leave 1 " 25 "
- " Schools 1 " 13 "

Total: 2, 58

Camp Strength as at 2400 on 14/8/18 → 30, 829

Decreases
- Died of wounds – Off 1 OR
- Wounded – " 3 "
- Sick 2 " 19 "
- Det Duties – " 4 "
- Leave 1 " 30 "
- Schools 2 " 8 "
- Rest Camp / NYDN 1 " 5 "

Total: Off 6, OR 71 → 24, 758

Increases
- From Hosp (S) – Off 9 OR
- " Det Duty – " 8 "
- " Leave 1 " 11 "
- " Schools 1 " 4 "
- " Rest Camp – " 3 "
- " Pioneer Coy – " 32 "
- M.O. 1 " – "

Total: 3, 67 → 27, 825

Decreases
- Killed 3 Off 30 OR
- Missing – " 3 "
- Wounded 10 " 319 "
- D of W – " 7 "
- NYDN – " 14 "
- Hosp. – " 15 "
- Det Duty 2 " 13 "
- Leave – " 32 "

Total: 15, 433 → 12, 392

Increases
- From Hosp (S) Off 14 OR
- " " (W) – " 1 "
- Det Duties 1 " 4 "
- Leave 1 " 19 "
- Schools 1 " 3 "
- Rein. – " 2 "
- NYDN

Total: 3, 45 → 15, 437

P.T.O.

D. D. & L., London, E.C.
(10340) Wt W3300/P713 750,000 5/18 E 2688 Forms/C2118/16

COPY No. 5

AMENDMENT TO BATTALION ORDER No 22
BY
LIEUT-COL J. ANDERSON C.M.G. D.S.O. COMMDG 1/6TH BN H.L.I.

1st AUGUST 1918

(1) (a) Rations will be transported by Light Railway from Ecoivre as follows:—

HD QRS. to TUNNEL DUMP, B.15.c.5.3.

All Coys to B.16.c.2.1. & whence by push truck to two front line Coys to B.22.c.8.0.

The N.C.O. & 5 men per Coy. will report at B.16.c.2.1. at 2100 nightly

(B) Water is laid on in area. Water points are as under

B.21.a.7.0.	1 tank	400 gallons
B.21.a.8.3.	1 "	400 "
B.21.a.7.7.	1 "	400 "
B.16.c.2.4.	2 tanks	400 "
B.15.c.5.2.	1 tank	300 "

Reserve water is also held at Coy. HQrs & Battn HQrs as follows:—

at each Coy H.Qr.   15 filled tins
"   "   Battn. H.Q.   30 filled tins

2. R.E. MATERIAL

Indents for R.E material for ensuing 24 hours must reach Battn HQrs by 0830.

3. SALVAGE

Divnl. Salvage Dump is at ROCLINCOURT A.29.c.8.3. Coy. Salvage Dumps will be formed & all salvage will be sent to TUNNEL DUMP (B.15.C.5.3) receipts being taken for same.

4. MEDICAL

R.A.P. is situated at B.15.c.5.1.
Relay Post   "   " B.20.b.1.9.
A.D.S. (LENS ROAD) " " A.28.a.7.6.
Main Dressing Station MAROEUIL L.4.a.3.8.

5. BURIAL

The following cemetries are available:— ROCLINCOURT A.29.c.1.5.
                                          ANZIN   G.1.d.7.3.
                                          MAROEUIL   F.27.a.9.5

Bodies will be sent to TUNNEL DUMP & evacuated by light Railway. Immediately any death takes place Battn H.Q. will be advised. A card showing number, name, unit, religion & date of death must accompany the body after all personal effects have been removed.

VI CANTEENS

Y.M.C.A. canteen is situated at B.15.c.6.1.

VII AMMUNITION

Brigade Ammunition & Ration Dumps are situated as follows:—

PILL BOX   B.21.a.25.80.
Hd. Qrs. DUMP B.14.a.65.10.
CAMPBELL "   B.20.a.8.1.

The latter dump is in BRIERLY HILL TRENCH.

D. McMartin
LIEUT.
A/ADJT. 1/6TH H.L.I.

Issued at 1600 1st Aug 1918

Copy No 1 to O.C. "A" Coy
     2 -   " "B" "
     3 -   " "C" "
     4 -   " "D" "
     5 - H.Qrs R.S.M. + FILE
     6 - C.O. , FILE

SECRET.   BATTALION ORDER Nº 2A.   Copy Nº 7
                            By
        LIEUT-COL. J. ANDERSON. C.M.G. D.S.O. Comm'dg. 4/6th Bn. H.L.I.

REF. MAPS. – TRENCH MAP. 51B.N.W. MARŒUIL & 00. WILLERVAL. 1/10,000   5th AUGUST. 1918.

1. The 52nd Division Southern Boundary will be altered to run as follows:— B.30.a.2.3 – H.3.6.8.2. – H.3.k.0.0. – H.2.c.0.8. – G.6.c.0.9. – G.3.6.9.3.
    Simultaneously with the above the Inter-Brigade Boundaries will be altered as follows:—
    (a) Between RIGHT (156TH) and CENTRE (157th) Brigades – A line from B.23.6.5.5. due WEST to point of junction of BACK TR. with POST LINE (inclusive to 156th Brigade) – down road through BAILLEUL – B.21.d.5.8. (inclusive to 156th Bde.) – B.21.c.6.6. – due WEST.
    (b) Between CENTRE Brigade (157th) and LEFT Brigade (155th) – from B.10.6.6.9. along TIRED ALLEY to its junction with BROWN LINE (inclusive to 157th Brigade) – TIRED ALLEY (inclusive to 155th Bde) as far as its junction with GREEN LINE – thence due WESTWARDS.
    (c) The Inter-Battalion Boundary – TOMMY ALLEY (inclusive to RIGHT Battalion)

2. Companies will take over areas as under:-
    (a) OUTPOST.
        OUTPOST LINE – BOW TRENCH – 2 Platoons.
        OUTPOST SUPPORT – BOW SUPPORT – 2 Platoons.
    "C" Coy. will take over all above line between Battalion Boundaries. Coy. or ½ Coy localities will be selected in and around BOW TRENCH for purposes of defence. The positions of localities selected must not be obvious to the enemy.
    (b) MAIN LINE.
        (1) "A" Coy. will take over POST LINE from junction with BACK TRENCH (exclusive) to B.22.a.55.95. (inclusive.)
            2 Platoons in POST LINE
            2 Platoons Support at Coy. H.Qs.
            Company HQs – B.21.6.65.20.
        O.C. "A" Coy. will arrange mutually with O.C. Left Coy. 1/7th Royal Scots as to hour at which he will relieve "A" Coy. in present area.
        (2) "B" Coy. will take over POST LINE from B.22.a.55.95 (exclusive) to its junction with OUSE ALLEY (inclusive)
            2 Platoons in POST LINE
            2 Platoons in Support at Coy. H.Qs.
            Company HQs situated at B.22.a.5.8.
        (3) "D" Coy. will take over POST LINE from junction with OUSE ALLEY (exclusive) to junction with TOMMY ALLEY (inclusive)
            3 Platoons & 1 Section in POST LINE.
            2 Sections in HULL POST – B.16.a.
        O.C. "D" Coy. will arrange mutually with the O.C. RIGHT Coy. 1/7th H.L.I. as to hour of taking over this POST.
            Company HQs in POST TRENCH.
    Relief will commence as early as possible after breakfast and will be completed by 1500.

3. TRENCH & AREA STORES.
    Area & Trench Stores will be left in areas as at present distributed and handed over to, or taken over by relieving Corps, receipts being taken or given for same.
    Duplicate copies of stores taken or handed over will be rendered to reach Orderly Room by 1800.

3. (CONTD).
Companies will organise the distribution of Trench Stores in their Coy area, if necessary on 6th inst. after relief ready for handing over to 1/5th H.L.I. on relief on 7th inst. All Lewis Guns & L.G. Magazines, Dixchies and other Regtl. & Coy Equipment will be manhandled to new areas.

4. SANITARY.
Usual clearance certificates re sanitation will be taken.

5. Completion of above alteration will be wired or sent by runner to Battalion H.Q. using Code Word "COAL".

D. Chamberlain
Lieut
C/Adjt. 1/6 H.L.I.

Issued at 2300 5.8.18.
Copy No 1 To O.C. A Coy
    2 - " B "
    3 - " C "
    4 - " D "
    5 - O.C. H.Qs Coy & S.M. & T.M.
    6 - C.O.

SECRET.   BATTALION ORDER No 25.   COPY No 5.
                                BY
        LIEUT-COL. J. ANDERSON. C.M.G. D.S.O. COMMDG. 1/6TH BN H.L.I.

REF MAPS - MARŒUIL. 1/20,000   &   WILLERVAL. 1/10,000   6TH AUGUST, 1918.

I. INFORMATION.
  (a)   The 5th H.L.I. will relieve 6th H.L.I. in RIGHT SUB SECTOR of
        OPPY SECTOR on 7th August.
           Relief will commence at 0900 and will be completed
        by 1400.
  (b)   A Coy. 5TH H.L.I. will relieve B Coy. 6TH H.L.I.
        B   "   "   "   "   A   "   "   "
        D   "   "   "   "   D   "   "   "
        C   "   "   "   "   C   "   "   "

II. DISPOSITIONS.
           On relief, 6th H.L.I. will take over same dispositions
        as those at present held by 5th H.L.I. as under:-
        A. Coy. - BROWN LINE from B.21.d.3.8. (exclusive) to junction
                  with OUSE ALLEY (inclusive) at present held
                  by B Coy. 5TH H.L.I.
        C. Coy. - BROWN LINE from LEFT of A. Coy. to junction with
                  AIRPLANE TRENCH (exclusive) at present held by C
                  Coy. 5TH H.L.I.
        B. Coy. - BROWN LINE from LEFT of C Coy. to junction with
                  TIRED ALLEY (inclusive) at present held by D Coy
                  5th H.L.I.
        D. Coy. - BRIERLY HILL TRENCH (B.14 a & c) from junction with
                  OUSE ALLEY (inclusive) to junction with TIRED
                  ALLEY at present held by A. Coy. 5TH H.L.I.
        BN. H.Qrs - is situated at B.15.a.25.30.
                    H.Q. personnel will move to new area in 3
                    parties at 10 minutes interval.

III. GUIDES.
  (a)   Corps will arrange to supply guides of 1 N.C.O. per Platoon
        for 5th H.L.I. as under:-
        1000 -- B. Coy. at junction of OUSE ALLEY & BROWN TRENCH.
        0930 -- A. "   "   "   "   "   "   "   "
        0900 -- C. "   "   "   "   "   " & POST TRENCH.
        0900 -- D. "   "   "   " TOMMY ALLEY & POST TRENCH.
  (b)   Guides (1 N.C.O per platoon) will be provided by 5th H.L.I. to be
        at points as under:-
        For A Coy. at junction of OUSE ALLEY & BROWN LINE.
         " D   "   "   "   "   "   "   "   "
         " C   "   "   "   "   "   "   "   "
         " B   "   "   "   " TOMMY ALLEY   "   "
  (c)   Route -
           Right, Centre, Post Line Coy. & Outpost Line Coy. will
        use OUSE ALLEY C.T.
           Left Post Line Coy will use TOMMY ALLEY.

IV. ADVANCED PARTIES.
           1 Officer per Coy, 1 N.C.O per platoon, 2 Signallers per
        Coy & 1 N.C.O & 4 Signallers from H.Qrs Coy will proceed to
        new area at 0700 to take over Trench Stores, Maps etc.
           1 Guide per Coy will be provided by 5th H.L.I. at positions
        as stated in para 3 b. at above hour.
           Advanced Parties of 5th H.L.I. will arrive on afternoon of 6th
        August.

V. LEWIS GUNS.

Each Company will hand over 176 Lewis Gun Magazines, taking over the same number in the new area. Receipts will be taken & given. The balance of magazines and all buckets will be taken to new area. O.C. H.Qs Coy. will take all the H.Qs Magazines and buckets to new area. O.C. Coys. will ensure that all magazines handed over are in a thoroughly clean condition.

All other stores will be manhandled to new areas.

VI. TRENCH STORES.

All Trench Stores, Log Books, Special Maps & plans will be handed & taken over, receipts being taken and given.

Duplicate receipts will be forwarded to reach Orderly Room by 2000 on 7th inst.

VII. SALVAGE.

Each man after relief of Battalion, when coming out of the trench will bring some salved article with them and take it to Salvage Dump.

O.C. Coys will ensure that this is made known to all ranks.

VIII. SUPPLIES.

Rations arrive nightly as under:-
A Coy - by Rail to TUNNEL DUMP.
C, B, & HQs - by Rail to LONGWOOD DUMP.
D Coy - by Limber to Coy H.Qs.

Rations for consumption on 7th are being sent up to 5 S.H.L.I. area tonight as per separate instructions issued.

Water is laid on in Coy Areas.

IX. WORK IN HAND.

All work in hand and work projected will be handed over in writing.

X. SANITARY.

Trenches & Coy Areas will be left in a scrupulously clean & sanitary condition. Usual clearing certificates will be taken.

XI. COMPLETION OF RELIEF.

Completion of Relief will be wired or sent by runner "Priority" to Battalion H.Qs, using the code word "TIRED".

XII. ACKNOWLEDGE.

Issued at 2000. 6-8-18.   Y/Adjt 1/6 H.L.I.

Copy No 1 To O.C. A Coy
  "   " 2 - " B "
  "   " 3 - " C "
  "   " 4 - " D "
  "   " 5 - C.O. HQs Coy, R.S.M & File
  "   " 6 - Q.M, T.O. & FILE

SECRET.

BATTALION ORDER No. 26.
By
MAJOR W. M. ANDERSON, M.C. Comdg. 1/6th Bn. H.L.I.

Copy No. 6.

REF MAPS - MAROEUIL 1/20,000 & WILLERVAL 1/10,000.   12th AUGUST 1918.

1. INFORMATION.

The 6th H.L.I. will relieve the 7th H.L.I. in the left SUBSECTOR of 157th Bde. SECTOR.
Relief will be completed by 1400.

2. DISPOSITIONS.

(1) A Coy. 6th H.L.I. will relieve   D Coy 7th H.L.I.
    "B"   —   —   —   "B" —   —
    "C"   —   —   —   "C" —   —
    "D"   —   —   —   "A" —   —

Battalion Boundaries
Right - TOMMY ALLEY - (exclusive)
Left - B.10.b.6.9. down new un-named extension of TIRED ALLEY leading from PLUMER Extension to YUKON thence down TIRED ALLEY as far as its junction with the GREEN LINE (all exclusive)

Battalion Head Quarters - B.15.c.6.5.
R.A.P. - B.15.c.45.15.

Guides of 1 N.C.O. per platoon for above Coys. will be at points as under:-

For "A" Coy. 0900 - junction of TOMMY ALLEY & BROWN LINE.
    "D"   0930 -   "   " TIRED ALLEY & BROWN LINE.
    "C"   0900 -   "   " AIRPLANE SWITCH & BROWN LINE.
    "B"   0930 -   "   " AIRPLANE SWITCH & BROWN LINE.

(2) D Coy 7th H.L.I. will take over dispositions of "A" Coy 6th H.L.I.
    "B" —   —   —   —   —   —   —   —   "C" —
    "A" —   —   —   —   —   —   —   —   "B" —
    "C" —   —   —   —   —   —   —   —   "D" —

Guides will be provided by Coys as under for 7th H.L.I:-

"A" Coy - junction of BROWN LINE & TOMMY ALLEY
"B" —   "   " AIRPLANE SWITCH & BROWN LINE.
"C" —   "   " TOMMY ALLEY & BROWN LINE.
"D" —   "   " TIRED ALLEY & BROWN LINE.

3. COMMENCEMENT OF RELIEF.

Companies will commence relief as under:-

"A" Coy. -0900. Route - BROWN LINE & TOMMY ALLEY
"D" "   -0930. Route - TIRED ALLEY.
"B" "   -0930. Route - TIRED ALLEY - BROWN LINE & AIRPLANE SWITCH.
"C" "   -0900. Route - AIRPLANE SWITCH.

4. ADVANCED PARTIES.

Advanced parties have proceeded as already detailed.

5. LEWIS GUNS.

Each Coy. will hand over & take over 192 Magazines (loaded) without buckets and H.Q. 48 Magazines (loaded) without buckets, receipts being taken & given for same.
O.C. Coy. will ensure Magazines are in a thoroughly serviceable and clean condition.

6. **TRENCH STORES.**
Trench Stores, Log Books, Special Maps & Plans will be handed & taken over & receipts taken & given. Duplicate receipts will be forwarded to each Orderly Room by 2000 on 13th inst.
If 7th H.L.I. Advanced Parties do not arrive before Coys are due to leave present area an officer or N.C.O. will be left to hand over Area Stores.

7. **S O S Posts etc.**
All details re SOS, Sentry & Gas Posts will be carefully taken over and also a detailed statement of work in progress & projected in writing.

8. **SUPPLIES**
Rations come up nightly by Lorry & Train to TUNNEL DUMP and from there are pushed forward on Trolleys to Coy. Areas. Usual Ration Parties under C.Q.M. Sgts. will be sent to above Dump at 2100 nightly.
Water is laid on in the Areas.

9. **SALVAGE.**
An Salvage Dump is situated at TUNNEL DUMP where all salvage from Coys will be sent.

10. **SANITATION**
The usual Clearance Certificates re sanitation will be taken & given. O.C. Coys will ensure their Area is left in a thoroughly clean and sanitary condition.

11. **REPORTS**
Completion of Relief will be wired or sent by Runner "Priority" to Battalion Headquarters using the Code word "ADONIS".

12. **ACKNOWLEDGE**

D H Mackenzie
Lieut.
A/Adjt. 1/6th H.L.I.

Issued at 1615 12.8.18.

Copy No 1 — to O.C. A Coy
       2 —   "   B "
       3 —   "   C "
       4 —   "   D "
       5 — CO, HQ, RSM & File
       6 — QM & TO
       7 — WAR DIARY

SECRET.   BATTALION ORDER Nº 29.   Copy Nº 7.
BY
MAJOR W. M. ANDERSON. M.C. COMMDG. 1/6TH BN. H.L.I.

REF. MAPS. MARŒUIL 1/20.000, & LENS 1/100.000.   16TH AUGUST. 1918.

1. INFORMATION.
   (a) The 52nd Division will be relieved in the line by the 8th & 51st Divisions.
   (b) The 21st Infantry Brigade will relieve the 157th Infantry Bde. in the OPPY SECTOR.

2. (a) 1st Bn Worcestershire Regt. will relieve 1/6th H.L.I.
   (b) A. Coy 1st Worcesters. will relieve C Coy 1/6 H.L.I.
       B "   do.   do.   B   "   "
       C "   do.   do.   A   "   "
       D "   do.   do.   D   "   "
   After relief, Companies will proceed independently to Embussing Point at A.11.a.7.8. at whence they will be conveyed by Motor Lorry to DURHAM & LANCASTER CAMPS, ST. ELOI.
   LIEUT. C. BRUCE is appointed embussing Officer & 2/LIEUT. D. HOGG debussing Officer. The latter will proceed with the 1st bus to ST. ELOI and the former by the last.

3. ROUTE
   For both relieving unit & Battalion, when relieved, route to be used is PLANK ROAD and TIRED ALLEY.
   A distance of 200 yards between platoons will be maintained when crossing the ridge before dark.

4. GUIDES.
   Each Coy will detail 1 Officer & 1 N.C.O. per platoon, H.Qrs. 1 Officer & 1 N.C.O. to meet relieving Battalion at head of TIRED ALLEY at 6 P.M. Route – TIRED ALLEY.

5. ADVANCED PARTIES
   Advanced parties will arrive on morning of 16th from 1st Worcestershire Regiment.

6. AREA STORES.
   All Area Stores, Defence Schemes, Log Books, Sketch Maps, Photographs will be handed over & receipts taken. Details of pending gas operations will be carefully handed over.
   Duplicate receipts will be furnished to reach Orderly Room by 1200 on 17th inst.

7. WORK IN HAND S.O.S. ETC.
   Details of Work in progress and Work Policy and also full details re S.O.S. Sentry & Gas Posts, Patrols etc. will be handed over.

8. TRANSPORT.
   No Transport will be available. All Lewis Guns & L.G. Magazines, Dixies & Cooking Utensils will be manhandled from Coy Areas to embussing Point. Greatcoats & W.P. Sheets will be neatly rolled & tied securely to the Waist belt.

9. RIFLES, INSPECTION OF.

All Rifles will be unloaded prior to leaving the trenches and carefully inspected by platoon Commanders. S.B.R's will be worn in the Alert position as far as line drawn between ROCLINCOURT (Inclusive) and NEUVILLE ST VAAST (exclusive) after which they may be carried in the "Ready" position.

10. ALARM.

In the event of an alarm or enemy attack during the relief, troops will halt and man the nearest defences, reporting their dispositions at once to Brigade HQrs.

11. SUPPLIES.

Rations will be drawn as at present from Supply Dump at ECOIVRES.

12. TRANSPORT & Q.M. PARTIES ETC.

These will remain at their present positions in ECOIVRES. Pipe Band & Orderly Room will rejoin on morning of 17th inst. All personnel of Brigade Pioneer Coy & Nucleus will rejoin on the morning of 17th inst. They will be rationed up to and including 18th inst.

13. DISCIPLINE.

Battalion Bounds will be marked by Battalion Boards. No man will leave his battalion area without a pass & without being properly dressed.

14. SANITATION.

Trenches Dugouts, & Coy Area will be left in a thoroughly clean and sanitary condition.

The usual clearance certificates will be obtained.

15. REPORTS.

Completion of Relief will be wired to Battn HQrs "Priority" or sent by runner using Code Word "JOCK".

16. ACKNOWLEDGE.

Issued at 0700 16.8.18.

Lieut
A/Adjt 1/6 H.L.I.

Copy No 1 to O.C. A Coy
" " 2 — — B "
" " 3 — — C "
" " 4 — — D "
" " 5 — C.O. HQ Coy R.S.M. & File
" " 6 — Q.M. & T.O.
" " 7 — WAR DIARY.

SECRET.   Copy No. 2

157th Infantry Brigade Order No. 122.

Ref. Map. 1/40,000 36 B.&.C.   15th August, 1918.
    1/40,000 51 B.&.C.
    1/100,000 LENS 11.

1. The 52nd Division will be relieved in the line by the 8th and 51st Divisions in accordance with Table "A" on the reverse.

2. The 24th Infantry Brigade will relieve the 157th Infantry Brigade in the OPPY Section.

3. All details of relief, including guides, will be arranged between C.O.s concerned.

4. Defence Schemes, Log books, Maps, 1/10,000 and 1/20,000, Photographs, and all trench stores will be handed over, and receipts taken. Details of pending gas operations will be carefully handed over.

5. During the relief there will be no movement EAST of the PONT du JOUR - THELUS Ridge line before 6 p.m.

6. (i) In the event of an alarm or enemy attack during the relief, troops will halt and man the nearest defences, reporting their dispositions at once to Brigade Headquarters.
(ii) C.O.s will remain with their opposite numbers and await orders.

7. Brigade Headquarters will close at A.28.b.30.35 on completion of relief.

8. Completion of relief will be wire "Priority" to Brigade Headquarters, using the code word "ACHA".

9. A C K N O W L E D G E.

            C.S. Stirling-Cookson.
                   Captain,
           Brigade Major, 157th Infantry Brigade.

Issued at H.P.m. on 15/8/18.

Copy No. 1 to 5th H.L.I.
    2 6th H.L.I.
    3 7th H.L.I.
    4 157th L.T.M.B.
    5 2nd L.F.A.
    6 413th Fld. Coy. R.E.
    7 220th Coy. A.S.C.
    8 52nd Division.
    9 24th Infantry Bde.
    10 8th Division.
    11 155th Inf. Bde.
    12 156th Inf. Bde.
    13 "A" & "Q".
    14 Bde. Sig. Officer.
    15) War Diary.
    16)
    17 File.

TABLE "A".

Serial No.	Date of Relief.	From. Unit.	From.	Relieved To.	Relieved by.
1	16/17th August.	157th Bde. Hqrs.	A.28.b.30.35.	WHITE HOUSE, Mt. St. ELOY.	24th Bde. Hqrs.
2	"	5th H.L.I.	Front Line (Right).	ROCLINCCURT West Camp.	2nd Northampton. Regt.
3.	"	6th H.L.I.	Front Line (Left).	DURHAN and LANCASTER Camps.	1st Worcestershire Regt.
4.	"	7th H.L.I.	BROWN LINE (Support).	FRASER Camp.	1 Sherwood Foresters.
5.	"	157th L.T.M.B.	Line.	FRASER Camp.	24th L.T.M.B.

Reliefs will take place in following order :- Serials 2, 3. Simultaneously No. 2 using CONCRETE Road and OUSE ALLEY, No. 3 using Plank Road and TIRED ALLEY. No. 4 using OUSE and TIRED ALLEYS, No.5 under their own arrangements.

A distance of 200 yards between platoons will be maintained when crossing the Ridge before dark.

SECRET.

157th Infantry Brigade Administrative Instructions No.113.
Issued with reference to Brigade Order No. 122.

15th August, 1918.

On relief by the 24th Infantry Brigade, Battalions will move to Camps as under :-

5th H.L.I.	ROCLINCOURT WEST
6th H.L.I.	DURHAM & LANCASTER CAMPS, MT.ST.ELOI.
7th H.L.I.	FRASER CAMP, MONT ST. ELOI.
157th L.T.M. BTY.	" " " "
Brigade Hqrs.	WHITE HOUSE, " " "

MOVE.

5th H.L.I. will move by march, route the remainder of the Brigade by Busses which bring up relieving Battalions.

TRANSPORT & Q.M. PARTIES.

These will remain at their present positions in ECOIVRES.

SUPPLIES.

Rations will be drawn as at present from Supply Dump at ECOIVRES. Rations for 5th H.L.I. will be sent up by Battalion Transport.

AREA STORES.

All Trench and Area Stores will be handed over and receipts taken. Duplicate lists of stores handed over will be forwarded to Brigade Hqrs by 1800 on 17th inst.
Duplicate lists of Area Stores taken over will also be forwarded to Brigade Hqrs.

DUTIES.

Battalion on Duty 17th August.	7th H. L. I.
" " " 18th "	6th H. L. I.

DISCIPLINE.

Battalion Bounds will be marked by Battalion Boards. No man will leave his Battalion Area without a pass and without being properly dressed.

NUCLEUS & BRIGADE PIONEER COY.

All personnel of the Brigade Pioneer Coy., and NUCLEUS will rejoin their units at Mont St ELOI on 17th inst. They will be rationed up to and including the 18th.

ADVANCED PARTIES.

1 Officer & 6 O.R. per Battalion (less 5th H.L.I.) and 1 Officer from L.T.M. Bty., will report to Brigade Hqrs representative at WHITE HOUSE, MONT ST. ELOI at 3 p.m. on 16th inst., to take over Camps. An Officer and Billetting party from 5th H.L.I. will report at present Brigade Hqrs at 3 p.m. on 16th inst., to take over Camp.

ACKNOWLEDGE

H M Hewison
Staff Captain, 157th Infantry Brigade.

"A" Form
MESSAGES AND SIGNALS.

Army Form C. 2121
(in pads of 100.)

Prefix	Code	m.	Words.	Charge.	This message is on a/c of	Recd. at	m.
Office of Origin and Service Instructions.		Sent			Service.	Date	
		At	m.			From	
		To					
		By		(Signature of "Franking Officer.")	By		

TO — 6th H.L.I.

| Sender's Number. | Day of Month. | In reply to Number. | AAA |
| OK 282 | 15 | | |

Please arrange following guides tomorrow aaa 1 to be at Bde Hq at 8 am to meet advance party of relieving Battn and guides at head of TIRED ALLEY at 6 pm to meet relieving Battn.

From	157th
Place	
Time	

SECRET   BATTALION ORDER No. 30.   Copy No. 5

By

MAJOR W. M. ANDERSON M.C. Commdg 1/6 H.L.I.

17th AUGUST, 1918

REF MAPS — LENS 11. 1/100,000 & LENS 36 B. 1/40,000

1. INFORMATION.

The 6th H.L.I will move to CHATEAU DE LAHAIE Area on 17th Aug. & will be accommodated in CANADA CAMP X 7.a.

2. BATTALION PARADES.

Battalion will parade on Alarm Post (vacant ground S.W. of LANCASTER Camp, ready to move off at 2.15 p.m. Band will parade with Battalion.

Dress:- Full Marching Order, Tam o'Shanter, Steel Helmet securely fastened on back of Pack (with exception of Band, who tie inside packs). Greatcoats neatly rolled round the Pack, W.P. Sheet neatly rolled & tied to Pack, Water Bottles filled & kept filled. Equipment must be thoroughly cleaned & brass work polished.

Dress:- Officers — Sam Browne Belt & Revolver, Field Dressing, Steel Helmet, Iron Rations, Water Bottles Filled. This does not apply to mounted Officers.

3. MARCH DISCIPLINE

The strictest March discipline will be maintained. Coys will march in fours & keep to right of road - each four being covered off from front to rear. Distances to be

(2)

maintained on the march – Between Platoons 5 yards – Between Coys 100 yds – Between Transport & Battalion 100 yds Between Battalions 500 yds.

There will be a 10 minutes halt at each clock hour.

4. ADVANCED PARTIES

Advanced Parties proceeded as already detailed.

5. TRANSPORT

Transport will accompany Battn. All Lewis Guns & Magazines will be stacked on Main Road opposite LANCASTER Camp by 1100. The RSM will detail a Loading Party & Baggage Guard from men unfit to march (not to exceed 1 NCO & 6 Other Ranks). The T.O. will arrange to have all Limbers at this point by 1300 & loaded by 1330.

All Officers Kits, Mess Stores, Coy Boxes & Stores, Cooking Utensils etc will be at side of Road opposite to entrance to FRASER CAMP by 1230 ready for loading & loaded by 1300. One Lorry will report at Bde HQ at 1200 for conveyance of this baggage. The T.O. will have remainder of Transport ready loaded up to move with the Battalion by 1400.

6. SANITATION

Camps will be left in a scrupulously

+sanitary 5
clean for action. Camp will be
ready for Commanding Officers
inspection by 1300.

ᵐ ACKNOWLEDGE.

DLMacmillan
                    Lieut
               a/Adjt 16H.L.I

Issued at _____ 17.8.18

Copy N° 1 — OC A
     „ „ 2 — „ B
     „ „ 3 — „ C
     „ „ 4 — „ D   Teh
     „ „ 5 — CO, Adj, Sgy RSM
     „ „ 6 — QM + O.

"A" Form.
MESSAGES AND SIGNALS.

Army Form C. 2121.
(In pads of 100.)

TO: 5th 6th 7th LTMB

Sender's Number.	Day of Month.	In reply to Number.	A A A
BM 1/55	23		

Cancel verbal instructions as regards locations selected for units following will now be occupied aaa 5th HLI to Square M 32 c+d 6th HLI to BRICKWORKS S.2 d & 3 c. 7th HLI as before aaa at Passing point R 34 b 58. BLAIREVILLE WOOD units will march Eastwards in Artillery formation aaa Bde HQrs. will be old Bn HQrs. S 2 (+4). Brickworks

Recd 1800
WMG

From: 147 Bde
Place:
Time: 5.55 pm.

Mosley Capt

Copy N°

154th Infantry Brigade Order N° 130.
Reference Sheet 51 B. S. W.

Secret.   24th Aug 18.

1. The Army will advance to allow the enemy no respite in this retreat. Accordingly the 52nd Division will conform to the movements of troops on its flanks.

2. The 154th Brigade will pass through the line at present held by the 156th Brigade & which runs approximately from T.2.c.5.0. to T.1.a.8.8. The 154th Brigade will attack eastward maintaining touch with the 51st Div which will be attacking on our right. The 154th Brigade will finally assault and consolidate that portion of the Hindenburg line between T.5.a and N.34.d. Both front and support systems to be captured. ~~This 5th line will~~

3. The 156th Brigade will advance on the left of the 154th Brigade at 7 a m to the road N.32.b.7.6 and to N.26 Cent conforming to movement of 154th Brigade and being echeloned in left rear. ~~~~

4. The 6th H.L.I will attack on the right. The 5th H.L.I will attack on the left. The 7th H.L.I and 157th L.T.M.B. (less 2 Sections) C Company 52nd Battalion, M.G.C (less 1 Section) will be in Brigade reserve.

5. The approach march will be timed to bring the two assaulting Battalions into line held by the 156th Brigade by 6.45 A.M. The attack will be carried forward from this line punctually at 7 A.M in conjunction with the 56th Division on our right and our troops on our left, the 156th Brigade following echeloned behind our left FLANK. For the approach march, the 6 & 5th H.L.I will start in artillery formation from the W side of the Railway running North & South from Ooarc. The 6th H.L.I on the right with its right at the junction of the road with the Railway at S.3.d.8.8 (S.9.c.8.2) and a frontage of approximately 800 yards. The 5th H.L.I forming up on the left. Advance from here to commence at 4.15 A.M. The advance to be regulated so that the leading lines do not

pass through the 156th Brigade lines will at 6:45 A.M.

6. The 7th H.L.I. and other troops in Brigade Reserve will move to a position of assembly, so as to follow about 1½ miles in rear of 6th H.L.I. when the latter move forward at 4:15 A.M. During the advance the 6th H.L.I. will direct.

7. O.C. 154th L.T.M.B. will detail 2 Guns to 6th H.L.I. and 2 Guns to the 5th H.L.I. to report on the Railway line at 4 A.M. O.C. 154th L.T.M.B. will be prepared to reconnoitre and place the remainder of the guns in position to cover consolidation.

8. O.C., M.G. Coy will detail 1 Section of Guns for an independent mission as a Battery of opportunity. He will, with the remainder of his guns take every advantage of covering the advance. 1 Section to be always in Brigade reserve following in rear of 7th H.L.I. After the capture of the final objective he will dispose his guns in depth to cover the consolidation & repel counter-attacks.

9. On arrival in the 156th Brigade lines the 6th H.L.I. will at once gain close

contact with left, 56th Division maintaining it throughout the attack.

10. During the attack the 6th H.L.I will assist. All company officers will work on compass bearings.

11. Rations for 24th plus 1 day's Iron Rations will be carried on the man.

12. Frequent information & situation reports will be sent to Brigade H.Qrs.

13. Prisoners will be sent back under a small escort to behind the railway at starting point.

14. Brigade H.Qrs will be at S 5 d 8 3

15. Acknowledge.

J. Stirling-Cook
Captain
Brigade Major, 157th Inf Bde

MESSAGES AND SIGNALS.

Army Form C. 2121
(In pads of 100.)

TO O.C. 6th Highland Light Infantry Bn.

Sender's Number.	Day of Month.	In reply to Number.	AAA
101 X	15		

Bde Orders as to move up via PLANK Rd and TIRED Alley. Will you please have guides i.e. one per platoon and one per Coy and Bn HQ at the junction of Tired Alley and the Plank Road by 5/45 P.M.

W C Stevens Capt
Comdg 1/Worc R

Secret.   BMx/301

154th Infantry Brigade Order No. B2.

25/9/18.

1. The 154th Bde will alter & establish its dispositions as follows to-day with the intention of carrying out a prepared attack on the HINDENBURG LINE (not to-day) in conjunction with the troops on our RIGHT.

2. Dispositions:-
   (a) Observation line to be about 250 yds from HINDENBURG LINE
   (b) Main Line of Resistance (sunken rd T3b & T.4c)
   (c) Reserve Line (Road through T.3A. c & D.)

   The 6th & 7th A.&S.H. will be in (a) & (b) & (say (b)) suitably placed between (a) & (c). The 5th A.&S.H. in (c).

3. The adjustment will be carried out gradually to-day without attracting attention, the 7th A.&S.H. taking over from 5th A.&S.H., the latter going into the RESERVE Line.
   The adjustment will be arranged between all 3 C.Os.

4.

1. Strong Patrols must be sent out by day and night to reconnoitre & bring in information regarding the HINDENBURG LINE which is to be systematically attacked.

2. 1st K.O.Y.L.I. will occupy SUMMIT TRENCH & if possible FMT SWITCH & T 1 d & 15 c respectively without serious fighting.

3. 1st K.O.Y.L.I. will be in close touch with the Troops of the Division on our RIGHT Flank.

J.R. Stirling
Captain
Brigade Major 101st Inf. Brigade.

Secret

154th Infantry Brigade Order No. 131.

24/9/18

1. Units will maintain their present line & watch the outer flanks, both of which are exposed.

2. Positions will be strengthened against counter attacks. Present front line will be Main Line of Resistance.

3. 12 M.G's are disposed in depth on the Brigade front.

4. Defensive Patrols will ~~cover the front~~ be sent out to cover the front. 7th H.L.I. will send a patrol to be in touch with 156th Bde. on the left.

5. 9 Bdes of Field Artillery are ~~covering~~ presently covering the Bde Front & will put down an S.O.S. on HINDENBURG Line when called for.

6. Bde Hqrs will remain at T.2.c.2.8.

7. 154 Bde will be prepared to attack early to morrow morning. Order of Battle:- 5th H.L.I. in Reserve, 6th H.L.I. on RIGHT, 7th H.L.I. on LEFT, M.G. LINE as for to-day.

8. Acknowledge.

B. Stirling Cook
Captain
Brigade Major, 154th Inf. Bde.

B.M.X.1304

Secret.

5th. 6th. 7th. H.L.I. (Lt.M.B. for information)

I. O.C. Bns. will send out one officer's patrols at once to work in the direction of the HEMIK Hill & HINDENBERG LINE to see if the enemy will show his hand.

As the Leavies are still firing on Hindenberg line the patrols must not go too close up to that line.

This patrolling will be constantly kept up, the patrols however must not get involved but are to obtain information, this information to be wired to Bns Hqrs. as soon as received.

II. The 155. Bde have captured the Hindenberg line and are working down that line to cross our front clearing the Hindenberg line as they go.

As soon as the 155 Bde. are seen approaching our front Each Bn. will then send out 2 or 3 patrols, these patrols will not however get mixed up with the 155. Bde but are merely to make enemy think we are about to launch an attack.

III. MONCHY has been captured by the
Canadians & our troops are on the
E. outskirts of Guémappe

IV. Acknowledge

S Stirling Cookson Capt
Bde. Major 11th? Bde.

Ref. 1235

26/8/18.

5th. Hold their patrol to
SKETIN Hill
6th & 7th. Hold to their own
fronts
M

Widely extended order; return 1600.
Send back runners with information

Secret.

157. Bde. order No. 134.   26/Aug/18

I. The 155 Bde. is cleaning HINDENBERG LINE as far as SENSEE River and will cross the river and establish itself about FONTAINE-CROISILLES.

The 156. Bde. with objective the Road in U.1.d. 8.9 to Q.32 central will be Echeloned to the left rear of the 155. Bde.

Recd 1910

II. The 155. Bde. is dropping one Battn. at HENIN HILL.

III. The 7th H.L.I. will take over HENIN HILL from this Battn. of 155. Bde. 7th H.L.I. to face N & E.

IV. The 6th H.L.I. will concentrate in the area T.4.a. T.3.b. & d. (Exclusive of Sunken Rd. in T.3.d) & T.4.c.

V. The 5. H.L.I. will be located in the vicinity of the Sunken Road T.3.d. T.3.c. & if necessary in T.9.b.

VI. The 157. Bde. is in Divisional Reserve.

VII. Acknowledge.

J. S. Stirling Cookson Capt.
Bde. Maj. 157. Bde

Secret. Addendum to 157. Bde. order
                    No. 134.

1. O.C. C. Coy 52. Bn. M.G.C. will detail
4. Machine Guns to be placed at the
disposal of O.C. 7. H.L.I.
The remainder of C. Coy. 52 Bn. M.G.C
will concentrate in the area allotted
to 5. H.L.I.

2. The L.T.M.B. will concentrate also in
area allotted to 5 H.L.I.

                    J. Stirling Cooke Capt
                    Brig.Maj: 157. Bde.

26/8/18.

Secret.

154th Inf. Bde. Order No. 135.

24/8/18.

1. 154 Bde. will attack at 9.20 a.m. to day under barrage & will capture FONTAINE CROISILLES & continue advance S.E. and take RIENCOURT. V.24.

2. 6th & 4th A.L.I. will be the assaulting Baths. 6th A.L.I. on right 4th A.L.I. on Left & 5th A.L.I. in Reserve.

3. Assault Baths will assemble along the line of SUMMIT TR. from T.4.d.6.0 to junction with HINDENBURG SUPPORT Line at N.35.c.3.4. Approach to this line to be concealed from FOOLEY TRENCH.

4. Frontage for 6th A.L.I. will be from the RIGHT of this line to where the track crosses it in T.5.c.3.9. Frontage for 4th A.L.I. from there to LEFT, ~~ready to advance from there~~

5. Baths will be ready to advance at 9.20 a.m.
at 9.30 am Barrage will come down on FOOLEY TR. from T.11.a.3.4 to ~~T.5.b.~~ T.5.b.1.9 & remain down to 9.36.a.m. by which time the assaulting Baths will have moved forward ~~to the~~ close up under the barrage. At 9.36 a.m Barrage & assaulting troops will move forward at 100 yds per 4 mins direct on FONTAINE CROISILLES. 4th A.L.I. ~~directing~~ will direct

6. 155 Bde will mop up HINDENBURG LINE behind our attack as far as FOP LANE. The Left of 4th A.L.I. will be directed on S. end of FONTAINE CROISILLES.

7. 156th Bde will be attacking under a separate Barrage on our

LEFT. The Right of this Bde is being directed on N. end of FONTAINE CROISILLES.

8. The Barrage for 52nd Division will remain on general line of UNA TR. EAST of FONTAINE CROISILLES for 30 minutes after when it will lift & 154 Bde will push on to RIENCOURT & 156 Bde to HENDECOURT.

9. On approaching FONTAINE CROISILLES, 5th A.L.I in Reserve will close up 1 Coy close behind 4th A.L.I. to mop up FONTAINE CROISILLES. This Coy will follow the Bde when its mission is finished.

10. While Barrage is on general line UNA TR for 30 minutes, the Assault Battns will re-organise & get their direction for RIENCOURT, the advance to which should be continued without further orders the moment the barrage lifts.

11. 5th A.L.I in reserve will form up behind the junction of 6th & L.I. & 4th A.L.I. WEST of SUMMIT TRENCH & follow the advance one mile behind.

12. L.I.H. Bty will follow as soon as transport can be ~~obtained~~ provided. 4 M.Gs will follow close behind the leading wave. The remainder of the guns will support the advance under separate orders fr their C.O.

13. Advance Bde. HQrs will be established in FAT SWITCH where track crosses it in T.5.C.3.9. Frequent reports showing location of front lines & progress must be sent in.

14. 56th Divn will be attacking on our RIGHT, forming up in

SUMMIT TR. post 2 of 6th A.L.I.
15.   Acknowledge.

J S Tillingcook
                        Captain
          Brigade Major 154th Inf Brigade.

On His Majesty's Service.

157/52/

6th M.D.L.I
Sep. 18

12-H
80 rebels

WAR DIARY / INTELLIGENCE SUMMARY

(Erase heading not required)

6 HILL Volume 3. SEPTEMBER 1918. REF. MAP FRANCE 51B SW 1/20,000 865 EDITION (See Appx. 1.9.18)

Place	Date	Hour	Summary of Events and Information	Remarks and references to Appendices
MERCATEL.	1/9/18	0030	Orders received to attack following over from FAT SWITCH.	Appx. 1/9/18
		0500	Reveille.	
		0715	Battalion moved by route march to FAT SWITCH, TCC 119 arriving there 1015.	
		1300	Commanding Officer and Adjutant went to shot demonstration and conference.	
		1600	Commanding Officer, R.S.M., signallers and all officers (see Appx. 3/9/18)	
		1900	Orders received for moves and following (see Appx. 3/9/18) 2030 R.S.M. call. 2100 Lights out.	
			Lost C.H. HILLS to R.A.F.	
FAT SWITCH 2/9/18		0330	Reveille.	Appx. 2/9/18
		0530	Battalion moved by route march to trenches in B.18 a, arriving there at 0600.	
		0625	Orders received to move to new area. (see H.Q. 29 B.)	
		0830	Battalion moved via HINDENBURG LINE I, D.20.a enemy was found at 0915	
		1615	Warning order received to be prepared to take over 157 Inf. Bde. Line — Commanding Officer and	
		1700	OC Companies reconnoitred front line — BULLECOURT — TANK AVENUE. (see Appx 2/9/18) Appx 2/9/18	
			Was received the V Corps Staff Commander Dividing Officer and	
			V.2.d and D. Heavy artillery. Remade CASTRICOURT RIES DU BOUCHET, with cavalry	
			new positions high ground by Railway anap. 63–64 steering railway in D.4. V.23, V.29	
		1930	Moving orders received.	
		2015	Orders received to stand down.	
CROISILLES. 3/9/18		0015	Warning order received that 157 Inf Bde were to attack in the morning.	Appx 3/9/18
		0300	Operation Orders received (see Appx. 3/9/18)	
		0330	Reveille.	
		0500	Battalion moved by route march via BULLECOURT to REINCOURT, there dump issued "A" & "B" Companies. Thence it moved to artillery formation in T.B. 125° to the HINDENBURG SUPPORT LINE	Appx 3/9/10
			V.15 a and c. (Map Ref. France 51 NE 1/20000) being in position by 0930.	
		1000	QUÉANT AID PROVIDED (Map Ref. France 51 NE above) found to have been evacuated by the enemy.	
		1100	Orders received to take up and form whilst the remainder went immediately forward into position. (Appx. 3.9.10)	

WAR DIARY
INTELLIGENCE SUMMARY.

(Erase heading not required.)

Army Form C. 2118.

Instructions regarding War Diaries and Intelligence Summaries are contained in F.S. Regs, Part II. and the Staff Manual respectively. Title pages will be prepared in manuscript.

Place	Date	Hour	Summary of Events and Information	Remarks and references to Appendices
PRONVILLE	3/9/18 (contd)	1530	Batt. still in position on attitude HINDENBURG SUPPORT LINE. A and B Coys in Shelter Road D.4.d. Battalion Hqrs (A and B Bn) (D10) Light Railway D.3. Map Ref. France 57c. N.E. 1/20,000	Appendix 3/9/18.
		1645	Orders received to move up to MELBOURNE STREET — D.10.a.+.c. (see App. 3.9.18.)	
		1930	Move completed.	
		2130	Warning order received that 52nd Division would form Corps Support (XVII Corps)	
			W.O. received that 63rd (Naval) Division was forming on the line of the Canal du NORD.	
			Casualties: 4 Other Ranks (wounded)	
	4/9/18	0400	Reveille.	
			Congratulatory message received from Field Marshal Commander in Chief.	
			During the day Company Inspections and Salvage were carried out.	
			Warning order received that 52nd Division would go into Corps Reserve on night of 5th/6th Sep., changing over with the 56th Division.	
		1900	Heavy enemy barrage put down on road E.7 — D.8 — D.24. Enemy counterattacks heavy without success.	Appx. 4/9.
	5/9/18	0600	Reveille.	
			Company inspections and Salvage were carried out during the day in 2D.10.	
		1100	Move orders received. (see App. 5/9/18.)	Appendix 5/9/18
		1230	Move orders cancelled.	
			Casualties: 1 O.R. wounded (and remaining on duty.)	
	6/9/18	0400	Reveille.	
			Company inspection and Salvage in 2D.10. A/t PRONVILLE carried out during day.	Appendix 6/9/18.
		1000	W/O received that 63rd Division relieve Bn F.2 a/c, E.8.b/c, E.4.a/c, E.3.a/c, E.4.b/c, SWAN LANE.	
		1120	Warning order received to withdraw on following day to area B.2.5.5.7.8. (See App. 6.9.18.)	
		2030	Warning order received to withdraw to 7.30.a.c. on following day.	
		2330	Move orders received. (see App. 7/9/18)	

LIEUT. J.W. BRUCE, E.A. HITCHCOCK, and J.M. STEWART report for duty.

WAR DIARY
or
INTELLIGENCE SUMMARY.
(Erase heading not required)

Army Form C. 2118.

Instructions regarding War Diaries and Intelligence Summaries are contained in F.S. Regs., Part II. and the Staff Manual respectively. Title pages will be prepared in manuscript.

Place	Date	Hour	Summary of Events and Information Map Ref. S1/2 S.W / 1/20,000 5 1/2 N.E 5 4/2 N.W	Remarks and references to Appendices
PROIVILLE	7/9/18	0400 0600	Reveille. Battalion moves by Route march to T.30.C. via QUÉANT, MOREUIL, LONGATTE arriving there at 0915. Bivouac area allotted and prepared.	Appendix 7/9/18
		1930 2000	Commanding Officers conference with all Officers. Lieut. N. MARTIN to III Army School (H) Lieut. H.G. SPENCE rejoins from 2 Army Rest Camp Capt. J. FARQUHAR and 2/Lieut. T. CRAIG report from Nucleus 2/Lieuts. J. McNICOL, J.H. SMITH, 2/Lieut. H.J. RYPER and J.C. MOODIE join unit for duty. 2000 - Roll Call. Capt. J.F. KING to U.K. on furlough.	
CROISILLES	8/9/18	0700 0900 - 1130 12.30 8.00 - 16.30 16.00 18.30 20.30	Reveille. Battalion Baths & R.T.I.D.2.II. Company Inspections. Commanding Officer to conference at Brigade H.Qrs. Hunter Parades by Companies. Commanding Officer holds conference with Company Commanders 20.00 Roll Call. Voluntary Church Service on Klaxon Post. Lights out.	
	9/9/18	0600 0900 0930 0930-1230 1400-1500 1800-1900 2000 2030	Reveille. Inspections. Preparations for Corps Commandant visit. Company Commandant's visit cancelled. Salvage in T.30.a. by D.Coy. 'A','B','C' Coys. Steady Drill, Saluting, Musketry. 'D' Coy. Practice Attack under Artillery Barrage. Completed. Squadron Training. Attacks (Less squadron) Lewis Gun Training. Roll Call. Lights out. Lieut. P.A.S. McCRACKEN rejoins unit from furlough to U.K.	
	10/9/18	0700 0930-1130	Reveille. Company Training. Close order and Salutary Drill. Artillery Formations and Musketry. Specialist Training. Officers Signals Semaphore + Lecture.	

D. D. & L., London, E.C.

Army Form C. 2118.

WAR DIARY
or
INTELLIGENCE SUMMARY.
(Erase heading not required.)

Instructions regarding War Diaries and Intelligence Summaries are contained in F. S. Regs., Part II. and the Staff Manual respectively. Title pages will be prepared in manuscript.

Place	Date	Hour	Summary of Events and Information	Remarks and references to Appendices
CROISELLES	10/9/18 (contd.)	10.15	Brigade Lecture for all Officers and N.C.Os., and Demonstration of How a Platoon Attacks a Strong Point.	
		20.00	Roll Call	
		20.30	Lights Out	
	11/9/18	07.00	Reveille	
		08.00–08.30	Gas Inspection	
		08.30–09.30	Company Training	
		09.30–10.30	"A" & "D" Coys. Tactical drill. Platoons in "B" "C" Coys. Field Drill and Colour Drill at Hay Dumping the Attack	
		10.30–11.30	"B" & "C" Coys. Tactical drill. Platoons in "A" "D" Coys. Practice demonstration of the Attack	
		14.00–15.00	Specialist Training for Signallers and Scouts under specialist officers	
		16.00–17.00	N.C.Os. Parade	
		20.00	Roll Call	
		20.30	Lights Out	
	12/9/18	07.00	Reveille	
		08.00	Company Inspections	
		08.30	Bayonet Fighting & Rifle Exercises. Tactical Schemes by Platoons	
		09.30	B.A.T. & Lewis Gun formation Stunts and by Signallers	
		11.00–11.30	Specialist Training Lewis Gun Training : All ranks. N.C.Os. Parade	
		14.30–15.30		
		20.00	Roll Call	
	13/9/18	07.00	Reveille	
		08.00	Company Inspections	
		09.00	Company Training. T.O.T. Medical Inspect. Gas drill Musketry. Platoon Tactical Schemes.	
		10.00–11.30	Specialist Training. Boots and Respirators	
		14.30–15.30	N.C.Os. Parade. Lewis Gun Training	
			Compulsory Sports. Practice demonstration of attack to Lieut Berry.	
		20.00	Roll Call	
		20.30	Lights Out	

WAR DIARY
INTELLIGENCE SUMMARY

(Erase heading not required.)

Army Form C. 2118.

Instructions regarding War Diaries and Intelligence Summaries are contained in F.S. Regs., Part II. and the Staff Manual respectively. Title pages will be prepared in manuscript.

Place	Date	Hour	Summary of Events and Information	Remarks and references to Appendices
CROISILLES	14/9/18	0600	Reveille	
		0700	Breakfast	
		0830	Clothing Parade. 0830 Coy C.n.t.h. Inspection. 0900 C.O. inspection of men on Mess Parade	HJ
		1000	Brigade Parade	
		1020-1100	Inspection and address by Corps Commander	
		1130	Commanding Officer, I.O. and O.C. Companies visit the post line about Incay, which to the m/l shortly take over, returning 1930	
		1330-1620	N.C.Os. Parade. Lewis Gun Training	
		Noon	Roll Call	
		2030	Rifles out	
	15/9/18	0700	Reveille	
		1030	Church Parade. 1100 Advance Party under Lt McCracken proceed to new area	
		1130	O.C. Companies Parade. C.O. Parade	
		1430	Brigade Parade. Parade taken by Lt M. Johns & 240723 Sjt F. Gosfield, 240381 Pte M. Smart, 240487 Sjt J. Smith, 240362 Cpl J. McDonald att. 2nd Lt M.B., 240877 A/Cpl R. Brown, 241077 Pte S. McCallister, 28201 Pte T. Vernah	BJm
		Noon	Roll Call	
		2030	Rifles out	
	16/9/18	0600	Reveille	
		0700	Breakfast	
		1100-1300	Advance Parties (NCOs & men per Coy) S.O. I. Lewis & Lt Squillen leave for Front line	
			Drawing up of Loads & drawing up Baggage etc.	
		1330	Inspection of Guns by Commanding Officer	Aldershot 16/9/18 BJm
		1445	Battn paraded & proceed by route march to front line at INCHY-EN-ARTOIS moving Here at 2145 (see Appendix) relieve 9th King's Liverpool Regt.	
		2345	Relief Complete. 1 Officer (Lieut P.A.E McCracken) (killed) and 2 O.Rs wounded	
INCHY-EN-ARTOIS	17/9/18	0030	S.O. visited the mortars. D. Coy returning at 0300	
		0500-0600	Stand to Arms – Situation unchanged – Morning hrly. artillery fire during night	
		1100	C.O. visited the Outpost line C. Coy.	

Army Form C. 2118.

WAR DIARY
or
INTELLIGENCE SUMMARY.
(Erase heading not required.)

Instructions regarding War Diaries and Intelligence Summaries are contained in F. S. Regs., Part II. and the Staff Manual respectively. Title pages will be prepared in manuscript.

Place	Date	Hour	Summary of Events and Information	Remarks and references to Appendices
INCHY-EN-ARTOIS	20/9/18	0700	Reveille	
		0900	Instruction by Platoon & Coy Commanders.	
		1000-1300	Cleaning of kit, clothing, equipment etc.	Shew
		1500-1630	Lecture Gas Training - Cleaning of brass on all equipment	
		2030	Lights out	
MOREUIL	21/9/18	0700	Reveille	
		0730	Platoon Musketry Parades - Inspection of kit, equipment etc.	
		1000-1200	Coy Training - Lewis Gun Training - Handling of arms - Saluting Drill.	
		1400-1530	All NCOs attended Lecture under Lieut Little - Methods of filling returns etc.	B.Ly
		2030	Lights out.	
		2180	Warning orders issued by Bde to be prepared to move as per Bde Order 143. Batt would proceed to line x 22/23 inst.	Appendix 21 7R
	22/9/18	0700	Reveille -	
		0800	L.O. & C/Sgt & O.C. Coys reconnoitred Lines to be taken over infront line relieving, at 11000	Appendix 22/9/18
		0700-1000	Church parade on the Alarm post.	
		1100-1600	Cleaning of Camp, Stowing of baggage etc.	
		1845	Batt proceeded by route march and relieved 1st Battalion Lynch in the line taken in the MOEUVRES Area, coming under orders of 1 B.G.E. 156 Bde. (Lt Uppenink) Dispositions B Coy - Left outpost Coy; A Coy - Right outpost Coy; C and D Coy Batt Reserve. Casualties Pte Kyffin (Lieut A MACINTEE) wounded and 10 O.R. wounded.	

WAR DIARY
INTELLIGENCE SUMMARY
(Erase heading not required.)

Army Form C. 2118.

Instructions regarding War Diaries and Intelligence Summaries are contained in F. S. Regs., Part II. and the Staff Manual respectively. Title pages will be prepared in manuscript.

Place	Date	Hour	Summary of Events and Information	Remarks and references to Appendices
INCHY-EN-ARTOIS	17/9/18 (contd)	1700	S.O.S. fired from Right Bttn sector. Enemy opened a barrage line to hour later in front of INCHY. No hostile attacked materialised on Bttn Front, but MOEUVRES was taken by the enemy who was driven out later by a counter attack.	Ref. map 57C NE. 1/20,000. B/b..
		2100	Barrage died out & artillery fire became normal.	
		2030	Stand to arms.	
			Casualties — 5 O.R. (wounded) and N.Y.D.N.) 2/Lt PATERSON left Unit for leave 9am tomorrow	
	18/9/18	0530	Stand to arms. — Work in Battle Positions carried out by Support Coy.	
		0600	Night Quiet. Normal mutual artillery activity (normal)	D/b
		1100	B.O. visited Support Coy and Left Outpost Coys.	
		1630	MOEUVRES (on night 17th Inst.) retaken by the enemy.	
		2030	Stand to Arms. — All Coys.	
		2300	Patrol 1/1 off 13 O.R. gained touch with Left Bttn, Right Bttn. "A" Coy relieved "C" Coy in the Outpost line at 2200. "C" Coy going into Bttn Reserve.	
	19/9/18	0530	Stand to Arms. — Night quiet. —	Appendix 19/9/18
		0600	B.O. visited Outpost Coys. — Work on Battle Positions, Supports & Coy Containment.	B/b
		1000		
		1900	MOEUVRES retaken by the Right Bttn under a heavy Barrage and all positions consolidate.	
		2100	Bttn relieved by 2/4 Lancashire (landOperative)	
		2845	Relief complete. Bttn relief Bttn proceeded independently trans area at MOREVIL. Weather fair. Enquacken	

Casualties: 1 O.R. Killed & O.R. wounded. 2/Lt J.T. MORRISON resumed from leave to Bn. Capt MELENSNER, 2/Lt MOSLEY and FLETT joined Unit. D/b..

D. D. & L. London, L. C.
(1052n) Wt W43000F/771 750,000 9/15 E 2688 Forms/C2118/10

WAR DIARY
INTELLIGENCE SUMMARY

CONFIDENTIAL — 1/6 H.L.I.

Place	Date	Hour	Summary of Events and Information	Remarks and references to Appendices
MOEUVRES	23/9/18	0145	Relief complete — Bn HQrs at E19a 1/9.	copy
		0500-0600	Stood to Arms. — B.O. radji recce the whole Bttn Area. Hostile Artillery activity slightly above normal + intermittent m.g. during the day.	
do	24/9/18		CASUALTIES — 60 OR wounded 1 OR died of wounds. Stood to arms. Gallery normal.	
		0930	Bn O.O. 144 issued (orders to march to Westmin near Moeuvre in relief)	Appendix I 24-9-18
			3rd 5th 7th & 9th Inft. Battn Order No 30 issued accordingly. (weather)	Appendix II
		2230	Recce Complete	App II 24-9-18
		2345	Coys commenced to arrive in Camp. CASUALTIES — Nil.	
NOREUIL (in reserve)	25/9/18	1000	Batt resting and cleaning up in morning out of line. Bn Order No 31 issued giving orders for the attack to be launched on the	Appendix I 25-9-18
		1600	BEAULT DU MORD morning S. of PRONVILLE ? Emergency Orders for the night issued. Bttn instructions with reference to Bn Order No 145 received	Appendix II 25-9-18 hrs ?
		11pm	CASUALTIES Nil	
	26/9/18		Bttn remained in former area S. of PRONVILLE awaiting further instructions. Bttn instructions for attack issued.	Appendix I 26-9-18
		1745	Bn instructions No.1 4.7 issued marching out to form up in places of assembly attacking Brown line.	Appendix II 26-9-18 copy
		1800	Moved to position of assembly SAND LANE (Hindenburg Front Line) CASUALTIES — Nil.	

M. Maury. Capt.

Army Form C. 2118.

WAR DIARY
or
CONFIDENTIAL INTELLIGENCE SUMMARY.

1/6th H.L.I.

(Erase heading not required.)

Instructions regarding War Diaries and Intelligence Summaries are contained in F. S. Regs., Part II. and the Staff Manual respectively. Title pages will be prepared in manuscript.

Place	Date	Hour	Summary of Events and Information	Remarks and references to Appendices
SAND LANE (Hindenburg Trench) Ref Map 57C NE Hargicourt	27/9/18	0520	Zero hour – heavy barrage opened up & 3rd Germans attacked. Zero +15 minutes in accordance with Bde Orders No 145 the Bn attacked the Hindenburg front line about E.20 & 7.1 Heine turning S. down Hindenburg line mopping up as far as K.3 cntlt approx. Remaining 2 companies went on from SAND LANE (E.20c – E.25c) accompanied by 4 Tanks & mopping Hindenburg line amongst Sapts and followed the 2 leading Companies while the 7th MGs made good the tail of the Copse to the east. All objectives were taken to programme. By midday all opposition N. of the Canal Du Nord was at an end and battalion was pushing forward fighting with the Canadians attacking BOURLON WOOD from the North. The 23rd Division wanting South East towards GRAINCOURT.	Appendix I 27-9-18 Appendix II 27-9-18
			CASUALTIES (see appendix)	
			PRISONERS TAKEN 10 Offrs 183 OR. Material Captured (see appendix)	

Mws Wallace Capt.

– CONFIDENTIAL –

WAR DIARY or INTELLIGENCE SUMMARY

1/6th S.L.I.

Army Form C. 2118.

(Erase heading not required.)

Place	Date	Hour	Summary of Events and Information	Remarks and references to Appendices
CAMBRAI Rd CANAL DU NORD	28. 9 - 17		Day spent in clearing up the area which Battn. attacked through yesterday – salving MG's dead bodies and collecting our own and enemy dead. Battn. still held responsible for this of CANAL which is the present line of resistance although other attacking troops have gone through on line. Disposition made accordingly. CASUALTIES Nil	Unsey
-do-	29/9/17	0900	Programme of training between non-executions of platoons and Coy games and inspection of kits by Coy and Coy Officers. Two was countilled on Bag was writing the Battn. to cut the battle area.	
		1600	Line received to start a rectangular area bounded on the North by the BAPAUME - CAMBRAI Rd. and with South by the line drawn between ANNEUX and GRAIN COURT hwy. Coys engaged in actually making Nissen huts more sortable	
		1700	made (15½) 15/38 and to effect that Coy coils shift to more comfortable quarters so long as they could remain their battle positions in times deserving. CASUALTIES – Nil	Appendices 29-9-18
-do-	30/9/18	0830	Programme of training again consulted and was chief off 9. proceeded. Clearl Lines presently allotted to Coys friendly out some Shallenia area being S. of MOEUVRES.	dispatch
		0900	Bag warming was received that Bag would again move East tomorrow 1st Oct.	
		1200	Battn. cookers hot midday meal out to Coys salvage area.	
		1400	Coys returned to Camp. CASUALTIES Nil	

M D. Wherry Capt.

WAR DIARY
or
INTELLIGENCE SUMMARY.

Army Form C. 2118.

PAGE 1

TABLE SHEWING INCREASES & DECREASES IN BATTN CAMP STRENGTH DURING MONTH OF SEPTEMBER 1918

Place	Date	Hour	Summary of Events and Information			Remarks and references to Appendices
				OFF.	O.R.	
			Strength shown on last month's summary	18	404	
			Less Salvage Party: 31-8-18		31	
			Camp Strength as at 1st September 1918 →	18	373	
			Decreases Wounded		1. O.R.	
			" Sick to Hosp.		13	
			" To Detl Duty		27	
			" Courses (Offrs)	1½	2	
			" On Leave		43	
			" To Rest Camp		2	
			" Home Establ.		1	
				2	89	
				16	284	
			Increases From Hosp (Sick)		9 O.R.	
			" Detl Duties		33	
			" Leave		22	
			" Courses		3	
			" Rest Camp		5	
			" Reinforcements	4	67	
			" From Hosp (Wound)		4	
				8	143	
			Camp Strength as at 2400 on 7-9-18 →	24	427	
			Decreases To Hosp (Sick)		5 O.R.	
			" Detl Duties		8	
			" Courses	1		
			" On Leave		49	
					63	
				24	364	
			Increases From Hosp (Sick)		3	
			" Detl Duties		11	
			" Leave		37	
			" Courses		2	
			" Hosp (N York)		7	
			" Hosp (Wound)		1	
			" Reinforcements		28	
			" Joined for Duty	3	2	
				3	91	
			Camp Strength as at 2400 on 14-9-18 →	24	455	

				OFF.	O.R.	
			Decreases Killed		3	
			" Wounded		11	
			" To Hosp (Sick)	1	14	
			" Detl Duties	2	17	
			" Courses	2	1	
			" On Leave		20	
				5	82	
				22	373	
			Increases From Hosp (Sick)		16 O.R.	
			" Detl Duties		12	
			" Leave	1	44	
			" Courses		2	
			" Rest Camp		2	
			" Hosp (Wound)		6	
			" Reinforcements	3	2	
				4	74	
				26	447	
			Camp Strength as at 2400 on 21-9-18 →			
			Decreases Wounded		1 O.R.	
			" To Hosp (Sick)	1	18	
			" Detl Duties		16	
			" Courses		23	
			" Home Estab.	1	0	
			" accid. injury		2	
				2	60	
				24	387	
			Increases From Hosp (Sick)		8 O.R.	
			" Detl Duties		26	
			" Leave		3	
			" Courses		5	
			" Hosp (Wound)		31	
			" Reinforcements	2		
				2	75	
			Camp Strength as at 2400 on 26-9-18 →	26	462	

Carried Forward to Page 2.

Army Form C. 2118.

WAR DIARY
or
INTELLIGENCE SUMMARY.
(Erase heading not required.)

PAGE 2

Instructions regarding War Diaries and Intelligence Summaries are contained in F. S. Regs., Part II. and the Staff Manual respectively. Title pages will be prepared in manuscript.

Place	Date	Hour	Summary of Events and Information	Remarks and references to Appendices
			Off. O.R.	
			Carried Forward from Page 1	
			Comp. Strength as at 24.00 on 26-9-18 → 26 462	
			Decreases. Killed Off. 1508.	
			Wounded 5" 112"	
			Died of Wounds 1" 7"	
			Missing 12"	
			Sick to (Hosp) 3"	
			To Course of Inst. 6"	
			Accidentally Inj. 2"	
			___ ___	
			6 111	
			20 351	
			Increases. From Hosp.(Sick) 6"	
			" Hosp. (Wound) 5"	
			" Reg'tl. Duties 1 14"	
			" Leave 18"	
			Reinforcements 2" 0"	
			___ ___	
			3 43	
			23 394	
			Comp Strength as at 24.00 on 30-9-18 →	
			NETT INCREASE FOR THE MONTH 5 OFF.	
			" DECREASE " " 10 O.R.	

Appendix
1-9-18

Secret   Copy No 2

157th Infantry Brigade Order No 136

31st August 1918.

1. The 52nd Division will take over the battle line at BULLECOURT from 56th Division starting on the night 31st August/1st Sept.

2. The 157th Infantry Brigade will move to HENIN HILL Area on 1st September in the following order:-

    Bde. H.Qrs. leaving present Camp   7.30 am.
    5th H.L.I. leaving present Camp   6.45 am.
    7th H.L.I.   "   "   7.00 am.
    6th H.L.I.   "   "   7.15 am.
    157 L.T.M.B.   "   "   7.30 am.

    A distance of 200 yards between Battalions on the march and 100 yards between companies will be maintained.

3. One officer per Battalion and L.T.M.B. will proceed in advance to HENIN HILL today, to be allotted their respective bivouac areas by Captain Spiers.

4. From 7 o'clock on the night 31st Aug./1st Sept. the 157th Infantry Brigade will be ready to move at one hours notice.

5. Brigade Headquarters will close at its present site at 7.30 am on 1st prox. and open at T.4.b.8.6. at ...... time.

6. Acknowledge.

J.S. Cunningham
Capt.
Brigade Major 157th Infantry Bde.

Issued at 11.30 am on 31/8/17

Copy No 1   to   5 HLI
        2   6 HLI
        3   7 HLI
        4   157 L.T.M.B.
        5   413th Field Coy RE
        6   2nd L.H.
        7   52nd Division
        8   220th Coy A.S.C.
        9   Staff Capt
        10 }   War Diary
        11 }
        12.   File.

Secret   Copy N° 2

157th Infantry Brigade
Administrative Instructions issued with
Brigade Order N° 136.
_____

Ref. map. Sheet 51.b.   1/20,000   31st Aug 1918

1. Moves
   Divisional Train to S.6.d.
   Advanced Mob. Vety. Section to S.6.d.
   S.A.A. Section D.A.C. to T.13. Central.
   D.A.D.O.S. to BOYELLES. (T.13.C).

2. Supplies.
   Preserved meat will be issued to all
   troops in front line (i.e. Infantry, less
   transport, proportion of M.G. Battalion and
   R.E. Companies.) till further orders.

3. Ammunition
   Divisional S.A.A and Grenade Dump
   T.13.c.7.3.
   All demands to refill 1st line transport
   with ammunition etc. will be sent to
   Staff Captain, Rear Bde. Hdqrs.

4. R.E. Material.
   Dump. T.13.c.1.1.
   Applications for R.E. Material will be
   wired to Bde. Hdqrs. "Q"

2

5. **Prisoners of War.**
Divisional Cage T.17. central.
The 1/6H.L.I. will hold in readiness to report to Bde.H.Qrs. when ordered 2 NCOs and 10 men from nucleus. These men will take over prisoners from representative of units, and escort them back to the Divisional Cage.

Prisoners will be sent by units to Advanced Brigade Headquarters.

6. **Burials.** The Brigade will be responsible for Burying its own dead as far as possible, under the directions of the Divisional Burial Officer, who will be attached to the advanced Dressing Station.

Parties detailed as under, from nucleus, will proceed as per verbal instructions and report to P.ofW. Cage T.17. central, by 6 pm today.

Necessary cooking utensils will be taken.

This party will come under the orders of the Divisional Burial Officer.

5th H.L.I. 1 N.C.O. & 8 men
7th H.L.I. 1 "   & 7 men.

Units as early as possible, after an action, will have all bodies collected at at a central place, and will notify the location to Brigade Hdqrs "Q".

7. <u>Medical</u>.
Corps Main Dressing Station. BOIRY BECQUERELLE. T.I.C.
Positions of Divisional Dressing Stations will be notified later.

8. <u>Nucleus</u>. The nucleus, less those detailed for special employ, will proceed at once to Divisional Reception Camp. MONCHIET.

9. <u>Returns</u>. The following returns will be wired daily to Bde Hdqrs. "Q."

Nature	Due Daily	Note.
1. Detailed Casualty Return.	10. a.m.	(a).
2. Estimated Casualty Return	4.30 p.m.	(b).
3. Estimated number of prisoners taken and material captured.	5. p.m.	(c).

<u>Notes</u>.
(a). Officers names and initials to be given in BLOCK LETTERS. Dates when casualties occurred in case of officers, to be given.

(b). Officers and other ranks to be shown. Estimate should be within 5% of the correct number. Casualties for each day being added on to the preceding casualties from 1st Sept.

(c) Guns, ammunition Dumps etc, Machine Guns, trench Mortars. Approximate location of guns, Dumps and Machine Guns to be given.

10. Carrying Parties. Each Battalion will hold in readiness, 6 men to report to the Brigade S.A.A. Officer when ordered.

This party will be responsible for carrying ammunition etc. from Brigade advanced Dump to Battalions, when necessary.

11. All parties detailed to report to Bde Hdqrs. will bring with them the unexpired portion of the days ration, and rations for the following day, after which they will be rationed by Bde Hdqrs

12. ACKNOWLEDGE.

Patrick Spens
for Staff Capt 157th Inf Bde.
Capt

Issued at 6.30pm on 31/8/18.

Copy No 1 to 5 Inf.
        2   6 Inf.
        3   7 Inf.
        4   15th L.M.B.
        5   Brig Major
        6   413th Field Coy RE
        7   2nd L.H.
        8   220th Royal SS
        9 } War Diary
       10 }
       11   File.

"C" Form.
MESSAGES AND SIGNALS.

Army Form C. 2123.
(In books of 100.)

No. of Message ....

Prefix	Code	Words	Received. From	Sent, or sent out.	Office Stamp
				At .... m.	S8 Lu
Charges to Collect			By	To	1/9
Service Instructions S8 Lu				By	

Handed in at .... Office 9.45 m. Received .... m.

TO   S8 L A

*Sender's Number	Day of Month	In reply to Number	AAA
SC6	1		

Location	ADS	T23a	5·7
Car	relay	posts	
U7c9·9	and	U19d	9·7

FROM PLACE & TIME   S8 TU

*This line should be erased if not required.
(27802). Wt. W14832/M1523. [E 930] 100,000 Pads—3/17. M.R.Co.,Ltd. Forms C./2123.

DELA
6 ALI

Appendix
2-9-18

ADS. U 20 d 9-4.   Copy No 2

Secret   137th Infantry Brigade Order No 137.

1st Sept. 1918

1. (a) The Canadian Corps of the First Army, on our left, will attack will attack the DROCOURT-QUEANT line S. of the SCARPE tomorrow.

(b) The 3rd Division, of 6th Corps on our right will capture LAGNICOURT and push on towards BEAUMETZ - les - CAMBRAI.

(c) The XVII Corps will co-operate with the attack of the Canadian Corps on Right of 1st Army, and by pushing its left forward, endeavour to gain position to attack QUEANT from the N.

(d) The 57th Divn. on left of XVII Corps will not make a frontal attack on QUEANT - DROCOURT line but will pass through the gap made by the Canadian Corps in V.13. and then turn S.E.

2. The 52nd Divn will conform to movements of 57th Divn and move forward to assault when it is known that 57th Divn is advancing.

3. The 155th Infantry Bde. is attacking this evening, objective being roughly. C. 5. d. central. to

2

MIN: SANS SOUCI

to U.29.d.7.7. — ~~inclusive.~~
where 57th Division will maintain touch with their line, running roughly Northwards.

4.(a). The 156th Inf.Bde. will attack tomorrow through 155th Inf.Bde. and clear area MIN. SANS SOUCI to the road in U.30.b. as far as cross roads in V.25.a.6.2. — D.1.a.5.1. — C.6.b.9.0.
Zero hour for this attack will be notified later.

(b). The 155th Inf.Bde. will move its right to keep touch between 3rd Division on its extreme right, and the right of the attack of the 156th Inf.Bde.

(c) The 153rd Inf.Bde will attack through 156th Inf Bde as far S. as QUEANT — LAGNICOURT Road.

5. The 157th Inf.Bde will stand by, prepared to move up to push through 156th Inf.Bde and attack HINDENBURG SUPPORT LINE as far as the Communication trench from V.26.d.1.9. to V.26.d.1.4.

6. Consequent on the above, the 157th Inf.Bde

The 157th Inf/Bde will move as under, tomorrow 2nd September.

Bde Hdqrs to U.7.c.95.80.
5th H.L.I. to trenches in U.13.b. being present site at 5. a.m.
6th H.L.I. " "   " U.13.a.   -do- 5.20. a.m.
7th H.L.I. " "   " U.7.d.   -do- 5.10 "
157 L.T.M.B. " " " U.13.a.   -do- 5.30 "

7. On arrival in the new areas the 157th Inf/Bde will be prepared to move at <u>half an hours notice</u>.

8. Acknowledge.

L. S. Stirling-Cookson
Capt
Bde Maj 157th Inf/Bde.

Issued at 7.15 p.m. on 1/9/18.

Copy No 1 to 5 H.L.I
        2   6 H.L.I
        3   7 H.L.I
        4   157 L.T.M.B.
        5   2nd L/F.A.
        6   443rd Field Coy.
        7   155th Bde.
        8   156th Bde.
        9 } War diary
       10 }
       11   File.

Secret.
OC 5th K.O.Y.L.I.
6th K.O.Y.L.I.
9th K.O.Y.L.I.
137 T.M.B.

BM 15/25

Ref 137th Inf/Bde. Order No 137.

para 4. a.

ZERO hour will be 0845

A. Stanley Cooke

2/9/18

Bde Maj 137th Inf/Bde.

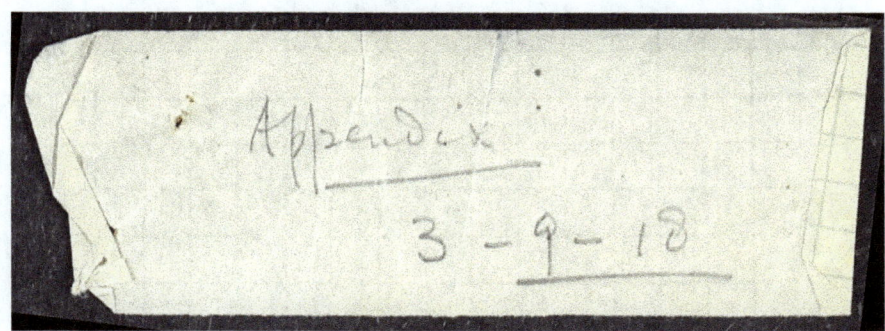

BM 15/24

O.C. 5 H.L.I.
6 "
7 "
157th L.T.M.B.

Battns and L.T.M.B. instead of halting and remaining in their present areas will proceed at once into new areas which are as follows:-

6 H.L.I. into trench system in U.20.a
L.T.M.B.   "   "   "   " U.20.a.
5 H.L.I.   "   "   "   " ~~U.21.a.~~
                           U.21.a.4.8 to
                           U.26.b.7.4.
making use of trenches and sunken road in U.20.d. and U.26.b.
7th H.L.I. into the trench system in U.21.a & as far South as U.21.a.4.8
May also make use of ~~trenches in~~ TRIDENT ALLEY in U.21.b.

Notification will be sent when B.H.Q. moves from its present site at U.7.c.95.80
Report arrival in new areas.

7/8/18.
                    A.S. Stirling Cochran Capt
                    Bde Maj 157th Inf Bde.

5 HLI Secret BM 15/26.
6 HLI 9/9/18.
7 HLI
157 LTMB

The 157th Inf.Bde. may have to proceed into the line this evening. It is therefore necessary that reconnaissances should be made.

O.C. Battns. will each detail a few a small number of officers to reconnoitre forthwith, they will be away for as short a time as possible.

The 7th H.L.I will reconnoitre as far forward as TANK SUPPORT (U.28.G. and U.22.d) and N. of FOX SUPPORT. & if possible

The 5th H.L.I. will reconnoitre as far forward if possible, as TANK SUPPORT & and S. of FOX SUPPORT. TANK AVENUE.

The 6th H.L.I. will reconnoitre also, as far forward as TANK SUPPORT, if possible.

If the Bde. does go into the line in relief of the 155th Inf.Bde. The 7th H.L.I. will be on the LEFT, the 5th H.L.I. on the RIGHT and the 6th H.L.I. in Reserve (probably).

In order to give rough idea of present dispositions of 155th Inf.Bde. copy latest situation wire is forwarded herewith.

2.

Situation 12 noon aaa 4th R.S.F in WOLF ALLEY and trench from U.30.a.0.6. to U.30.b.5.3. aaa Support Coy in MU ALLEY aaa Reserve Coy at U.22.d.9.2. aaa 5th R.S.F. 1 Company in HOBART SUPPORT held up by heavy M.G. fire from C.17.b. and C.18.a. aaa 1 Coy in trench C.5.c. to C.11.a. in touch with small party 3rd Divn. at C.10.b.9.2. aaa 2 Coys in trenches in C.5.b. aaa 4th KOSB TANK AVENUE aaa added 52nd Divn reptd. flank Bdes.

2/9/18.　　　C.S. Stirling Cooker
　　　　　　　Bde Maj 157th Bde

SECRET

157. Inf. Bde. Operation Ordr. No. 138.   Copy No. 2

2 Sept, 1918.

1. The 63rd Divn. on our left are holding the HINDENBURG SUPP. line from V.26.d.7.7 to D.3.6.6.6. thence along railway to V.29.a. On Right of 52nd Divn. front of 3rd. Div. is in C.R.6 & d.

2. The 157. Inf. Bde. will attack today under a barrage at 11.a.m. from HINDENBURG line in V.26.d and V.27.c S and S.E. thro' QUÉANT and PRONVILLE eventually taking up a line from D.14.a & b – D.15.a. & b thence along MELBOURNE STREET – D.10. central covering QUÉANT and PRONVILLE from S and E & connecting up with the Canadn. Div. at D.14 central.

3. Units will leave camp in following order –
   7. A.S.I.   5. H.L.I.   6. Sco. R.   1/7. Lomds.
   The 7. H.L.I. starting punctually at 0500, others units following at 300 yds interval. Route via BULLECOURT towards RIENCOURT along BULLECOURT – RIENCOURT Rd. Immediately before reaching RIENCOURT (about Bull dog SUPPT.) Units will turn E. just S. of RIENCOURT and adopting artillery

formation will march on a compass bearing to the two lines of HINDENBERG SUPPORT LINE in V.25.c & V.25.A. From here Y. Btl. will move down HINDENBERG Suppt line to where it crosses the Sunken Rd. at D.3.b.1.9. & where the left of Y. Btl. will rest, its right being 300 yds W. of this. The 5 Btl will follow the Y. Btl. & will face S. its left in touch with Y. Btl. and its right about where the road crosses the trench in V.26.d.6.3.

These 2 Battns. will form the assaulting Battns. attacking as follows — 5 Btl on Right due S. thro' E. end of QUEANT to the HINDENBERG LINE in D.14.a&b and D.15.a. Y. Btl. on left attacking S.E. thro' PRONVILLE. The latter Battn. on leaving HINDENBERG SUPPT LINE will get its direction for attack parallel to SUNKEN Rd. running thro' D.3.A.

The 6. Btl in Brigade Reserve will follow from RIENCOURT about one mile behind the assaulting columns and will halt in HINDENBERG Supp't Line in V.25. a and c.

3.

On assaulting Battns. going forward 2. Coys. of G. Hdl. will be prepared to follow echeloned behind the right of the 5. Hdl & to Left in mopping up dug-outs. The remaining 2. Coys. to await orders from Bde. H.Qrs. except in case of an emergency when the C.O. will use his own discretion.

Artillery. 4. The assault will made under a barrage going down on line D.2. Central — D.3. Central at 11. a.m. for 8. minutes & moving forward at 100 yds. every 3. minutes —

M.G. 5. O.C. M.G. Coy. will detail one section of guns to each of the assaulting Battns. & to come under their orders. One section to Bde. Reserve and one section as a battery of opportunity to follow leading waves of the assaulting Battns. Good covering fire from M.Gs should be obtained from the high ground on the HINDENBURG SUPPORT Line. A M.G. barrage has been arranged by Div. (exclusive of guns with 157. Bde) to cover advance

4.

of assaulting Battn. Each assaulting Battn. will detail 8 men as carriers for M.Gs. allotted to him. The Bn. in B. de Reserve will detail 16 carriers, 8 for battery of opportunity & 8 for Reserve Line.

L.T.M.B.

6. OC. 157. L.T.M.B. will detail 2. L.T.M.s to each of the assaulting Battns., remainder being in Bde. Reserve.

Consolidation

7. After passing thro' QUEANT and PRONVILLE the 5th Bde. will consolidate along HINDENBURG Front line from Road running N & S. in D.14.A. to where Road crosses HINDENBURG TR. in D.15.b.1.7. The Y. line from latter point along HINDENBURG LINE to D.16.a.9.2. thence Northward along MELBOURNE ST. Immediately this line has been reached strong patrols will be sent out to gain touch with 63rd Div. in INCHY & in HINDENBURG SUPPT. Line.

8. Units will take S.A.A. on packs animals as far as possible.

9. Attention is drawn to the HIRONDELLE RIVER running thro' QUEANT & then S. of PRONVILLE state of-

the same is not known.

10. Motor Ambulance relay posts near U.22.c.4.2 and U.27.d.2.6

11. Advance Bde. Report Centre will be where Railway cuts HINDENBERG LINE in C.6.b.9.1. All runners will be directed to strike the railway & go W. along it.

12. Bde. HQrs. will open at U.27.d.2.4 at 7.30. a.m.

13. O'sC. Bns. & Coy. Comdrs will loose pigeons immediately they reach the final objective. In addition Golden rain rockets will be fired —

14. Acknowledge —

Issued at 2.30. a.m. on 3/9/18

S Stirling Cookson
Capt.
Bde. Maj. 157. Bde.

"C" Form.
MESSAGES AND SIGNALS.

Army Form C. 2123.
(In books of 100.)

Prefix	Code	Words	Received.	Sent, or sent out.	Office Stamp
	£ s. d.		From	At m.	
Charges to Collect			By 1400	To	
Service Instructions	Recd			By	

Handed in at .... Office .... m. Received .... m.

TO ABLA

Sender's Number	Day of Month	In reply to Number	AAA

Present Line Prossville in
our Enemy reported
holding our objective in
Hindenburg front line the
may also be occupying
Hindenburg Supp line from
D4d eastward but letter
is doubtful as 630
here reported there AAA
at moment all 3
tattoo at in original
pushing off position col
Gibbons will give orders
to carry out original
move & occupy Hindenburg
front line & Melbourne
street AAA C6 AAA

FROM
PLACE & TIME

*This line should be erased if not required.
(27802) Wt. W14832/M1523. [E 930]. 100,000 Pads—3/17. M.R.Co., Ltd. Forms C./2123.

"C" Form.
MESSAGES AND SIGNALS.

Army Form C. 2123.
(In books of 100.)

*Sender's Number	Day of Month	In reply to Number	AAA
instead	following	following	behind
right	will	move	off
to	take	&	take
up	position	&	Sunken
road	DUC	towards	Pronville
& behind	&	Rly Embankment	
D3c	&	&	AAA
no	artillery	barrage	but
if help	up	at	notify
the ration of	from	zero	now
artillery	Linsen	offers	also
being	and	you	
BHQ	when	rolling	fire
requires	JAM	notify	Brigade
report	when	the rolling	front
me	occupies	&	be
prepared	mop up	up	further

*This line should be erased if not required.

"C" Form.
MESSAGES AND SIGNALS.

Army Form C. 2123.
(In books of 100.)

| Prefix | Code | Words | Received. From... By... | Sent, or sent out. At... m. To... By... | Office Stamp. |

Charges to Collect
Service Instructions

Handed in at............ Office......m. Received......m.

TO

*Sender's Number	Day of Month	In reply to Number	AAA
reference to MGB	5th	N21
must	keep touch	15th
Bde	now along	sixteen
Road	N &	S
in	D8c	D14a	MGB
Lose	no time	taking
off	& notify	Bde
MGB	prepare	information
to act	for	above
previous	orders	held good

FROM
PLACE & TIME   6th   10 am

"C" Form.
MESSAGES AND SIGNALS.

Army Form C. 2123.
(In books of 100.)

No. of Message _____

Prefix	Code	Words	Received.	Sent, or sent out.	Office Stamp.
			From	At ___ m.	
Charges to Collect			By	To	
Service Instructions: Urgent Opn Pty				By	

Handed in at: SETJ Office ___ m. Received ___ m.

TO: CHHJ

*Sender's Number	Day of Month	In reply to Number	AAA
GM 1120	3		

Directly you reach objective HINDENBURG LINE you will be relieved by 155 Bde AAA Immediately after relief move Eastwards along HINDENBURG LINE and start mopping up from left at HLJ D16 a 3.3 had mop up as far as Bty central by HLA will hold position originally ordered ie HINDENBURG LINE and MELBOURNE STREET added

5 HLD repeated to 6
7 HLD 155 & 156 Bdes
7 & 52 Div

FROM PLACE & TIME: SETJ

"A" Form
MESSAGES AND SIGNALS.

Sender's Number.	Day of Month.	In reply to Number	AAA
BM 1510	3		
Guards	Divn	now	on
high	ground	N of	BOURISIES
J.C.C	aaa	Seha	will
maintain	touch	with	them
by	patrols	this	cancels
previous	orders	aaa	Seha
will	move	from	MELBOURNE
STREET	and	HINDENBURG	trench
as	now	held	and
will	move	E	and
be	responsible	for	HINDENBURG
line	between	D16A33	and
Div Central	but	will	be
accomodated	as far	as	possible
in	D16B	occupying	front
line	and	supports	aaa
Sigs	will	also	move

"A" Form
MESSAGES AND SIGNALS.

E	holding	HINDENBURG	line
from	D1/B30	to	TADPOLE
COPSE	exel.	after	this
line	is	cleared	up.
Batth	will	be	located
in	D1VB	and	D18A
aaa	Sela	will	move
from	present	position	and
will	hold	MELBOURNE	Trench
aaa	LTMB	will	remain
with	SELA	and	MGs
as	at	present	disposed
aaa	Move	to take	place
forthwith	OCs	to report	when
moves	complete	aaa	Addsd.
Sela	Seha	Segu	repeated
155	156	and	52 Div

From
Place: Seh.
Time

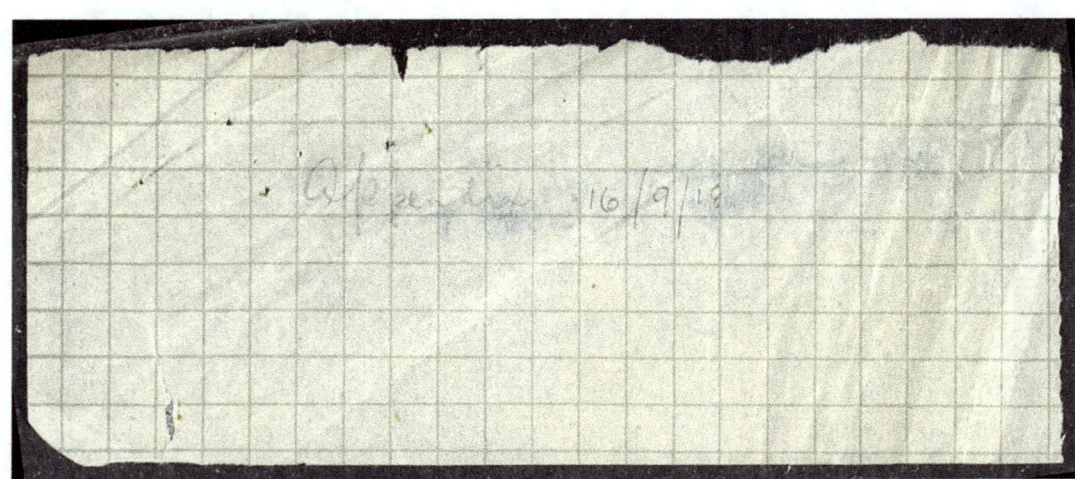

Alexandria 16/9/18

SECRET.   Copy No. 8

BATTALION ORDER

BY

MAJOR W.MENZIES ANDERSON, M.C. Commdg., 1/6th Bn.High.L.I.
                                                16/9/18.

Reference Maps 51 C N.E. 1/20,000 & 51b 1/40,000.

1. INFORMATION.

(a) The 52nd Division will relieve the 57th Division in the Front line on 15/16th and 16/17th Sept., 1918.
(b) The 157th Brigade will relieve the 172nd Brigade in the left section on 16/17th Sept., 18.

2. 6th H.L.I. will relieve 9th Kings Liverpool Regt., on 16/17th Sept., taking over dispositions as held by unit relieved.
5th H.L.I. will be on the Right and Canadians (Battn. will be notified later) on the right *left*.
Units will not pass EAST of MELBOURNE STREET in in D.10 a and c before 8 p.m.
6th H.L.I. will enter the front line by HINDENBURG SUPPORT LINE and track running through D.4 c and d., D.5.C and d. and D.6 c and d.

3. DISPOSITIONS.

Outpost Line.
    C. Coy   Left Outpost Line Coy.
    D "   Right   "   "   "
    A "   Left Support Coy   ) Battn
    B "   Right   "   "   ) Reserve.

Battn H.Qrs   D.6 d 6.9.

4. HOUR OF PARADE.

Battalion will parade on Alarm Post ready to move off at 1445 prompt - Order of march C, D, A, B,
Dress - Steel Helmets F.M.O (less Haversacks) Packs only to contain authorised articles. S.B.Rs, Water Bottles filled.
Route - Units will march via ECOUST - MOREUIL - QUEANT Road.

A halt will be made about 1 mile W. of Queant in HIRONDELLE VALLEY where evening meal will be served.

5. Owing to the danger of Gas shelling during the relief the greatest care will be taken to conceal any extra movement by daylight especially on the High Ground between MOREUIL and ECOUST and immediately W. of QUEANT.
Closing up on the march will be especially guarded against.
A distance of 500 yards will be maintained between Battns. 100 yards between platoons and every 4 vehicles on the march.

6. ALARM.

In the event of Alarm or enemy attack during the relief - Troops will man the nearest defences reporting their dispositions to Brigade H.Qrs.

7. LEWIS GUNS.

All Lewis Guns, 20 Magazines per gun in Canvas Carriers, Spare Parts etc., will be taken into the line with exception of 3 H.Qrs guns which will be left at Q.M. Stores in charge of Lewis Gun N.C.O.(Battn)
Magazines surplus to 20 Mags. per gun and all Lewis Gun cases
Tin Boxes etc., will be dumped at Q.M. stores by 1000 prompt.

LEWIS GUNS (Cont).

All Lewis Guns will be transported on Lewis Gun Limbers.
A and B Coys and H.Qrs Lewis Guns will be taken to near Battn. H.Qrs on Limbers.
From this point where limbers leave Battalion in or near PRONVILLE A.& B.Coys will manhandle C. and D. Coys Lewis Guns with 20 Mags per gun to near Battn.H.Qrs and arr on arrival there will hand same over to C. & D. Coys who will carry same with them into Outpost line.

8. TRANSPORT.

All S.A.A. Grenade, and Tool Limbers with Very Lights, Flares etc., will move with Battalion to Battn.H.Qrs. 2 Kitchens (evening meal will be cooked en route) and 2 Water Carts filled will also accompany Battalion.
20 Degchies will be taken up with the 2 Cookers to Battn.H.Qrs
2 remaining Cookers will be sent to Transport Lines.
Maltese Cart and Officers Mess Cart will accompany Battn.

9. BATTLE STORES.

All Battle Stores includg. Petrol Tins and 13 Trench Shelters will be taken over and receipts given for same.
Copies of receipts will be handed in to Orderly Room by 0700 on 17th inst.

10. SENTRY POSTS, PATROLS etc.

All details re Sentry and Gas Posts, Patrols etc will be carefully taken over.
Each Coy, Platoon, and Section Commander will be in possession of 2 Ground Flares. These will be carefully retained.

11. TENT SHELTERS.

All Tents and shelters in present area will be handed over in Situ to unit taking over.
The Q.M. will arrange to leave 2 men in charge to hand same over and obtain receipts. These receipts will be forwarded to Orderly Room as early as possible.

12. The U/m Officers and Other Ranks will not proceed with the Battn into the line.

Officers -
% Capt. G.P.Speirs.   % 2/Lt R Paterson
* 2nd Lt. G. Martin.   * 2/Lt J C Moodie.
% Lieut. J.H.Smith.

Other Ranks -
A. Coy.
* No 240160 Sgt. McGhee.
* " 241041 L/Cp. Hair.
* " 46085 Pte. Cumming.
* " 38828 " Kenworthy.
* " 25137 " Wilson.
* " 37877 " Baillie (Sigs)
" " 55035 " Clark

B. Coy.
* No 240890 Cpl. Allan.
* " 331438 L/Cpl. McConachy.

* No 5436 Pte. Keyes.
* " 240820 " Stewart.
* " 5391 " Taylor.
* " 37485 " Allison.

B.O. Sheet 2.

 C. Coy.

   ※ No 240467 Sgt. Smith.
   ※ No 240255 Cpl. McMillan.
   ※ No 241055 L/Cpl. Brown.
   ※ No 9400 Pte. Burns.
   ※ No 45422 Pte. Casey.

 D. Coy.

   ※ No 8821 L/Sgt. Pollock.
   ※ " 42984 Pte. Bates.
   ※ " 243513 Pte Harrow.

 H.Qrs. Coy.

   ※ No 240351 Cpl. Callaghan (Instructor)
   % " 240806 Sgt. H.J. Beveridge)
   % " 243460 Pte. J. Ward   ) O.Room.
   % " 56286   "   H. Henson   Runner.
   % " 240477 L/Cp. Ritchie   Off.Mess Cpl.)
   % " 240154 Pte. T. Scott   O.S.

  % Band.

   ※ Gas.Instructor. Sgt. Gibb.
   ※ P.T. & B.F.   L/Cp. Brown.
   % L.G.Sgt.   Sgt. Bowes.

Officers and men marked ※ proceed to Nucleus Camp.
They will parade at Orderly Room at 1400 fully equipped and carrying days rations under 2nd Lt. Martin and Proceed to Div. Reception Camp BOISLEUX AU MONT.

Officers and men marked % will proceed to Battn Transport Lines.
They will parade on Battn Alarm Post at 1430 (fully equipped and carrying days rations) under Lieut. Smith and proceed to Battn. Transport Lines with Transport.

13. CARRYING PARTIES, RUNNERS ETC.

  A. & B. Coys will each detail 4 Orderlies to be attached to C. & D Coys respectively to act as runners from Outpost Lines to Battn H.Qrs on night of 16/17th inst. These runners should dump their packs with their own Coys near Battn H.Qrs.
  On arrival at new Battn H.Qrs A & B Coys will provide necessary carrying parties for Water Ammunition and Rations to C. & D Coys respectively.

14. SURPLUS, KITS HAVERSACKS.

  All Officers Valises, Haversacks, and surplus Kit, will be sent to Q.M.Stores by 0900 prompt and stacked by Coys.
  Kits of Officers proceeding to D.R. Camp will be sent down later under arrangements to be made by Q.M.

15. SUPPLIES.

  The attached Location List shews the position of Divisional and Other units after the Completion of Relief.
  O.C. Div Train will deliver Rations to 1st Line Transport of un units on completion of move.
  Water Points are as stated on attached Location List.

16. Move- (a) Baggage waggons of the train will rejoin units by 6 a.m. on the morning of the move.
  (b) 2 Lorries will be available from 9 a.m. on 16th inst. to move surplus baggage of units. All surplus baggage of unit will be dumped at Transport Lines.

MEDICAL ARRANGEMENTS.

17. Medical Arrangements

        Medical Arrangements are as follows -
- Car Collecting Posts   D. 6.d.6.1. and D 6 d 5.2.
- Trolley Posts.   D 11. d 5.0.
- Wheeler Posts   D.19 b. 4.1. and D 12.b. 6.0.
- A.D.S.   D. 1 d. 6.8.
- Corps MAIN Dressing Stn.   V 25 central.

18. BURIALS.

        A Cemetry for British Troops has been opened at - D. 1 d. 3. 8. QUEANT.

19. AMMUNITION.

        Brigade Ammunition Dumps are situated as follows -
        V 29.a.4.3. and D 11.b.8.0.

20. GUIDES

        Guides for relieving Coys will be supplied by 9th Liverpool Regt. at Battn. H.Q. on arrival.

21. Completion of Relief.

        Completion of Relief will be sent by Runner or wired Priority to Battn H.Qrs using Code Word " Jock " No time will be lost in getting into position as the Outgoing Brigade has to be out before daylight.

22. ACKNOWLEDGE.

    Issued at...0700...16/9/18.   [signature] Lieut.
                                      A/ Adj. 1/6th Bn. H.L.I.

```
Copy No 1 To O.C A Coy.
  "    " 2 "   "  B.  "
  "    " 3 "   "  C   "
  "    " 4 "   "  D   "
  "    " 5 "   "  H.Qrs Coy, R.F.M.
  "    " 6 "   Q.M.
  "    " 7 "   T.O.
  "    " 8 "   C.O.
```

LOCATION LIST.

```
157th Inf. Bde .H.Q.              V 28.d.00.
5th Bn, H.L.I.     "              E.7.c.10.10.
6th Bn. H.L.I.     "              D. 6.d. 60.90.
7th Bn, H.L.I.     "              D.6 c.60.65.
157th L.T.M.B.                    D.6.c. 3. 9.


Transport Lines All Units.        U.28 Central.
-------------------------------------------------

Divisional H.Qr                   D.7 a 5. 7.
413th Field Coy.  R.E.            C.5. b. 8.8.
Div. Train H.Qrs                  C.1.d. 8.3.
 "     "    No 4 Coy              C. 1 d. 8.3.

Refilling Point.                  C 1 d. 8.3.

D.A.P.M.                          D.7.a.5.7.
D.A.D.O.S                         C. 7 a. Central.
Div. Salvage Officer.             C. 16 b. 0.9.
Div. Burial Officer.              D. 7 c.
  (With Pioneer Battn.)

Divn. Reception Camp.             BOISLEUX au MONT.
Divn. Bulk Canteen.               ECOUST.
Div. BATH. Officer.               ECOUST.

Adv. Clothing Exchange.           C, 7 a Central.

Reinforcement Railhead.           BOISLEUX.
Proposed P.of W. Cage.            D. 2 a 7.1.
        Water Points
--------------------

Location.
BOISLEUX AU MONT.  S 9 d. 7.4.   Water Cart R.P. 2 Standpipe & Troughs
BOYELLES           S 13. b 5.0.    "      "    "   1      "         "
CROISELLES         T 4 a. 5.5. (a) "      "    "   1      "         "
                      24       (b) 3 Wells
BULLECOURT         U.20.d. 8.4.   Troughs
  (Factory)        U.22 b. 0.6.   Water Cart R.P. 2        "         "
ST. LEGER.         T. 28 c.7.5.    "      "    R.P. 1      "         "
QUEANT             D.1 d. 7.5.    Troughs
                   D.8 a. 2.9      "
ECOUST.                           3 Wells with troughs Water Cart R.
LONGATTE           C.9 b. 2.7.    Troughs                ( P.
NOREUIL                           2 Wells with troughs Water Cart Refilling Point.
```

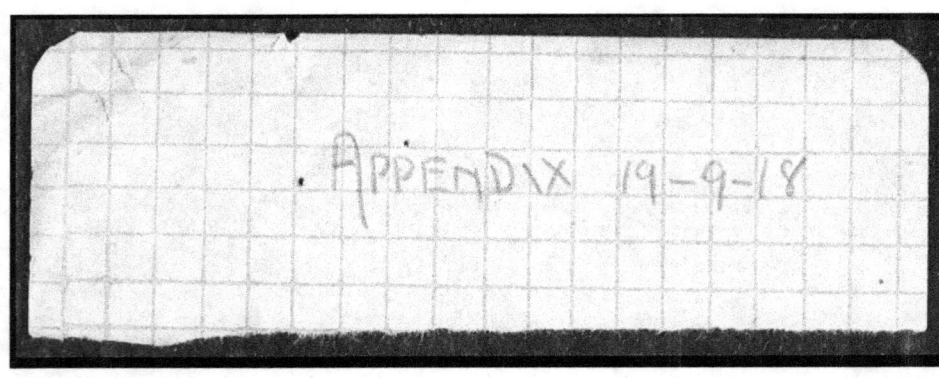

SECRET.

O.C. 5th Bn. H.L.I.	Headquarters, 155th Inf. Bde.
6th Bn. H.L.I.	156th Inf. Bde.
7th Bn. H.L.I.	5th Canadian Inf. Bde.
157th L.T.M.B.	O.C. 1/7th Scottish Rifles.

H.Q., 157TH INFANTRY BRIGADE.

Warning Order.

1. The 5th Canadian Infantry Brigade will relieve the 157th Infantry Brigade in the INCHY Sector on the night of the 19th/20th September, 1918.

2. (a) The 25th Canadian Infantry Battalion will relieve all troops of 5th H.L.I. also the 3 Companies of 7th H.L.I. in the Right Section of the 157th Infantry Brigade Front.

   (b) The 26th Canadian Infantry Battalion will relieve the 6th H.L.I. and the 2 Companies of 7th Scottish Rifles in the BUISSY SWITCH.

   (c) The 24th Canadian Infantry Battalion will relieve the remaining Companies of 7th H.L.I. located in D.6.d., also the 2 Companies of 7th Scottish Rifles in ADELAIDE STREET - also making use of the HINDENBURG SUPPORT LINE in D.5.d. if necessary.

   (d) The 5th Canadian L.T.M.B. will relieve the 157th L.T.M.B.

3. The 25th Canadian Infantry Battalion will enter the front line by the track running through D.10.a. and b. and D.11.a. and b.
   The 24th and 26th Canadian Infantry Battalions entering the front line by the HINDENBURG SUPPORT LINE and track running through D.4.c. and d., D.5.c. and d., D.6.c. and d.
   The 5th Canadian L.T.M.B. using whichever track is more suitable.

   Order of Relief :- 5th., 6th, 7th H.L.I., 7th Sco Rifles, 157th L.T.M.B.

   First troops of 5th Canadian Infantry Brigade will not pass MELBOURNE STREET in D.10. a. and c. before 8. p.m.

4. Advance Parties. Small advance parties from units of 5th Canadian Infantry Brigade will proceed to Battalions' and L.T.M.B. Headquarters. Guides from units will meet these advance parties at the points stated below and will conduct them to the respective Headquarters.
   Guide from 5th H.L.I. to meet Advance Party at Cross Roads S. of PRONVILLE at D.9.d.1.2.
   "   " 6th, 7th H.L.I. and 157th L.T.M.B. to meet Advance Party at PRONVILLE in street at D.9.b.central.
   Guides to be at Meeting Points at 8.30 a.m.

   Guides for units in the evening at the rate of 1 per platoon, under an Officer.
   Guides for 24th and 26th Canadian Infantry Battalions and 5th Canadian L.T.M.B. to meet incoming units at D.9.b.central (PRONVILLE).
   Guides for 25th Canadian Infantry Battalion to meet that Battalion at D.9.a.7.5. (N.W. end of PRONVILLE).
   O.C. 7th H.L.I. will arrange Guides from Companies of 7th S.R.
   Guides to be ready waiting at meeting place at 7.30 p.m.

   The roads and way into the line to be previously reconnoitred by the Officer in charge, and guides.

5. ACKNOWLEDGE. (Units of 157th Inf. Bde. only)

18th September, 1918.

Captain,
Brigade Major, 157th Infantry Brigade.

SECRET.   Copy No..........

157th Infantry Brigade Order No. 142.

18th September, 1918.

1. Warning Order forwarded under this office B.M.2/53 of to-day's date is confirmed.

2. After Relief, the 157th Infantry Brigade will withdraw to bivouac in the Area between PRONVILLE and NOREUIL.
   Representatives of Units are being taken by the Staff Captain, on morning of 19th September, to be shewn bivouac sites allotted.

3. Orders regarding the Listening Set at E.7.c.0.1., all trench stores and orders regarding defences etc., will be handed over.

4. Completion of relief will be wired "Priority" to Brigade He-Headquarters by using the code word "GOOD BISS".

5. 157th Infantry Brigade Headquarters will close at V.22.d.0.0. on completion of relief, and will open at same time at a place which will be notified later.

6. In the event of alarm or enemy attack during the relief :-
   (a) Troops will man the nearest defences, reporting their dispositions at once to Brigade Headquarters.
   (b) C.O.s will remain with their opposite numbers and await orders.

7. A C K N O W L E D G E.

Captain,
Brigade Major, 157th Infantry Brigade.

Issued at 9.30 pm on 18/9/18.

Copy No. 1 to 5th H.L.I.
         2   6th H.L.I.
         3   7th H.L.I.
         4   157th L.T.M.B.
         5   5th Canadian Infantry Brigade.
         6   155th Infantry Brigade.
         7   156th Infantry Brigade.
         8   7th Scottish Rifles.
         9   Staff Captain.
        10   I.O.
        11) War Diary.
        12)
        13   File.

"A" Form
MESSAGES AND SIGNALS.

Army Form C. 2121
(In pads of 100.)

TO: HILA LIND HTJO HIQI

Sender's Number: OX209.21

Ref BM1430 of today aaa 6th K.O.S.B will be prepared to come under orders of B G O C 156th Inf Bde in the attack tomorrow evening aaa Remainder of 157th Inf Bde will remain in Divisional Reserve

From Place: LIME

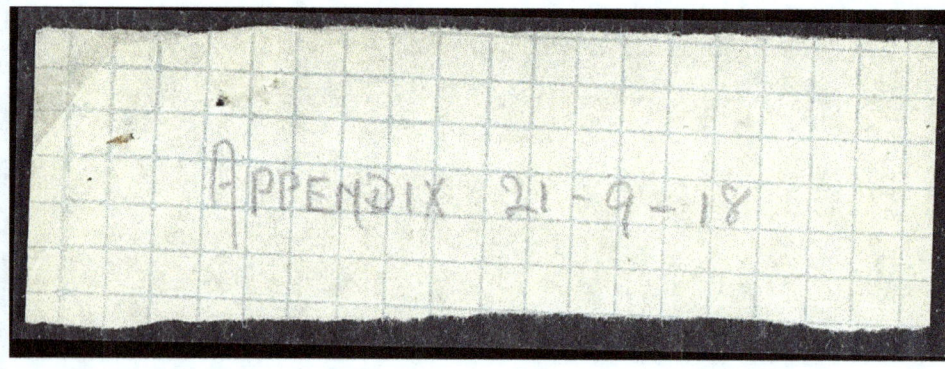

Appendix 21-9-18

"C" Form.

MESSAGES AND SIGNALS.

Army Form C. 2123.
(In books of 100)

No. of Message..........

Prefix ... Code ... Words 43

Received. From ... By ...

Sent, or sent out. At .... m. To .... By ....

Office Stamp
305
21/9/18

Charges to Collect

Service Instructions

Handed in at **RIKU** Office 2212 m. Received 2225

HIJO

Sender's Number	Day of Month	In reply to Number	AAA
S195	21	—	
One	coy	DUQU	detailed
assist	HIJO	tomorrow	night
to	dig	posts	aaa
Officer	DUQU	reporting	HIJO
0800	tomorrow	22nd	to
arrange	work	required	and
guides	aaa	Addsd	L180
Repto	LIME	aaa	HIJO
aaa	QIFI	aaa	DUQU
aaa	RIKU		

FROM PLACE & TIME **QIJO**

"A" Form
MESSAGES AND SIGNALS.

Prefix	Code	m	Words	Charge	This message is on a/c of	Recd.
			Sent			Date
			At......m.		Service	
			To			From
			By		Signature of Franking Officer	By

TO H150

Sender's Number	Day of Month	In reply to Number	AAA
Porr 2225	21		

Ref	Porr	14.30	of
today	please	instruct	2 Col
Anderson	and	Coy	Comdr
to	report	at	L150
HQrs	D.15.b.7.7	at	9.45 am
tomorrow	22nd	inst	aaa
L150	will	give	instructions
re	taking	over	Sir
line	aaa	Ym	will
probably	have	to	take
over	from	1st	Guards
Bde	their	HQrs	being
at	D.27.b.4.8	aaa	It
is	not	known	what
instructions	there	L150	will
give	you	but	am
informed	there	is	possible Bn HQrs

From at D.24.c.7.7 aaa
Place Lime
Time

SECRET.   157th Infantry Brigade Order No. 143½   Copy No. 1

21st September, 1918.

Ref. Map. 1/20,000 . 57 c. N.E.

1. The 52nd Division will extend its front Southwards to-morrow 22nd inst. as far as the line K.11.b.0.7. - K.3.c.0.8. - D.30.b.0.3. - D.22.a.0.7.

2. The 6th H.L.I. will relieve troops of the 1st Guards Brigade in the new area after dark to-morrow.
The 6th H.L.I. will come under orders of B.G.C., 156th Inf. Bde. at present commanding the MOEUVRES Sector at 6. p.m. to-morrow.

3. O.C. 6th H.L.I. and his Company Commanders will report at Headquarters 156th Inf. Bde. at D.15.b.7.7. at 9.45 a.m. to-morrow morning.

4. The present Front Line, Outpost Line and Main Line of Resistance and Barrage Line are shewn on map issued to 6th H.L.I.
The Guards Main Line of Resistance is the Old British Line in J.5. and D.29. from where the spurs to the N.E. are heavily swept by M.G. fire. The Guards will not move their Machine Guns at present.
Owing to the above method of holding the ground, the Outpost and Main Line of Resistance marked in our new area are not dug, except where trenches are shewn on map. 1 Company 17th North'd. Fus. (P) will be placed at the disposal of the B.G.C. 156th Inf. Bde. to assist in this matter.

5. O.C. 52nd M.G. Bn. in consultation with O.C. Guards Division M.G. Bn. and B.G.C., 156th Inf. Bde. will place as many Machine Guns as necessary in the new area up to half a Company. These Machine Guns will come from Divisional Reserve.

6. O.C. 6th Bn. H.L.I. will report completion of relief to 156th and 157th Inf. Bde. Hqrs., by Priority wire using the code word "CAMBRAI".

7. 1st Guards Brigade, 156th Inf. Bde. and 6th H.L.I. please acknowledge.

Captain,
Brigade Major, 157th Infantry Brigade.

Issued at 11.45 pm

Copy No. 1 to 6th H.L.I.
   2 156th Inf. Bde.
   3 1st Guards Bde.
   4 52nd Division.
   5 5th H.L.I.
   6t 7th H.L.I.
   7 157th L.T.M.B.
   8 155th Inf. Bde.
   9 Staff Captain.
   10) War Diary.
   11)
   12 File.

Copy No. 8

BATTALION ORDER No. 50.
By
Lt. Col. W. Menzies Anderson, M.C., Commdg., 1/6th H.L.I.
24 : 9 : 18.

This Battn. will be relieved by the 5th H.L.I. tonight 24th/25th inst.

On relief A & B Coys will proceed independently to K.1.a.4.3. i.e. on CAMBRAI RD. 300 yds. WEST of Cross Roads where 1 Limber will be waiting for each Coy. On limbers being loaded up Coys will proceed independently to bivouac area at C.11.a.8.1. (57c N.W. 1/20000). A & B Coys. will be met by Guides at C.23.b.6.4 (Junction of Cross Roads).

C & D Coys & HQ will proceed independently to TADPOLE COPSE DUMP where they will meet 1 L.G. Limber per Coy. C & D Coys & HQ will be met by Guides at Cross Roads at C.11.c.8.5.

Tea will be ready for Coys on arrival in new area.

Coys. will report Relief Complete at this end by 2 Runners to Battn. HQ. These Runners will attach themselves to & march with Battn. HQ.

Medical Officer is responsible for loading up Panniers on medical cart at Tadpole Dump.

Signalling Officer for loading up Sig. Equipment on limbers at Tadpole Dump.

Sgt. Major responsible for collecting & loading up tools etc. on limbers, also for collecting & loading up all Petrol Tins on Water Carts also Cooking Utensils if any.

All Carriers Ration Bags will be brought down out of the Line by Coys & carried on L.G. Limbers.

OC. Coys. must ensure that all L.Ps. & L.G. Ammn. are taken with them also that every man leaves the Trenches with 120 rounds S.A.A.

<u>Trench Stores</u>. All S.A.A, Grenades, Very Lights, S.O.S Rockets & Ground Flares will be handed over to 5th H.L.I. by Coys.

D. McIntyre. Lieut.
Adjt. 1/6th H.L.I.

Issued at 1500. 24/IX/18.

Copy No. 1 - To OC. A Coy
  " 2 - "   " B "
  " 3 - "   " C "
  " 4 - "   " D "
  " 5 - "   HQ, R.S.M & File
  " 6 - "   Medical Officer & Return
  " 7 - "   Commdg. Officer
  " 8 - "   War Diary

SECRET.   Copy No. 2

155th. INF. BRIGADE ORDER No.119.

24th September, 1918.

1. 1/5th. H.L.I. will relieve 1/6th H.L.I. in the Right Battalion Area during the night 24th/25th September.

2. Details of relief will be arranged between Commanding Officers.

3. Completion of relief will be wired to this office by code word "GIBBS".

4. 1/6th. H.L.I. will acknowledge.

McClement   Captain,
Bde. Major 155th Inf. Brigade.

ISSUED at 0900 through Signals to :-

Copy No.	
1	157th Inf. Bde.
2	6th. H.L.I.
3	4th. R.S.F.
4	5th. R.S.F.
5	4th. K.O.S.B.
6	155 L.T.M. Bty.
7	7th. Royal Scots.
8	7th Scottish Rifles.
9	52nd Bn. M.G.C.
10	Right Group Comdr. R.F.A.
11	2nd Guards Bde.
12	52nd Division.
13	File.
14-15	War Diary.

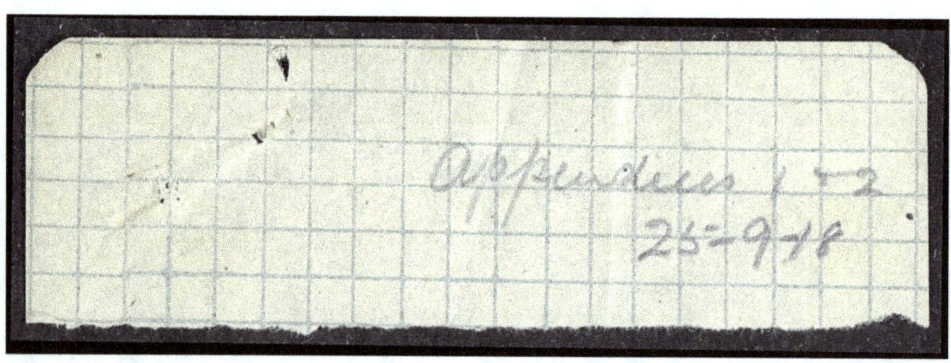

Appendices 1 & 2
25-9-78

OC 6th W.L.
7th K.L.

A.I.

Please make the following amendments to Bde. Order № 14 5 of today:-

Para 4. Line 4. for "they will assault" read "they will assemble"

Para 7. (a). Line 16. after "touch," add "136th Brigade."

Line 17. after "patrols;-" add "to get in touch with 15th Bgde."

[signature]

25/9/16.   for Bde. Maj. [?]

SECRET.   Copy No.......

157th Infantry Brigade Order No.145.

Ref. Map MOEUVRES Special Sheet
Parts of 57.c.N.W., N.E., S.W., and S.E., 1/20,000.

1. On a day and at a Zero hour to be notified later the British 1st and 3rd Armies will attack.

   (a) The Canadian Corps (1st Army) on our left, attacking BOURLON WOOD from the North and West will direct.
   In conformity with their action the 63rd Division, XVII Corps will attack with its left on the Corps Northern Boundary and its right on the MOEUVRES-GRAINCOURT ROAD (E.21.c., E.27.b., E.28.c. and d, K.5.a) exclusive.
   The 52nd Division will conform to the action of the 63rd Division and attack with its left on the MOEUVRES-GRAINCOURT ROAD (inclusive).
   On the South the Guards Division is likewise attacking, but not as a part of the concerted movement of the Canadian and XVII Corps.

   (b) The objectives are given on Maps issued to C.O's.

1st objective			RED
2nd do,		Canadian	GREEN
		Remainder	BROWN
3rd do.			BLUE.

   (c) (i) The XVII Corps barrage for the attack of 156 Infantry Brigade will come down at Zero on line E.26.b.2.8. - E.20.d.3.9. and at Zero plus 15 minutes will roll eastwards at the rate of 100 yards in 3 minutes to a line running north from E.27.a.5.5. Here it will pivot and swing round to a general line from E.27.a.5.5. to E.21.c.5.5. - E.17.c. which it will reach at Zero plus 110 minutes. The barrage will then again roll forward south eastwards at the rate of 100 yards in 4 minutes.
   (ii) The 9th Brigade R.F.A. will place a block barrage on the line E.26.b.9.4. - E.26.a.8.6. at Zero for 157th Inf. Bde.
   (iii) At Zero plus 40 minutes the block barrage will swing southwards at 100 yards per 5 minutes to the line South end of lock - K.3.a.7.5. - K.2.b.6.6. where it will pause for 5 minutes and then cease at Zero plus 95 minutes.
   (iiii) Consequent on the above the 156th Inf. Bde. will attack and make good the line of the Canal by Zero plus 28 minutes. The assaulting troops of the 157th Infantry Brigade (6th and 7th H.L.I.) will attack simultaneously with 156th Inf. Bde. at Zero plus 15 minutes and will capture and form a defensive flank down ALF Trench under which the remainder of the assaulting troops of 6th and 7th H.L.I. will form up, afterwards attacking southwards under the block barrage which will move forward at Zero plus 40 minutes.

   (d) The 63rd Division will attack under the barrage with its right on the MOEUVRES - GRAINCOURT ROAD (exclusive), clear the HINDENBURG LINE and capture GRAINCOURT and ANNEUX.

   (e) In conformity with the action of the 63rd Division the 52nd Division will attack as follows:-
   (i) The 156th Inf. Bde. will take LEOPARD AVENUE from the MOEUVRES-GRAINCOURT ROAD (inclusive) to the bend at E.27.a.2.5. to which the barrage, while pivoting, will form a protection.
   (ii) The 156th Bde. will then advance and clear the area shaded pink on map. The line KANGAROO TRENCH-SOW AVENUE must be made good and from here they will push forward on to high ground in K.4.a. and K.4.c.

   (f) The 155th Inf. Bde. will hold their present line.

2. (a). The 157th Inf. Bde will mop up the HINDENBURG FRONT LINE and both banks of the CANAL in E.26., K.2.b., K.3.a. under a block barrage. (vide para 1 sub para c and sub para 3.)

(b) The remainder of the area between 157th Inf. Bde. and Guards Division will be cleared without a barrage.

(c) It is most important that the 157th Inf. Bde. area be cleared of the enemy at the earliest possible moment.

3. 157th Bde.
The HINDENBURG FRONT LINE and the CANAL will be mopped up from North to South as follows:-
The 6th H.L.I. on the right, mopping up both lines of trenches and the Communication trenches between them.
The 7th H.L.I. on the left, dealing with the CANAL (including both banks) and the Communication Trenches leading from the most Easterly of the two Trench Lines to the CANAL.
The 5th H.L.I. will be in Brigade Reserve in their present position, but after the attack by the 157th Brigade has started the two rear Companies will close up into the two trenches running Northwest from each end of SAND LANE, one Company in each.

4. Prior to the assault the 6th and 7th H.L.I. will assemble in SAND LANE and front line of HINDENBURG FRONT LINE running running South east from the Northern end of SAND LANE.
They will assault here in accordance with the arrangement made at the Conference this morning.
To make room for this, the 5th H.L.I. will temporarily close down to the Southern end of SAND LANE and the trench running South from it, opening out again when the assaulting troops have moved forward.

5. The forming up trench will be ALF Trench (E.26.a.95.70. to E.26.b.60.55.) and North of it.
Only the leading Companies of 6th and 7th H.L.I. can form up here; the remaining Companies must push down from SAND LANE as far as possible and be ready to come into position behind the leading Companies as these latter move forward, as arranged at to-day's conference.
For this purpose gaps will be cut in the wire from E.26.a.8.9. to E.26.a.9.5., by the tanks.
The forming up place is at present in the hands of the enemy, the leading troops therefore, must expect, and be prepared to fight their way down; they will then form a defensive flank under cover of which the leading assault Companies will form up. The method of forming the defensive flank will be as arranged at the conference to-day.

6. The assault will be carried out as follows:-

(a) The barrage, consisting of shrapnel, thickened up by Machine Gun and Trench Mortar Fire, will move forward from the line given in para 1, (c), (iii), at the rate of 100 yards in 5 minutes. The depth of the barrage from North to South will be 100 yards and the breadth will stretch across both lines of trenches and the CANAL. It will be an oblique barrage.

(b) Immediately behind the barrage will follow 4 tanks in line abreast, one tank being just West of the trenches, two tanks between the two lines of trenches, and one tank between the trenches and the CANAL. The tanks will move from North to South but will zigzag about. Two of these tanks, on reaching the CAMBRAI Road, will cross to the East of the CANAL, the other two continuing to our Southern boundary.
The Infantry will keep close behind the line of tanks.

(c) The 7th H.L.I. will mop up the canal from West to East, taking it in sections; the leading Company taking the 1st section, the 2nd Company leapfrogging through the 1st Company

(a) (c) Contd.

1st Company and taking the second section, and so on, care being taken in carrying out the leap frog principle not to lose the barrage.

The 6th H.L.I. will not leap frog, but will work straight down the trenches dropping moppers up as they go.

In both cases very detailed arrangements will be required; every man must know what his particular task is.

O.C. 7th H.L.I. must make special arrangements for dealing with the crossing over the canal by the CAMBRAI Road end, and also with the Lock at K.3.7.7. & the spoil heap in E.27.c.4.2.

Two tanks will, in the first case, deal with the former and one with the latter, Lock.

7. (a) As soon as the areas have been captured, the 156th Inf. Bde. will secure the line SOW AVENUE - KANGAROO TRENCH.

(b) The 157th Inf. Bde. front will be divided into two areas; The Right Area from our Southern Boundary to COW ALLEY (exclusive). The Left Area from COW ALLEY (inclusive) to the forming up place AIM TRENCH.

(c) Immediately it is seen that the 156th Inf. Bde. are occupying SOW AVENUE and KANGAROO TRENCH, the new dispositions will be taken up:-
The 6th H.L.I. occupying the Right Area.
The 7th H.L.I. occupying the Left Area.

Each Battalion will be organised in depth, the CANAL being the Main Line of Resistance.

(d) Both Battalions will at once obtain close touch with the units on their flanks, i.e. the Guards on the Right and troops occupying MOEUVRES on the Left.

The 6th H.L.I. will send out troops to gain touch with the 2nd Guards Brigade at the following points, reporting when contact gained:-
(i) BEAR Trench L.3.a.5.2.
(ii) WORM Trench and Canal L.3.a.8.3.

The 7th H.L.I. will send out troops for a similar purpose to:-
(iii) PIG AVENUE.

The Guards will be at these points at Zero plus 60 minutes and will commence working North as soon as our barrage lifts at Zero plus 95 minutes.

The 6th H.L.I. will also arrange to send a patrol to get in touch, and report having done so:-
(a) In LION Trench.

Similarly the 7th H.L.I. will send patrols: to get in touch with 156th Bde
(b) On the CAMBRAI Road.
(c) In ZEBRA Trench.
(d) In KANGAROO Trench.

(e) Consolidation will be started and carried out as quickly as possible after capture of the area. Tools for this must be taken.

(f) While the 157th Inf. Bde. is capturing its area, the Heavy Artillery and the 52nd Bn. M.G.C. will be engaging LEOPARD AVENUE - LION, SOW and KANGAROO Trenches and the HINDENBURG SUPPORT LINE in Squares E.22. and 28.

8. (a) 6 Light Trench Mortars placed in position in the approximately at the following points :- E.26.a.0.0. - E.26.c.6.6. - E.26.c.1.1., will fire on the enemy trenches, thickening the block barrage, their fire moving Southwards with that of the

8. (a) Contd.
with that of the barrage.

(b) Two Light Trench Mortars will follow the Assaulting Companies moving down LILY Trench, thence down the trench running parallel to the Canal and next East of WOLF and FOX Trenches.

9. On Y/Z night the 157th Inf. Bde. will move into position prior to forming up for assembly, by track "Q" marked on the map, and marked "157th" on the ground, in luminous paint. This track will not now run along the Light Railway in E.19.c;d.1. as previously arranged, but will run via Sunken Road running North and South through E.25.b. It will run Westwards from about E.25.a.5.9. to Sunken Road about E.25.b.6.9. thence to LILY Trench.
The above track will be thoroughly reconnoitred beforehand.

The 156th Inf. Bde. will move by track "M" on map and marked "156" in luminous paint on the ground.

10. An officer from Brigade Headquarters will be sent to each Battalion Headquarters to synchronise watches.

11. Medical Arrangements. - Issued with Administrative Instructions.

12. Signal Instructions, including position of Advanced Brigade Report Centre, routes for runners, etc. will be issued separately.

13. 157th Inf. Bde. Hqrs. will be at D.29.b.8.2.

14. ACKNOWLEDGE.

P.S. Stirling Cookson
Captain,
Brigade Major, 157th Infantry Brigade.

Note.
Ref. Para. 3. Troops should get square behind this line, (ALF Trench) if time and space permit and, if the 155th Inf. Bde. have by then made room.

			Coy	
325/05	Pte	Robertson A	A	H Royal Sig
200224	"	Traward W	Dly	"
42884	"	W Bates	Dly Runners	
56908	"	R Law	D. Carrier	
30135	"	R McKean	C. Runner	
203206	"	C Carter	C. Carrier	
54911	"	W Allison	A. Carrier	
243524	"	T McGuire	B. Carrier	
140330	L/Cpl	Lancto	H	Salvage Coy
29114	Piper	McCormack	Dly	
240976	"	Chapman	Dly	
202363		Wilson A	S.a. Rigger	
203121		Jacquis A		
241193		Banks R	2nd Row	
55608		Edwards W	Pealrow	
240625	Pte	McDonald G	A Coy	

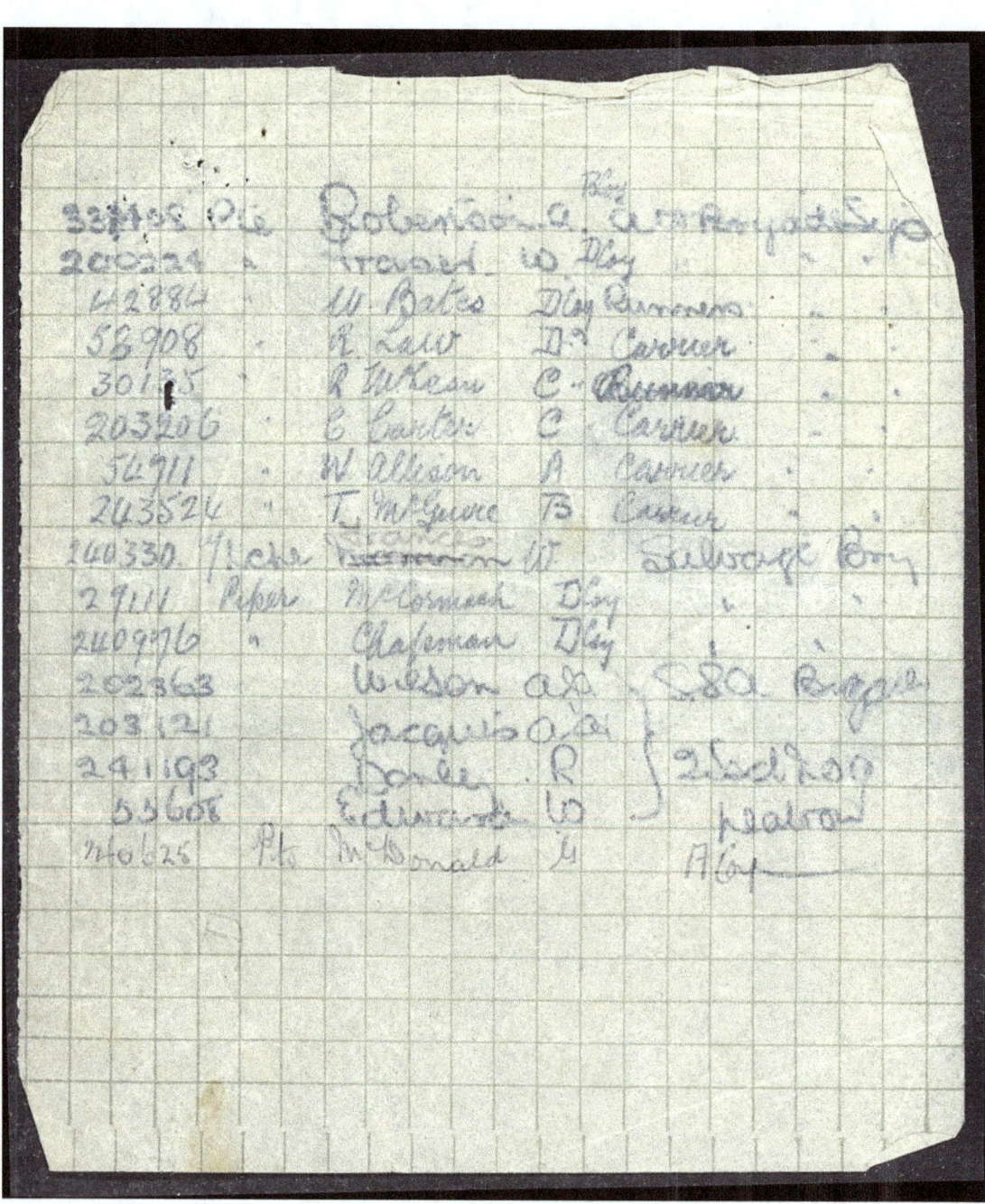

S E C R E T.   Copy No. 2

157th Infantry Brigade Administrative Instructions
Issued with Reference to
157th Infantry Brigade Order No. 145 of 25/9/18.

---

1. **Supplies.**

    Railhead   -   BOISLEUX AU MONT
    Refilling Point -   ECOUST (C.1.d.9.9.)

    (a) Preserved Meat will be issued (less a proportion of Fresh Meat for Transport Details) for consumption on 'Z' day.

    (b) Supply Situation on Morning of 'Z' Day.

    On the Man { One day's Rations. P. Meat.
                { One Iron Ration.

    Commanding Officers will ensure that the above rations have been distributed to and are carried by individuals prior to the advance.

2. **AMMUNITION.**

    S.A.A. & Grenade Dumps.

    Brigade Dumps are established at the following points:-

    (i)   Forward Dump   E.20.c.6.3
    (ii)   "   "   E.26.c.7.0
    (iii) Main Dump   D.30.c.9.7.

    These Dumps contain a supply of S.A.A., Grenades, Lewis Gun Magazines, S..S. Rockets, 1" D.I. Lights & Ground Flares. Box Respirators and Chloride of Lime, and will be under charge of Lt. J.. STEWART, who will be situated at Main Dump (D.30.c.9.7.)

3. **WATER.**

    "A" Men.

    (a) An advanced Dump of Drinking Water will be established at the Main Ammunition Dump (D.30.c.9.7.). For this purpose 20 Petrol Tins will be withdrawn from each Unit. In addition to these the Dump will contain 150 Petrol Tins and 250 Full Water Bottles, i.e. a total of 210 Petrol Tins and 250 Water Bottles.

    (b) Empty Petrol Tins should be sent back to the Dump. No man should come back without one.

    "B" Animals.

    (a) Available Water Points :-

        PRONVILLE.   (E.9.a.2.8.)
        QUEANT.   (D.1.d.central)

    It is hoped to open up a water point at LOUVERVAL as early as possible.

4. **TRAFFIC.**/-

4. TRAFFIC.
(i)
(A) As operations proceed the Main Line of Supply for the Division will become CROISILLES - LAGNICOURT - LOUVERVAL Road

(B) MOEUVRES will be controlled by 63rd Division.

(C) Troops and empty H.T. must use Cross country Tracks as far as possible.

(D) Animals proceeding to and from water must on no account use Lorry Routes. All Transport Officers must be prepared to reconnoitre new routes to water and if necessary will cut wire or fill in old trenches to accomplish this end.

(E) Vehicles must not halt on Main Lorry routes. They must pull clear of the Road or down a side road.

(F) The QUEANT - PRONVILLE - MOEUVRES Road will be used as little as possible by Transport of this Division

(ii)
The following Road is allotted to this Brigade for Supply purposes from 'Z' day inclusive:-

LAGNICOURT - LOUVERVAL - CAMBRAI Road.

5. PROVOST.

(A) Stragglers.

(i) Brigade Stragglers Posts will be established at the following points:-

(a) Trench junction in E.20.c.3.3.
(b) Trench Junction in E.25.b.70.35.

Any Stragglers stopped by those posts will be sent back direct to their Units.

(ii) Behind those Brigade Posts a line of Stragglers Posts and a Straggler collecting station will be established under Divisional Control.

(B) Prisoners of War.

Divisional Cage, D.13.c.1.

Battalions will establish P. of W. collecting stations and will send back prisoners to Brigade Headquarters (D.22.b.8.2.)
(i) From ALF along trench in E.20.c., to North end of SAND LANE. Routes used should be down SAND LANE and along trench running through E.25.a & b, to Light Railway at E.19.c.5.1., thence along Light Railway to Bde. Hqrs. - and
(ii) Down APE Trench E.25.c. to trench running through E.26.c. past South end of SAND LANE on to Light Railway, and Bde. Hqrs. as for (i).

6. MEDICAL.

Locations. 1/1st Lowland Field Ambulance D.1.d.8.9.
(Divisional Advanced Dressing Station)

Relay Posts.	Regtl. Aid Posts.
D.17.d.3.8.	E.13.d.0.8.
D.18.c.5.8.	D.18.d.2.6.
D.18.d.2.6.	E.19.a.8.3.
E.13.a.0.9.	E.19.c.1.0.
E.19.a.8.3.	

3.

6. **MEDICAL (Contd.)**

      Trolley Post.   Horsed Ambulance Post.

      D.17.a.5.9.   D.17.b.1.3.

           Motor Car Post.

           D.18.d.5.5.

7. **VETERINARY.**

      Advanced Collecting Station will be situated at D.7.a.5.8.

8. **BURIAL.**

      The Burial Parties, detailed in this Office Z/3928 of 21.9.18, will report to Brigade Transport Officer at Transport Lines at 2 p.m. on 'Z' minus 1 day. They will be rationed to 'Z' day inclusive after which day they will be attached for Rations to 17th Northumberland Fus.

9. **SALVAGE.**

      (A) As soon as the Tactical situation permits, Battns., will at once start Salvage operations in their immediate vicinity. The Salvage area allotted to this Brigade is - the Area to be captured.

      Lists of material salved should be made out, particularly for Guns, Machine Guns, etc.

      (B) Wherever possible Battn Salvage Dumps should be situated near a Road or Track.

      (C) Every effort must be made to Salve British Rifles in serviceable condition. If left exposed to weather they deteriorate rapidly. These Rifles must therefore, when collected, be placed under extemporised cover at once.

      (D) Returning vehicles of 1st Line Transport will be systematically used to evacuate salvage to Divnl. Salvage Dump. British Rifles and equipment must be evacuated first.

      (E) All Roads or Tracks must be cleared of loose boxes or rounds of ammunition.

10. **TENTAGE.**

      (A) For the purposes of these operations the following number of Tents and Shelters may be retained by Units for Transport Lines etc.

	Tents.	Shelters.
Brigade Hqrs.	1	7
Each Battalion.	2	13
L.T.M. Bty.	1	4

      (B) Every precaution must be taken to prevent loss of this Tentage during operations as it cannot be replaced at present. Units will be held responsible for any losses.

      (C) All/-

10. **TENTAGE (Contd.)**

(C) All tentage in excess of the scale laid down in para (A) will be returned to D.A.D.O.S. by noon 'Z' minus day. Units will report when this has been done and the amount returned.

11. **RECEPTION CAMP.**

From 'Z' day inclusive, reinforcements and personnel returning from Leave will remain at Divnl. Reception Camp, pending Orders to rejoin their Units.

12. **PERSONNEL FOR ADMINISTRATION PURPOSES.**

The parties who have already been earmarked (reference Z/392B of 21/9/18) for the above duties will report as follows:-

Duty.	Unit.	Number	Report to.
Escort for P. of W.	5th H.L.I.	1 N.C.O. & 5 men	Bde. Hqrs. at Transport Lines at 0900
	7th H.L.I.	1 N.C.O. & 5 men	
Salvage.	6th H.L.I.	1 N.C.O. & 2 men	do.
Burial.	5th H.L.I.	10 men.	
	7th H.L.I.	1 N.C.O. & 10 men	do.
Pack Dump.	Each Unit.	1 man.	do.
Bde. S.A.A. Carrying party.	5th H.L.I.	4 men	
	6th H.L.I.	4 men	do.
	7th H.L.I.	4 men	

13. **ACKNOWLEDGE.**

H.M. Hewison
Captain,
Staff Captain, 157th Infantry Brigade.

Issued at .... 25/9/18.

```
Copy No. 1 to 5th H. L. I.
         2    6th H. L. I.
         3    7th H. L. I.
         4    157th L. T. M. Bty.
         5    D.G.O.
         6    Hqrs. 155th Inf. Bde.
         7    Hqrs. 156th Inf. Bde.
         8    B. T. O.
         9    S. A. A. Officer.
        10  )
        11  ) Battn. Quartermasters.
        12  )
        13  (
        14    War Diary
        15    File.
```

SECRET   OPERATION ORDER Nº   COPY Nº 5
BY
Lt. Col. H Menzies ANDERSON, M.C. Comdg 6G. H.I.L.O
Army Form 57. M.E. 1/20000.   26-IX-18

1.(a) On a day & at a Zero hour to be notified later the
      6 attack 1st + 3rd Armies will attack.
  (b)   The 156th Bde will attack on the left of & the Guards
      Division on the right of the 154th Bde.

II.   The assaulting Troops of the 154th Bde. (6th & 7th H.L.I.)
      will attack simultaneously with the 156th Bde. at Zero
      + 15 & will capture & form a defensive flank down
      AL. Trench, under which the remainder of the
      assaulting Troops of the 6th & 7th H.L.I. will form up,
      afterwards attacking Southwards under the Black
      Barrage which will move forward at Zero plus
      40 minutes.

III.   Dispositions of Coys for the Attack will be as under
      Leading Line A & D Coys
      A Coy on the Right, D Coy on the Left.
      Each Coy will go forward in two lines, each line
      consisting of two platoons with a distance of
      150 yds between each line.
      Moppers Up.   B & C Coys will each detail one
      platoon to mop up for A & D Coys respectively.

Their platoons will go forward in one line 50 yds in rear of the rear line ~~of the~~ of the Coy. They are mopping up for & will be responsible for mopping up all Trenches & deep dug outs as required.

RESERVE

B & C Coys (less 2 Platoons each) will be in Battn. Reserve & will advance in rear of A & D Coys respectively in similar formation, except there will only be 1 Platoon in the rear line, & at a distance of 200 yds behind the rear Platoon of the attacking Coys.

The Platoons in the rear line of the Reserve Coy will be used as Moppers Up if required.

IV (a) The method of reaching the Position of Assembly & A.L.F. Trench will be as follows:-

At Zero - 60 the 7th H.L.I. will have 2 Coys in WILLY TRENCH followed by 2 Coys 6th H.L.I. (D & A Coys). Two Coys 7th H.L.I. will be in SAND LANE immediately South of WILLY TRENCH followed by two Coys 6th H.L.I. (C & B Coys). After Zero & before Zero + 15 the 7th H.L.I. 2 forward Coys will attack A.L.F. Trench & proceed along it as far as the 156th Barrage will allow. D & A Coys 16th H.L.I. will follow closely behind in the Trench.

At Zero + 15 the 2 forward Coys 7th H.L.I. will

push along ALF Trench to the CANAL DU NORD followed closely by D & A Coys in the Trench. D & A Coys will then get into position for the attack as detailed in para. III (a).

At Zero + 20, C Coy followed by B Coy will come out of SAND LANE Trench near Junction with WILLIE Trench & will proceed towards ALF Trench through gaps in wire which will have been cut by Tanks (from E 26 a 8·9 to E 26 b 60/55 or North of it) if this has not been done wire must be cut by hand. These two Coys will get into ALF Trench if vacated by A & D Coys or if A & D Coys are still in ALF Trench they will get into position for the attack Southwards immediately North of ALF Trench in the open. Care must be taken by B & C Coys to avoid the Block Barrage when crossing from SAND LANE to ALF Trench.

The mopping up Platoons to advance with A & D Coys should proceed with A & D Coys to WILLIE Trench at Zero - 60.

V (a) D & A Coys will advance Southwards along the HINDENBURG LINE between the two Trenches running almost parallel to the CANAL DU NORD (both inclusive) until touch is established with the Guards Divsn. Moppers up will be used.

required.

VI. The new dispositions when consolidating to be taken up will be as follows:-
Front line D & C Coys.   D Coy. Right   C Coy. Left
Reserve A & B   A   "   B   "

VII (a) Only 4 Lewis Guns with 20 magazines per gun will be taken forward, the remainder will be dumped here.

(b) Each man will carry 6 detonated Grenades 4 of these in his pockets. Less Signallers, Nos. 1 & 2 of the L.G. Teams & Coy. HQ's who will carry 2 grenades per man.

(c) Rations for Zero day & also Iron Rations will be carried on the man. All Water Bottles must be filled before moving off on Zero – 1 night

VIII Prisoners. All Prisoners will be sent to Batln HQ's. When possible slightly wounded men should be detailed as escort.

IX Batln HQ will be situated in Pill Box about E.20.c.3.4.

X ACKNOWLEDGE
Issued at   26.9.16   Patrick Spens
                                    Major
                              for Adjt. 4 & JC

157th Infantry Brigade Instructions No.1.

1. 4 Tanks for employment with the 63rd Division will cross our front about Zero plus 16 minutes and move Northwards. All ranks are to be warned that these will not be our Tanks going to the wrong place. The 4 Tanks working with the 157th Brigade will cross the Northern end of SAND LANE, probably after most of the 6th H.L.I. & 7th H.L.I. have started off for the forming up place. Before crossing SAND LANE the Tanks will halt for a second or two and Troops in the Trench must clear up and down the trench to leave sufficient space for the Tanks to pass over.

2. Tank signals are to be known by all ranks. They are as follows:-

    (a) A Green and White Flag flown from the Tank means "Come on".

    (b) A Red White and Blue Flag means Tank going home.

    (c) A Red and Yellow Flag means Tank Broken Down.

3. In addition to the signals given in para 2, the 2 Tanks which go right down to our Southern Boundary will, when the barrage lifts off our area at Zero plus 95 minutes, go quickly ahead and locate the Left of the 2nd Guards Brigade. The moment they have done this they will fly the Green and White Flag to signify they are in touch with the Guards Brigade.
    For this the 2nd Guards Brigade will mark the Left of their position by placing Red and Yellow Flags in the parapet.
    All ranks are to be cautioned most carefully against firing into the area occupied by the 2nd Guards Brigade.
    The 2nd Guards Brigade on our Right will be sending the 1st Coldstreams to the EAST Bank of the CANAL and the 3rd Grenadiers will be on the WEST Bank up to our Southern Boundary.

4. The 7th H.L.I. will assist the 156th Brigade whenever possible. This Brigade will be working EAST of the CANAL and parallel to our advance.
    Assistance can be given by clearing up the crossing of the CAMBRAI Road and the CANAL and in particular at the Spoil Heap (the loop trench EAST of the CANAL running from Square E.27.c.6.0 to E.27.c.3.3.), also by clearing the enemy from the Western end of ZEBRA and KANGAROO TRENCHES.
    All ranks must be warned to watch the progress of the 156th Brigade so that there can be no chance of firing into them. Every assistance possible must be given to them.

5. The 6th H.L.I. must watch SQUIRREL TRENCH (K.2.b. & K.3.a.) which is reported to be strongly held as far West as K.2.b.5.0.

6. The Staff Captain is arranging for scaling ladders for 7th H.L.I. in case they should be necessary for getting out of the CANAL on the Eastern Bank. O.C., 7th H.L.I. will arrange to draw and carry them.

7. All ranks are to be warned that a percentage of the shells used in the barrage will be smoke shells, consequently they may find themselves enveloped in a smoke cloud.

Secret   Copy No. 2

7th K.O.S.B. Instructions &c.

1. The 1st K.O.S.B. will leave present billets at 9pm tonight and will bivouac in trench system in O.28.a.
   From here they will move to Assembly area starting at 12.30 am 27th inst.

2. 7th K.O.S.B. will start dribbling up into their Assembly area from their present camp at 9pm tonight.

   5th Y.K.L.I. will make room in WILLY trenches for 7th K.O.S.B. moving their men down to South end of SANO LANE, as the latter come up.

   From the time of arrival till Zero hour the troops occupying WILLY trenches will be responsible for its defence.

   Col. 7th K.O.S.B. will report arrival in assembly area by phone or runner using code word "TEEK".

3. Tanks
   Arrangements have been made

2/

the tanks of the 3rd Divn. at ZERO hour or shortly after to cut gaps in the wire on E.26.a.7.7. and thereabouts. These tanks will probably go to STAND LINE about its centre. This is not to prevent wire cutting continuing by 5th Tk Bn tonight.

(b) Div tanks will deal with SQUIRREL trench and 5th Tk Bn will send sappers up behind this track.

3. Machine Guns
    As agreed at conference today, 5 M.G.s will capture enemy M.G. posts in E.26.a.9.7. and in E.20.c.80.15. immediately between ZERO and ZERO plus 5 minutes. This margin of 5 minutes is allowed for the 4 wire cutting tanks to carry it, as they will probably pass over the enemy M.G. posts, the tanks having been warned that our men may be there, and if we have attacked before arrival of tanks, the men must endeavour to signal to the tanks.

4/ To ensure the capture of the

3.

capture of the forming up place. 2 L.T.M.s fire southern the most western of the 2 trenches running S.W. from W. end of ALF. trench for 5 minutes commencing at ZERO + 5 ~~minutes~~. At ZERO plus 5 minutes they will cease fire and another mortar will at once open on 2nd trench any parallel E of it. At ZERO plus 10 this mortar will cease fire and a 4th mortar will fire down ALF trench from its junction with the last mentioned trench to the Canal. This trench mortar fire will cease at ZERO + 14 minutes.

During this period the leading coys of 7th, 6th & 4th L.F. will keep pushing down towards ALF. trench their head being as close to mortar fire as possible and as explained at the conference.

5. Consolidation must commence immediately any portion of a trench has been taken, and it must be clearly understood that the canal is our Main Line of Resistance and must be fought for to the last.

6/

4

5. 1 Offr and 10 O.R. of the 177th
Tunnelling Coy. will be attached to
the Bn. & 157th Bde. as follows:-

1 Off & 5 OR to 7th H.L.I.
5 OR " 5th H.L.I.

These tunnellers will be used for
the purpose of looking for booby
traps.

S. Stirling Cochran
Lt
26/7/18   Bde Maj 157th Inf Bde

Issued at 5.45 p.m. to all
recipients of 157th Bde Order N° 145.

1/6th H.L.I.

ENEMY MATERIAL CAPTURED ON 27-9-18

Machine Guns	14
Bombs (Various)	386
M.G. Belts with S.A.A.	84
" Belt Carriers	53
" Barrels	2
" Carriers (Metal)	4
" Mountings	2
" Belt Filler	1
" Case & Cleaning Rod	1
Very Pistol	1
" Lights	6 bags
Rifles	80
Gas Shells	12 boxes
Bandoliers	31
Large N°s of S.O.S. Signals	

30/9/18   Lieut Col.
                Commdg. 1/6th H.L.I.

Casualty Report   27/9/18

Officers — 5 Wounded & 1 Died of Wounds

Other Ranks:—

	Killed	D. of Wounds	Missing	Wounded	N.Y.I.N.	Wounded at Duty	Total
A Coy	3	1	2	14	1	—	21
B "	6	—	6	20	1	—	33
C "	3	—	5	24	1	—	33
D "	3	—	—	14	—	2	19
	15	1	13	72	3	2	106

O.C. 5th H.L.I.
    6th H.L.I.
    7th H.L.I.

> H.Q.,
> 157TH INFANTRY
> BRIGADE.

    The line of the CANAL DU NORD is still the Main line of resistance of the Brigade, but as long as the troops can man their battle positions in a quarter of an hour or half an hour, battalions can make their own dispositions.
    The usual morning and evening "stand to" is not necessary.

29th Septr, 1918.
                              Capt.
    Bde. Major, 157th Inf. Bde.

Appendix
29-9-18.

157/52

13-H.

On His Majesty's Service.

16th M.L.9
Oct. 1918

1/6th Battalion, Highland Light Infantry.

War Diary for Month of October, 1918.

CONFIDENTIAL. - WAR DIARY or INTELLIGENCE SUMMARY. 1/6th H.L.I. - OCTOBER 1918. - (Sheet No. 1)

Army Form C. 2118.

Place	Date	Hour	Summary of Events and Information	Remarks and references to Appendices
CANAL DU NORD Ref Sheet 57c 1/40000 To CANTIGNEUL MILL (F 30a)	1/10/18 morning		From reveille preparing to move up to CANAL DE L'ESCAUT to relieve Bn in Reserve 63rd (NAVAL) Div.	
		1400	Battalion moved across the CANAL DU NORD (in accordance with Bde Order BM 157/62 of 30th September & Bde Note Appendix "A" 1/10/18) at FADDENHAME and marched via GRAUICOURT and CANTAING crossing the RIVER ESCAUT and CANAL DE L'ESCAUT about 1700.	
		1700	Shortly after (1715) arrived at CANTIGNEUL MILL (F30a) where Battalion Halted. Companies manned shallow trenches immediately E of CANTIGNEUL MILL. Battalion Transport (except B.G. Limbers & mobile Ammunition) moved into a sunken road column and parked as a Bn at L 3.6 (CANTAING)	
		1800.	Conference of Company Officers at Bn H.Q. in the Mill. — 155 Bde had already gone through to the attack.	
			At Conference it was learned that the 157th Bde at dawn (having previously moved up into positions) would attack due E (South of CAMBRAI taking the village of NIERGNIES as a first objective and an unusual objective.	
			Battalion had no Casualties moving up but shortly after the arrival Major G.P. SPEIRS was on the mess moved to & OC killed by a 5.9 Shelling being above normal especially a canal Bridgeheads. CASUALTIES includes R.S.M. RAINS and Signalling Sergeant.	Appy.
		2130	Cn. of own 9 OC. Coys at Bn HQ. re the attack. Company officer instructed to take no action till arrival of further orders. CASUALTIES 5 officers wounded (subsequently killed), 1 O.R. killed, 9 O.R. wounded	
CANTIGNEUL MILL (F 30a)	2/10/18	0130 0900 10-0-0	(BM0/15) Information received from Bde that Bde attack was cancelled for time being. A further information was received that Major G.P. SPEIRS had been killed on his way to brigade statn for further orders. Attack definitely cancelled. Sent round Coys with Command.	Appendix 2/10/18
		1500	Officer — Continuous shelling (HE) although not very heavy. Comm 29 officer invited O.P. on RD leading into PROVILLE (suburb of CAMBRAI) in order to see the actors which Bn would actually be moving into the line	Appy.
			CASUALTIES 1 O.R. Killed (or 1st)	

M. Mackay. Capt.

- CONFIDENTIAL - WAR DIARY

INTELLIGENCE SUMMARY 1/6th HIGH. L.I.

(Erase heading not required.)

OCTOBER (Sheet 2) 1918.

Army Form C. 2118.

Place	Date	Hour	Summary of Events and Information	Remarks and references to Appendices
PILLBOX at CANTIGNEUL MILL (F30a)	3/10/18	1000	Day spent by Companies improving the existing trenches. Company Officers making Companies especially familiar with La Folie Wood.	
		Evening	Patrols also received Bde. of 155th Bde. patrols met with no resistance of 3rd H.L.I. would push out fighting patrol for a considerable distance and keep touch with the enemy.	Appendix 1 3/10/18.
		2230	Shelling pretty heavy — 4.2 burst at entrance to Battn H.Q. killing 2 officers servants and wounding 2 Division Staff. received that Major A. Spain wounded yesterday had died from wounds. enquiry. CASUALTIES – 2 OR killed 3 OR wounded.	
PILLBOX in CANTIGNEUL MILL (F30a)	4/10/18	0940	B.M. 900 received to effect that 157th Bde would relieve the 155th Bde in the line tonight.	Appendix 1. 4/10/18
		1400	Conference of Company Officers at Bn. H.Q.	
		1500	Bde. Order No 156 received metal crossfires as to relief & O.C. Coy at 1100 Company Officers and OC 75 and D Coy moved to RSF H.Q. (Bn which we relieve) and arranged as to guides etc.	Appendix 2 4/10/18
		1930	Companies moved in Artillery formation with the respective guides — A & B Coys to front line C Coy (counter attack coy) to strong point 500 yards E of Bn HQ and C Coy & reserve	
Copse.		2200	200 yards in front of Battn H.Q. B/T H.Q. to Copse A 26. d 5.0 Relief rather Complete. Enta without shelling during relief. Number of gas shells Battn H.Q. wounded. 2 O.R. killed.	Appx 1

M. W. Acres Capt.

(A9175) W. W2358/P360 600,000 12/17 D.D. & L. Sch. 52a. Forms/C2118/45.

Army Form C. 2118.

WAR DIARY
or
INTELLIGENCE SUMMARY.

CONFIDENTIAL

1/6th High. L.I.
October (Sheet 3) 1918

(Erase heading not required.)

Place	Date	Hour	Summary of Events and Information	Remarks and references to Appendices
COPSE. A26 d 3.9	5/10/18	0530	Stand to Arms - Coy. Offrs visited C and D Coys. No conversation with front line Boys in daylight except by 'phone. Area round copse very much gassed for respirators having to be worn much of the time	
		1330	B.G.C. and Bde Major visited Headquarters and orders were issued for a minor operation to be carried out by B Coy (less 2 Platoons) before dawn next morning (See G.S. Or No.147) Minor operation to consist of capture + consolidation of a small group of house about 400 yards S. of M. of our front line pot.	Appendix 1 5/10/18.
		1500	Zero hour fixed at 0400. 6" wh. (See Brass Notes received (relief of 5th by 7th to carried out	Appendix 2
		1830	Bde Orders issued re operation to be B.Coy.	6/7 6/7 and
		1840	Bde wire OR 1730 received cancelling the operation.	
		1900	Bde Order received to effect that Bn would be relieved tonight	
		2000	IO of 2/14th. Imp. Regiment arrived + stated that his battalion would not be in about half an hour	
		2030	Relieving battery commenced to arrive	
		2145	Relief completed refer Bde HQ msg No 149	Appendix 3
		2230	Coys. Inclination independently back to area immediately N. of Canal du Nord vacated by us on 30th inst. CASUALTIES 1 Killed + 2 Wounded OR	5-10 -18
CANAL DU NORD (K2.b)	6/10/18	0130	Coys reported arrival in area	
		0300	Men rested + cleaned up during day. B.G.C. visited area morning Bdr of a probable move tomorrow	Appx.

A.M. MacVicar

CONFIDENTIAL WAR DIARY
                or
INTELLIGENCE SUMMARY.

Army Form C. 2118.

16th High. L.I.
OCTOBER 1916 (SHEET 4)

Place	Date	Hour	Summary of Events and Information	Remarks and references to Appendices
CANAL DU NORD (R.3.6)	7/10	0200	Bn Orders No 150 received intimating that the Bn would move to the Houvin area	APPENDIX 7/10.
			Moving present area at 1500 & entraining for Houvin from VAULX-VRAUCOURT of 1915. Transport travelled by Road to destination.	
			Morning spent preparing to move	
		1430	Bn Paraded on side of CAMBRAI RD 300× N.W. CANAL DU NORD	
		1445	B2 moved off.	
		1645	B2 reached VAULX VRAUCOURT STN	
		2000	B2 entrained — Entraining Strength 23 O/s. 377 O.R.	Heavy.
		2130	Left for PETIT HOUVIN.	
IN TRAIN PETIT HOUVIN	8/10/18	0910	Arrived at Petit Houvin & marched to HOUVIN-HOUVIGNEUL our destination but were ordered to make for GRAND RULLECOURT via LE CAUROY.	
GRAND RULLECOURT		1430	Arrived GRAND RULLECOURT — Battn settled down in billets by 1630.	
		1630	Transport Arrived —	
do—	9/10/18	0700	Battn engaged in scrubbing equipment & cleaning up	
			Commdg Officer & 6 other offrs Commdg Company Officers Conference at Divl HQ. LE CAUROY to take place at 0900.	
		1300	Commdg Officer returned	
			Coys went in parties of 30 throughout the day to the Divisional Baths inside the Grand Rullecourt Church.	

Army Form C. 2118.

- CONFIDENTIAL - **WAR DIARY**
or
INTELLIGENCE SUMMARY. 1/9th HIGHLAND LIGHT INFANTRY
(Erase heading not required.) OCTOBER 1918 (SHEET No 5)

Instructions regarding War Diaries and Intelligence
Summaries are contained in F. S. Regs., Part II.
and the Staff Manual respectively. Title pages
will be prepared in manuscript.

Place	Date	Hour	Summary of Events and Information	Remarks and references to Appendices
GRAND RULLECOURT	10/10/18	0700	Reveille	
		0900	Platoon Officers Inspection	
		0930 to 0945	O.C. Coys Inspection on Training Ground	
		0945 till 11.15	Sqdy Drill Saluting Artillery Formation Bullet & Bayonet Lectures Rapid Loading - Training of Scouts & Signallers under Specialist Officers	
		11.15	B.C.O. & Bn Major inspected training	W/Day
		0945	Lewis Gun Class under 16 Scholils Instructors	
		1400 to 13.30	N.C.O.s Class under Cart Capt & H/R.S.M.	
- do -	11/10/18	0700	Reveille 0745 Inspection of Platoon by Platoon Commanders 0800 Breakfast	
		0900	Platoons inspected prior to moving to "B" area (area allotted 6th H.L.I.)	
		0930 to 0945	Coys inspected on Training Ground B.G.C. & B.M. Visited Incident Training	
		0945 to 11.15	Squdy Drill Saluting Rapid Loading Lecture on Saluting and March Discipline Signalling & Scout Training Artillery Formation Bullet & Bayonet	
		1400 to 14.00	Bn Major inspected Bn's Lewis Gun Classes	
		14.00 to 15.30	Lewis Gun Training, for all n.c.o. of Coys under 16 Scholils Gun Instructors	W/Day
		15.30	Remainder of Bullion N.C.O.s under Cart Adjutant and H/R.S.M.	
		1700	Guard Mounting 2100 Light Out Orders issued re entertainments & fire piquet	
- do -	12/10/18	0630	Reveille 0700 Breakfast 0800 Platoon inspected by Platoon Commanders	
		0930 to 11.30	Companies paraded on Training Ground & carried out Training as laid down in "Instruction" Training Programme drawn as yesterday General Wavell & Col. McLeish (G.S.O.1) visited various Platoons drilling	
		11.30	Dinner Hour	
		14.00 to 15.30	L.G. Training - 1 Signalling Training - 14.30 Company Officers inspected Platoon Commanders (by Platoons) handling their platoons mo parade of Shelter Trench & Entering Entrenchments	W/Day
			L.G.'s were inspected in parade by Bde Armour Sergt.	

W. D. Wallace, Capt.

Army Form C. 2118.

WAR DIARY
INTELLIGENCE SUMMARY.
(Erase heading not required.)

1/6th HIGHLAND LIGHT INFANTRY
OCTOBER 1918 (SHEET No 6)

CONFIDENTIAL

Instructions regarding War Diaries and Intelligence Summaries are contained in F.S. Regs., Part II. and the Staff Manual respectively. Title pages will be prepared in manuscript.

Place	Date	Hour	Summary of Events and Information	Remarks and references to Appendices
GRAND RULLECOURT	13/10/18 SUNDAY	0730	Reveille	
		0830	Platoon Commanders Inspection	
		0945	Batt'n in Parade for Service in "B" Area	
		1100	C.O's Commanders Inspection of B's by Companies in Full Marching Order by Coys	
		1230	Followed by medical inspection	
		2100	Light Out	
	14/10/18	0630	Reveille	
		0715	Platoon Commanders Inspection	
		0930	Coy Commanders Inspection in Training Ground	
		0945-1030	Platoon Tactical Scheme carried out according to a programme drawn up for Coy Officers approval.	
		1030-1115	B'n two Officers under Asst. Adjt. and O/RSM. (Steady Drill).	
		1330	Lecture at CHATEAU GRAND RULLECOURT for all Officers and NCO's, by Lt-Col. James R.A.F. Subject Co-operation of Aeroplanes with other Branches of the Service. — Very interesting instructive lecture for the men.	
		2100	Light Out	
	15/10/18	0630	Reveille	
		0800	1 Coy (B Coy) proceeded to E Range (near DENIER) & proceeded to fire several practices including 5 rounds with live magazines	
		0930 to 1130	Training (as per Hints on Training) for other three companies which included Platoon 487 Tactical Schemes.	

MajDMacaulay Capt.

WAR DIARY

INTELLIGENCE SUMMARY. 1/6th HIGH. L.I.
OCTOBER 1918 (SHEET No 7)

Army Form C. 2118.
— CONFIDENTIAL —

Place	Date	Hour	Summary of Events and Information	Remarks and references to Appendices
GRAND RULLECOURT	15/10/18	1400	B Coy returned from E Range.	
		1400 to 1530	Lewis Gun Training for all men of Battn. – Scouts & Signallers Training. N.C.O's class under Asst Adjutant.	MSY
	16/10/18	0630	Reveille. Platoon Inspection. Breakfast	
		0930 to 11.30	Marched to Battn Training Ground & Carried on Training which included Sentry Drill – Bn Refresher Drill – Lecture & Demonstration on the use of the No 36 Grenade – Bayonet Fighting (with back of Enemy State) and between 1015 and 1100 Company Tactical Schemes	
		1400 to 1530	Lewis Gun Training under instructors. All N.C.O's has instruction under Asst Adj. and A/R.S.M. Scout Training under Intelligence Officer and Signalling under Signalling Officer. Parade of Stretcher Bearers under M.O. (Lectures).	MSY
	17/10/18	0630	Reveille. Platoon Inspection. Breakfast	
		0930 to 1015	Inspection by OC Coys – Sentry Drill – Box Respirator Drill (Gas Helmet & Handled)	
		1015 1130	Lett 1130 Company Tactical Schemes are carried out, the various phases of the attack being practised	
		1130 1145	Lecture by Platoon Commanders on use of 36 Grenades	
		1345 – 1500	Lewis Gun Training – Asst Adjutants Class for N.C.O's – M.G's Class for Instructor Buzzers. Gas instructions were carried out for men who had not been inoculated for MSY.	MSY

Mowacy. Capt.

CONFIDENTIAL.

WAR DIARY
or
INTELLIGENCE SUMMARY. 1/6th HIGH. L.I.
(Erase heading not required.)
OCTOBER (SHEET 8) 1918.

Army Form C. 2118.

Place	Date	Hour	Summary of Events and Information	Remarks and references to Appendices
GRAND RULLECOURT	18/10/18	0630	Reveille	
		0715	Platoon Commanders inspection	
		0800	A Coy proceeded to Range (I.14.C central) and fired several practices including practice with Box Respirator on.	
		0930	Remaining Coys carried out training as per programme submitted by Company Comdrs which includes Sentry Drill – Instruction in use of 36 Grenade & Smoke Bomb Demonstration	
		1130	Platoon Tactical Schemes were also carried out & patrolling was practised (during night also)	
		1130	B Coy & A Coy marched back to Camp.	
		1400	Musketry Party returned.	
		1345	Inoculation & Dental Parade of D Coy	
			Training starts (E of Ker(S) St 11) that Division would move tomorrow and on arrival at destination (E of Ker(S)) would be at disposal of VIII Corps.	Appendix 1 18-10-18
		1445	Inoculation for men of C Coy.	
		1345 to 1500	Lewis Gun training for Officers & men of B Coy under L.G. instructors.	
		2130	B.M. 20.35 received giving our destination for tomorrow's march as ST ELOI Orders issued accordingly.	Appendix 2 18-10-18
		2215	Bn Ordy No 151 net giving detailed orders for move – Bn Orders issued accordingly.	Appendix 3 18-10-18
GRAND RULLECOURT to ST ELOI	19/10/18	0420	Reveille	
		0545	Breakfast	
		0800	Coy & Men Parade Grounds ready to move	
		0830	Battn complete with transport ready to move	
		0845	Moved from GRAND RULLECOURT via AVESNES LE COMTES – HABARCQ – AVESNES – ST ELOI	
		12.00	Principal Commander inspected column 2 kilos out of AVESNES column immediately afterwards halted for midday meal	
		1345	Moved on again – 1600 arrived in FRASER CAMP ST ELOI having done about 15 miles.	

M. Williams Capt.

Army Form C. 2118.

WAR DIARY or INTELLIGENCE SUMMARY.

CONFIDENTIAL

(Erase heading not required.)

1/6th High. L.I.

October 1916 (Sheet 9)

Instructions regarding War Diaries and Intelligence Summaries are contained in F. S. Regs., Part II. and the Staff Manual respectively. Title pages will be prepared in manuscript.

Place	Date	Hour	Summary of Events and Information	Remarks and references to Appendices
ST ELOI	19/10/18	1600	MAJOR P. STORMONTH DARLING 10th R.H. arrived and assumed duty as 2/Command.	
		1730	Evening Meal	
		1900	Mens feet inspected by Platoon Commanders.	
		2100	Lights Out	
		2200	Co. Order 152 received giving detailed orders for tomorrow's move – also S.C. 16 issued therewith	Appendix 19-10-18
"			Tomorrow's destination HÉNIN LIÉTARD.	
	20/10/18	0630 Reveille		
		0730 Breakfast		
		0900	Fell in with Transport ready to move off.	
		0915	Passed B.H.Q. starting point (white house St Eloi) & marched via NEUVILLE ST VAAST - THELUS -	
			WILLERVAL - ARLEUX-EN-GOHELLE.	
		1245	Halted at road named place for midday meal.	
		1345	Continued march and at 1540 reached Eastern edge of HÉNIN LIÉTARD where orders were given to	
HÉNIN LIÉTARD			halt & billet for the night. Bn. civilian inhabitants in the village.	
		1600	Received warning of duties near tomorrow morning.	
		2200	Bce. Order No 153 received	Appendix
		2245	B.M. 69/1/3 rec'd (warning against yellow X Gas) Bn. order issued accordingly	20-10-18 10 Sep
	21/10/18	0500 Reveille		
		0645 Breakfast		
		0840	Batt. with Transport paraded & marched off.	
		0915	Reached Bde. Starting Point at X Roads in HÉNIN LIÉTARD - passed through MOYELETTE	
		1215	& reached FIERS where Batt. got into billets.	
		1730	Midday Meal	
		1730	Orders that Bn. would be in this area for three or four days.	
			Evening Meal	
			Men warned as to light fire Requests etc.	ivory

M. D. Macey
Capt.

Army Form C. 2118.

WAR DIARY
or
INTELLIGENCE SUMMARY.

CONFIDENTIAL

1/6th HIGH. L.I. OCTOBER 1918 (SHEET 10)

(Erase heading not required.)

Place	Date	Hour	Summary of Events and Information	Remarks and references to Appendices
FLERS	22/10/18	0730	Reveille	
			Men were employed all day cleaning up litter scrubbing equipments.	
			During morning a special kit-drying parade was held as many men's feet had suffered with the 3 days marching.	
			C.O.s. inspected their Coys. 1600 Comm Offrs Shelter Trenching Ground	Nosey
		appx.		
		1730	Evening meal	
		2030	Lights Out	
- do -	23/10/18	0630	Reveille	
		0730	Breakfast	
		0900	Coys carried out training which included Bayonet Drill — Practice in use of 36 Grenades	
		1115	Rapid Loading. Each Coy carried out a Tactical Scheme for 1 hour D Coy having the co-operation of a section of the L.T.M. Battery.	
		1130	Rec'd Warning Order (B2.) to effect that Division would march in 24 hrs east of	
			Concentrate in neighbourhood of FLÊTRES.	
		1400	Rec'd B.M. 1435 recd saying Divn would for tomorrow via DOUAI → MONTREUIL	Appendix 1
		1700	B.M. 1720 rec'd. to effect that starting point for Batt. would be 2nd Park of DOUAI	Appendix 2
		2100	Batt. Orders No. 134 that 91st Bde would be employed in attack if none — 19th Orders issued according to	
		2223	Received notification that 91st Bde would be employed marching ROADS in MONTREUIL area.(Divis 1272 (BM 5/753))	Nosey Appendix 3
FLERS to MONTREUIL	24/10/18	0600	Reveille 0700 Breakfast 0900 Paraded at FLERS Church ready to march off	
		1040	Reached Bgde Starting Point at S. end of the N. exit of DOUAI.	
		1400	Passed through DOUAI (Sacked & shewn in ruins) FAUBOURG MORELLE – RACHES – PT BAILLON – MORELLE – RACHES – PT BAILLON – and reached MONTREUIL 13-10-18	Nosey
			at about 1400 pm where Coys. advanced parties with guides had Cops & their billets.	Appendix 3
			No further	M.H. Murray Capt.

Army Form C. 2118.

WAR DIARY
or
INTELLIGENCE SUMMARY. 1/6th HIGHLAND LGHT INFANTRY.
OCTOBER 1918 (SHEET No 11)

CONFIDENTIAL — (Erase heading not required.)

Place	Date	Hour	Summary of Events and Information	Remarks and references to Appendices
MONTREUIL (FLINES APPDX)	25/10/18	0630	Reveille	
		0830	Whole Battn. road repairing and clearing — 1 Coy in MONTREUIL and remaining 3 Coys working on FLINES - MARCHIENNES Rd. Coys took their cookers with them and remained out during the day. — To relieve monotony of road making training was carried on alternately by Coys i.e. exercise laid down in training being carried out	APPENDIX 23.10.18 APPENDIX 24-11-18
		0900	Commdg Officer, 1 Coy Commander, 1 2/Command visited the front line area motoring to St AMAND & from there proceeding on foot.	nil
-do-	26/10/18	0630	Reveille	
		0830	Battalion again on road repairing all Coys on FLINES. MARCHIENNES ROAD.	
		0830	that wet morning most of portable men — Road repairing cancelled —	
		1000	Training in billeting area. Group of Officers & all available N.C.Os formed	
			from every Battn. being ordered to Brigade were instil.	
		1400	Word rec'd from Bgde that Bn. would have to parade tomorrow morning,	nil
		1730	ready to Bat. and get further orders as to Starting period time of passing & location — M/3A22 at 1020.	
			at another Bat. & to Bay Bumf FLINES in charge of 1 Cpl.	
MONTREUIL TO LANDAS.	27/10/18	1600	Reveille	
		0930	Left MONTREUIL & reached LANDAS in the early afternoon passing through COUTICHES and ORCHIES — billeted in LANDAS	
		1400	Lst inspection and bandaging parade — Mens feet have suffered somewhat owing to the amount of marching the Bn. has done in the last 10 days.	
		1700	Short Orders issued as regards lights (screening of etc) Best training of portable men tomorrow	APPENDIX 27/10/18
		2100	Bn. Orders No 157 iss'd giving details of move tomorrow	

M.W. Mason Capt.

Army Form C. 2118.

― CONFIDENTIAL ―

WAR DIARY
or
INTELLIGENCE SUMMARY. 1/6ᵗʰ HIGHLAND LIGHT INFANTRY.
OCTOBER 1918 (SHEET No 12)

(Erase heading not required.)

Place	Date	Hour	Summary of Events and Information	Remarks and references to Appendices
Ref Map Sh.44 1/40,000 LANDAS	28/10/18	0630	Reveille - Platoon Commanders Inspection - Breakfast. - Companies getting ready to move.	
		1200	Battalion Paraded and moved off to LECELLES via RUMEGIES	
		1235	Battalion passed Bde starting point	
		1430	Arrived at LECELLES and billeted there Mr 15.c.5 Bn moving up into the line and making room for one Bn. which became Divisional Reserve.	W37
		1800	Kit Inspection & bandages parades	
		2030	Lights Out.	
"	29/10/18	0630	Reveille - Inspections - Breakfast.	
		0930	Training in Smartening up Drill etc (as per "Little Brown Book")	
		1130		
		1500	Lewis Gun training	
		1630	and NCOs Class under Capt Aj't.	
		2030	Enemy commenced to shell village (about 30 rounds 5.9)	W37
			CASUALTIES LIEUT A.I. HENDERSON wounded.	
RUMEGIES	30/10/18	0400	Village again shelled with 5.9's – none of 6ᵗʰ casualties although 7ᵗʰ H.L.I. had a few.	
		0630	Reveille - Inspection. Breakfast.	
		C93ᵒ & 1130	Coy training on ground N. of LECELLES CHURCH. Coy Tactical Schemes carried out.	
		1230	Afternoon parade cancelled by BM.	
		1300	Notified that Batt. would move during afternoon back to RUMEGIES - Batts still being in Divisional Reserve.	
		1400	Left LECELLES	
		1445	Arrived RUMEGIES & were guided to billets by I.O. & scouts.	W37
		1700	Guard mounting &c	
		2050	Lights Out.	

M. A. McLeur

Army Form C. 2118.

WAR DIARY
or
INTELLIGENCE SUMMARY.

— CONFIDENTIAL —

1/6th HIGHLAND LIGHT INFANTRY.
OCTOBER 1918. (SHEET No 13)

(Erase heading not required.)

Place	Date	Hour	Summary of Events and Information	Remarks and references to Appendices
RUMEGIES	31/10/18	11.30	Divisional Inspection. Breakfast.	
		09.30 to 11.30	Training and Company Tactical Schemes carried out in Training Ground at East end of village.	WOW
		09.00	2 Officers proceeded to front line to reconnoitre forward areas.	
		14.30 & 15.30	Lewis Gun Training. Signalling Training.	
			2nd Lieuts Beavis & Brunnell inoculated. Medical Officer	

M.M. Maciver Capt.

WAR DIARY
or
INTELLIGENCE SUMMARY.
(Erase heading not required.)

Army Form C.2118.

Instructions regarding War Diaries and Intelligence Summaries are contained in F. S. Regs., Part II. and the Staff Manual respectively. Title pages will be prepared in manuscript.

TABLE SHEWING INCREASES & DECREASES IN BATTN. CAMP STRENGTH DURING MONTH OF OCTOBER 1918.

Place	Date	Hour	Summary of Events and Information	OFF	O.R.	OFF	O.R.	Remarks and references to Appendices
			Camp Strength as at 1st October 1918 ⇒	23	394			
			Decreases					
			Wounded					
			Sick to Hosp. 24/8	21 O.R.				
			To Det. Duty	22 "				
			To Courses of Instn.	3 "				
			On leave	2 "				
			Killed 19/8					
			Died of Wounds	2 "				
			Increases			3	54	
			From Hosp.(Sick)	14 O.R.		20	334	
			" " Batt'n	32 "				
			Leave	55 "				
			Courses 10/8	10 "				
			Reinforcements 10/8	+5 "				
			Camp Strength as at 24.00 on 7/10/18 ⇒			26	459	
			Decreases					
			Wounded	6 O.R.				
			Sick to Hosp. 13/8	8 "				
			To Det Duty	4 "				
			To Courses of Instn.	15 "				
			On Leave 2/8	35 "				
			Died of Wounds	1 "				
			To Rest Camp	3 "				
			Increases			3	72	
			From Hosp. (Sick)	14 O.R.		23	474	
			" " Batt'n	4 "				
			Leave	17 "				
			Courses	4 "				
			Reinforcements 4/8	3 "				
			Camp Strength as at 24.00 on 14-10-18 ⇒			24	465	
			Decreases					
			Wounded	1 O.R.				
			Sick to Hosp. 19/8	9 "				
			To Courses of Instn.	2 "				
			On leave 19/8	49 "				
			To Det Unit	1 "				
			Increases			2	62	
			From Hosp.(Sick)	9 O.R.		25	403	
			" " Batt'n	2 "				
			Leave	5 "				
			Courses	1 "				
			Reinforcements 19/8	14 "				
			Camp Strength as at 24.00 on 21-10-18 ⇒			24	431	
			Decreases	Off. & 6 Hosp. 17/8 12/8 22 O.R.				
			On leave	91 "				
			To Det Batt	5 "				
			To Sick Wait.	1 "				
			Increases			1	65	
			From Hosp.(Sick) 12/8	14 O.R.		26	327	
			" " Batt'n	14 "				
			Leave	12 "				
			Courses	1 "				
			Reinforcements	2 "				
			Camp Strength as at 24.00 on 28-10-18 ⇒			29	373	
			Decreases Sick to Hosp. 12/8	3 O.R.				
			Wounded	5 "				
			To Courses of Instn. 13/8	1 "				
			On leave	1 "				
			To Sick Batt.	2 "				
			Increases			3	32	
			From Hosp. (Sick) 19/8	19 O.R.		29	393	
			" " Batt.	2 "				
			Leave	13 "				
			Courses	2 "				
			Reinforcements				15	
			Camp Strength as at 24.00 on 31-10-18 ⇒			30	403	

NETT INCREASE FOR THE MONTH - 7 OFF. 9 O.R.

SECRET.

O.C. 5th Bn. H.L.I.	Bde. I.O.
6th Bn. H.L.I.	Staff Captain.
7th Bn. H.L.I.	B.T.O.
157th L.T.M.B.	Sigs. Officer.

B.M. 15/62.
30/9/18.

WARNING ORDER :-

1. In continuation of B.M.1800 of to-day, 157th Inf. Bde. will move East and take over the line from the 63rd Division in F.30. and be in Support to 155th Inf. Bde.

2. 5th H.L.I. will be on the Right, 6th H.L.I. on the Left and 7th H.L.I. in Reserve.

3. Order of March from present Area :- 6th, 5th, 7th H.L.I. 157th L.T.M.B. head of the column to pass over the canal at E.27.c.1.3. at 2. p.m. tail of column to pass junction of roads CANTAING L.3.b.2.4. at 5. p.m. 500 yards distance will be maintained between Battns. and 100 yards between Companies.

4. Battalion I.O.s will meet Brigade I.O. mounted, at Canal crossing CAMBRAI Road E.27.c.1.3. at 9. a.m. to-morrow 1st prox. They will proceed in advance to reconnoitre L'ESCAUT CANAL and river crossings, and best route from East of CANTAING.

5. O.O.s and Coy. Commanders will meet the B.G.C. at canal crossing E.27.c.1.3. mounted, and accompanied by the necessary grooms, at 11. a.m.

6. Lewis Gun and S.A.A. wagons will accompany Battalions on the march, remainder of Transport will move under Brigade Arrangements.

7. A C K N O W L E D G E.

30/9/18.

Captain,
Brigade Major, 157th Infantry Brigade.

SECRET.

157th Infantry Brigade Administrative Instructions No. 5.

Issued with reference to B.M.15/62 of 30th Sept. 1918.

1. **Transport.**

Limbered G.S. wagons carrying Lewis Guns and S.A.A. will accompany Battalions. The L.T.M.G.S. wagons will move with the L.T.M. Battery.

The remaining Transport, i.e. Field Kitchens, water carts, tool carts and baggage wagons will march under the orders of the Staff Captain after all units have passed the Starting Point.

Transport will move in same order as units viz:

6th H.L.I. 5th H.L.I. 7th H.L.I.

Transport of 6th H.L.I. will be drawn up on road running through K.2.b. with head of column clear of main CAMBRAI Road, ready to move at 2.30 p.m. Transport of 7th H.L.I. will draw up on road running through E.26.d. with head of column clear of main CAMBRAI Road, ready to move off at 2.30 p.m. Transport of 5th H.L.I. will form up on road running through K.1.b. and E.25.d. Head of column at junction of main CAMBRAI Road, ready to move off at 2.30. p.m.

2. **Cookers.**

Arrangements will be made by Battalions to have hot meals in cookers ready for men when transport arrives at the new area.

3. **Nucleus.**

Nucleus will remain at Battalion Transport Lines and not return to Divisional Reception Camp.

4. **Rations.**

Rations will be issued on arrival at new Transport Lines.

5. **Water Carts.**

Water carts will move full. Water has been ordered for 12. noon to enable this to be done.

6. **Greatcoats.**

Greatcoats will be carried on the man in the pack.

If leather jerkins are issued before units move, these must not be worn but carried in the pack.

7. **March Discipline.**

Strict march discipline must be maintained. All vehicles must keep to the right and no man will march at the side of vehicles.

30th September, 1918.

Captain,
Staff Captain, 157th Infantry Brigade.

O.C. 5th H.L.I.
     6th H.L.I.
     7th H.L.I.
     157th L.T.M.B.

> H.Q.,
> 157TH INFANTRY
> BRIGADE.
> No. BM 15/63
> Date 1/10/18

        This Office BM.15/62 of 30th September is confirmed. Units will march via GRAINCOURT and CANTAING.

        On completion of relief Brigade Headquarters will open at F.30.c.5.3. LA HARTERRE.

Arrival in new area will be reported immediately by units.

1st October, 1918.
                                                  Capt.
                  Brigade Major, 157th Infantry Bde.

To all recipients of B.M.15/62.

Addendum to Warning Order.

1. Reference para 3. The tail of the column will pass the junction of the roads CANTAINO not later than 5. p.m.

2. Strict march discipline will be maintained with the usual 10 minutes halt every clock hour, when all ranks must be clear of the road.

3.

SECRET

BATTALION ORDERS
BY
Lt Col H Menzies Anderson MC Commanding 1/6 H.L.I.
1-10-18

I. In continuation of warning order issued yesterday evening the 157th Inf Bde are moving EAST today & taking over the line from the 63rd Div in F.30 & are to be in support to the 155th Inf Bde.

II. The 6th H.L.I. will rendezvous ready to move off in vicinity of Bde Dump at 1345 & at 1400 the head of the column will pass over CANAL CROSS CAMBRAI ROAD (G.27.c.1.3) March discipline will be strictly adhered to & 100ᵡ distance between Coys will be maintained.

III. The usual halts will be given (10 mins every clock hour)
Lt McNicol will be at CANAL CROSSING CAMBRAI ROAD E.27.c.1.3 mounted at 0900 to meet Bde Intelligence Officer and proceed with him to reconnoitre CANAL DE L'ESCAUT & river crossing etc.

IV. All O.C. Coys will meet the Commanding Officer at Bde Dump in CAMBRAI Rd at 1045 where their mounts will be awaiting them & proceed to reconnoitre the route.

V. Dispositions in new area 6th on left 5th on right & 7th in reserve.

VI. With the exception of Lewis Gun SAA Limbers which will move with the Battn Transport will move under Bde arrangements.
Lewis Gun & SAA limbers will report at Bde Dump at 1215 from which point guides will take them to their Coy areas. Each O.C. Coy will detail a loading party for these limbers also a guide to report to Q.M.S. not later than 1200.

VII. Transport of 6th H.L.I. less SAA & LG limbers will be drawn up on road running through K.2.b with head of column clear of main CAMBRAI Rd ready to move at 1430.

VIII. Rations will be issued on arrival at new transport lines.

IX. Q.M. will arrange to have hot meals in cookers ready for men when transport arrives in new area.

X. Water carts will now full. They will be filled at 1200 by Bde arrangements.
Q.M.S. will arrange for a water issue to Coys at the following hours. A Coy 0900 D Coy 0915 C Coy 0930 B Coy 0945 H.Q.rs 1000.

XI. Great coats weather proof sheets to be carried in the pack on the men. If leather jerkins are issued before moving they will also be carried in the pack.

XII. All Officers valises, mess boxes + surplus baggage to be dumped at CANTEEN TENT by 1100 today.

XIII. DRESS Steel Helmets + Full marching order.

XIV. ACKNOWLEDGE

XV. NUCLEUS.
Nucleus will remain at ~~~~ Battn. Transport lines + will not return to Divl. Reception Camp. Further orders later.

Issued at   1-10-18.   W. D. Maclean Capt a/Adjt
                                        1/6 H.L.I.

Copy No. 1. To O.C. A Coy
   "   " 2.   "   B
   "   " 3.   "   C
   "   " 4.   "   D
   "   " 5.   HQrs RSM + FOE
   "   " 6.   QM + T.O.
   "   " 7.   C O
   "   " 8.   War Diary.

BATTALION ORDER No 56
BY
LT. COL. W. MENZIES ANDERSON. D.S.O. M.C. COMMDG 1/6TH BN. H.L.I.

COPY No 8

7TH OCTOBER 1918

DRESS

Kilt, Kilt Apron, Tunic & Tam o' Shanter.
Full equipment with Steel Helmet secured on back of pack & Box Respirators resting on top of pack.
Haversack at side (containing rations) Waterbottle filled.
Greatcoat & messtin will be carried inside the pack — no article must be left hanging.

COY INSPECTIONS

Coy Commanders will hold an inspection of their coys prior to parade, to ensure that all men are dressed in conformity with the above. Special attention should be paid to the height of hosetops & the wearing of Tam O'Shanters in the regimental manner.

PARADE HOUR

1440 — Markers will be put out on Battn. parade ground (which will be pointed out to Ordly Sgts by A/RSM.

1445 — Coys will fall in on Battn. parade ground in close column of Coys, ready to move off.

ORDER OF MARCH

Pipe Band, H.Qrs. Coy, A, B, C, D.

MARCH DISCIPLINE

The strictest march discipline will be kept throughout the march.
Coys will march in fours — not threes as hitherto — outside men changing over after each halt.
O.C. Coys will specially bring to the notice of recently joined drafts the rigid orders re smoking & drinking of water.

W. D. Shearer Capt.
A/Adjt 1/6th Bn. H.L.I.

P.T.O.

Issued at 1130   7/10/18

Copy No 1   to   O.C. A Coy
  —   — 2   —   —   B —
  —   — 3   —   —   C —
  —   — 4   —   —   D —
  —   — 5   —   —   H.Q. Coy
  —   — 6   —   Q.M.
  —   — 7   —   T.O.
  —   — 8   —   C.O, File

SECRET.   Copy No. 2

                    157th Infantry Brigade Order No.151

Ref. Map. LENS 11, 1/100,000.   18th October, 1918.

1.   The 52nd Division will move EAST from present Area, commencing to-morrow, 19th inst.

2.   The 157th Infantry Brigade Group will proceed by Route March on the 19th inst. to MONT ST. ELOY Area.
        The Starting Point will be the meeting of the roads immediately West of AVESNES-LES-COMTE, i.e. where the LIENCOURT - AVESNES-LES-COMTE and GRAND RULLECOURT - AVESNES-LES-COMTE Roads meet.

3.   The following will be the order of march :-

Bde. Hqrs.	Time to pass Starting Point	0945
6th H.L.I.	------- Do -------	1000
7th H.L.I.	------- Do -------	1020
5th H.L.I.	------- Do -------	1040
413th Field Coy. R.E.	------- Do -------	1100
2nd L.F.A.	------- Do -------	1120

        The 157th L.T.M.B. will follow immediately in rear of the 7th H.L.I.
        The 220th Coy. A.S.C. will follow in rear of the Field Ambulance, leaving GIVENCHY-LE-NOBLE at 1100, joining the AVESNES-LES-COMTE - HABARCQ Road by the most direct route.

4.   A distance of 500 yards will be maintained between units and 100 yards between Companies.   Transport will accompany units.

5.   Route as follows :-   Starting Point, HABARCQ,- Junction of Roads South East edge of BOIS de HABARCQ, HOUTE - AVESNES, MONT ST. ELOY.

6.   O.C. 2nd L.F.A. will detail one horse Ambulance wagon to be attached to, and to follow in rear of each Battalion, joining the Battalions at the Western entrance to AVESNES-LES-COMTE, the remainder of Ambulance following in rear of the column.

7.   A halt of one hour will be observed approximately from 1300 to 1400.   This halt will be ordered by Brigade Headquarters in the most suitable place.

8.   The mid-day meal must be ready for issue from cookers immediately the halt takes place.   On no account will the halt be extended.

9.   A rear party under an officer will be left by each unit to clean up the Billeting Area.   The Officer will obtain a certificate from the Area Commandant that billets have been left clean.   This will be sent to Brigade Headquarters on arrival at MONT ST. ELOY.

10.   A C K N O W L E D G E .

                                                       Captain,
                                     Brigade Major, 157th Infantry Brigade.

Issued at 2215 on 18/10/18.

Copy No. 1 to 5th H.L.I.   Copy No. 6.A. 220th Coy. A.S.C.
         2   6th H.L.I.   7   52nd Division.
         3   7th H.L.I.   8   Area Commandant Gd. Rlct.
         4   157th L.T.M.B.   9   Staff Captain.
         5   413th Field Coy. R.E.   10) War Diary.
         6   2nd L.F.A.   11)
                                            12   File.

"A" Form.
MESSAGES AND SIGNALS.
Army Form C. 2121.
(In pads of 100.)

Prefix	Code	Words	Charge	This message is on a/c of:	Recd. at ... m.
Office of Origin and Service Instructions		Sent At ... m. To By		.... Service. (Signature of "Franking Officer.")	Date ...... From ...... By ......

TO
5 HT 137 LTMB 225th field Coy
6 HT 226th Infbde
7 HT 2nd 90

Sender's Number	Day of Month	In reply to Number	AAA
AC 18	19		

Administration instruction Suffolk orders
No 12 aaa baggage will
be carried as it
was today aaa tractor
horses will report at
0700 as follows
to 5th HT 2 to
6th HT 2 to
7 HT 1 to Suffolk
aaa LTMB aaa the
lee lty lorry will be
available for 5th HT after
it has completed /
aaa aaa motor wagons
will be detached to
report at 0700 as

From		
Place		
Time		

The above may be forwarded as now corrected. **(Z)**

Censor. Signature of Addressor or person authorised to telegraph in his name.

*This line, except **AAA**, should be erased if not required.

MESSAGES AND SIGNALS.

A Form. Army Form C. 2121. (In pads of 100.)

TO — 2

Sender's Number	Day of Month	In reply to Number	AAA
as	following	1	to
each	Bttn	and	1
to	LTMB	2	to
Bde	Hqrs	aaa	rations
drawn	tonight	must	be
reduced	and	carried	on
the	men	aaa	fresh
meat	may	be	carried
on	sae	half	turkey
ordinary	load	of	which
should	be	distributed	on
other	sae	timbers	aaa
great	care	must	be
taken	in	packing	the
tins	to	make	the
most	of	all	available
offer	kaca	supplies	aaa

MESSAGES AND SIGNALS.

Army Form C.2121.
(In pads of 100.)

Prefix	Code	m.	Words	Charge	This message is on a/c of:	Recd. at .... m.
Office of Origin and Service Instructions.			Sent			Date ....
			At .... m.		.... Service.	From ....
			To			
			By		(Signature of "Franking Officer.")	By ....

TO	3		

Sender's Number.	Day of Month.	In reply to Number.	AAA
Railhead	for	20th and	Inclusive
THELUS	AAA	supplies	will
be	Drawn	by	follow
tomorrow	(A)	Supplies	for
2nd inst)	arriving	at	Railhead
by	pack	train	on
gos and	will	be	21st
by	held	Railway	to
LA	CouLOTTE	(N3) (Central)	21st
(By	Supplies	for	21st
inst	will	be	delivered
to	exists	by	train
wagons	before	tomorrow	march
aaa	being	supplies	can
be	taken	to	meet
sug	in	horse	allotted
for	return	line	etc

From		
Place		
Time		

The above may be forwarded as now corrected.   **(Z)**

Censor.   Signature of Addressee or person authorised to telegraph in his name.

*This line, except **A A A**, should be erased if not required.

MESSAGES AND SIGNALS.

Prefix....... Code....... m.	Words.	Charge.	This message is on a/c of:	Recd. at ...... m.
Office of Origin and Service Instructions,	Sent			Date.......
	At........ m.		.................Service.	From.......
	To......			
	By......	(Signature of "Franking Officer.")	By.......

| TO | 4 | | |

| Sender's Number. | Day of Month. | In reply to Number. | AAA |

aaa Note aaa the following are
weak posts in new area aaa
CANAL DE LA HAUTE DEULE aaa
O.26.c.75   O.27.a.54
O.27.b. — Numerous pumps in
houses aaa Roads near
all times will be the
road LIEVIN — LENS HENIN
LIETARD aaa have parties
EG outings ZZ and
met Shores short
reception Camp HHH Camp
NEUVILLE ST VAAST by
1700 tomorrow aaa acknowledge
parties shower not
report before 1700 aaa
acknowledge

From
Place 137th Bde
Time

The above may be forwarded as now corrected. (Z)
Censor.   Signature of Addressee or person authorised to telegraph in his name.

SECRET.   Copy No. 2

157th Infantry Brigade Order No.152.

Ref. Map. LENS 11, 1/100,000.   19th October, 1918.

1. The Division will continue its move towards BERLIN to-morrow 20th October, 1918.
    The 157th Infantry Brigade Group will proceed by route march to the HENIN - LIETARD Area where it will bivouac for the night.

2. The Starting Point will be Brigade Headquarters (The WHITE HOUSE).
    The following will be the order of march :-

Unit		Time	Amended
Brigade Headquarters.	Will pass Starting Point	0830	0830
7th H.L.I. followed by 157th L.T.M.B.	Do	0835	0835
5th H.L.I.	Do	0900	0905
6th H.L.I.	Do	0910	0915
412th Field Coy. R.E.	Do	0925	0930
1/2nd L.F.A.	Do	0940	0945
220th Coy. A.S.C.	Do	1000	

    The 157th L.T.M.B. will follow immediately in rear of 7th H.L.I.

3. A distance of 500 yards will be maintained between units and 100 yards between Companies.

4. March discipline must be improved, particularly as regards keeping well to the right of the road. Transport must not be allowed to straggle.

5. Route. From the Starting Point - NEUVILLE ST. VAAST - THELUS - WILLERVAL - ARLEUX-EN-GOHELLE - DROCOURT - HENIN LIETARD.

6. O.C. 2nd L.F.A. will detail one horse ambulance wagon to be attached to and follow in rear of each Battalion, joining Battalions at the Starting Point.

7. A halt of one hour for the mid-day meal will take place about 1230 on receipt of orders from Brigade Headquarters.
    Brigade Headquarters will be at the head of the column.

8. Brigade Headquarters will close at the WHITE HOUSE at 0830.

9. Advance parties as for to-day will report to the Staff Captain at Brigade Headquarters (WHITE HOUSE) at 0830, mounted on bicycles.

10. A rear party under an officer will be left by each unit to clean billets. Each Officer will obtain a certificate from the Area Commandant or his representative that the billets have been left clean. Certificates to be forwarded to Brigade Headquarters.

11. Each unit of the Brigade Group will detail an orderly to report to Brigade Headquarters at 1900 to-morrow.

12. A C K N O W L E D G E .

                                                    Captain,
                                    Brigade Major, 157th Infantry Brigade.

Issued at ...2200... on 19/10/18.

Copies to all recipients of Brigade Order No.151, and S.A.A. Sect. D.A.C. and Mob. Vet. Section.

Appendix I
19-10-18

OC 5th /24
6th /
7th /
8th / S.M.B.

B.M. 4/43
20/10/18

Following has been received from Division, and is forwarded for information:—
"Warning aaa Dugouts, cellars, Straw
"on floors of houses, bits of furniture
"have been found contaminated
"with yellow cross liquid aaa Many
"dugouts have small sign of cross
"in chalk, preceded by a numeral
"but sign not invariably found.
"aaa"

20/10/18.

(Sgd) C.S. Sheils, Capt.
Bde Major, 157th Inf Bde.

Copy No 8

BATTN. ORDER No 60
BY
LIEUT-COL. W. MENZIES ANDERSON D.S.O. M.C.
Commdg 1/6th Ath H.L.I.
20th Octr, 1918

I. Battalion will move from present billets by route march tomorrow, 21st October, Karadzsgin Square (front of Q.M's Store) ready to move @ 0800.

II. Orders already issued are cancelled & the following substituted:—
    0500 Reveille.
    0600 Blankets } rolled in bundles of 10
          Waterp's } handed to Q.M. Stores.
    0630 Breakfast
    0900 Commdg Officer's Inspection.

III. O.C. Coys will ensure that Blankets & Waterp'ts are neatly rolled & that no foreign articles are inserted in the bundles.

IV. O.C. Coys will detail men party-carry as follows—
    personnel to be issued new O.C. to march, to report at

(Page 2)

... at Morrison at Orderly Room at 0800

V. L/C McNicol & 2 Other Ranks will report at
O.gg.4.y.4. on bicycles at 0730 leaving
line at 0645 — same men as Today

VI. O.C. Coys will ensure that men are properly trained,
in every respect for 0800 parade.

VII. Transport — 1 Doctor Lorry will report to H.Q.1 for
carrying Kitbags at 0700. Regt. Transport
will accompany Battalion.

VIII. Leave Party Parade at Orderly Room at 0730.

IX. WARNING Dugouts, cellars, straw & bits
of Furniture have been found to be containing Shell Yellow X Liquid. Many dugouts
do show small sign of a man preceded
by warning, but has been in case
invariably found.

M. D. Maguire Capt
Adjt 76th H.L.I.

20 10/18 Copies #1 1, 2, 3, 4 & 5 — T.O. Coys A B C D H.Q.
                    6, 7, 8 & 9 — T.Q.M. T.O. S.Q. & R.M.E.

Ref. Bde. Order No.153.   After Order.

Motor lorries will report at 0700 to units as follows :- 2 to
7th H.L.I. and 157th L.T.M.B., 2 to 5th H.L.I., 1 to 6th H.L.I. and
1 to Bde. Hqrs., for carrying baggage.

                                              Captain,
                                    Brigade Major, 157th Infantry Bde.
20th October, 1918.

SECRET.   Copy No. 2

157th Infantry Brigade Order No. 153.

Ref. Map. 44A. 1/40,000.   20th October, 1918.

1. The 52nd Division will continue its move Eastwards to-morrow.

2. The 157th Infantry Brigade Group, less 413th Field Coy. R.E., and Hqrs., and 2 Sections of 1/2nd L.F.A., will proceed by route march to FLERS, PLANQUE, and WAGNONVILLE.

3. The Starting Point will be point O.29.b.7.4. (i.e. roads junctions in HENIN LIETARD where the road turns due East and near which point on the left hand side is a large Y.M.C.A. marquee.)
The following will be the order of march :-

    Brigade Headquarters.
    5th H.L.I.
    6th H.L.I. immediately followed by 157th L.T.M.B.
    7th H.L.I.
    220th Coy. A.S.C.
    1 Section 2nd L.F.A.

Brigade Headquarters will pass the Starting Point at 0900 and units will follow in the order of march at the regulation distance of 500 yards between each unit and 100 yards between Companies.
The Section of the Field Ambulance to join the tail of the column by the most direct route.

4. Route. From Starting Point - Main HENIN LIETARD-DOUAI Road - FLERS, PLANQUE and WAGNONVILLE.

5. Advance parties as for to-day will report to the Staff Captain at the Y.M.C.A. tent at the Starting Point at 0730.

6. A rear Party under an Officer will be left by each unit to clean billets.

7. Brigade Headquarters will close at its present site at 0830. to-morrow.

8. On reaching destination after move each unit will invariably send an orderly to Brigade Headquarters.

9. A C K N O W L E D G E.

                                Captain,
              Brigade Major, 157th Infantry Brigade.

Issued at 2130 on 20/10/18.

Issued to all recipients of Brigade Order No.152, less S.A.A., Sect. D.a.c Mob. Vet. Sect., 413th Field Coy. R.E.

Appendix
20/10/18

BATTN. ORDER No. 61.   Copy No. 5

By
LIEUT-COL. W. MENZIES ANDERSON, DSO, MC.
                    Commdg. 16th Bn. H.L.I.
                          23rd October, 1918.
~~~~~~~~~~~~~~~~

The Battn. will move tomorrow 24/10/18, by route march to FLINES area via DOUAI.

- 0530 ... Reveille.
- 0600 ... Sick Parade
- 0615 ... Platoon Commander's Inspection.
- 0630 ... Breakfast.
- 0715 ... Advance Party of 1 Officer (to be detailed by "A" Coy) & 2 O.R. on Bicycles report at Orderly Room ready to move off.
- 0715 ... O.C. Coys inspect Billets.
- 0730 ... { Officers' valises, mess boxes etc. } { to be stacked at }
           { Men's blankets rolled otherwise in bundles of 10 } { Q.M.S. Store }
           { Greatcoats tightly packed in bundles of 10 }
- 0815 ... Commdg. Officer will inspect Billets.
- 0845 ... Markers (1 per Coy) report to R.S.M. at junction of roads at Church.

Battn.

Page 2.

Battn. parade (in F.M.O.) with Transport ready to move off.
Parade ground will be notified later.
Balmorals to be worn & rations to be carried on the man.

0845 ... Rear Party (1 N.C.O & 4 men per coy) will report at Ordly Room to Officer i/c (2nd Lt R. Paterson M.C.)

a/Adjt. 6th H.L.I.

Issued at 2000. 23/10/18

Copies Nos 1, 2, 3, 4 & 5 — To O.C Coys A, B, C, D & H.Qrs resptly.
"   6, 7 & 8 — To Q.M, T.O & Comdg Officer, resptly.

SECRET. Copy No. 2

157th Infantry Brigade Order No.154.

Ref. Map. 44A. 1/40,000.   23rd October, 1918.

1.   The 52nd Division will concentrate in the FLINES Area, commencing to-morrow, 24th October, 1918.

2.   The 157th Infantry Brigade Group, less 413th Field Coy. R.E., will proceed by route march to billets at MONTREUIL.
The Starting Point will be the road junctions at W.21.c.0.2. West of the North end of DUAI.

3.   The following will be the order of march :-

Brigade Hqrs.	Head of unit to pass the starting point	0915.
157th L.T.M.B.	(Immediately followed by 157th L.T.M.B.)	
5th H.L.I.	Head of unit to pass the starting point	0930.
7th H.L.I.	------ Do ------	0945.
6th H.L.I.	------ Do ------	1010.
1/2nd L.F.A.	------ Do ------	1025.
220th Coy. A.S.C.	------ Do ------	1040.

4.   A distance of 500 yards will be maintained between units and 100 yards between Companies.
Brigade Headquarters, 157th L.T.M.B., and 1/2nd L.F.A. will march to the starting point by the WAGNONVILLE - DOUAI Road running approximately North and South through W.14.b., W.15.a. & c. W.21.a. & c. to starting point.

5. ROUTE.
FLERS - DOUAI - FAUBG. MORELLE, (W.17.d.) - RACHES - PT. BAILLON (R.33.b.) - MONTREUIL.
The route through DOUAI will be carefully reconnoitred beforehand.

6.   A rear party under an officer will be left by each unit to clean billets.

7.   The usual advance parties, mounted on bicycles, will report to the Staff Captain by 0800. *at Brigade Headquarters*

8.   Brigade Headquarters will close at present site at 0830.

9.   A C K N O W L E D G E.

                               Captain,
              Brigade Major, 157th Infantry Brigade.

Issued at 2030. 23rd October, 1918.

Copy No.				
1	to 5th H.L.I.	7	52nd Division.
2	6th H.L.I.	8	Staff Captain.
3	7th H.L.I.	9	Bde. Sigs. Officer.
4	157th L.T.M.B.	10)	War Diary.
5	1/2nd L.F.A.	11)	
6	220th Coy. A.S.C.	12	File.

157th Infantry Brigade Administrative Instruction issued with
reference to 157th Infantry Brigade Order No.154.
----

1. **Supplies.** Railhead for 24th inst. VITRY-EN-ARTOIS.
   Refilling Point for Bde. Group. WARENDIN.
   Supplies will be drawn from Railhead by M.T. and taken to the
   Refilling Point.
   Train Companies will deliver rations to-morrow for the 25th inst.
   in new Brigade Areas.
   220th Coy. A.S.C. will march with the Brigade in accordance with
   B.O.154, and will subsequently concentrate under O.C. Divnl. Train
   at WARENDIN.

2. **Divisional Reception Camp.** This unit will entrain to-morrow at
   ZIVY Station and proceed to VITRY-EN-ARTOIS.

3. **Damp.** Blankets and all extra stores and kits in excess of Mobile
   Scale will be dumped at FLINES, probably on the 25th inst.
   Separate orders will be issued later.

4. **Lorries.** 3 lorries will rendezvous at FLERS Church at 0700 tomorrow.
   O.C. 7th H.L.I. will detail an officer to dispatch these lorries as
   follows :- 1 to 5th H.L.I., 1 to 6th H.L.I. and 1 to 7th H.L.I.
   After it has completed one run, the O.C. 5th H.L.I. will
   arrange for the lorry which carried 5th H.L.I. baggage, to return
   to Brigade Headquarters to lift baggage of Brigade Hqrs., and
   L.T.M.B. It will then be returned to 5th H.L.I. if required.

KM Newrick
Staff Captain, 157th Infantry Brigade.

23rd October, 1918.

Captain,
157th Infantry Brigade.

Issued to all recipients of Brigade Order No.154.

MESSAGES AND SIGNALS. Army Form C. 2123

Prefix	Code	Words	Sent, or sent out.	Office Stamp.
Received from	By		At ___ m.	HIF 23/10/18
Service Instructions			To ___ m.	
			By	

Handed in at **ZOG** Office **1448** m. Received **1458** m.

TO **6th H.L.I.**

*Sender's Number.	Day of Month.	In reply to Number.	AAA
BM1420	23		
Ref	BM1435	of	today
order	of	march	and
timed	to	pass	S.P.
at	W21c02	as	follows
Bde	Hqrs	followed	by
L.Tmp.	0915	5 H.L.I.	0930
7 H.L.I.	0945	6 H.L.I.	1010
fld	amb	1025	220
coy	asc	1040	aaa
orders	will	follow	as
soon	as	possible	advance
parties	will	report	to
staff	Capt	at	Bde
Hqrs	at	0800.	

FROM **157 Bde**

PLACE & TIME

"C" FORM.
MESSAGES AND SIGNALS.

Army Form C. 2123
(In books of 100.)
No. of Message..........

Prefix: Sm   Code: 2153   Words: 48

Received from: ZOG   By: McIntosh

Service Instructions: ZOG

Sent, or sent out.
At........ m.
To........
By........

Office Stamp: HIF 23/10/18

Handed in at .... Office .... m. Received 2223 m.

TO 6th K.L.I

Sender's Number	Day of Month	In reply to Number	AAA
1312	23	—	

after reaching new area tomorrow company commanders will be prepared to go out and reconnoitre main roads in FLINES and MONTREUIL to MARCHIENNES (Exclusive) as work on these roads will be started by the brigade on morning of 25th inst

FROM 154 Inf Bde
PLACE & TIME

O.C. 5th H.L.I.
    6th H.L.I.
    7th H.L.I.
    157th L.T.M.B.

B.M.5/155.
23/10/18.

Subject :- <u>Road Work.</u>

Further to this office wire B.12, of to-day.

1.   On the 25th inst. the Division will carry out work on roads in the new area.

2.   The following roads are allotted to this Brigade :- They will be divided into Battalion areas by the Acting Brigadier, who will proceed in advance of the Brigade to-morrow morning.
    Main Roads in FLINES and MONTREUIL. MONTREUIL - MARCHIENNES Main Road to MARCHIENNES exclusive. Craters are located at S.3.b.6.6. and S.5.a.9.6.

3.   Brigade and Battalion tools will be supplemented by the following tools which will be delivered at each Brigade Headquarters to-morrow afternoon after 1500 under Corps arrangements :-

    Shovels 150)
    Rammers 20)
    Picks 50)
    Hammers 10) Each Brigade.
    Brooms)
    Scrapers) Numbers not yet known.)
    Wheel-)
    barrows)

The above are minimum numbers which may be increased.

4.   The work required is roughly:-
(a) Generally to improve roads.
(b) Filling in craters and completing work on partially filled ones. Craters to have two layers of bricks on the top. Bricks to be laid with their long sides at right angles to the sides of the road.
(c) Removing mud from the road proper.
(d) Removing mud from the side walks where necessary in order to allow drainage of the road.
(e) Drainage generally. It should not be generally necessary to dig out ditches except in certain places.
    <u>N.B.</u> (i) Mud must be thrown over and not into the ditches.
        (ii) If bricks are not available without doing so, the nearest garden wall, etc., must be demolished and used.

5.   In order to obtain some training and to relieve the monotony of the work, Battalion Commanders will ~~come down~~ combine work with training.
    Training will be carried out on the march to and from the work and for two half hours (Brown Book) during the work.

6.   A report will be forwarded each evening to reach Brigade by 1730, stating particularly the work done and work still required.

7.   Instructions will be issued later as regards drawing extra tools required.

23rd October, 1918.

Captain,
Brigade Major, 157th Infantry Brigade.

O.C. 5th H.L.I.
     6th H.L.I.
     7th H.L.I.
     157th L.T.M.B.

ROAD WORK.

1.   In continuation of BM.5/155 of yesterday's date, areas are allotted for work as follows:-

5th H.L.I. One Company clearing and widening the street in FLINES Village at the blown up factory, one Company filling in the crater at M.25.c.2.8., and two Companies clearing and draining the FLINES - MARCHIENNES Road as far as the road junctions at M.32.b.5.7.

6th H.L.I. One Company clearing and draining roads in MONTREUIL, and three Companies clearing, draining, etc., the FLINES - MARCHIENNES Road from S.3.b.6.4. eastwards along the road mentioned.

7th H.L.I. One Company clearing and draining the roads in FLINES village, and three Companies clearing and draining the FLINES - MARCHIENNES Main Road from M.32.b.5.7. to S.3.b.6.4.

157th L.T.M.B. Clearing and draining roads (a) street in FLINES marked KURZE STR. i.e., from point R.23.b.7.0. to R.23.b.8.4., (b) Road from R.24.c.3.5. (near Brigade Headquarters) running parallel to railway, commencing at the point mentioned and working north.

2.   The duration of work, including march to and from work is 6 hours. Parties to march off at 0830.

3.   Ref. BM.5/155, dated 23rd instant, para 3 (c).
    Mud will be removed from the road proper, i.e., from off the cobbles. The mud on the sides of the road will not be scraped away where there is not a metalled bottom to the road. Water will, however, be drained away into the ditches on both sides of the road. Mud removed in making these drains to be thrown over the ditches and not into them.

4. **Tools.** Battalions will utilise the tools in regimental establishment. Very few picks will be required. Each unit will detail one limber to report to Brigade Headquarters at 0730 tomorrow morning to draw tools, and then return to Battalions.

5.   Attention is drawn to para 6 of BM.5/155 regarding reports.

6.   Acknowledge.

24th October, 1918.

                                                  Captain,
                            Brigade Major, 157th Inf. Bde.

"A" Form.
MESSAGES AND SIGNALS.

Army Form C. 2121.
(In pads of 100.)

Prefix	Code	m.	Words	Charge	This message is on a/c of:	Recd. at m.
Office of Origin and Service Instructions.			Sent			Date
			At m.		Service.	From
			To			By
			By		(Signature of "Franking Officer.")	

TO

Sender's Number.	Day of Month.	In reply to Number.	AAA
BM 830	20		

Ref Bm 5/156 of yesterday tools from Corps have not yet arrived aaa they with 1/e sent to Bns. on arrival aaa Men can change about from work to training using available tools till others from Corps arrive

War Diary

From
Place
Time

The above may be forwarded as now corrected.   (Z)

Censor.   Signature of Addresser or person authorised to telegraph in his name.

*This line, except AAA, should be erased if not required.
Wt. W 3253/P511. 500,000 Pads. 1/18. B. & S. Ltd. (E2389.)

"C" FORM.
MESSAGES AND SIGNALS. No. of Message..........
Army Form C. 2123. (In books of 100.)

Code......... Words........	Sent, or sent out.	Office Stamp.
By..........	At........m.	H1F
...ructions	To..........	22/10/18
ZUY	By..........	

at.................. Office......m. Received......m.

6ᵗʰ H L I

...der's Number.	Day of Month.	In reply to Number.	A A A
12	22		

warning order aaa division will march on 24ᵗʰ inst and concentrate in FLINES area

Ward

FROM 157 BDE
PLACE & TIME

* This line, except A A A, should be erased, if not required.

"A" Form.
MESSAGES AND SIGNALS.
Army Form C. 2121. (In pads of 100.)

TO: BHQ

Sender's Number.	Day of Month.	In reply to Number.	AAA
Rm 1830	26		
Warning	order	Ref Bm	1600
of	today	aaa	Following
is	order	of	march
and	time	to	pass
Starting	point	M.13.c.7.2	sheet
44	aaa	Bde	HQ
1015	6 MG	1020	7 MG
1035	5 MG	following	by
Bombs	1100	C. Coy	M.G. Bn
1115	1/2 LFA	MGO 1125	220
Coy	A&Q	MGO 1135	aaa
advance	parties	on	bikes
to	report	Staff	Capt
at	Bde HQ	at	0830

From: By Bde

"A" Form.
MESSAGES AND SIGNALS.

Army Form C. 2121.
(In pads of 100.)

Priority

TO: 6 A.S. / 4 A.S. / 5 A.S. / 7 A.S. / C Coy 5" M.G. / R.E.

Sender's Number.	Day of Month.	In reply to Number.	AAA
B32	26		

In continuation of BM 1600 and BM 1830 the co-ordinate of starting point should read M13d.y.2 aaa. The times for passing starting point will be approximately 2 hours later than time stated in BM 1830 aaa. Orders will follow as soon as possible. A meal should be given troops before marching off

From / Place: 154th Inf. Bde.

"A" Form
MESSAGES AND SIGNALS.

| TO | 5 HLI | 6 HLI | 7 HLI | |

| Sender's Number. | Day of Month. | In reply to Number. | AAA |
| B 23 | 25 | | |

Ref	BM 1750	of	today
aaa	Each	Battn	will
send	3	Officers	instead
of	2	tomorrow	26th
inst.			

From / Place: 157th Inf Bde.

Wm Cameron Capt

SECRET.

G.4/7/39.
25/10/18.

G.O.C. 157th Inf. Bde.

Subject :- RECONNAISSANCE OF FORWARD AREAS.

1. As soon as the leading Divisions of VII Corps have crossed the JARD CANAL, which may take place almost at once, the 52nd Division will probably go into the line.

2. Although the Division will not take over W. of the above Canal, the G.O.C. considers that it will be useful for a proportion of officers to see the country and also the local conditions obtaining in the forward area.

3. For this purpose, one motor lorry will be put at the disposal of each Infantry Brigade, and will be at Brigade Headquarters at 0830 on the 26th and 27th inst.

O.C. M.G. Bn. may send two officers with the lorry for 155th Inf. Bde. and C.R.E. may send two officers with each of the other lorries.

4. The lorries should go to ST. AMAND from which place officers should proceed on foot in parties of not more than three as much of the country forward of ST. AMAND is under enemy observation and movement is apt to be heavily shelled.

5. The senior officer of each lorry load should report at the Brigade Headquarters of the forward Brigade as follows :-

	26th inst.	27th inst.
155th Infantry Brigade.	24th Bde. 8th Div. P.7.d.2.3.	37th Bde. 12th Div.
156th Infantry Brigade.	37th Bde. 12th Div. J.31.central.	24th Bde. 8th Div.
157th Infantry Brigade.	37th Bde. 12th Div. J.31.central.	37th Bde. 12th Div.

(sgd) H.V. Curtis, Major,
General Staff,
52nd Division.

25th October, 1918.

Copy to C.R.E.

O.C. 5th H.L.I.
6th H.L.I.
7th H.L.I.
157th L.T.M.B.

Cancelled for 27.

Forwarded for information in continuation of this office wire B.M.1750 of to-day. The following is the allotment of officers to proceed by lorry leaving Brigade Headquarters at 0830 on 27th inst.

Brigade Hqrs.	2 Officers.	7th H.L.I.	2 Officers.
5th H.L.I.	2 "	R.E.	2 "
6th H.L.I.	2 "		

Captain,
Brigade Major, 157th Infantry Bde.

25th Oct. 1918.

SECRET.   Copy No....2..

157th Infantry Brigade Order No. 156.

27th October, 1918.

Ref Map. Sheets 44 and 44A, 1/40,000.

1.   The 52nd Division will relieve the 12th Division in the
Front Line on the night of 28th/29th.

2.   The 157th Brigade Group, less the 413th Field Coy. R.E.,
but plus 'C' Coy., 52nd Bn. M.G.C., will march to the LANDAS
Area on the 27th October. The starting point will be the
Road Junction at M.13.d.7.2. (i.e. where the LE HEM Road joins
the LA PLACETTE - FLINES - ORCHIES Rd.)

3.   The following will be the order of March :-

    157th Bde. Hqrs.   Head of Unit to pass Starting Point at 1130
    6th Bn. H. L. I.   "   "   "   "   "   "   "   " 1135
    7th Bn. H. L. I.   "   "   "   "   "   "   "   " 1200
    5th Bn. H. L. I.,
    followed by L.T.M.B.   "   "   "   "   "   "   "   " 1215.
    'C' Coy 52nd Bn. M.G.C. "   "   "   "   "   "   "   " 1230
    1/2nd L. F. A.   "   "   "   "   "   "   "   " 1240

        Route.-
            From Starting Point - COUTICHES - ORCHIES - RUE
                D'ORCHIES - LANDAS.

4.   A distance of 500 yards between Units and 100 yards
between Coys will be maintained.

5.   SUPPLIES.

    (a) The 220th Coy A.S.C. will load supplies for 28th inst
at 1000 on 27th., and will subsequently march to new Brigade
Area by same route as the Brigade Group.
        Meeting Place (where Unit representatives will meet
Train at end of march)
            220th Coy. A.S.C.   LANDAS Church.
    (b) Above Train Coy., will not pass through COUTICHES before
1300.
        After delivering supplies to Units the Coy., will
Concentrate at LES ARCINS (on ORCHIES - MARCHIENNES Road)
    (c) Refilling Point for 27th inst.
            Unit.   Refilling Point.
        157th Brigade Group.   On ORCHIES - MARCHIENNES Road
                                    in neighbourhood of LES ARCINS
    (d) Supply arrangements for 29th inst will be notified
later.

6.   The usual advance parties on bicycles will report to the
Staff Captain at Brigade Headquarters at 0830.

7.   BLANKETS.

        Blankets, extra Stores and Kits which cannot be carried
on Normal Transport Echelons, will be sent to Divisional Blanket
Dump, FLINES, before the march.
        One man per Unit will be left as Guard to these stores.
These men will be rationed from 28th inst. inclusive by Town
Major, FLINES.
        A nominal roll of these men (in duplicate) will be sent
to Brigade Headquarters on receipt of these Orders.

2.

Lt. Smith

8. RECEPTION CAMP.

The Reception Camp will start moving to the new site selected in DOUAI on 27th inst., in preparation for the move of Railhead to that place, which will probably take place on 29th inst.

O.C. Reception Camp, will, however, arrange to leave an Officer and sufficient men at VITRY to receive and despatch personnel of the Division, until the Div. Railhead leaves that place.

9. A rear party under an Officer will be left by each Unit to clean Billets. Each Officer will obtain a certificate that the billets have been left clean - certificates to be forwarded to Brigade Headquarters.

10. Brigade Headquarters will close at FLINES at 1100.

11. A C K N O W L E D G E.

Captain,
Brigade Major, 157th Infantry Brigade.

Issued at....0430........

Copies No. 1 to 5th H. L. I.
          2   6th H. L. I.
          3   7th H. L. I.
          4   157th L.T.M.B.
          5   'C' Coy., M.G.C.
          6   1/2nd L. F. A.
          7   220th Coy. A.S.C.
          8   Hqrs. Division.
          9   )
         10   War Diary.)
         11   File.

"A" Form.
MESSAGES AND SIGNALS.

Army Form C. 2121.
(In pads of 100.)

Prefix ... Code ... m.	Words.	Charge.	This message is on a/c of:	Recd. at ... m.
	Sent			Date ....
Office of Origin and Service Instructions.	At ... m.		.... Service.	From ....
	To			
	By		(Signature of "Franking Officer.")	By ....

TO 5th H.Q. 154th L.T.M.B.
    6th H.Q. C Coy 52nd M.G.Bn.
    4 H.Q. 2nd L.F.a. 220th Coy A.L.C.

| Sender's Number. | Day of Month. | In reply to Number. | AAA |
| B34 | 24 | | |

B36 cancelled.

From
Place   154th Inf Bde
Time

(Z) Lt/Col Antony Cochan

Censor.   Signature of Addressee or person authorised to telegraph in his name.

*This line, except **AAA**, should be erased if not required.
Wt. W 3253/P511. 500,000 Pads. 1/18. B. & S. Ltd. (E2389.)

"A" Form.
MESSAGES AND SIGNALS.

Army Form C. 2121.
(In pads of 100.)

TO	5HLI 137/LTMB 330 60y all
	6HLI C Coy 22nd Bn MGC
	7HLI 9th Fd Amb 330 chase

Sender's Number.	Day of Month.	In reply to Number.	
B36	27		AAA

Warning order aaa 137th Bde group will move to LECELLES tomorrow aaa to clear VIEUX CONDÉ by 1000 aaa Orders follow

From
Place: 137 Bde
Time:

Copy No. 2

157th Infantry Brigade Order No. 157.

Ref. Map. Sheet 44. 1/40,000.   27th October, 1918.

1. The 52nd Division will continue its march East to-morrow, 28th, the 156th Inf. Bde. taking over the front line on the night of 28th/29th inst.

2. The 157th Inf. Bde. Group will march from LANDAS to LECELLES to-morrow 28th inst. Starting Point will be the Cross Roads at H.25.b.7.4. East of VIEUX CONDE.

3. The following will be the order of march :-

   Brigade H.Q.   Head of Unit to pass Starting Point at..... 1215
   7th H.L.I.   Do   1230
   6th H.L.I. followed)
   by 157th L.T.M.B.   )   Do   1245
   5th H.L.I.   Do   1300
   "C" Coy. 52nd Bn. M.G.C.   Do   1315
   2nd L.F.A.   Do   1325

4. **Route.** From Starting Point - North end of VIEUX CONDE (H24.a.6.9.) - through H.18.d. - Cross Roads H.13.c.4.4. - RUMEGIES (Church) - LECELLES.

5. The usual distances will be maintained between Battalions and Companies on the march.

6. Advance Parties as for to-day will report to the Staff Captain at Brigade Headquarters LANDAS (N.28.b.3.3.) at 0900.

7. A rear party under an officer will be left behind by each unit to clean billets, the officer to obtain certificate that the billets have been left clean. Certificates will be forwarded to Brigade H.Q.

8. Brigade Headquarters will close at present location at 1115.

9. A C K N O W L E D G E.

10. Separate orders will be issued to 220 Coy. A.H. by Bn.
11. Troops will have midday meal before marching off.

A.S. Whinyloohen
Captain,
Brigade Major, 157th Infantry Bde.

Issued at 2100 on 27/10/18.

Copy No. 1 to 5th H.L.I.
        2   6th H.L.I.
        3   7th H.L.I.
        4   157th L.T.M.B.
        5   2nd L.F.A.
        6   "C" Coy. 52nd Bn. M.G.C.
        7   52nd Division.
        8   52nd Bn. M.G.C.
        9   Staff Captain.
       10) War Diary.
       11)
       12   F I L E.

220 Coy A.H.

WAR DIARY
or
INTELLIGENCE SUMMARY. 6 Highl. L.I.
November 1918 (Sheet No 1)

Army Form C. 2118.

(Erase heading not required.)

Place	Date	Hour	Summary of Events and Information	Remarks and references to Appendices
RUMEGIES	1/11/18	0630	Reveille Inspections Breakfast	
		0930 to 1115	Coy Training including Saluting Drill	
		1115 to 1130	Battn Tactical Scheme	
		1200	Draw & Issue	Army
		1400 to 1530	Lewis Gun Training Signalling Medical & Gas Training	
-do-	2/11	0630	Reveille Inspections Breakfast	
		0930 to 1130	Coy Training as per programme sent to MC for approval by Coy	
			Offrs including a Coy Tactical Scheme	
		1200	Midday Meal	
		1230 to 1530	Lewis Gun, Signalling, Gas, & Medical Training	
		1400 to 1530	Coy to purchase of foreign gifts saved fat all men issued	10/-
		1700	Draw & purchase arrangements of gifts since daily	
		2100	Lights Out.	
-do-	3/11	0700	Reveille Church Parade etc cancelled. Blok Party	
			due 30 men for signalling demonstration with aeroplane, on account of	
			rendering the roads unfit that Bn will not must proceed to CRESPIN &	
		1215	having only sent that Bn SUPPORT.	
			MIDDLESEX 5th Coys in SUPPORT.	
		1930	Orders for the morrow issued	

W.W. Nolan Capt

- CONFIDENTIAL -

WAR DIARY
or
INTELLIGENCE SUMMARY.
(Erase heading not required.)

Army Form C. 2118.

6th High. L.I.
NOVEMBER 1918. (Sheet No 2)

Place	Date	Hour	Summary of Events and Information	Remarks and references to Appendices
RUMEGIES	4/11/18	0630	Reveillé – Inspection – Breakfast. – Bn. order Programme cancelled.	Weather
P17 & 88			Preparing to move during morning	
HYDROPATHIC		1330	Moved off P17 L.88 where Batts. were billeted. HYDROPATHIC Lys	
			Arrived at P17 L.88. H.Q. was in & at	
		1700	HQ Mess and Orderly Room B2 in Support to 7th HLI	
			Front Line on the JARD CANAL. C & D manned the gap on the H.Day	
– do –	5/11/18	0630	Reveillé – Inspection – Breakfast.	
			Corps in Progress all day Cleaning up billets. One 1 Platoon per Coy the	
			allotted in groups of eight for supply & stand to the Lewis Gun Limbers	
		1230	Midday meal.	All Day
			Afternoon – Sorting of equipment. OC Corps reconnoitred route to front	
			Line. Men Bathing in the Hot Baths.	
– do –	6/11/18	0630	Reveillé – Inspection – Breakfast.	
		0930 to 1130	Coy training including Saluting, Gun Drill & Platoon Tactical Schemes	
		1230	Midday meal.	
		1400	Remainder of Officers reconnoitring routes to the front line. Men Bathing in	Very
			the Hot Coy	
– do –	7/11/18	0630	Reveillé – Inspection – Breakfast.	
		0900	Inspection of Billets by Commanding Officer	
		0930	Inspection of Battn on Training Ground by Comm. 95 Offr. (Bgen F.P.G)	
		1000 to 1130	Training – Battn on Gas training	
		1400 to 1530	Lewis Gun signalling & Bayonet training	
		1700	Recd message from Bde that Bn was likely to return to be ready to move forward. Immediate to Major M.L. Macie Capt.	

CONFIDENTIAL

WAR DIARY or **INTELLIGENCE SUMMARY**

Army Form C. 2118.

1/6th Argyll & S. L.
NOVEMBER 1918 (Sheet No 3)

Place	Date	Hour	Summary of Events and Information	Remarks and references to Appendices
CROISETTE (HYDRAULIC) NEAR St AMAND	8/11	0630	Reveille – Inspection – Breakfast	
		0830	Received Code word "HUNT" forward to get on the move and follow the retreating enemy	Appendix II
		0930	Batt'n with moved off Launebat to follow enemy B'de arrangements	
		1125	Reached Engs Roads & Bridges. Bridge over canal had not been completed. Left Transport & Brigade delay got across river but Transport could not	
			not then completed	
		1345	Eventually completed and all Batt'n safely in East side of JARD Canal	
		1510	Bay rest in Mahie on Western side of Neuville Bourgonval. No attack until K.30.d.6.3. too late to take any action	
		1530	Objective same up school I reported bosche at Newman's Bois Nichsle worked & after Cyclist party went to pass them never arrived – my B'de sent up from the Right and pushed through. Enemy had killed up to K 30 at K 21 crossing the Canal	
		1610	Arrived at LORETTE and met with no opposition Boche cavalry patrol reported to have been up the march before us.	
		1700	Reported Situation & disposition to Brigade took up Outpost Line presently guards – D Coy OP Hq MCGee all night line Bray	
		2300	Others not disturbed rest of day pass Brigade – CASUALTIES Nil. PRISONERS CAPTURED 2 OR	
			In CONDE-Slight slight	
LORETTE (OUTPOST LINE)	9/11	0100	Nature arrived lorry been delayed by enemy in the roads	
		0530	Stood to Arms – Bde Order not to the effect that we would move off at 0830 and advance our line as far as the WEST ANTOINE CANAL	
		0830	Col Paynter Comdg. B. & BN arrived – Battn commenced moving East. – LINE of ADVANCE – LORETTE – LA CIGOGNE – COURBOIS – R d Junction G.25.b - G.29.b – G.30.b.4.6 – G.27.a.5.1 (river Canal Bank) – G.14.c G.27.b G.27.central – 627 central	
		1100	Reached line G.14.c G.27.b G.27.central Front line B Coy (Capt King) left D Coy (Capt Farquhar) Right A Coy (Lt Henderson) Support. C Coy (Lt Thompson) Support	

W.J. Maciver Col

Army Form C. 2118.

WAR DIARY
or
INTELLIGENCE SUMMARY.

CONFIDENTIAL

(Erase heading not required.)

6th High. L.I.   NOVEMBER 1918 Sheet No. 4

Place	Date	Hour	Summary of Events and Information	Remarks and references to Appendices
LORETTE VILLE	9/11/18	10/00	Passed through BERNISSART + formed East entrance and flank for just in advance the morning of the 8th by the 3rd Canadian Patrol.	
POMMEROEUL		11/15	Aeroplanes reported enemy clear of ST ANTOINE CANAL.	
			Cyclists crossed canal by Lock No. 1.	
		11/20	Cavalry seen crossing Canal by Lock No. 1.	
		11/30	Two of our troops ordered to cross.	
		12/15 12/30	Our Patrols across - formed up to advance to E. Bank of Canal towards VILLE POMMEROEUL - No front.	
			Our troops met 150th men just left Hank, G.226 - G.23 a and d. Hence thought canal to be of advance minus G.226 - G.36 a + c. M66 + 1.	Wire
		13/15	Entered VILLE POMMEROEUL - No sign of enemy. Found that Cavalry (by an officer of the 7th) reconnoitred as far as M66 + 1 - Settled in billets for the night. Patrols out.	
			After my own report our proposition for transport running to reach	
		14/00 20/00	Orders received that we would probably have next morning. CASUALTIES. His.	
	10/11	05/30	Reveille and stand arms	
			Bn. Orders rec'd to effect that we would advance, the 7th leading followed by 5th supported by 6th. Objective HERCHIES.	
		11/30	Stood to started	
		12/00	6th Marched.	
		12/00	5th cleared SIRAULT. B.2 was held up + had lunch. Restore HAUTRAGE + SIRAULT.	
		13/10	Moved forward again rec'd orders that the 5th would do advance guard. We would go in front of T.1, 5 and 6 and T.1. On the way message rec'd that cavalry were held up by M.G's in front and 7th of our were in. Ordered in C.15, 24 and 30. Rose by 5th men + push to Engineers + bde of our supports and 7th to attack M.G's they could cut off any Boche climbing at + 5 m. were held up in front by heavy M.G. fire.	
		16/30	From the front 5 m. we had info that they received I.G. central II/S cited.	

M. O'Neill Capt.

WAR DIARY or INTELLIGENCE SUMMARY

Army Form C. 2118.

1/8th High. L.I.

NOVEMBER 1918 (Sheet No 5)

Place	Date	Hour	Summary of Events and Information	Remarks and references to Appendices
VILLE POMMEREUL to VACRESSE	10/11/18	1622	6th Wounded from F attacking North in direction of HERCHIES	
		1640	Moved off MG fire fairly heavy. Light Shelling.	
		1730	Found VACRESSE (subject of HERCHIES) clear of the enemy. Pushed patrols out towards HERCHIES. 1156 Bay occupied HERCHIES. Detachment of MG and LTMs reported. Recce agt HQ village for the night BGC taxied 2nd	
		2300	To arrived with cookers cost a lot of men along route + had to Z down and had evidence / roads were enforced that returns will not be till tomorrow noon.	
-do-	11/11/18	0830	Rec'd Orders that Bn. would advance CASUALTIES 1 OR KILLED 3 ORs wounded in support of 5th Gordon that	
			the Bn. would deploy fasting at IHCentral by 0830. Instructions accordingly	
		0830	Got news that ARMISTICE HAD BEEN SIGNED BY GERMANY and that hostilities would cease at 1100 along the whole front	
			Had Breakfast + got cleared up	
		1010	Moved off again. B Coy as advance of the keeping close touch with 3rd. Who were entering ERBISOEUL	
		1200	Arrived at HERBISOEUL. 3rd had gone on to line of forest edge. to take up an Outpost Line	
ERBISOEUL			Billeted behind the village	
		1600	all transport + rations arrived	ADMY
-do-	12/11/18 0730		Reveille. Rifles + cleaning equipment throughout	
		0900	Conference of Coy & Officers with GC Coys.	ADMY
		1230	Muster Meal 1230. Extra Meal.	
			BM 2/60 ace. of effect that Batth held subject to orders to proceed to Rosters afternoon...	
		1800	...	

M. J. McCrum Capt.

Army Form C. 2118.

WAR DIARY
or
INTELLIGENCE SUMMARY.

CONFIDENTIAL

1/5th Highland L.I.

NOVEMBER 1918. Sheet No. 6.

(Erase heading not required.)

Instructions regarding War Diaries and Intelligence Summaries are contained in F. S. Regs., Part II. and the Staff Manual respectively. Title pages will be prepared in manuscript.

Place	Date	Hour	Summary of Events and Information	Remarks and references to Appendices
ERBISOEUL	13th	0600	Reveille – Inspection Breakfast.	
		1100	Bn'n prepared to move to a new area. Move cancelled.	
		1200	move cancelled	
		1400	Bn'n fell in and marched with transport to front line HQ was N. of Mon's Turbise Rd. – B and C Coys manned outpost system.	Appx No III
		1700	Evening meal. Night Quiet.	Msry
Mons Turbise Rd	14th	0630	Reveille to outpost coys	
HQ Turbise		0730	Reveille to remainder – Inspection Breakfast	
		0830	Evening inspection B.C.O. & Bn Major called at HQ	
		0900	Company Officers inspected B & D Coys in command of CHATEAU in Mons	
		1100	TURBISE Rd in F.M.O.	
		1300	orderly Room	
			B.M. 57/95th Regt subsequent to entering received of a formal procession of the Army through Mons. Except 100 all ranks HQ 2.5 arm	Appx No IV
			Relation from Each Coy & an officer of A.T.B.	
		1730	Evening meal – Night quiet.	45-1
do –	15th	0530	Reveille – Inspection Breakfast	
		0730	Party of 100 men to Mons procession inspected by Commdg Officer in	
			CHATEAU GROUNDS	
		1130	Party Marched Off.	
		1230	Midday Meal	
		1600 to 1630	Bn'n Com'd Offr rode was carried out B & D Coys took over the Outposts	
		1730	and Coy C and A Coys inspected	

W.D.Weir Capt.

WAR DIARY
or
INTELLIGENCE SUMMARY.

Army Form C. 2118.

Codford 1/6 Batt. SLR'S
November 1915 Sheet No. 7

Place	Date	Hour	Summary of Events and Information	Remarks and references to Appendices
RAV 2 (Hut Lines)	10/11/15	0630	Orderly Trumpeter sounds to Reveille. Instruction - Breakfast	
		0700	Sick Parade	
		0730	Commanding officer inspects N.C.O's Cooks & Chateau de Vimbre du F.N.O	
			Throughout morning — Companies commenced parading. Coached in Extended Order & Company Drill &c &c.	
do	11/11/15	0530	Orderly Trumpeter sounds to	
		0630	Reveille Instruction Breakfast	
		0900	Guard Mounting	
		0930	Major Coats & Officers Band & Sgt or LCpl 100 attended Divisional Thanksgiving Service at PLOUYS	
		1306	Brigade wire 10/12/1 Reserved outpost to withdrawn to 2/200 reinforcement 1900.	Appendix VI 10/11/15
do	11/11/15	0530	Reveille Instruction Breakfast	
		0600	Orderly Trumpet	
		0630		
		1130	C.O made his Coy on Coy Battle inspection of Coy Billets Cookers commencing with 1 Coy D & B C	
			throughout morning & afternoon	
do	10/11/15	0530	Reveille Instruction Breakfast	
		0630	Guard Mounting	
		0930	Company arriving & c	
		1100	Commanding Officers Parade (Command Drill & Maine regimt unit SM R. attended Tournee Course 11 officers & 15 Burgess & 156 officers arrived Course)	

WAR DIARY
or
INTELLIGENCE SUMMARY.

Army Form C. 2118.

(Erase heading not required.)

Place	Date	Hour	Summary of Events and Information	Remarks and references to Appendices
RAVE	20/11/18	08.30	Reveille. Individual Breakfast.	
		09.00	Guard mounting	
		10.00	B.G.C. inspected Battalion, British soldiers, Wagons, Horses and stables	
NAMONI		11.00	Continued Forage	
		12.00	Sheds	
			Military transport animals	
	21/11/18	06.30	Reveille. Individual Breakfast	
			Guards mounting	
			As yesterday except Animal exhibitn	
		11.00	Brass tacks. Continues Parades	
			Preliminary individual equipment	
	22/11/18	06.30	Reveille. Individual Breakfast	
		09.00	Company training. C.O. arranging	
		09.30	Ceremonial Parade. Rehearsal of horses for tomorrow	
		14.00	Stables	
			Training animals Battalion	
	23/11/18	06.30	Reveille	
		08.00	Breakfast	
		08.00	"A" Parade Order for C.O. Parade	
		09.30	C.O. takes for Battalion training	
		10.00	Brigade marched to DRILL GROUND on N.W. CHATEAU ROAD. Battalion marched past 7,2,3,0,5 w.e 250 yd. Band W.E. 300. Inspected on N.W. of CHATEAU ROAD. Inspected by B.G.C. marched off hook in column. Clear column reformed twice and advanced in Ouvge order.	
		14.00	Stable.	
		16.00	Guard mounting	
			Nature. Musical battens	

[signature]

Army Form C. 2118.

WAR DIARY
or
INTELLIGENCE SUMMARY.

Confidential. 1/6 Batt Duke of Lancs Own
November 1918

(Erase heading not required.)

Instructions regarding War Diaries and Intelligence Summaries are contained in F.S. Regs., Part II. and the Staff Manual respectively. Title pages will be prepared in manuscript.

Place	Date	Hour	Summary of Events and Information	Remarks and references to Appendices
PAVE	24/11/18	0630	Reveille	(Appendix III)
		0930	Church Parade	
N of MONS			Nothing unusual worked	
	25/11/18	0630	Reveille Preliminaries Breakfast	
		0900	Commencing training for A B + D Coys C Coy on range fatigue on Brigade MG range K8 a+b about 45	
		1330	orderly room	
		1400	Shoots under Coy arrangements A B/V Z(1) in Battalion mtr coy competition	
		1800	Concert by Divisional Concert Party	
	26/11/18	0630	Reveille Breakfast	
		0830	Battalion Route March through MONS and back	
		1330	orderly room	
		1400	Shoots under Coy Arrangements B/D V D in Battalion mtr coy competition	
	27/11/18	1430	Lecture by Brigadier General on Homeless of Pealoom	
		0630	Reveille Preliminaries Breakfast	
		0900	Battalion on Coy Training except O Coy. O Coy on range at K 12 a + b about 45	
		1330	orderly room	
		1400	Shoots under Coy Arrangements A and B Battalion Combine D Sec/A 3-2	
	28/11/18	0630	Reveille Preliminaries Breakfast	
		0730	D Coy 2 officers & 5 pts to OR fatigue on Brigade lewis Gun range K8 a+b about 45	
		0900	A C Coy tactical scheme march out to DRILL GROUND at R 3 4 q + b one company scheme	
		1000	B Coy 2 officers + 5/6 OR fatigue on Brigade lewis Gun range K8 a + b about 45	
		1400	Shoots under Coy arrangement	

WAR DIARY
or
INTELLIGENCE SUMMARY.

Army Form C. 2118.

12th Bn. Hghrs. L.I.
November 1918 Sheet No. 10

Place	Date	Hour	Summary of Events and Information	Remarks and references to Appendices
PAVE nor MONS	29.11.18	0630	Reveille Inspection Breakfast	
		0900	Ceremonial Parade add month look in column of column	
		1130	Natives in Reading Room by R.A.F. flew on fright Bombers flew over the word	
			Enjoyed attendance. So all ranks attended Catholic	
		1330	Dining Room	
		1400	Draft under Cap. Armstrong 5 Sgts 9 V Cpls 9 L/Cpls in Bath Ground.	
	30.11.18	0630	Reveille Inspection Breakfast	
		0900	B Coy on Battalion Range A.C.D. Coy training	
		1330	C Room	
		1400	Store under Coy Arrangements	
		1600	St Andrews days concert	

WAR DIARY or INTELLIGENCE SUMMARY

Army Form C. 2118.

(Erase heading not required.)

1/6th Bn Highd L.I.
London/November 1918 Rest Roll

TABLE SHEWING INCREASES & DECREASES IN BATTALION CAMP STRENGTH DURING MONTH OF NOVEMBER 1918

Place	Date	Hour	Summary of Events and Information			Remarks and references to Appendices
				OFF.	O.R.	
			Camp Strength as at 1st November 1918	30	403	
			DECREASES			
			Wounded	2 –	6	
			Sick to HOSP.		3	
			to Detd Duties		38	
			On Leave		1	
			to Cadet Unit			
				2 –	48	
				28	355	
			INCREASES			
			From HOSP. Sick		5	
			" Wounded		5	
			" Detd Duties		12	
			" Leave		38	
			" Courses of Inst.		5	
			" Leave VIA HOSP		1	
			" Divnl Rec. Camp		2	
			" Rest		2	
			Reinforcements		1	
					71	
			Camp Strength as at 24.00 on 4-11-18 →	28 –	426	
			DECREASES			
			Wounded		2	
			Sick to HOSP.		18	
			to Detd Duties		5	
			" Courses of Inst.	2 –	4	
			On Leave		6	
			Died of Wounds		1	
			1.B.D CALAIS			
				2 –	27	
				26 –	399	
			INCREASES from HOSP. Sick	3 –	4	
			" Wounded		3	
			" Detd Duties	2 –	8	
			" Leave	1 –	24	
			" Courses of Inst	1 –	0	
			" Divnl Rec. Camp			
				8 –	44	
				34 –	433	
			Camp Strength as at 24.00 on 14-11-18 →			
			DECREASES Sick to HOSP.	1 –	7	
			On Leave	2 –	12	
				3 –	19	
				31 –	414	
				OFF.	O.R.	
				0 –	10	
			" Wounded		5	
			" Detd Duties	1 –	35	
			" Leave	1 –	20	
			" Courses of Inst	2 –	29	
			" Reinforcements		4	
			Casualties			
				4 –	119	
				35 –	533	
			Camp Strength as at 24.00 on 21-11-18 →			
			DECREASES Sick to HOSP.		3	
			to Detd Duties		5	
			" Leave	8 –	9	
			" Courses of Inst.		2	
			On Leave		2	
			" VIA HOSP			
			" IMKEST EGYPT.		1	
			Reinforcements			
				8 –	21	
				27 –	512	
			Camp Strength as at 24.00 on the 28-1-1-18 →	27 –	52	
					564	
			DECREASES Sick to HOSP.		2	
			to Detd Duties		1	
			" Courses of Inst	1 –	2	
			On Leave			
			to Rest Camp Paris Plage	1 –	0	
				2 –	6	
				25 –	558	
			INCREASES from HOSP. Sick	1	3	
			" Wounded		4	
			" Detd Duties		1	
			" Leave	1	10	
			" Divn. Rec. Camp		2	
			attd for Instruction			
			Reinforcements			
				2 –	41	
				2 –	50	
			Camp Strength as at 24.00 on 30-11-18 →	27 –	629	

NETT. DECREASE FOR THE MONTH → OFF. 3
INCREASE " O.R. 226

"G" FORM.
MESSAGES AND SIGNALS. Army Form C. 2123.

Prefix	Code	Words	Sent, or sent out.	Office Stamp.
Received from	By		At ... m. To ... By	

Handed in at 20G Office 0943 m. Received 1004 m.

TO

Sender's Number.	Day of Month.	In reply to Number.	AAA
B45	4		
ref	BOO	order	178
billets	will	move	of
from	present	area	at
Wasser	by	times	AAA
Billets	must	however	be
cleared	by	1200	to
allow	100	hide	-

FROM: Line

PLACE & TIME

"A" Form
MESSAGES AND SIGNALS.

Army Form C. 2121
(In pads of 100.)

Prefix......Code......m.	Words	Charge.	This message is on a/s of :	Recd. at......m.
Office of Origin and Service Instructions	Sent			Date.............
....	At ....m.		................Service.	From ....
....	To			
....	By		(Signature of "Franking Officer")	By..............

TO	OHU	157 LTMB	156 Bde	
	CHU	2nd FA	30 Br Inf Bde	
	9HU	155 Bde		

Sender's Number.	Day of Month.	In reply to Number.	AAA
896	4		

Bde	Hdqs	closes	at
present	site	at	1230
and	opens	P19 b 6.7 at	
same	hour		

From
Place 157 Bde
Time

The above may be forwarded as now corrected.   (Z)
Censor.   Signature of Addressor or person authorised to telegraph in his name

Order No. 1625. Wt. W2252/   P 511. 27/2. H. & K., Ltd. (E. 2634).

SECRET.

O.C. 5th H.L.I.   O.C. 2nd L.F.A.
    6th H.L.I.   D. Coy., 52nd M.G. Bn.
    7th H.L.I.   220th Coy, A.S.C.
    157th L.T.M.B.

WARNING ORDER.

Reference Map Sheet 44.

The 157th Infantry Brigade will relieve the 23rd Infantry Brigade (on right of 156th Infantry Brigade) on the night of the 4th/5th November.

The 5th H.L.I. will relieve the 2nd Devons in reserve (Battalion Headquarters at P.8.a.2.1.)

The 6th H.L.I. will relieve the 2nd Middlesex Regiment in support (Battalion Headquarters at P.17.b.8.8.)

The 7th H.L.I. will relieve the 2nd West Yorks in the front line (Battalion Headquarters at Q.2.d.9.9.)

157 L.T.M.B will relieve 23rd L.T.M.B. (H.Q. P.17. A.0.9.)

C.Os. and Company Commanders will visit their opposite numbers tomorrow morning as early as possible and arrange all details of relief.

Times marching off will be notified later.

Acknowledge ✓

3rd November, 1918.
                                          Captain,
                          Brigade Major, 157th Infantry Brigade.

"C" FORM.
MESSAGES AND SIGNALS.

Army Form C. 2123.
(In books of 100.)
No. of Message ....

Prefix .... Code .... Words	Sent, or sent out.	Office Stamp.
Received from .... By	At .... m.	A I F
Service Instructions	To	2/8
	By	

Handed in at 15½ Bde Office 10.18 m. Received 9.10 m.

TO 6th H.L.I.

* Sender's Number.	Day of Month.	In reply to Number.	AAA
612	2		
Your	Battalion	required	to
work	on	roads	tomorrow
as	strong	as	possible
aaa	report	dd-	road
junction	I/4 D22	at	0930
to	pioneer	officer	aaa
tools	abs	shovels	will
be	drawn	from	Bde
aaa	Cookers	to	be
taken	aaa	task	1000
1200	and	1300	to
1500	aaa	work	on
RUMIGIES	SAMEON	LANDAS	ROAD

FROM
PLACE & TIME 4/M.E

* This line, except AAA, should be erased, if not required.

SECRET.   Copy No...?..

157th Infantry Brigade Order No. 158.

Ref. Map. Sheet 44, 1/40,000.   3rd November, 1918.

1.   The 52nd Division will take over the whole VIII Corps front by relieving 8th Division in the Right Sector of the Corps.
        The Policy will continue to be that of closely watching the enemy by patrols, so as to detect at once and follow up any retirement of the enemy from his line on the JARD CANAL.

2.   The 157th Infantry Brigade will relieve the 23rd Infantry Bde. in the Front Line in accordance with Table "A" on the reverse.

3.   All details of relief, including guides, will be arranged mutually between C.O.s concerned.

4.   All maps, defence schemes, trench stores, etc., will be taken over.

5.   Completion of Relief will be wired "PRIORITY" to Brigade Hqrs., using the code word " TURK ".

6.   The 157th Infantry Brigade Hqrs., will close at RUMEGIES and open at P.17.b.6.7. at an hour to be notified later.

7.   Orders as regards time units will march off from their present billets will be notified later.

8.   A C K N O W L E D G E .

                                    [signature]
                                                           Captain,
                                    Brigade Major, 157th Infantry Brigade.

Issued at ...2330... on 3rd November, 1918.

            Copy No.   1 to 5th H.L.I.
                       2   6th H.L.I.
                       3   7th H.L.I.
                       4   157th L.T.M.B.
                       5   2nd L.F.A.
                       6   220th Coy. A.S.C.
                       7   23rd Inf. Bde.
                       8   155th Inf. Bde.
                       9   156th Inf. Bde.
                      10   52nd Bn. M.G.C.
                      11   52nd Division.
                      12   Staff Captain.
                      13   Bde. Sigs. Officer.
                      14) War Diary.
                      15)
                      16   File.

TABLE "A".

Serial No.	Date.	Unit.	From.	To.	Relieving.	Remarks.
1.	Novr. 4/5th.	157 Bde.H.Q.	Rumegies. (I.20.b.5.9.)	Line. (P.17.b.6.7.)	23rd Inf. Bde. H.Q. (P.17.b.6.7.)	
2.	4/5th	5th H.L.I.	Bour Botin (H.Q.I.35.a.)	Brigade Reserve (H.Q. P.8.a.2.1.)	2nd Devon Regt.	
3.	4/5th	6th H.L.I.	Rumegies (H.Q.I.14.d.1.5.)	Brigade Support. (H.Q.P.17.b.8.8.)	2nd Middlesex Regt.	
4.	4/5th	7th H.L.I.	Rue Lasson. (H.Q.J.19.a.3.5.)	Front Line. (H.Q. Q.2.d.9.9.)	2nd West Yorks Regt.	
5.	4/5th	157 L.T.M.B.	Rue Lasson. (H.Q.J.19.c.2.2.)	Front Line. (H.Q.P.17.a.0.9.)	23rd L.T.M.B.	

"C" FORM.
MESSAGES AND SIGNALS. No. of Message............

Army Form C. 2123.
(In books of 200.)

Prefix 10	Code O845 Words 7	Sent, or sent out.	Office Stamp.
Received from LIME By Hola		At m.	HIJO
Service Instructions		To	8/11/18
OPERATION PRIORITY		By	

Handed in at LIME Office O845 m. Received O844 m.

TO   HIJO

*Sender's Number.	Day of Month.	In reply to Number.	AAA
OK18	8		
HUNT	(aa)	acknowledge	

Appendix II

FROM   LIME
PLACE & TIME

To all recipients of 157th Infantry Brigade Order No.100.

        RATIONS........................... 1500.

                                    M. Cummins Lt for
                                                    Captain,
7/21/20   Brigade Major, 157th Infantry Brigade.

```
Copy No.  1. to  5th H.L.I.
          2.     6th H.L.I.
          3.     7th H.L.I.
          4.     157th L.T.M.B.
          5.     52nd Division.
          6.     C.R.A.
          7.     D.Coy., 52nd M.G.Bn
          8.     33rd Bde. R.F.A.
          9.     7th Canadian Inf. Bde.
         10.     156th Inf. Bde.
         11.     X/26 T.M.B.
         12.     Staff Captain.
         13 )    Sigs. Officer.
         14)     War Diary
         15)
         16.     File.
```

SECRET.   Copy No. 2

157th Infantry Brigade Order No.100.

Ref. Map. 44 C.E., 1/20,000.   7th November, 1918.

1.   The 157th Infantry Brigade will clear the ground between the River ESCAUT and the CONDE + TOURNAI Road as far NORTH as the Corps Boundary to-morrow, 8th November.

2.   1 Coy. 5th H.L.I. will make good the ground SOUTH of a line EAST and WEST through R.26.central.
     1 Coy. 7th H.L.I. will establish posts at the Copse at about R.20.b.7.8. and FORT MAHY, and thence patrol NORTHWARDS. All of the above points are held by the enemy.
     At ZERO hour the Coy. of 5th H.L.I. will attack due EAST from about R.20.a.5.8. followed by the Company of 7th H.L.I. which will attack along the road R.20.a.5.8. - R.20.d.2.2. (a post will be established at the latter point) - through the copse entering FORT MAHY from the SOUTH-WEST.

3.   Machine Guns will support the attack from R.20.c.y.5 and R.26.b.0.y

4.   Trench Mortars. 1, 6" Trench Mortar will demolish the three most NORTHERLY houses of WARDS (R.14.c.05.10.) on the EAST side of the BRUNEAU - CONDE Road before ZERO.

5.   ARTILLERY. (a) Two preliminary bombardments of half an hour each are being put down by the Heavy Artillery on to FORT MAHY and Copse at R.20.b.70.90. Also on to the house R.20.b.70.35. The Artillery is also directing steady fire on to these points up to ZERO plus 5.

     (b) Neutralising fire will be directed by Howies on to houses at R.15.a.65.5.0. also on to group of houses R.14.b.5.4., and FORT BRASSERY R.14.b.20.50. The above firing being carried out from ZERO to ZERO plus 30.

     (c) Hows 4.5" Hows. are demolishing the three houses at R.20.d.8.0. and also bombarding the two houses at R.20.d.10.95, and R.20.c.50.90.

     (d) 4.5" Hows. are neutralising FORT MOULIN A VENT from ZERO to ZERO plus 30. From which hour an eighteen Pounder barrage will be directed against this point.

     (e) A standing barrage of 18 pdrs. is being put down on the Copse and house R.20.b.75.90. and R.20.b.70.35. respectively, also on FORT MAHY.

     (f) A standing barrage of 18 pdrs. and Howies is being put down on the following line from ZERO to ZERO plus 20 :- from the Railway Crossing R.8.d.1.0. to the River bank at R.15.a.5.0. thence SOUTH along the EAST bank of the river ESCAUT to R.20.b.5.0. This standing barrage will, however, continue till ZERO plus 30 along the line mentioned NORTH of FORT DU PRESUNIUR.

6.   The artillery is cutting gaps in the existing wire about R.26.b.cent. and about R.26.central.

7.   Artillery fire ceases at ZERO plus 30.

8.   O.Cs. 5th and 7th H.L.I. will arrange O.P.s in our present lines and make frequent reports as to progress.

9.   ZERO hour will be notified later by the code word "RATIONS"

10. ACKNOWLEDGE.

                                                     S. Hutchinson
                                                     Captain,
                              Brigade Major, 157th Infantry Brigade.

Issued at 2100 on 7/11/18.

O.C. 5th Bn. H.L.I.
     6th Bn. H.L.I.
     7th Bn. H.L.I.
     157th L.T.M.B.

BM.2/62.
7/11/18

Warning Order BM.2/61 of 6th inst. is confirmed.

     The relief will take place on night of 7th/8th instant. After relief you will, in conjunction with 7th H.L.I., clear the new area of the enemy west of the Escaut River.

     Attached map shews the new boundary between the Canadian and VIII Corps as it will be after relief.

7th November, 1918.

(Sgd) C.S.Stirling Cookson Captain,
Brigade Major, 157th Inf. Bde.

Copies to 6th H.L.I., and 157th L.T.M.B.

Map to 5th H.L.I. only

SECRET.   Copy No. 2

Addendum No.1, to 157th Infantry Brigade Order No.159.

Ref. Map. Sheet 44, 1/40,000.   7th November, 1918.

Reference Brigade Order No.159 dated 6th inst. the following amendments are made :-

Para. 3, (a), (ii)
One Section of D Coy. 52nd Bn. M.G.C. will accompany the Left Coy. of the Front Line Battalion across the Canal.

Para. 3, (b).
One Section of D Coy. 52nd Bn. M.G.C. will cross East of the Canal with the leading Coy. of the Support Battalion (6th H.L.I.)

The above two Sections will be withdrawn, for the purpose of crossing the Canal, from the Left of the Brigade Front.   On reaching East Side of the Canal, the two sections will take up positons on the Line K.29.central - Q.6.a. where they will halt till the arrival of the remainder of the Machine Gun Company.

Para. 3, (d).
Cancel the paragraph as far as the 52nd Battalion M.G.C. is concerned.

Para. 11.
As soon as the river bridges are opened, Brigade Hqrs., will open at ODOMEZ (Q.3.c.5.5.) and not at HAUTE VILLE.

At present the 7th H.L.I. is the Front Line Battalion, 6th H.L.I. is in Support and 5th H.L.I. in Reserve.

O.C. 8th Corps Cyclist Battalion will report through O.C. Support Battalion.

The Support Battalion will gain touch with the 7th Royal Scots, of the Left Brigade, at the following points during the advance;-
(1) K.29.central, (2) The CONDE - PERUWELZ Railway at L.25.a.8.9.,
(3) the CONDE - BONSECOURS Road at L.21.d.5.6. in the event of the advance being made through the BOIS DE L'ERMITAGE.
O.C. Support Battalion will detail a liaison officer to accompany his Left Platoon for this purpose.   Reports will be sent to Brigade Hqrs., when touch has been gained.

Officers from Brigade Hqrs., Lieut. Cumming and Lieut. Kennedy, will be present during the crossing of troops across the bridges G. & K. and L. & M. respectively.   Any reports for Brigade Hqbs., should be handed to these officers.

A C K N O W L E D G E .

Captain,
Brigade Major, 157th Infantry Brigade.

Issued at..10.02. on 7/11/18.

Copies to all recipients of 157th Infantry Brigade Order No.159.

O.C. 5th Bn. H.L.I.
6th Bn. H.L.I.
7th Bn. H.L.I.
157th L.T.M.B.

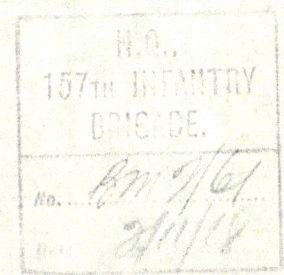

WARNING ORDER.

The 157th Infantry Brigade will be prepared to extend its boundary tomorrow and take over up to the railway which runs through R.25.c.2.9.and R.21.central.

The 5th H.L.I. will be prepared to move forward tomorrow, 7th instant, to take over the front line with two Companies as follows.

(a) One Company to take over dispositions of the present Right Company of the 7th H.L.I.

The Company of the 7th H.L.I. thus relieved to take over billets from the Company of the 5th H.L.I. now billeted in Q.9.b.

(b) One Coy. to take over dispositions of left Coy. of left Bn. 8th Canadian Inf Bde.

The remaining Company of the 5th H.L.I. will, for the time being, remain billeted in St.Amand, but on receipt of the code word "HUNT" will move forward to join its Battalion. O.C. 5th H.L.I. will arrange details of relief with OO.C. Battalions concerned. He will arrange to reconnoitre and select a Battalion Headquarters as near as possible to those of 7th H.L.I., at the same time selecting an area into which he will place one of the three forward Companies which will be his Battalion reserve Company in the Line.

The location of the Left Canadian Battalion Headquarters will be forwarded as soon as it is known.

6th November, 1918.

Captain,
Brigade Major, 157th Inf. Bde.

SECRET.   COPY No. 2....

157th Infantry Brigade Order No. 159.

Ref. Sheet 44. 1/40,000   6th November, 1918.

1. It is not intended to force a crossing of the JARD CANAL, active patrolling will, however, be carried out from dusk till dawn to ensure that the enemy does not retire without our knowledge.

2. When the enemy withdraws, the 52nd Division will follow him up to gain and maintain touch with his main force. It is not the intention that Battalions should become heavily engaged.

3. (a) As soon as the enemy's withdrawal from the JARD CANAL is ascertained, the following will be the procedure :-

   (i) Single file bridges will be thrown across the river and canal as under:-
   (Q.5.c.25.85.   to be known as   G Bridge.
   (Q.5.b.7.7.   ---do---   K do.

   (K.34.d.5.1.   ---do---   L do.
   (K.34.d.7.7.   ---do---   M do.

   (ii) Covering parties for each of the above pairs of bridges (G.& K., L.& M.) will be found from the left Company of the front line battalion: two platoons to each pair.
   These platoons will ferry across the river in the rafts and make good the ground between the river and canal. Similarly on arrival of the rafts for the canal bridges these two platoons will ferry across the canal and make good a bridgehead along the line K.34.b central - K.36.a.25.70. - along the road running S.E. through RIEUX DE CONDE to about K.36.c. central - about Q.6.b.0.6. - canal.
   The centre Company of the front line battalion will be responsible for watching the ground between the river and the canal in Q.6.c.& d. from positions along the southern bank of the river. This Coy. will also have one anti-aircraft Lewis gun mounted.

   (iii) Carrying parties for material of the above bridges will be found as follows:-
   For G. and K. Bridges by the Reserve Company of front line Btn.
   For L.& M. bridges by one Coy. of reserve Battalion.
   The latter Coy. being billeted in Q.9.b.
   The above Companies will provide not less than 40 carriers each. On completion of work the carrying parties will return to their billets and stand by.
   Anti-aircraft Lewis guns will be placed in the vicinity of the bridges by Companies furnishing the carrying parties.

   (iv) Bridging operations will be supervised by an officer and one section to be detailed by O.C. 413th Field Coy., R.E.

(b) Support Battalion. When the bridges are completed the Support Battalion will push over one Coy. through the Coy. of the front line Battalion (vide para 3 (a) sub-para (ii)) to link up with the right of the left Brigade at K.29.central and to take up the line K.29.central. - Q.6.a. The Coy. will halt on this line.
The remainder of the Support Battalion accompanied by the section of D. Coy., 52nd Bn. M.G.C., at present in Brigade Reserve, and one section, 157th L.T.M.B., will then cross to east of the canal, push forward through the line Q.6.a. - K.29.central. - K.16.central. and advance on a two Company front making good the following successive objectives, taking over each from the VIII Corps Cyclist Battalion,(less one Coy.) which will have already crossed east of the canal by bridges on the left Brigade front:-
    (1) VIEUX CONDE - PERUWELZ Railway
        (R.1., L.31., L.25., L.19., L.13.)

(ii) CONDE - MONT DE PERUWELZ - PERUWELZ Road.
(L.32., L.26., L.20., L.14., L.8.)

(iii) CONDE - CHATEAU de L'ERMITAGE - BOUQUET Road.
(L.33., L.27., L.21., L.15., L.8.b.& d.)

(iv) The line LORETTE - BONSECOURS - PERUWELZ.

Battalion Headquarters moving forward on the RIEUX de CONDE - GD. QUENOY - CHENE RAOUL Road.

Touch will be maintained throughout with the left Brigade who are advancing on to the same objectives on our immediate left.

Reports will be rendered on gaining touch with troops on flanks:-

(a) On line Q.6.a. - K.29.central. - K.16.central.
(b) VIEUX CONDE - PERUWELZ Railway.
(c) On line LORETTE - BONSECOURS - PERUWELZ.

(c) Reserve Battalion. One Coy. as in para 3 (a), (iii).
One Coy. will be detailed to proceed through CONDE either by light bridges or by rafts down the ESCAUT Canal, in order to cover the construction of bridges in CONDE by C.E. VIII Corps.
This Battalion, less two Coys., will remain in Brigade Reserve and concentrate about Q.3.d.central.

(d) D Coy. 52nd Bn. M.G.C.) Less Sections mentioned in para 3,(b),
    157th L.T.M.B.   ) will concentrate in Brigade Reserve
                            at about Q.3.d.2.0.

4. As soon as the Bridgehead is taken over by the Support Battalion, the Left Front Line Coy. of Battalion in Line, vide para 3, (a), (ii), will block the Western and Northern exits from VIEUX CONDE, reconnoitre VIEUX CONDE and report as to its occupation or otherwise by hostile troops.

5. Orders for the concentration of the Front Line Battalion will be issued by Brigade Hqrs.

6. Action of Artillery. In addition to the Artillery at present supporting the Brigade, the 9th Brigade R.F.A. will come forward from NIVELLE to HAUTE RIVE preparatory to pushing 1 Battery to East of the Canal when the Heavy Traffic Bridges "A" & "B" and "X" & "Y" have been completed by the C.R.E. at K.27.d.3.1. and PONT DE LA VERNETTE respectively. After crossing to East of the Canal this Battery will swing Southwards to assist the advance of the Support Battalion to whose Hqrs., it will send a liaison Officer.

7. Boundaries. Northern Brigade Boundary:-

P.3.central - K.35.central - K.36.b.2.7. - K.33.d.0.5. - K.28.d.2.0. - L.25.a.0.7. - L.22.central - L.23.central and then due Eastwards.

Southern Brigade Boundary and Corps Boundary :-

The Southern Boundary is as follows :- Q.9.c.2.4. - Q.16.c.9.5. - R.13.c.5.4. - R.20.a.1.1. - R.9.c.9.1. - along HAISNE River, but with the exception of one Coy. of the Reserve Battalion detailed to push through CONDE, no troops of the Brigade will move into or South of the CONDE - BOLT FACTORY - LE COCQ Railway unless tactically necessary.

8. The Code word " H U N T " will bring the above orders into operation without further orders.

3.

9. A central Visual Signalling Station will be established by Division about K.25.a.10.8. Furtehr Orders as regards communications will be issued later.

10. First Line Transport will cross to East of the Canal as soon as practicable and on ordersfrom Brigade Hqrs.

11. Brigade Headquarters will open near HAUTE VILLE as soon as the River Bridges are open.
   The exact location will be notified later.
   On moving East of Canal Brigade Headquarters will be in the vicinity of the ROEUX de CONDE - GD. QUENOY - CHENE RAOUL Road.

12. A C K N O W L E D G E.

B. Stirling Cookson
Captain,
Brigade Major, 157th Infantry Brigade.

Issued at....1800.... on 6/11/18.

Copy No. 1 to 5th H.L.I.
         2   6th H.L.I.
         3   7th H.L.I.
         4   157th L.T.M.B.
         5   2nd L.F.A.
         6   413th Field Coy. R.E.
         7   220th Coy. A.S.C.
         8   "D" Coy. 52nd Bn. M.G.C.
         9   155th Inf. Bde.
        10   156th Inf. Bde.
        11   8th Canadian Inf. Bde.
        12   9th Bde. R.F.A.
        13   33rd Bde. R.F.A.
        14   G.R.A.
     15   52nd Division.
        16   VIII CorpsCyclist Battalion.
        17   IV Hussars.
        18   52nd Bn. M.G.C.
        19   Staff Captain.
        20   Brigade Major.
        21   G.O.C.
        22   Bde. Sigs. Officer.
        23) War Diary.
        24)
        25   F I L E.

Secret   Appendix III.   Copy No 2

137th Infantry Brigade Order No 161.

Ref. Map. Sheet 45.   18th November 1918.

1. **Information** Small bodies of the enemy have been located in woods ~~woods~~ on woods E. of WILLEROT also E. of TERTRE, which village, a Coy of a Canadian Batt- Holds. These Canadians are crossing our Corps boundary today.

2. (a). The Division will continue the advance today.

(b). The 7th R.I. leaving present billets at 0700 will advance on a 2 Coy. front and cover 137th Brigade front, up to the line O.10.b.05. - Railway line through O.4 - I.34.d.c.8.a. - I.27.d - thence up road I.27.a. to I.21.a.2.0. from which point the 156th Infbde. continues the line N. along NEUF MAISON Road.

(c) 5th S.L.I. will march at 0700 by road. HARCHIES - VILLE POMMEROEUL - HAUTRAGE

2.

at last place they will halt till further orders.

(d). 6th H.L.I. will be prepared to move to HAUTRAGE after 0800 on receipt of orders.

(e). One section 157th L.T.M.B. at present with 6th H.L.I. will accompany the 7 H.L.I., remainder of the Battery will accompany 6.H.L.I.

(f). "D" Coy 52nd Bn M.G.C. will assist 7 H.L.I. in their advance. Sections not detailed for this purpose will march in rear of the 157th L.T.M.B.

(g) 7th H.L.I. Hdqrs will advance along the POMMEROEUL – CHENE – TERTRE road.

(h) Bde Hdqrs will remain at POMMEROEUL (Rue du Bois) until 9.30 am. when it will open at HAUTRAGE.

3. Boundaries
(1) Corps Boundary. On N. runs C.9. and E along canal to H2c.6.5. thence S. of STAMBRUGES – NEUF MAISON Road to C.20.c.0.6. – N. of HERCHIES to

3

D.10.b.b.b. (approx)
Southern boundary. O.11.central - RIVAGE
(exclusive) to S. outskirts GHELUVELT to R.19.d.6.5.
(ii) Inter Bde. boundary at present unaltered.

4. The 8th Div. take over part of the corps front to-day, time uncertain, but probably not before we reach our objective given in para 2.(b).

When this relief is complete the inter Div. boundary will run :- H.22.c.00 due E. to I.22.c.00 thence I.17.c.00 to I.18.c.00 up railway as far as road crossing I.12.a.5.6. - along road inclusive to 8th Div - to J.6.a.0.3.

Inter Bde. boundary after relief by 8th Div. will be H.10.c.00 - H.12.c.00. thence N.E. to C.29.b.00. - Railway at D.22 central.

The moves consequent on this rearrangement will be notified later.

5/ Transport.

4

5. Transport will accompany units, except that of "7th H.L.I." which will only accompany the Batt. as far as H.30.c Central, where it will halt. 7th H.L.I. Hd qrs probable final destination WILLEROT.

6. ACKNOWLEDGE.

            J S Chumleigh
            Capt
         Brigade Maj. 157 Inf Bde.

Issued at 0145 on 24/11/18.
Copy No 1   5 HLI
       2   6 HLI
       3   7 HLI
       4   157 LTMB
       5   D Coy 55th Bn M.G.C
       6   9th Bde R.F.A
       7   O.C Mounted Troops
       8
       9

SECRET.

O.C. 5th H.L.I.
     6th H.L.I.
     7th H.L.I.
     157th L.T.M.B.
     D.Coy., 52nd Bn. M.G.C.

Appendix IV

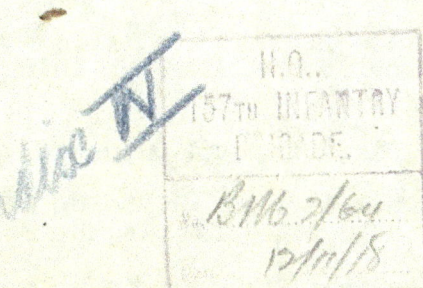

1. The 6th H.L.I. will relieve the 5th H.L.I. in the front line tomorrow, 13th instant. Relief to be completed by 1600.

2. O.C. D.Coy., 52nd Bn. M.G.C. will arrange relief of the M.G. sections in the front line.

3. On relief 5th H.L.I. will take over billets and inlying picket from the 6th H.L.I.

4. Details of relief to be arranged by Os.C. concerned.

5. Completion of relief to be reported by wire to Brigade Headquarters.

6. A C K N O W L E D G E.

12th November, 1918.

Captain,
Brigade Major, 157th Infantry Bde.

O.C. 5th H.L.I. O.C. 157th L.T.M.B.
    6th H.L.I.   D.Coy., 52nd Bn.M.G.C.
    7th H.L.I.

OUTPOSTS DURING THE ARMISTICE.

Appendix IV

Os. C. Battalions will arrange to carry out the Outpost system in accordance with F.S.Reg. Part I., as far as possible.

With the present available strength it is necessary to form one Outpost Company by combining two Service Companies.

The Outpost Line will be held by two Outpost Companies finding groups, Picquets, and Supports.

The Battalion at ERBISOEUL will find one Company in Reserve to be ready at 10 minutes notice from 8.0 p.m. to 7.0 a.m.

The principle object in view is to prevent any surprise on the part of the enemy, and to keep the British front carefully watched.

All military precaution to be taken as during the War.- No British troops to be allowed beyond the Picquet line except groups and their reliefs.

Civilians are not to be allowed to cross the Outposts either from front or rear - any person endeavouring to cross is to be taken to the examining post to be established by the D.P.M.

Local Defence for Groups and Picquets must be arranged, but digging is to be avoided if possible.

The Picquet line will be the line of Resistance.

Groups may be reduced to one Sentry by day 0600 to 1800 but must have two sentries by night.
M.G's. - one Sentry always.

Touch to be maintained by Patrols with Battalions on Right and Left.

As many men as possible to be under cover of a roof, but ready for immediate action.

12th November, 1918.   (Sgd) B.G.PRICE, Brigadier General,
                                 Commanding, 157th Infantry Brigade.

A	B	C	D
4	1	1	1
2	5	8	8

A 4
B 6 — + Kennedy
C 7
D 4

O.C. 5th H.L.I.
    6th H.L.I.
    7th H.L.I.
    2nd L.F.A.

Appendix I

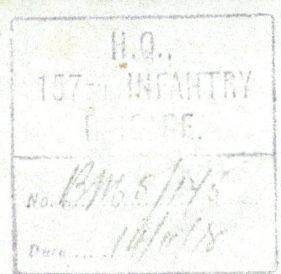

    The following orders with reference to the Army Commander's entry into MONS tomorrow supercede and cancel previous orders.

    The 5th H.L.I. will find 150 men, divided into 3 platoons, 6th H.L.I. 100 in 2 platoons, each platoon under an Officer.

    The parade will be commanded by Major Fowlis. Pipers and Drummers of 5th and 6th H.L.I. will attend in addition.

    Party of 6th H.L.I. will report to Major Fowlis at the Cross Roads J.6.a.0.3. at 0815. Dress - Fighting Order as per Divisional Standing Orders.

    O.C. 2nd L.F.A. will detail party of one Officer and 29 Other Ranks to join above party at J.6.a.0.3. at 0815. The whole party will meet the Staff Captain at Q.2.a.7.2. at 0940.

    Units will make their own arrangements re food, no cookers to go South of K.25.b.7.7.

    Motor lorry will call at 5th H.L.I. Hqrs. about 0845, and at 6th H.L.I. Hqrs. about 0900 to convey Officers wishing to attend.

14th November, 1918.
                                                    Captain,
                                    Brigade Major, 157th Infantry Bde.

"C" FORM.
MESSAGES AND SIGNALS.

Army Form C. 2123.
(In books of 100)
No. of Message ....

Prefix B	Code 1647	Words 25	Sent, or sent out.	Office Stamp.
Received from	By Reid		At .... m.	HJO
Service Instructions			To	17/11/18
	Appendix II		By	

Handed in at L_____ Office 1647 m. Received 1806 m.

TO HJO

*Sender's Number.	Day of Month	In reply to Number	AAA
10131	17		
2nd	Army	have	taken
over	responsibility	for	
front	aaa	outposts	will
be	withdrawn	by	2200
today	aaa	acknowledge	
aaa	report	completion	
	Relief complete 1900		

FROM Lime
PLACE & TIME

*This line, except **AAA**, should be erased, if not required.
(3287) Wt. W54/P738 691,000 Pads. 3/18. A.P.Ltd (E3013)

Copy No. 6

1/6th Bn. HIGHLAND LIGHT INFANTRY

TRAINING PROGRAMME FOR WEEK ENDING 30/11/18. By MAJOR P. STORMONTH-DARLING, Comdg. 1/6 Bn. HIGH. L.I.

DATE	0715	0900 to 1000	1000 to 1100	1100 to 1130	1130 to 1230	1130 to 1230	1400 to 1600	1400 to 1500	1500 to 1700	LECTURES
MONDAY 25/11/18	Platoon Commanders Inspection. Note. Any permanent orderly man or orderlies will be daily in that article daily and inspected	Coy Training – "Hints on Training"			Guard Drill Saluting	Voluntary Educ. Classes	Sports inside Coy arrangements	Defaulters Parade in F.M.O.	Defaulters fatigues	
TUESDAY 26/11/18		Batln. Route March. Batln. formed up on Mars facing North on D Coy's Parade Ground. Route :- To Mon's and Return.								1730. Lecture by B.S.C. to all Offrs + Platoon Sgts in Bn Educational Room. "Tactical Employment of Platoon."
WEDNESDAY 27/11/18		Coy Training Right ½ Coy. Squad Coy Training under all Coy L.G. Instructors Left ½ Coy. Musketry with short lectures on care of Arms, Ammun etc.	Left ½ Coy. Squad Coy Training Right ½ Coy. Musketry		Rifle Grenade Practice etc.	Voluntary Educ. Classes				
THURSDAY 28/11/18		Coy Training with ½ hours break			Ceremonial Drill					
FRIDAY 29/11/18	0830 to 1230 Parade	Coy Training. Coy Tactical Scheme to be carried out on Drill Ground K.3.4.9+10. The use of Ground + Cover etc. on taking up Outpost positions to be included in scheme. Schemes to be submitted to Orderly Room by 1200 on Wednesday.			Ceremonial Drill	Voluntary Educ. Classes				
SATURDAY 30/11/18	Platoon Commanders Inspection	Ceremonial Drill.			-					Note. Seeing by private days O.C. Coys will finish as their programme with ½ hrs ceremonial Drill.

DRESS { For all Parades on Monday, Wednesday, Thursday + Saturday } – Skeleton Order with Steel Helmet
{ except as otherwise stated }
{ for all Parades on Tuesday + Friday except as otherwise stated } – Full Marching Order

Issued at 10.30 — 24/11/18

Signed
Major
Adjt

COPY NO.

TRAINING PROGRAMME for WEEK ENDING 7/12/18 — 1/6 Bn. HIGHLAND LIGHT INFANTRY —
by Major P. Stormonth-Darling, Commdg. 1/6 Bn. High. L.I.

DATE	0715	0900 TO 1100	1100 TO 1130	1130 TO 1230	1400–1600 / 1400–1500	1500–1700	LECTURES
MONDAY 2/12/18	Platoon Commanders Inspection	A & B Coys. – Coy Training – "Hints on Training" C. Coy. – Range. D. Coy. – Duty with N° 20th Batty. R.F.A. — Separate instrs. issued	—	A & B. Coys. – Coy Training – Instructing up Drill. B. Coy. – Voluntary Education Classes. C. Coy. – Range.	Sports under Coy. arrangements		
TUESDAY 3/12/18	No Parade	0830 Battalion Route March – Battalion formed up on line facing Chateau at 0830. Route – To Cross Roads J.6.a.0.3. Cross Roads K.I.B.6.0. MASNUY ST JEAN – JURBISE – ERBISŒUL – Separate instrs. issued					
WEDNESDAY 4/12/18	Voluntary Education Instructors Note – Coy Comrs. may nominate cadres daily, as & when desired, with instructed	C. Coy. – Duty with N°20th Batty R.F.A. – Separate instrs. issued A & B Coys. – Coy Training D. Coy. – Range B. Coy. – Duty with 20th Batty. R.F.A.	—	A. Coys. – Coy Training – Instructing up Drill. C. Coy. – Voluntary Education Classes. D. Coy. – Range.	Defaulters Parade in Full Marching Order		
THURSDAY 5/12/18		Ceremonial Drill on Coy Parade Ground. In Class formation of Companies, dispd. by 0900. A. Coy. – Duty with 20th Batty. R.F.A. – Separate instrs. issued 1130 – March home.	—	D. & C. Coys. – Coy Training. D. Coy. – Voluntary Education Classes.			
FRIDAY 6/12/18	No. Parade	0830 Battalion march to K.3. A.9.4.10. via J.6.A.B. K.I.A.B. K.2.C.D. K.3. 0930 Coy Training – Coy Tactical Scheme 1100 – the use of Ground & Cover etc, on taking up outpost positions to include an Scheme. Schemes to be submitted to Orderly Room by 1200 on Tuesday	—	B. & C. Coys. – Ceremonial Drill. A. Coy. – Voluntary Education Classes.	Signallers formed up under Battalion Signalling Officer for practice.		
SATURDAY 7/12/18	Platoon Commanders Inspection	Ceremonial Drill	—				

Dress – { For all Parades on Monday, Wednesday, Thursday & Saturday } Skeleton Order with Steel Helmet except as otherwise stated.
{ For all parades on Tuesday & Friday, except as otherwise stated – Full Marching Order }

Reveille at — 1/12/18

Army Form C. 2118.

1/6th High. L.I.
DECEMBER 1918 (SHEET No 1.)

CONFIDENTIAL — WAR DIARY or INTELLIGENCE SUMMARY.
(Erase heading not required)

Instructions regarding War Diaries and Intelligence Summaries are contained in F.S. Regs., Part II. and the Staff Manual respectively. Title pages will be prepared in manuscript.

Place	Date	Hour	Summary of Events and Information	Remarks and references to Appendices
PA.VA.	1.12.18	0700	Reveille Breakfast	
		0830	Battalion to baths by companies at J.35.b. Sheet 46 France 40000	
MONSEURRE ROAD	2.12.18	0630	Reveille Breakfast	
		0900	Training carried out as per training Programme	Appendix 1
		1330	(orderly) Room. Battn. Storm moved to Thoraeu J.6.a.0.3. Sheet 46 France 40000	
		1400	Shots under Company arrangements. D Coy & 9th & Y Coy 5th Hindu under Company Arrangements Cut ssail (J.1.-5.0.)	
	3.12.18	0630	Reveille Breakfast	
		0830	Battalion Route march (wet)	
		1330	Battalion Orderly Room	
		1400	Shots under Company arrangements	
	4.12.18	0630	Reveille Inspection Breakfast	
		0900	Training as per programme	Appendix 2
		1330	Orderly Room	
		1400	Shots under Coy arrangements	
	5.12.18	0630	Reveille Inspection Breakfast	
		0900	D Company Range (B) of Laugin work at Brigade M.G. range at K.6.a.t.b. A Company at Artillery Demonstration	
		1330	Orderly room	
		1400	Shots under Coy arrangements	
	6.12.18	0630	Reveille Inspection Breakfast	
		0830	Training Programme	Appendix 1
		1330	Orderly Room	
		1400	Shots under Coy arrangements	
	7.12.18	0630	Reveille Inspection Breakfast	Appendix 1
		0900	Training Programme	
		14.15	D Coy at 9th.9 & C Coy Y 9th.9 Lord of ante leel company of Battalion Cwh nevull 6th Jn 3 - 7th. 9.0.	

Army Form C. 2118.

WAR DIARY
or
INTELLIGENCE SUMMARY.

1/6ᵗʰ Bⁿ Ḥyⁿ L.I.
DECEMBER, 1918 (SHEET Nº 2).

(Erase heading not required.)

Instructions regarding War Diaries and Intelligence Summaries are contained in F. S. Regs., Part II. and the Staff Manual respectively. Title pages will be prepared in manuscript.

Place	Date	Hour	Summary of Events and Information	Remarks and references to Appendices
PAYA MONSTURBISE ROAD	8.12.18	0700	Reveille Breakfast	
		0900	Companies Commence inspection of Billets etc.	
		1400	Guard Room Mounted. Capt Maxwell M.C. returned from leave bringing COLOURS with him.	
	9.12.18	0630	Reveille Breakfast. Instructions	
		0900	Company Training. A+B Coys Runners or Range	
		1330	Orderly Room	
		1400	Sports under Coy Arrangements	
	10.12.18	0630	Reveille Inspection Breakfast	
		0900	Ceremonial Drill on Drill Ground K.3.9.q+10 Sheet 45	
		1330	Orderly Room. 6.O. returned from leave to U.K	
		1400	Sports under Coy Arrangements	
	11.12.18	0630	Reveille Breakfast Instructions	
		0900	Demonstration of Battⁿ Ceremonial Drill to Artillery on Drill Ground K.3.q+10 Sheet 45	
		1330	Orderly Room	
		1400	Games under Coy Arrangements	

CONFIDENTIAL – WAR DIARY
or
INTELLIGENCE SUMMARY.
(Erase heading not required.)

Army Form C. 2118.

1/6th Bn Highl. L.I.
DECEMBER, 1918 (SHEET No. 3.)

Place	Date	Hour	Summary of Events and Information	Remarks and references to Appendices
PAIA MONS-TURBIE ROAD	1918 Decbr. 12.	0630	Reveille Inspection Breakfast	
		0900	Company Training	
		1330	Orderly Room	
		1400	Musical Inspection B Coy moved to new area (vacated by H.T.M.B. of 157 Brigade.)	
	13"	0630	Reveille Inspection Breakfast	
		0900	Baths for Battalion at 5th H.L.I.	
		1330	Orderly Room	
		1400	Sports under Coy Arrangements	
	14"	0630	Reveille Breakfast Inspection	
		0900	Coy Commanders have Coys at their disposal after Skin inspection	
		1300	Orderly Room	
		1400	Sports under Coy Arrangements	
	15"	0630	Reveille Breakfast	
		1130	C.O. inspection all arrivals joined since 19.11.18	
	16"	0600	Reveille	
		0800	Bn on parade and marches to K9+10. Sheet 45	
		1000	Inspection of Bn by S.O.6. 52 Div. each coy performing a different duty	
		1320	Orderly Room	
		1400	Sports under Coy Arrangements	

Army Form C. 2118.

CONFIDENTIAL—

WAR DIARY
INTELLIGENCE SUMMARY.

(Erase heading not required.)

1/6th Bn. High. L.I.

DECEMBER, 1918 (SHEET Nº 4)

Place	Date	Hour	Summary of Events and Information	Remarks and references to Appendices
PAVA	Dec 1918 17th	0630	Reveille Breakfast Protection	
INONS-TURBISE ROAD		0900	Bullets cleaned materials by C.O.	
		1100	Education Classes	
		1330	Orderly Room	
		1400	Shots under Coy Arrangements	
	18th	0630	Reveille Breakfast Protection	
		0900	Company Training	
		1100	Education Classes	
		1330	Orderly Room	
		1400	Shots under Coy Arrangements	
	19th	0630	Reveille Breakfast Protection	
		0900	D Coy to Range. R.S.A. for range practice (shot 45)	
		1000	B.O. materials O/B. C. in Chateau at J.6.A.0.2 (sheet 45)	
		1100	Education Classes	
		1330	Orderly Room	
		1400	Shots	
	20th	0630	Reveille Breakfast Protection	
		0830	A Coy to Range R&a (sheet 45)	
		9.00	B.E.D Company training	
		1100	Education Classes	
		1330	Orderly Room	
		400	Officers v Sergts 1/6 Sh. D Football	

Army Form C. 2118.

CONFIDENTIAL—

WAR DIARY
of
INTELLIGENCE SUMMARY.
(Erase heading not required.)

1/6 & Bn. High. L.I.
DECEMBER, 1918 (SHEET No 5.)

Instructions regarding War Diaries and Intelligence Summaries are contained in F. S. Regs., Part II. and the Staff Manual respectively. Title pages will be prepared in manuscript.

Place	Date	Hour	Summary of Events and Information	Remarks and references to Appendices
PAVA	December 1918	0630	Reveille Inspection Breakfast	
MONS-TURBS ROAD	21st	0900	C.O. inspection of Billets	
		1030	Medical inspection.	
		1100	Educational Classes	
		1330	Orderly Room	
		1400	Shona	
		1600	Concert by 5th Sth.9 Concert Party in town Concert Hall	
	22nd	0700	Reveille	
			Sunday.	
	23rd	0700	Reveille Breakfast. Inspection	
		0930	Batten Route march	
		1330	Orderly Room	
		1400	Shona. Sgt Strans awarded M.M. with XXII C.R.O.1851 dated 18.12.18 instruction Africa opened under Major Corrie and clerical staff	
	24th	0700	Reveille Inspection Breakfast	
		0900	Company Training	
		1100	Educational Classes	
		1330	Orderly Room	
		1400	Shona.	
	25th		Christmas Day. Comren's Dinners and Sodden Inatches. Xmas Puddings and Shortbread Gochi Boxes were distributed to the troops transport held a very successful dummy festival. Simply	

Army Form C. 2118.

1/6th Bn Highd. L.I.

DECEMBER, 1918. (SHEET No. 6.)

CONFIDENTIAL WAR DIARY or INTELLIGENCE SUMMARY.

(Erase heading not required.)

Instructions regarding War Diaries and Intelligence Summaries are contained in F. S. Regs., Part II. and the Staff Manual respectively. Title pages will be prepared in manuscript.

Place	Date	Hour	Summary of Events and Information	Remarks and references to Appendices
PAVA MONS JURBISE ROAD	Dec 1918 26th	0700 0930 1130 1330 1400	Reveille. Breakfast Inoculations Coy Training Educational Classes Orderly Room Sports	
	27th	0700 0930 1130 1330 1400	Reveille. Breakfast Inoculations Coy Training. All drafts forming towards 19/11/18 under order. Coy. Educational Classes Orderly Room Sports	
	28th	0700 0930 1100 1330 1400 0700 0800	Reveille. Breakfast Inoculations Ceremonial parade & inspection Educational Classes Orderly Room Sports Reveille Breakfast	C.O. inspection of billets
	29th		Sunday	
	30th	0700 0930 1100 1330 1400	Reveille Inoculations Breakfast Coy Training & Draft training Educational Classes Orderly Room Sports	
	31st	0700 0900 1330 1400	Reveille Inoculations Breakfast Batt Ceremonial Parade K 9 to Sheet 47. Orderly Room Rugby mat. Belen Lonwenge & Frelinge Bach V Bn Back + Reserve More Shaft Regiment Back V Bn Back + Reserve More	

WAR DIARY

— CONFIDENTIAL —

INTELLIGENCE SUMMARY:— Nolm High & Stanley

(Erase heading not required.)

December (W.I.E. No. 4.)

Army Form C. 2118.

Instructions regarding War Diaries and Intelligence Summaries are contained in F. S. Regs., Part II. and the Staff Manual respectively. Title pages will be prepared in manuscript.

TABLE SHEWING INCREASES AND DECREASES IN BATTALION CAMP STRENGTH DURING MONTH OF DECEMBER 1918

Place	Date	Hour	Summary of Events and Information		Remarks and references to Appendices
				OFF. O.R.	
			Camp Strength as at 1st December 1918	39 - 629	
			DECREASES:	OFF. O.R.	
			Sick to Hosp.	10	
			On Leave	4 - 7	
			To Course of Instr.	12	
			Detached duty	1 - 1	
			Small T. Base Depot	4	
			Dept. Hosp.	1 - 7	
			To House E.	7	
				6 - 43	
			INCREASES:		
			From Hosp.	9	
			" Leave	10	
			" Course of Instr.	8 - 11	
			" Estd. duties	3	
			" Reinforcements	1 - 94	
			" M.E.	9	
				21 - 586	
			Camp Strength as at 2400 on 7/12/18	7 - 30 915	
			DECREASES:		
			On Leave	1 - 4	
			To Course of Instruct.	4 - 14	
			Detached duties	3	
			To Base	1 - 1	
			To Small T.B. Depot	1	
			Absentees	2	
			" Course Schools	1 - 3	
				10 - 32	
			Camp Strength as at 2400 on 14/12/18	20 - 693	
			INCREASES:		
			From Hosp. (S)	11	
			" Hosp. (W)	2 - 14	
			" Leave	2 - 6	
			" Montgomery	1	
			" Rest Camp	1	
			" Absentees	1 - 2	
			" Course Schools	1 - 5	
				6 - 44	
			Camp Strength as at 2400 on 14/12/18	26 - 724	
			DECREASES:		
			Sick to Hosp.	1 - 16	
			Leave	1 - 4	
			To Course Schools	1 - 5	
				4 - 25	
				22 - 699	
				OFF. O.R.	
			INCREASES	OFF. O.R. 22 699	
			From Hosp (S)	8	
			" Hosp (w)	2	
			" Leave	2	
			" Detailed duties	1 - 9	
			" Course of Instruction	1 - 1	
			" Egypt	2	
			" Reinforcements	14 - 31	
			Camp Strength as at 2400 on 21/12/18	24 - 930	
			DECREASES:		
			Sick to Hosp.	14	
			Leave	1 - 4	
			Course of Instruction	4 - 8	
			To Base for wintering	1	
			Detached duties	1	
				2 - 2 29	
			Camp Strength as at 2400 on 28/12/18	14 - 901	
			INCREASES:		
			From Hosp (S)	6	
			" Hosp (W)	1	
			" Leave	3 - 11	
			" Base H.Q	1	
			" Course of Instruction	6 - 9	
			" Rest Camp	1	
				10 - 29	
			Camp Strength as at 2400 on 30/12/18	24 - 930	
			DECREASES:		
			Sick to Hosp.	1	
			To Rest Camp	1 - 1	
			Leave	6	
			Warmed to U.K. for discharge	1 - 8	
				26 - 922	
			INCREASES:		
			From Course of Instruction	1 - 3	
			Leave	1 - 2	
				2 - 5	
			Camp Strength as at 2400 on 31.12.18	28 - 927	

1/6 Bn Highland Light Infantry

WAR DIARY
INTELLIGENCE SUMMARY

Army Form C. 2118.

16 9h.9 JANUARY 1919

Place	Date	Hour	Summary of Events and Information	Remarks and references to Appendices
PAYE	1919 JAN 1		New Years Day. Major Gen Hunter Weston KCB DSO Awarded full that men in Bn	
	2		Company Training. Educational Classes. Shots.	
MONS	3		Brigade Ceremonial Parade. Educational Classes. Shots.	
	4		Billets & Medical Inspections. Shots.	
JURBISE	5		Divine Service	
ROAD	6		Brigade Ceremonial Parade. Educational Classes. Shots.	
	7		Coy Training. Educational Classes. Shots. Brigade Rifle Races	
	8		Coy Training. Educational Classes. Shots. Parties Leave	
	9		Brigade Ceremonial Parade. Educational Classes. Shots.	
	10		Company Training. Educational Parade. Shots 6ths & 7ths & 9ths & Bn football team	
	11		Inspection of Billets - Bain to Baths. Shots.	
	12		Divine Service	
	13		Bain to Baths. Shots.	
	14		Brigade Ceremonial Parade. Educational Classes. Shots.	
	15		Battalion Shots. Educational Classes.	
	16		Company Training. Educational Classes. Shots.	

W Wallace Capt

Army Form C. 2118.

1/6 Bn. Highland Light Infantry.

WAR DIARY
INTELLIGENCE SUMMARY.
(Erase heading not required.)

JANUARY 1919.

Instructions regarding War Diaries and Intelligence Summaries are contained in F. S. Regs., Part II. and the Staff Manual respectively. Title pages will be prepared in manuscript.

Place	Date	Hour	Summary of Events and Information	Remarks and references to Appendices
PAYÁ	1919 JAN 17		Area Improvements. Educational Classes Shots.	
MONS	18		Divine and Ceremonial Parade. Educational Classes Shots.	
—	19		Divine Service	
TREISE	20		Route March Shots — Guard for Mons Rly Station mounted (Offrs Offrs)	
ROAD	21		Company Training. Educational Classes Shots.	
	22		Lewis Gun Carting (New section) Educational Classes Shots — Mons Str Guard in Return	
	23		Medical Inspection. Lewis Gun Instruction. Educational Classes Shots	
	24		Coy training Educational Classes Shots. Boxing team won Bri Cross Rose	
	25		Battalion medical Inspection. Educational Classes Shots Cross in BE Dr Hall	
	26		Divine Service	
	27		Coy training snow event to fall down. Educational Classes Shots	
	28		Coy training. Educational Classes Shots — Supply Guard mounted.	
	29		Coy training Educational Classes snow on ground	
	30		Coy training — Education — Medical Reclassification	
	31		Coy Training — Education	

M.J. McKie
Capt

Army Form C. 2118.

WAR DIARY
or
INTELLIGENCE SUMMARY.

(Erase heading not required.)

Instructions regarding War Diaries and Intelligence Summaries are contained in F. S. Regs., Part II. and the Staff Manual respectively. Title pages will be prepared in manuscript.

1/4th Bn High L.I. Infantry
Farmers (Sheet 410)

TABLE SHEWING INCREASES AND DECREASES IN BATTALION CAMP STRENGTH DURING MONTH OF JANUARY 1918

Place	Date	Hour	Summary of Events and Information		Remarks and references to Appendices
				OFF. O.Rs.	
			Camp strength as at 2400 on 31-12-18	28 724	
			INCREASES to		
			Hosp.	6	
			Courses	2 3	
			Detached duties	3	
			Reinforcements	1	
			Leave to U.K.	5	
			Short Leave		
				3 18	
				31 745	
			DECREASES to		
			Hosp.	6	
			Courses		
			Disposal	38	
			Detached duties	1-2	
			Leave to U.K.	1	
			Short Leave	3	
			Escort duty		
				2 50	
				28 695	
			Camp strength as at 2400 on 7-1-19		
			INCREASES to		
			Hosp.	15	
			Courses	2 5	
			Detached duties	5	
			Reinforcements	2	
			Leave to U.K.	2	
			Short Leave		
			Escort duty	3	
				5 30	
				33 725	
			DECREASES to		
			Hosp.	3	
			Courses	1	
			Disposal	1 38	
			Detached duties	8	
			Leave to U.K.	3	
			Short Leave	2 8	
				3 61	
				30 664	
			Camp strength as at 2400 on 14/1/19		
			INCREASES to	OFF O.Rs.	
			Hosp.	5	30 664
			Courses	2 2	
			Short Leave	2 14	
					5 21
					35 685
			DECREASES to		
			Hosp.	1	
			Courses	1 2	
			Disposals	19	
			Detached duties	4	
			Prison	6	
			Leave to U.K.	2	
			Short Leave	3 13	
					5 47
					30 638
			Camp strength as at 2400 on 21/1/19		
			INCREASES to		
			Hosp.	3	
			Courses	1 -	
			Detached duties	1 -	
			Reinforcements	1 48	
			Prison	9	
			Leave to U.K.	1 - 4	
			Short Leave	3 3	
			Escort duty	2 14	
					4 21
					34 659
			Camp strength as at 2400 on 28/1/19		
			DECREASES to		
			Hosp.	4	
			Detached duties	1 - 4	
			Short Leave	6	
					6 83
					28 576
			INCREASES to		
			Hosp.	4	
			Disposal	2 - 13	
			Detached duties	9	
			Leave to U.K.	1	
			Short Leave	4	
					1 9
					29 585
			DECREASES to		
					3 24
					26 561
			Camp strength as at 2400 on 31/1/19		

Net Decrease for month
OFF 2
ORs 166

Army Form C. 2118.

WAR DIARY
of
INTELLIGENCE SUMMARY. 6th HIGH. L.I.

FEBRUARY SHEET 1.

(Erase heading not required.)

Vol 11

17H
4 struts

Place	Date	Hour	Summary of Events and Information	Remarks and references to Appendices
PAYE nr MONS.	1919 FEBRUARY. 1		Comm'g Officers Inspection of Billets & Billeting area – Sports.	
	2 (Sunday)		Divine Service.	
	3		Company Training – Education – Repairing of Rifles by Bn Armourer & Lewis Guns by Bn Armourer Staff Sergeant.	
	4		Company Training – Education – Repairs of Rifles, Lewis Guns as above continued. – Boxing Tournament at Jurbise.	
	5		Coy Training – Education – Educational bus by Motor Lorry for 30 O.R.	
	6		Bn Coys proceeded to Baths Erbisn – L.G. Training & Education for remainder. Afternoon Boxing Tournament JURBISE – Bn representative Pte Crawford (Harlow weight) from North Br. in final trial.	
	7		Remainder of Bn. proceeded to Baths ERBIN – Education. Afternoon Sports Cross Country run – Cpl 3rd place.	
	8		Exam'n of Officers. Inspection of Billets & Billeting Area – Sports. Medal Inspection.	
	9 (Sunday) Nov 9		Divine Service. Inspection of Dress of 10 off, 120 O.R. proceeding to A.of.O.	
	10.		Lewis Gun training to Bn. (less Draft). Draft final kit inspection & pay. 1445 Bays paraded were addressed by B.J.C. moved off & taken at MONS.	
	11.		Reorganisation of Bn. – Absorbing 4 Coys into a two Coy. area.	

Wallace Capt.

WAR DIARY
of
INTELLIGENCE SUMMARY.

6th H.G.H.L.I.

FEBRUARY SHEET 2.

Army Form C. 2118.

Place	Date	Hour	Summary of Events and Information	Remarks and references to Appendices
JAVÉ MONS. near MONS.	FEBRUARY 1919 12.		Educational tour by Lorry to Brussels for N. of [?] 60 OR. - Education for Corporals	
	13.		Recruits Officers Inspection of Billeting Area - Education.	
	14.		Inspection of Baths in F.M.O.	
	15.		Working party of 40 OR. (N.C.O. & Officer) to River Convoi. - Education for Corporals.	
	16. (Sunday)		R.C. & C of E service - Coys of B" became merged into 1 Coy, known as the Composite Coy from to days date except for purposes of pay when they coys still retain their identity. - Platoons of Composite Coy known as A B C & D Platoons.	
	17.		Bn. proceed to Baths CHIN. - Working party to Receivoir 1 NCO 15 men	
	18.		Cleaning & Inspection of Billets - Education - Working party to Massevaux Pte Shackleland Tried by FGCM [?] [?]	
	19.		Cleaning & Inspection of billets - Education - Working party to Mass convoi.	
	20.		Cleaning & Inspection of Billets - Education - Working party to Receivoir.	
	21.		Cleaning & Inspection of Billets - Education - Working party to Mass convoi.	
	22.		Commdg Officers Inspection of Billets - Education - Working party Recommenced enquiry into cheft o/men.	
	23.		Cleaning of Billets.	
	24.		Cleaning & inspection of Billets & investigation of claims for Burned clamps.	
	25.		Cleaning of Billets.	

M J W Moore Capt.

Army Form C. 2118.

WAR DIARY
of
INTELLIGENCE SUMMARY. 6th HIGH. L.I. FEBY SHEET 3.
(Erase heading not required.)

Instructions regarding War Diaries and Intelligence Summaries are contained in F. S. Regs., Part II. and the Staff Manual respectively. Title pages will be prepared in manuscript.

Place	Date	Hour	Summary of Events and Information	Remarks and references to Appendices
GAVÉ near Mons	FEBRUARY 1919 26 Wed		Coys Race Meeting - Horses took men out to the Race course.	
	27		63rd Division Race Meeting - 2 lorries took 30 O.R. out Champ of Battle to Ramousies.	
	28		Billet Cleaning - Board of Offrs Aveilly P.R.I. P.M.C. Offrs.	

M.W. [signature] Capt.

Army Form C. 2118.

WAR DIARY
~~INTELLIGENCE SUMMARY~~
(Erase heading not required.)

TABLE SHEWING INCREASES AND DECREASES
IN
BATTALION CAMP STRENGTH
DURING
MONTH OF FEBRUARY 1919

Instructions regarding War Diaries and Intelligence Summaries are contained in F.S. Regs., Part II. and the Staff Manual respectively. Title pages will be prepared in manuscript.

Place	Date	Hour	Summary of Events and Information			Remarks and references to Appendices
				OFF	ORs	
			Camp Strength as at 24.00 on 31-1-19	26	561	
			INCREASES			
			From Hosp		4	
			" Absentee		2	
			" Leave (UK)		11	
			" Corps Ord Camp		1	
			" Escort Duty	2		
			" Detd Duty		3	
			" Courses of Instr		2	
					25	
			DECREASES			
			To UK for Dispersal	3	84	
			" Leave (UK)		7	
			" Leave (UK)	1	3	
			" Payroll (etHosp)		1	
			" Corps Ord Camp		2	
			" Comm Maths		1	
			" Hosp (Dental)		1	
			" Hosp		1	
				4	100	
			Camp Strength as at 24.00 on 7.2.19 →	22	486	
			INCREASES			
			From Hosp	1	1	
			" Leave (UK)	1	7	
			" Corps Ord Camp		6	
			" Courses of Instr		18	
			" Detd Duty	1		
			" L.T.M.B.		9	
				3	46	
				25	532	
			DECREASES			
			To UK for Dispersal	1	109	
			" Leave (UK)	2		
			" Leave (UK)		8	
			" Corps Ord Camp		5	
			" Hosp (Dental)		7	
			" Hosp		1	
			" Detd Duty		1	
			" Army of Occup	10	180	
				11	309	
				14	223	
			Camp Strength as at 24.00 on 14.2.19 →			
			INCREASES			
			From Leave (UK)	2	2	
			" Courses of Instr		5	
			" Detd Duty	3		
				16	232	
			DECREASES			
			To UK for Dispersal	1	108	
			" Detached Duty		2	
			" Conducting Pcty	1	0	
				2	110	
			Camp Strength as at 24.00 on 21-2-19 →	14	122	
			INCREASES			
			From Hosp		1	
			" Leave (UK)	2	4	
			" Courses of Instr		1	
			" Detd Duty		8	
			" L.T.M.B.	1	0	
				3	14	
				17	136	
			DECREASES			
			To UK for Dispersal		35	
			" Detached Duty		3	
			" Conducting Duty M.O.	1		
				4	38	
			Camp Strength as at 24.00 on 28.2.19 →	13	98	
			NETT DECREASE FOR MONTH	13	463	

WAR DIARY
or
INTELLIGENCE SUMMARY. 6th HIGH. L.I.
MARCH 1919.

Army Form C. 2118.

Place	Date	Hour	Summary of Events and Information	Remarks and references to Appendices
	MARCH			
MEGISE	1	1400	Musketry Parade in front of CHÂTEAU – Provisional CADRE selected.	WW
	2	1000	Bn. Kit Inspection.	WW
	3	1000	Bn. proceeded to Divl. Baths GHLIN	WW
	4	1015	Billet inspection by Commanding Officer. S.S. 611 (Fire Orders) read to all ranks at parade 1030	WW
	5		Cleaning of Billets & Rifle Inspection	WW
	6		do	WW
	7		do	WW
	8		—	WW
	9		Cleaning of Château & Packing of Regimental Equipment. Result of 2nd Army Pipe Championship announced Bn. winners. Pibroch 1st Pipe Major McKenzie 6th HLI. 3rd Pipe Major Broadwood 6th HLI. March Strathspey and Reel 1st Pipe Major Broadwood 6th HLI 2nd Pipe Major McKenzie 6th HLI.	WW
	10		Cleaning of Billets XVII Corps Race Meeting	WW
	11	6.50AM 1200	Batt. proceeded to Baths GHLIN. S.C. 793 recd. Entraining Bn tomorrow to MAIZIÈRES	WW

W. Wallace
Capt.

18 H
Harburg

Army Form C. 2118.

WAR DIARY
or
INTELLIGENCE SUMMARY.   6th HIGH. L.I.

(Erase heading not required.)   MARCH 1919.

Vol 12

Place	Date	Hour	Summary of Events and Information	Remarks and references to Appendices
TURBISE MAIZIÈRES	MARCH 1919. 12		Bn. moved to Billet at MAIZIÈRES - concentration point for 154th Bn. CADRES - arrived there by 1530.	
	13	1800	Cadre parade for Inspection Handling of Arms etc - Dismissed 10.00.	
	14	0800	do	
	15	0815	do	
	16. SUNDAY	1000	Church Parade	
	17.	0800	Cadre Parade till 14.00 -	
	18.	0810	Cadre Paraded & proceeded to Bath CALUA - Transport personnel reduced owing to horses being [last Sunday] 15th A/15/50 not ordinary mile horses on 21st to SOIGNIES	
	19	0800-1000	Cadre Parade 14.00-16.00 Defaulters Parade	
	20.	0800-1000	Cadre Parade 1100 Inspection of Billets by Comm'g Officer.	
SOIGNIES.	21.	1100	Moved to SOIGNIES CADRE RAILHEAD for 52nd DIV - All in Billets by 18.00.	
	22.	1000	Inspection of Billets by Comm'g Officer	
	23.		do — Last 3 horses on B: charge left to day.	
	24		Cleaning & Inspection of Billets	
	25		do	
	26		do	
	27		do	

M. Villar Capt.

18 H

Army Form C. 2118.

WAR DIARY
INTELLIGENCE SUMMARY: 6th HIGHLAND LIGHT INFANTRY
(Erase heading not required.) MARCH 1919.

Instructions regarding War Diaries and Intelligence Summaries are contained in F. S. Regs., Part II. and the Staff Manual respectively. Title pages will be prepared in manuscript.

Place	Date	Hour	Summary of Events and Information	Remarks and references to Appendices
	MARCH 1919			
SOIGNIES BELGIUM	28	0900	Inspection of Billets - 1300 Parade in Full Marching Order	
" "	29		do	
" "	30	0900	SUNDAY. Inspection of Billets by Comdg Offr - Church Parade 10·0	
" "	31	11·00	Parade of Coys & O.C. Coys for Inspection & Handling of Arms	Monday

W. Matthews

Army Form C. 2118.

WAR DIARY
or
INTELLIGENCE SUMMARY.

(Erase heading not required.)

Instructions regarding War Diaries and Intelligence Summaries are contained in F. S. Regs., Part II. and the Staff Manual respectively. Title pages will be prepared in manuscript.

TABLE SHEWING INCREASES AND DECREASES IN BATTALION CAMP STRENGTH DURING MONTH OF MARCH 1919

Place	Date	Hour	Summary of Events and Information	Remarks and references to Appendices

Camp Strength as at 2400 on 28/2/19 →   OFF. 13   O.R. 98 | OFF. 15   O.R. 84

INCREASES
 From Bde H.Q.   OFF 2   O.R —
 Ex detached duty   8
 Leave   1   3
                     ___ ___
                      1   11

DECREASES
 To ex for disband   1   15
 To Hosp.   1   1
 To Leave to ex   1   1
 To detached duty   —   1
                      ___ ___
                      1   18

Camp Strength as at 2400 on 1/3/19 → 12   91

INCREASES
 From Bde H.Q.   1   —
 absentee   —   1
 from leave   —   1
                      ___ ___
                      1   3

DECREASES
 To ex for disband.   —   9
 Detail dr. to Brussels 1   —
                      ___ ___
                      1   10

Camp Strength as at 2400 on 14/3/19 → 12   84

INCREASES
 from conducting duty 3   —
 from leave   —   2
 from detached   —   1
                      ___ ___
                      3   3

                          15   84

Camp Strength as at 2400 on 28/2/19 →   OFF 13   O.R 98

DECREASES
 To ex for disband.   3.   22
 To Hosp.   —   1
 absentee   —   1
 To Leave   —   5
 To Base E & ex on duty —   —
 To conducting duty   1   4
                      ___ ___
                      4   31

Camp Strength as at 2400 on 2/3/19 → 11   56

INCREASES
 From absentee   —   1
 from leave   —   1
 conducting duty   —   2
 detached duty   —   2
 Hosp.   1   1
                      ___ ___
                      1   4

DECREASES
 To Hosp.   —   1
 Leave   —   1
 conducting duty   —   —
 E.F.C. duty   —   10
 Ex for disband.   5   2
 detached duty   1   2
                      ___ ___
                      6   19

Camp Strength as at 2400 on 31/3/19 → 6   46

[signature]
Adjutant 1/4 Bn. Dk. of Cambridge

www.ingramcontent.com/pod-product-compliance
Lightning Source LLC
Chambersburg PA
CBHW080817010526
44111CB00015B/2572